SOUP OF THE DAY

KATE McMILLAN

PHOTOGRAPHY BY ERIN KUNKEL

weldonowen

CONTENTS

JANUARY 8

FEBRUARY 32

MARCH 56

APRIL 80

MAY 104

JUNE 128

JULY 152

AUGUST 176

SEPTEMBER 200

OCTOBER 224

NOVEMBER 248

DECEMBER 272

A SOUP FOR EVERY DAY

Hot, cold, smooth, chunky, creamy, brothy—soups come in myriad forms, yet always delight. Considered by many to be the ultimate comfort food, they are welcome additions to the dining table throughout the months, marking seasons and occasions with flavorful flair.

This book will encourage you to make soups on any day of the year. Using what's fresh as your guide, draw on seasonal ingredients—asparagus and peas in spring; corn, peppers, and tomatoes in summer; cruciferous vegetables and hearty greens during the fall; and root vegetables in winter—to inspire your creations.

Versatile, flexible, and easy to stretch, making soup is a smart way to cook. Some are perfect for casual weeknight meals, while others offer an elegant way to begin a dinner party. Soups are easy to dress up by adding texture, flavor, or a festive touch with simple garnishes—a topping of crisp garlic croutons; a swirl of pesto, olive oil, or crème fraiche; or a sprinkle of chopped fresh herbs. They are also easy to personalize to your own tastes by swapping in alternative ingredients, omitting cream or an herb you may not have on hand, or changing the texture by puréeing it or leaving it chunky. Many soups can be made ahead and reheated just before serving, while others can be prepared in large batches and frozen for quick meal options on busy nights. You'll learn these approaches and many more on the pages that follow.

The recipes in this book, 365 in all, are organized by calendar month and are designed to stimulate ideas for cooking any day of the year. You can use the calendar pages in the front of each chapter as a road map for your soup-making adventures, or feel free to meander through the recipes at your leisure, knowing that there will always be a dish to inspire you, no matter what the season. There are also dozens of full-color photographs to guide and entice you along the way.

The wealth of delicious recipes, colorful photographs, and daily culinary wisdom inside these pages are sure to satisfy a yearning for soup, no matter what the day brings.

1
SPICY SAUSAGE &
BROCCOLI RABE SOUP
page 11

2
FRENCH ONION SOUP
page 11

3
CAULIFLOWER & ROASTED
GARLIC PURÉE
page 12

4
FIVE-SPICE BEEF STEW
page 12

8
CHICKEN CHILI WITH
PIQUILLO PEPPERS
page 15

9
BEEF BORSCHT
page 16

10
CLASSIC CHICKEN NOODLE SOUP
page 16

11
MOROCCAN LAMB STEW
page 17

15
BARLEY-LEEK SOUP WITH
MINI CHICKEN MEATBALLS
page 21

16
MUSSELS IN TOMATO
& CREAM BROTH
page 21

17
SAVOY CABBAGE, FONTINA
& RYE BREAD SOUP
page 22

18
GINGERY BEEF BROTH WITH
SOBA NOODLES & BOK CHOY
page 22

22
KUMQUAT-CARROT PURÉE WITH
TOASTED FENNEL SEEDS
page 24

23
TORTELLINI & ESCAROLE SOUP
page 27

24
CRANBERRY BEAN & BARLEY SOUP
page 27

25
FENNEL-CELERY BISQUE
page 28

29
VEGETABLE-LENTIL
SOUP WITH SHERRY
page 30

30
SMOKED TROUT CHOWDER
page 30

31
OLD-FASHIONED TOMATO
& RICE SOUP
page 30

5
POSOLE
page 13

6
VEGETARIAN CHILI
page 13

7
AVGOLEMONO
page 15

12
KALE & WHITE BEAN SOUP
page 17

13
CREAM OF TOMATO SOUP
page 18

14
CIOPPINO
page 18

19
BROCCOLI & CHEDDAR SOUP
page 23

20
CITRUSY SEAFOOD SOUP
page 23

21
ROAST PORK &
UDON NOODLE SOUP
page 24

26
STEAK & POTATO SOUP
WITH FRIED SHALLOTS
page 28

27
TURKEY SOUP WITH
CHIPOTLE & LIME
page 29

28
LEEK & POTATO SOUP
WITH BLUE CHEESE
page 29

During the cold and dark start of the year, warming soups provide nourishment and comfort—and fill the house with delicious scents. Aromatic broths and spicy stews are the backdrop for January's sturdy vegetables, which include cabbage, broccoli, and cauliflower, ideal partners for beans, sausage, and noodles of all types. Winter citrus, from kumquats to Meyer lemons, offer hits of bright flavor to seafood and vegetarian dishes.

january

1

Tone down the spice in this soup by using half spicy and half sweet or all sweet Italian sausage. Serve with warm garlic bread.

SPICY SAUSAGE & BROCCOLI RABE SOUP

serves 4–6

1 lb (500 g) spicy Italian sausages

2 Tbsp olive oil

1 large yellow onion, chopped

5 cloves garlic, thinly sliced

6 cups (48 fl oz/1.5 l) chicken broth

½ bunch broccoli rabe, tough stems peeled, cut into ¾-inch (2-cm) pieces

2 Tbsp tomato paste

Salt and freshly ground pepper

Grated pecorino cheese for serving

In a frying pan, cook the sausages over medium heat, turning occasionally, until golden brown and cooked all the way through, about 15 minutes. Let cool, then cut into slices ¼ inch (6 mm) thick. Set aside.

In a large, heavy pot, warm the oil over medium-high heat. Add the onion and garlic and sauté until translucent, about 5 minutes. Add the broth and bring to a boil. Add the broccoli rabe, tomato paste, and sliced sausage, adjust the heat to maintain a simmer, and cook, uncovered, until the broccoli rabe is tender, 7–8 minutes. Season with salt and pepper and serve, topped with grated cheese.

2

Traditional French onion soup relies on rich beef broth for its deep, full flavor. You can find high-quality broth at meat markets or specialty-food stores.

FRENCH ONION SOUP

serves 6

3 Tbsp unsalted butter

1 Tbsp canola oil

2½ lb (1.25 kg) yellow onions, thinly sliced

Pinch of sugar

Salt and freshly ground pepper

2 cups (16 fl oz/500 ml) dry white wine

8 cups (64 fl oz/2 l) beef broth

1 bay leaf

6 thick slices country-style bread

3 cups (12 oz/375 g) shredded Comté or Gruyère cheese

In a large, heavy pot, melt the butter with the oil over medium-low heat. Add the onions and sugar, and season with salt and pepper. Cover and cook, stirring occasionally, until the onions are meltingly soft, golden, and lightly caramelized, 25–30 minutes.

Add the wine, raise the heat to high, and cook until the liquid is reduced by about half, 8–10 minutes. Add the broth and bay leaf, reduce the heat to medium-low, and simmer, uncovered, until the soup is dark and fully flavored, about 45 minutes. If the liquid is evaporating too quickly and the soup tastes too strong, add a little water, then cover the pot and continue cooking.

Preheat the oven to 400°F (200°C). Arrange the bread slices on a baking sheet and toast, turning once, until golden, 3–5 minutes per side. Set the toasts aside.

Remove and discard the bay leaf. Ladle the soup into ovenproof bowls arranged on the baking sheet. Place a piece of toast on top of the soup in each bowl and sprinkle with the cheese. Bake until the cheese is melted and the toasts are lightly browned around the edges, about 15 minutes. Serve.

3

CAULIFLOWER & ROASTED GARLIC PURÉE

serves 4–6

1 large head garlic

1 tsp olive oil

3 Tbsp unsalted butter

½ yellow onion, chopped

¼ cup (2 fl oz/60 ml) dry sherry

4 cups (32 fl oz/1 l) chicken or vegetable broth

1 head cauliflower, stemmed and cut into small florets

3 Tbsp heavy cream

Salt and ground white pepper

Chopped chives for garnish

The flavor of the garlic adds richness to this soup but it is subtle. If you are a real garlic lover, roast 2 heads of garlic for the recipe.

Preheat the oven to 400°F (200°C). Cut off the top of the head of garlic, drizzle with the olive oil, and wrap loosely in foil. Roast until tender when pierced with a knife, about 45 minutes. When it is cool enough to handle, squeeze the garlic flesh from the skins and set aside.

In a large saucepan, melt the butter over medium-high heat. Add the onion and sauté until soft, 5 minutes. Add the roasted garlic and, using a wooden spoon, mash it into the onions. Cook until the mixture is bubbly and starting to caramelize, about 3 minutes. Add the sherry and bring to a boil, stirring to scrape up any browned bits on the bottom of the pot, and let boil for 2 minutes. Add the broth and bring to a boil. Add the cauliflower and reduce the heat to medium-low. Simmer, uncovered, until the cauliflower is very tender, 20–25 minutes. Remove from the heat and let cool slightly.

Working in batches, purée the soup in a blender. Return to the saucepan over medium heat. Add the cream and return the soup just to a gentle boil. Season with salt and pepper and serve, garnished with the chives.

4

FIVE-SPICE BEEF STEW

serves 4–6

1 Tbsp canola oil

1½ lb (750 g) beef sirloin tip, cut into strips ½ inch (12 mm) thick and 3 inches (7.5 cm) long

2 cups (16 fl oz/500 ml) beef broth

¼ cup (2 fl oz/60 ml) soy sauce

2 Tbsp dry sherry or rice wine

1 unpeeled piece fresh ginger, about 1 inch (2.5 cm) long, thinly sliced lengthwise

½ tsp Chinese five-spice powder

½ lb (250 g) Chinese or daikon radish, peeled and cut into 2-inch (5-cm) pieces

4 green onions, white and tender green parts, cut into 2-inch (5-cm) lengths

5 or 6 napa cabbage leaves, cut crosswise into strips 2 inches (5 cm) wide

The Chinese radish is sweeter than its more popular cousin, the Japanese daikon, and both are easy to find at Asian markets. Any mild turnip may be substituted.

In a large, heavy pot, warm the oil over medium-high heat. Working in batches, add the beef strips and brown well on all sides, about 5 minutes per batch. Transfer to a bowl. Add the broth and stir to scrape up any browned bits on the bottom of the pot. Return the meat to the pot. Add the soy sauce, sherry, ginger, five-spice powder, daikon, and green onions. Bring to a simmer, reduce the heat to medium-low, cover, and simmer until the meat falls apart when tested with a fork, about 3 hours.

Using a large spoon, skim the fat from the surface of the stew. Add the cabbage, cover, and simmer over medium-low heat until the cabbage is very soft and wilted but not mushy, about 30 minutes longer. Serve.

5

POSOLE
serves 12

1 lb (500 g) dried posole or
2 lb (1 kg) presoaked dried posole

3 Tbsp olive oil

2 yellow onions, finely chopped

8 cloves garlic, finely chopped

1 Tbsp dried Mexican or regular oregano

1 tsp red pepper flakes

5 cups (40 fl oz/1.25 l) chicken broth

½–1 lb (250–500 g) boneless pork shoulder, trimmed and cut into ½-inch (12-mm) cubes

Salt and freshly ground pepper

Posole is a special comfort food of the Southwest. You can easily use canned hominy, but the authentic dried corn, soaked and simmered with a few simple seasonings, is far tastier. Look for dried posole in a well-stocked grocery or Hispanic market.

If using dried posole, in a large bowl, combine the posole with water to cover and let stand overnight, stirring occasionally. Drain and set aside.

In a large, heavy pot, warm the oil over medium heat. Add the onions, garlic, oregano, and pepper flakes, cover, and cook, stirring occasionally, until the onions and garlic are almost tender, about 10 minutes. Add 8 cups (64 fl oz/2 l) water, the broth, and the posole and bring to a simmer.

Meanwhile, place a large frying pan over medium-low heat. Scatter the pork in the pan and sauté until it has lost its pink color and has released a generous amount of liquid, about 10 minutes. Raise the heat to medium-high and cook, stirring, until the liquid evaporates and the meat is well browned, 10–12 minutes. Transfer the meat to the pot with the posole. Add 2 cups (16 fl oz/500 ml) of the posole cooking liquid to the frying pan off the heat and stir to scrape up any browned bits on the pan bottom. Return the liquid to the pot.

Bring to a simmer, cover partially, and cook, stirring occasionally, for 1 hour. Add 2 tsp salt and 1 tsp pepper and continue to simmer, partially covered, stirring occasionally, until the meat is tender and most of the posole kernels have burst, 1–1½ hours longer, adding more water as necessary to keep the consistency soupy. Season with salt and pepper and serve.

6

VEGETARIAN CHILI
serves 6–8

2 cups (14 oz/440 g) dried pinto beans, picked over and rinsed

3 Tbsp canola oil

2 yellow onions, finely chopped

5 cloves garlic, minced

1 Tbsp plus 1 tsp dried oregano

1 Tbsp plus 1 tsp ground cumin

1 tsp ground coriander

1 Tbsp paprika

¼ tsp cayenne pepper

¼ cup (1 oz/30 g) chili powder

1 can (15 oz/470 g) diced tomatoes

1 canned chipotle chile in adobo, minced

5 cups (40 fl oz/1.25 l) vegetable broth

1 Tbsp balsamic vinegar

3 Tbsp finely chopped cilantro

Salt

In some parts, traditional chili may require beef, but more liberal interpretations include beans and vegetables, for a lean but filling dinner-in-a-bowl. Cumin, cayenne, chipotle, and cilantro pack a nice Latin kick in this version.

Place the dried beans in a bowl with cold water to cover and soak for at least 4 hours or up to overnight. Drain and set aside.

In a large, heavy pot, warm the oil over medium heat. Add the onions and garlic and sauté until softened, about 7 minutes. Add the oregano, cumin, coriander, paprika, cayenne, and chili powder and stir to combine. Cook, stirring, for about 3 minutes.

Add the tomatoes, chipotle, broth, and beans and bring to a boil. Reduce the heat to low and cook, partially covered, until the beans are tender yet firm, 1–1½ hours. If the chili seems too thick, add a little water.

Add the vinegar and cook for 1 minute. Stir in the chopped cilantro and season with salt, then serve.

JANUARY 7

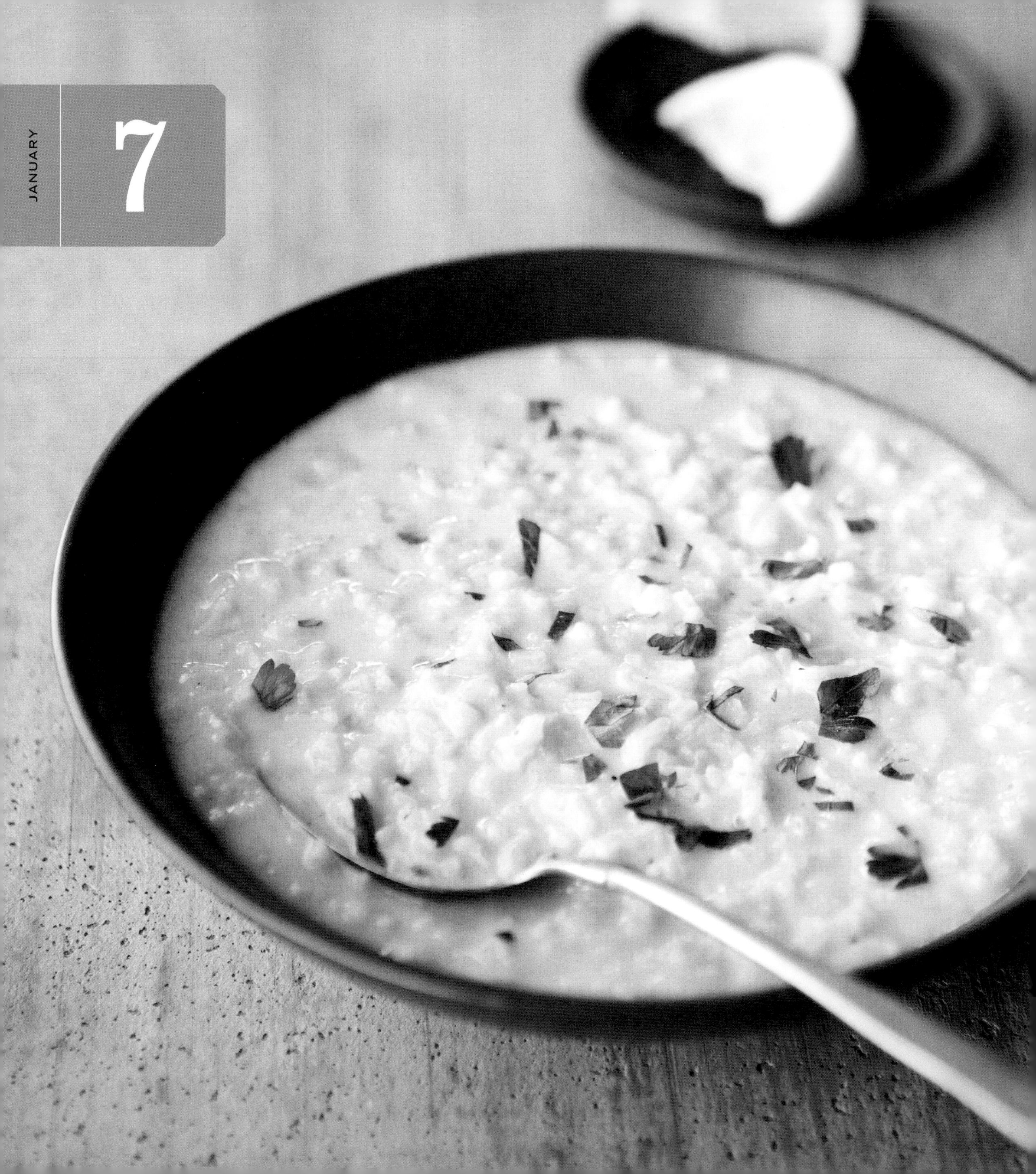

7

*This rich, lemony
chicken-and-rice
soup is a signature
dish of Greece.
To help prevent
the eggs from
curdling, they
must be tempered
by whisking a small
amount of hot liquid
into the yolks to heat
them slightly before
adding them to the
hot mixture.*

AVGOLEMONO

serves 4

6 cups (48 fl oz/1.5 l) chicken broth

½ cup (3½ oz/105 g) long-grain white rice

4 egg yolks, lightly beaten

¼ cup (2 fl oz/60 ml) fresh lemon juice

1 tsp finely chopped lemon zest

Salt and ground white pepper

2 Tbsp finely chopped flat-leaf parsley

In a large, heavy pot, bring the broth to
a boil over medium-high heat. Add the
rice and cook, uncovered, until tender,
about 15 minutes.

In a bowl, whisk together the egg yolks, lemon
juice, and lemon zest. Whisking constantly,
slowly pour 1 cup (8 fl oz/ 250 ml) of the hot
broth into the egg mixture. Reduce the heat
under the broth to medium-low and slowly
stir the egg mixture into the pot. Cook,
stirring, until the soup is slightly thickened,
3–4 minutes. Do not let it boil.

Season with salt and pepper and serve,
garnished with the parsley.

8

*Smoked paprika,
piquillo peppers,
and sherry vinegar
punctuate this chili
with a Spanish
twist. Serve with
Manchego cheese
and crusty bread.*

CHICKEN CHILI WITH PIQUILLO PEPPERS

serves 6

2 Tbsp olive oil

1 large yellow onion, chopped

3 cloves garlic, minced

1 lb (500 g) skinless, boneless chicken
breasts, cut into ¼-inch (6-mm) cubes

Salt

1 tsp smoked paprika

½ tsp chili powder

1 jar (5 oz/155 g) roasted piquillo or
red bell peppers, drained and sliced

1 can (15 oz/470 g) white beans, drained

1 can (28 oz/875 g) crushed tomatoes

1 cup (8 fl oz/250 ml) chicken broth

2 Tbsp tomato paste

1 Tbsp sherry vinegar

2 Tbsp chopped cilantro

In a large, heavy pot, warm the oil over
medium-high heat. Add the onion and garlic
and sauté until translucent, about 5 minutes.
Add the chicken and cook, stirring often,
until browned on all sides, 5–7 minutes. Stir
in 1 Tbsp salt, the smoked paprika, and the
chili powder and cook for 1 minute. Add the
peppers, beans, tomatoes, broth, tomato paste,
and vinegar. Stir well to combine and bring
to a boil. Reduce the heat to low and simmer
gently, uncovered, stirring occasionally, until
the flavors come together and the chicken is
cooked all the way through, about 30 minutes.

Stir in the cilantro, season with salt, and serve.

9

*This traditional
Russian beet soup,
ideally a vibrant
ruby red, is fit for
the winter months
when made heartier
with shredded beef
and a rich broth.*

BEEF BORSCHT

serves 4

3 beets (about 1½ lb/750 g)

2 Tbsp canola oil

1 leek, white and pale green parts, sliced

1 parsnip, peeled and chopped

1 large carrot, peeled and chopped

1 celery rib, chopped

2 cloves garlic, minced

6 cups (48 fl oz/1.5 l) beef broth

2 cups (12 oz/375 g) shredded cooked beef

⅛ tsp ground allspice

Salt and freshly ground pepper

2 cups (4 oz/125 g) chopped green cabbage

1 cup (6 oz/185 g) canned diced tomatoes

2 Yukon gold potatoes, peeled,
each cut lengthwise into 4 wedges

2 Tbsp red wine vinegar, plus more as needed

½ cup (4 oz/125 g) sour cream

1 Tbsp small dill sprigs

Preheat the oven to 350°F (180°C). Wrap
each beet in foil and roast until tender when
pierced with a knife, about 1 hour. Let cool,
still wrapped, for 15 minutes. Using a paring
knife, peel and discard the skins. Shred the
beets into a bowl. Set aside.

In a large, heavy pot, warm the oil over
medium-low heat. Add the leek, parsnip,
carrot, celery, and garlic and cook, stirring
often, until tender, about 10 minutes. Add
the broth, beef, allspice, 2 tsp salt, and ¼ tsp
pepper. Bring to a boil, reduce the heat to
low, cover, and cook until the vegetables
are tender, 25–30 minutes. Stir in the beets,
cabbage, and tomatoes. Raise the heat to
medium-low and cook, uncovered, until
the cabbage is tender, about 10 minutes.

Meanwhile, put the potatoes in a saucepan
and add water to cover and ½ tsp salt. Cover
and bring to a boil. Reduce the heat to medium-
low and simmer until the potatoes are tender,
15 minutes. Drain and keep warm.

Reduce the heat under the soup to low and stir
in the 2 Tbsp vinegar. If the soup tastes a little
dull, add a bit more vinegar, salt, or pepper.
Divide the potato wedges among bowls and
ladle soup over them. Garnish with the sour
cream and dill, then serve.

10

*Instead of pasta,
try adding ¼ cup
(2 oz/60 g) rice to
the soup 15 minutes
before it is done.
Or try other small
pastas, like orzo,
stelline, or ditalini.
A squeeze of lemon
brightens the
chicken flavor.*

CLASSIC CHICKEN NOODLE SOUP

serves 4

1 Tbsp canola oil

2 celery ribs, finely chopped

1 leek, white part only, halved
and thinly sliced

1 carrot, peeled and finely chopped

5 cups (40 fl oz/1.25 l) chicken broth

1 bay leaf

¼ tsp dried thyme

2 cups (12 oz/375 g) cooked shredded chicken

½ lb (250 g) dried egg noodles

Salt and freshly ground pepper

¼ cup (⅓ oz/10 g) minced flat-leaf parsley

In a large saucepan, warm the oil over
medium heat. When it is hot, add the celery,
leek, and carrot and sauté until softened,
about 5 minutes. Add the broth, bay leaf,
thyme, and shredded chicken. Bring to
a boil over medium-high heat. Add the
noodles, stir well, and cook just until
the noodles are tender, about 10 minutes.

Remove and discard the bay leaf from the
soup. Season to taste with salt and pepper
and serve, garnished with the parsley.

11

Fresh dates, with their thin skins and intense sweetness, are occasionally mistaken for a dried fruit. They're not— these characteristics merely come from growing in the desert. Here they add a depth of flavor to the stew and marry well with the pungent spices.

MOROCCAN LAMB STEW
serves 6

4 Tbsp (2 fl oz/60 ml) olive oil

2 yellow onions, finely chopped

3 carrots, peeled and chopped

½ cup (2½ oz/75 g) all-purpose flour

Salt and freshly ground pepper

3 lb (1.5 kg) cubed lamb for stewing

3 cloves garlic, minced

1 tsp ground cumin

¼ tsp saffron threads

1 Tbsp peeled and minced fresh ginger

2½ cups (20 fl oz/625 ml) beef broth

1 cup (8 oz/250 g) canned crushed tomatoes

1 cup (6 oz/185 g) chopped pitted dates

Grated zest and juice of 1 orange

2 Tbsp finely chopped flat-leaf parsley

Preheat the oven to 350°F (180°C). In a large, heavy pot, warm 1 Tbsp of the oil over medium heat. Add the onions and sauté until softened, about 7 minutes. Add the carrots and sauté until slightly softened, about 3 minutes. Transfer to a bowl.

In a resealable plastic bag, combine the flour, ½ tsp salt, and ½ tsp pepper. Add the lamb, seal the bag, and shake to coat. Add the remaining 3 Tbsp oil to the pot and warm over medium-high heat. Working in batches, remove the lamb from the bag, shaking off excess flour, and add to the pot in a single layer. Brown on all sides, 4–5 minutes per batch. Transfer to a bowl.

Return the onion mixture and browned lamb to the pot. Add the garlic, cumin, saffron, and ginger and stir to coat the meat and vegetables. Add the broth and bring to a boil, stirring to scrape up any browned bits on the bottom of the pot. Add the tomatoes, dates, and orange zest and juice and bring to a boil over high heat. Cover and bake until the meat is tender, 1½–2 hours.

Season with salt and pepper and serve, garnished with parsley.

12

Portuguese linguiça or chorizo is often the choice for soups with greens and beans, but using low-fat turkey kielbasa imparts the same smoky, spicy flavor.

KALE & WHITE BEAN SOUP
serves 4

1 bunch kale (about ¾ lb/375 g)

1 Yukon gold potato (about ½ lb/250 g)

2 oz (60 g) pork or turkey kielbasa sausage

2 tsp olive oil

1 large yellow onion, chopped

4 cloves garlic, chopped

⅛ tsp red pepper flakes

Salt and freshly ground pepper

1 can (15 oz/470 g) white beans, drained

Remove the tough stems from the kale and cut the leaves crosswise into strips ½ inch (12 mm) wide. You will have about 5 cups (10 oz/315 g). Cut the potato into 1-inch (2.5-cm) pieces. Slice the kielbasa. Set aside.

In a large, heavy pot, warm the oil over medium-high heat. Add the onion and garlic and sauté until translucent, about 5 minutes. Stir in the kale, potato, kielbasa, and red pepper flakes. Season generously with salt. Pour in 8 cups (64 fl oz/2 l) water. Bring to a boil, reduce the heat to medium-low, and simmer, uncovered, until the kale is almost tender, about 20 minutes.

Add the beans and cook until heated through, about 5 minutes. Season with salt and pepper and serve.

13

In the winter when tomatoes are not in season, canned tomatoes are the best choice for adding to soups. San Marzano tomatoes, a plum variety from Italy, are widely acknowledged as the gold standard of canned tomatoes.

CREAM OF TOMATO SOUP

serves 4–6

¼ cup (2 oz/60 g) unsalted butter

1 celery rib with leaves, finely chopped

½ cup (2 ½ oz / 75 g) chopped shallots

1 clove garlic, minced

⅓ cup (2 oz/60 g) all-purpose flour

1 can (28 oz/875 g) diced tomatoes

2 cups (16 fl oz/500 ml) chicken broth

2 cups (16 fl oz/500 ml) half-and-half

1 tsp chopped marjoram or oregano, plus sprigs for garnish

Salt and freshly ground pepper

In a large, heavy pot, melt the butter over medium heat. Add the celery and cook, stirring occasionally, until it begins to soften, about 2 minutes. Add the shallots and garlic and cook, stirring often, until the shallots soften, about 2 minutes.

Sprinkle the flour over the vegetables and stir well. Stir in the tomatoes with their juices, the broth, the half-and-half, and the chopped marjoram and stir well. Bring to a boil over high heat, stirring often. Reduce the heat to medium-low and simmer, uncovered, until the soup is slightly thickened, about 30 minutes.

Season with salt and pepper and serve, garnished with the herb sprigs.

14

The are many stories about the origins of this San Francisco specialty. Most locals believe it is related to the Italian cacciucco, a fish stew of Livorno, and to the fish stews of the Friuli region, which are made with red wine. Serve with grilled coarse country bread rubbed with garlic.

CIOPPINO

serves 6

½ cup (4 fl oz/125 ml) olive oil

3 large yellow onions, chopped

5 celery ribs, chopped

6 cloves garlic, minced

2 small bay leaves

2 thyme sprigs

2 tsp ground fennel seeds

1–2 tsp red pepper flakes

5 cups (40 fl oz/1.25 l) fish broth

3 cups (18 oz/560 g) canned diced tomatoes

1½ cups (12 fl oz/375 ml) dry red wine

½ cup (4 fl oz/125 ml) thick tomato purée

Salt and freshly ground pepper

18 clams, scrubbed

1 crab or lobster, cooked, cracked, and cut into 2–3-inch (5–7.5-cm) pieces

18 shrimp, peeled and deveined

18 sea scallops, tough muscles removed

18 mussels, scrubbed and debearded

¼ cup (⅓ oz/10 g) chopped flat-leaf parsley

In a large, heavy pot, warm the oil over medium heat. Add the onions and sauté until translucent, about 7 minutes. Add the celery, garlic, bay leaves, thyme, fennel seeds, and red pepper flakes and sauté until the celery is soft, about 5 minutes. Add the broth, tomatoes, wine, and tomato purée and simmer for about 10 minutes to blend the flavors. Season with salt and pepper.

Add the clams, discarding any that do not close to the touch. Add the crab, cover, and simmer briskly until the clams start to open, about 5 minutes. Add the shrimp, scallops, and mussels, discarding any that do not close to the touch, and continue to cook until the shrimp turn pink, the scallops are opaque throughout, and the mussels open, 3–5 minutes. Discard any unopened clams or mussels.

Season with salt and pepper and serve, sprinkled with the parsley.

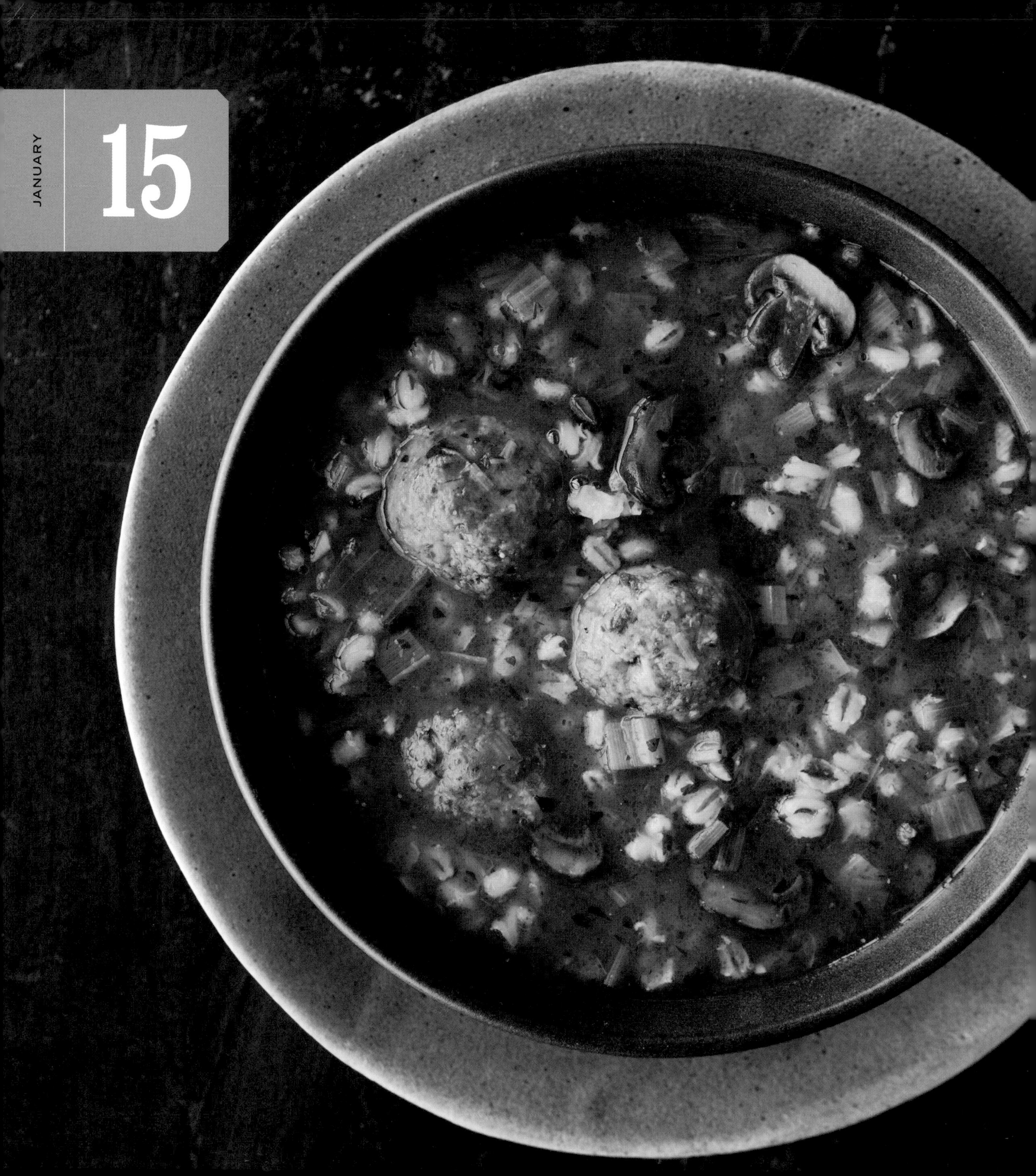

15

This is a great soup to make with kids, who will have fun forming the meatballs and love eating the end result. The meatballs are also delicious served with pasta or couscous. The meatballs can be made ahead and frozen.

BARLEY-LEEK SOUP WITH MINI CHICKEN MEATBALLS

serves 8–10

1 Tbsp unsalted butter

2 Tbsp olive oil

3 leeks, white and pale green parts, chopped

3 cloves garlic, minced

½ lb (250 g) cremini mushrooms, sliced

2 Tbsp tomato paste

¼ cup (2 fl oz/60 ml) dry white wine

2 cups (12 oz/375 g) pearl barley

8 cups (64 fl oz/2 l) chicken broth, plus more as needed

FOR THE MEATBALLS

1 lb (500 g) ground chicken

½ cup (2 oz/60 g) grated Parmesan cheese

¼ cup (1 oz/30 g) plain dried bread crumbs

2 Tbsp minced flat-leaf parsley, plus ½ cup (¾ oz/20 g) chopped parsley for garnish

1 Tbsp tomato paste

Salt and freshly ground pepper

In a large, heavy pot, melt the butter with the oil over medium-high heat. Add the leeks and garlic and sauté until very soft, about 5 minutes. Add the mushrooms and cook, stirring often, until they begin to soften, about 5 minutes. Add the tomato paste and wine, stir to combine, and cook for 4 minutes. Add the barley and 8 cups broth and bring to a boil. Reduce the heat to low, cover, and simmer until the barley is tender, about 45 minutes.

Meanwhile, to make the meatballs, preheat the oven to 375°F (190°C). Oil a baking sheet. In a bowl, combine the chicken, Parmesan, bread crumbs, 2 Tbsp parsley, and tomato paste. Add 1 tsp salt and ½ tsp pepper and stir to combine. The mixture will be very sticky. To form the meatballs, use two small spoons to scoop up the mixture and transfer it to the prepared sheet. Bake until the meatballs are cooked through and no longer pink in the center, 10–12 minutes.

Add the meatballs to the soup and stir in gently. If the soup is too thick, add more broth and heat through. Season with salt and pepper and serve, garnished with the ½ cup (¾ oz/20 g) parsley.

16

For a hit of spice, add a few drops of hot-pepper sauce to this creamy mussel soup. Mussels often have "beards," fibrous tufts with which they cling to rocks (farm-raised mussels may not have these). If present, scrape away the fibers with a paring knife or scissors before cooking.

MUSSELS IN TOMATO & CREAM BROTH

serves 4–6

2 Tbsp olive oil

1 shallot, minced

3 cloves garlic, minced

1 tsp ground cumin

½ tsp paprika

½ tsp ground ginger

¼ tsp ground cinnamon

1 cup (8 fl oz/250 ml) clam juice

2 cups (16 fl oz/500 ml) chicken broth

3 lb (1.5 kg) mussels, scrubbed and debearded

3 plum tomatoes, seeded and diced

½ cup (4 fl oz/125 ml) heavy cream

Salt and freshly ground pepper

2 Tbsp minced flat-leaf parsley

In a heavy-bottomed saucepan, warm the oil over medium heat. Add the shallot and garlic and sauté until soft, about 4 minutes. Add the cumin, paprika, ginger, and cinnamon and allow the spices to toast, stirring constantly, for 2 minutes. Add the clam juice and the chicken broth and bring to a boil. Add the mussels, discarding any that don't close to the touch. Cover the pan tightly and steam the mussels until they open, 5–7 minutes. Discard any unopened mussels.

Stir in the tomatoes and cream and return to a gentle boil. Season with salt and pepper, stir in the parsley, and serve.

17

High up in the Alps between France and Switzerland sits Italy's smallest region, the Valle d'Aosta. The cows that graze on the mountain slopes produce the milk for its famed Fontina. Here, it is used in a rustic soup traditionally made with the local dark rye bread, pane nero.

SAVOY CABBAGE, FONTINA & RYE BREAD SOUP

serves 4–6

Salt and freshly ground pepper

1 head savoy cabbage (about 1 lb/500 g), cut lengthwise into quarters and cored

1 lb (375 g) Fontina cheese

6 cups (48 fl oz/1.5 l) chicken broth

Pinch of grated nutmeg

Pinch of ground cinnamon

12 slices crusty rye bread, toasted

2 tsp unsalted butter, cut into bits

Bring a pot of water to a boil. Add a pinch of salt and the cabbage. Reduce the heat to low and cook, uncovered, until the cabbage is tender, about 30 minutes. Drain and let cool, then cut crosswise into thin slices.

Preheat the oven to 350°F (180°C). Coarsely shred enough cheese to measure ½ cup (2 oz/60 g). Thinly slice the remainder. In a large saucepan, combine the broth, nutmeg, and cinnamon and season with salt and pepper. Bring to a simmer.

Arrange 4 of the bread slices in the bottom of a deep 3-qt (3-l) baking dish. Cover with half each of the cabbage and the cheese slices. Repeat the layers, then cover with the remaining bread. Pour the hot broth over the top. Sprinkle with the shredded cheese and dot with the butter.

Bake until the soup is bubbling and browned, about 45 minutes. Let stand for 5 minutes, then serve.

18

Just 20 minutes and a handful of ingredients yields this ultraflavorful broth, to which you can add any combination of noodles and greens. The soup can be made ahead and frozen. When serving, tongs make easy work of dividing the noodles and bok choy among bowls; ladle the broth on top.

GINGERY BEEF BROTH WITH SOBA NOODLES & BOK CHOY

serves 4–6

2 green onions

3 cups (24 fl oz/750 ml) beef broth

2-inch (5-cm) piece fresh ginger, peeled and thinly sliced

1 large clove garlic, crushed

Salt

1 Tbsp canola oil

2 baby bok choy, quartered

¼ lb (125 g) cremini mushrooms, thinly sliced

5 oz (155 g) soba noodles

1 tsp soy sauce

Hot sauce, such as Sriracha, for serving (optional)

Thinly slice the green onions, reserving the white and pale green parts in one bowl and the dark green parts in a separate bowl.

In a large, heavy pot, combine the broth, 3 cups (24 fl oz/750 ml) water, the ginger, garlic, and the white and light green parts of the green onion and bring to a boil over medium-high heat. Reduce the heat to low and simmer for 20 minutes. Strain the liquid, discarding the solids, and return the broth to the pot. Season with salt and keep warm over low heat.

In a frying pan over medium-high heat, warm the oil. Add the bok choy and mushrooms and sauté, stirring frequently, until the vegetables begin to caramelize and soften, about 6 minutes. Set aside.

Return the broth to a boil and add the soba noodles. Cook, stirring occasionally, for 4 minutes. Add the bok choy, mushrooms, and soy sauce and stir to combine.

Serve, garnished with the dark green onion slices. Pass the hot sauce at the table, if using.

19

If you prefer, instead of puréeing you can finely chop the broccoli into small florets and peel and finely dice the stem for a chunkier consistency.

BROCCOLI & CHEDDAR SOUP

serves 6–8

2 Tbsp unsalted butter

1 yellow onion, finely chopped

¼ cup (1½ oz/45 g) all-purpose flour

5 cups (40 fl oz/1.25 l) chicken broth

1½ lb (750 g) broccoli, tough stems peeled, florets and stems coarsely chopped

1½ Tbsp fresh thyme leaves or ½ tsp dried

1 Tbsp fresh lemon juice

2 cups (16 fl oz/500 ml) milk

½ lb (250 g) sharp Cheddar cheese, shredded

Salt and ground white pepper

In a large, heavy pot, melt the butter over medium heat. Add the onion and sauté until very tender, about 8 minutes. Stir in the flour and sauté for 1 minute. Add the broth, broccoli, thyme, and lemon juice and bring to a boil. Reduce the heat to low, cover, and simmer until the broccoli is tender, about 20 minutes. Remove from the heat and let cool slightly.

Working in batches, purée the soup in a blender. Return to the pot, stir in the milk, and bring to a simmer over low heat. Stir in half of the cheese and continue stirring until melted. Season with salt and pepper. Serve, garnished with the remaining cheese.

20

A tangy mixture of fresh citrus juices gives this soup a wonderfully bright flavor, making it ideal for a cold winter evening. You can substitute calamari or shrimp for the clams.

CITRUSY SEAFOOD SOUP

serves 4–6

1 lb (500 g) firm white-fleshed fish fillets such as monkfish, flounder, or cod

Salt and freshly ground pepper

3 Tbsp olive oil

1 large yellow onion, chopped

2 cloves garlic, minced

1 tsp ground cumin

2 tsp paprika

4 cups (32 fl oz/1 l) fish broth or water

½ lb (250 g) small clams such as Manila, scrubbed

⅓ cup (3 fl oz/80 ml) fresh orange juice

2 Tbsp fresh lime juice

Chopped mint or flat-leaf parsley

Cut the fish into strips 1½ inches (4 cm) long and ½ inch (12 mm) wide and place on a plate. Sprinkle lightly with salt, cover, and refrigerate until ready to cook.

In a large, heavy pot, warm the oil over medium heat. Add the onion and sauté until tender, 5–7 minutes. Add the garlic, cumin, and paprika, reduce the heat to low, and sauté until the garlic is tender, about 5 minutes. Add the broth, raise the heat to medium, and bring to a boil. Reduce the heat to low and simmer for 15 minutes to blend the flavors.

Add the fish pieces and the clams, discarding any that do not close to the touch, and cook until the fish is opaque throughout and the clams have opened, 7–10 minutes. Discard any unopened clams. Stir in the orange and lime juices, season with salt and pepper, and serve, garnished with mint.

21

This soup is a great way to use leftovers, as you can make it with any meat or seafood and substitute just about any type of vegetable. Serve the soup with both a spoon and a fork or chopsticks.

ROAST PORK & UDON NOODLE SOUP

serves 4

½ lb (250 g) pork tenderloin

1 Tbsp olive oil

Salt and freshly ground pepper

1 Tbsp canola oil

3 oz (90 g) shiitake mushrooms, thinly sliced

2 baby bok choy, quartered lengthwise

5 cups (40 fl oz/1.25 l) chicken broth

5 Tbsp soy sauce

3 Tbsp mirin

6 oz (185 g) udon noodles

Preheat the oven to 400°F (200°C). Put the pork on a baking sheet, brush with the olive oil, and season with salt and pepper. Roast until an instant-read thermometer inserted into the thickest part registers 135°–140°F (57°–60°C), 20–25 minutes. Let the pork rest for at least 10 minutes and then chop into bite-sized pieces.

While the pork is resting, in a small frying pan, warm the canola oil over medium heat. Add the mushrooms and bok choy and sauté until they begin to caramelize, 5–7 minutes. Remove from the heat and set aside.

In a large, heavy pot, combine the broth, soy sauce, and mirin and bring to a boil over medium-high heat. Add the udon and cook, stirring occasionally, for 4 minutes. Add the pork, mushrooms, and bok choy and reduce the heat to a simmer for 5 minutes. Serve.

22

Kumquats are tiny citrus fruits that are packed with flavor. Do not peel them when you make this soup. The peel is the sweet part of the fruit and balances the tartness of the flesh.

KUMQUAT-CARROT PURÉE WITH TOASTED FENNEL SEEDS

serves 4

2 tsp fennel seeds

4 Tbsp (2 oz/60 g) unsalted butter

1 small yellow onion, chopped

2 cloves garlic, minced

1 cup kumquats, unpeeled, chopped, plus kumquat slices for garnish

2 lb (1 kg) carrots, peeled and thinly sliced

5 cups (40 fl oz/1.25 l) chicken broth

Salt and freshly ground pepper

In a small frying pan, toast the fennel seeds over medium heat just until fragrant, about 3 minutes. Transfer to a spice grinder and grind finely.

In a large, heavy pot, melt the butter over medium-high heat. Add the onion and garlic and sauté until translucent, about 5 minutes. Add the kumquats and carrots and sauté for 10 minutes. Add the broth and bring to a boil. Reduce the heat to low and simmer, uncovered, until the carrots and kumquats are very soft, 35–40 minutes. Remove from the heat and let cool slightly.

Working in batches, purée the soup in a blender. Return to the pot and stir in the ground fennel. Season with salt and pepper and serve, garnished with kumquat slices.

23

23

For easy variations, substitute other small filled pasta, such as ravioli, or use Swiss chard or spinach in place of the escarole.

TORTELLINI & ESCAROLE SOUP

serves 6

6 cups (48 fl oz/1.5 l) chicken broth
8 oz (250 g) fresh tortellini
1 small head escarole (6–8 oz/185–250 g)
Salt and freshly ground pepper
¾ cup (3 oz/90 g) grated Parmesan cheese

In a large, heavy pot, bring the broth and 2 cups (16 fl oz/500 ml) water to a boil over medium-high heat. Reduce the heat to medium, add the tortellini, cover, and cook until al dente, 4–5 minutes, or according to the package directions.

Meanwhile, cut the core end from the escarole. Remove the leaves from the head, rinse, and dry well. Pile the leaves on top of one another and cut into ¼-inch (6-mm) strips.

When the tortellini are done, add the escarole and season with salt and pepper. Simmer, uncovered, until the escarole is soft, about 2 minutes. Serve, garnished with the Parmesan.

24

Beans and barley are a classic combination in soup and one that yields a pleasant texture and earthy, almost meaty flavor. You can replace the barley with farro, wild rice, or Israeli couscous, and use different beans as well. Just keep in mind you may have to adjust the water amount and cooking time accordingly.

CRANBERRY BEAN & BARLEY SOUP

serves 4

1 cup (7 oz/220 g) dried cranberry or red kidney beans, picked over and rinsed
1 Tbsp olive oil
2 oz (60 g) sliced pancetta, finely chopped
2 celery ribs, chopped
2 carrots, peeled and chopped
1 yellow onion, chopped
2 cloves garlic, finely chopped
½ cup (4 oz/125 g) pearl barley, rinsed
Salt and freshly ground pepper
Extra-virgin olive oil for serving

Place the dried beans in a bowl with cold water to cover and soak for at least 4 hours or up to overnight. Drain and set aside.

In a large, heavy pot, warm the 1 Tbsp oil over medium heat. Add the pancetta and sauté until lightly browned, about 8 minutes. Add the celery, carrots, onion, and garlic and sauté until tender, about 10 minutes.

Add the beans and 8 cups (64 fl oz/2 l) water. Bring to a simmer over low heat and cook, uncovered, until the beans are very tender, about 1 hour.

Pour through a sieve placed over a clean pot; reserve the liquid. In a food processor, purée the beans and vegetables. Add the purée to the cooking liquid. Stir in the barley and season with salt and pepper. Bring to a simmer over medium heat, reduce the heat to low, and cook, uncovered, stirring often, until the barley is tender, about 30 minutes.

Season with salt and pepper and serve, passing extra-virgin olive oil at the table for drizzling.

25

Quick and simple to prepare, this soup also freezes well. Freshly cracked black pepper or small crackers make an elegant topping.

FENNEL-CELERY BISQUE

serves 4

4 Tbsp (2 oz/60 g) unsalted butter

2 shallots, minced

2 fennel bulbs, stalks and fronds removed, chopped

5 celery ribs, chopped

¼ cup (2 fl oz/60 ml) dry white wine

2 cups (16 fl oz/500 ml) vegetable broth

½ cup (4 fl oz/125 ml) heavy cream

Salt and ground white pepper

In large, heavy pot, melt the butter over medium-high heat. Add the shallots, fennel, and celery and sauté until the vegetables soften, about 10 minutes. Add the wine and cook for 5 minutes. Add the broth, bring to a boil, reduce the heat to low, and simmer until the vegetables are very tender, about 20 minutes. Remove from the heat and let cool slightly.

Working in batches, purée the soup in a blender. Return to the pot and add the cream. Bring the soup just to a boil over low heat. Season with salt and pepper and serve.

26

To make the fried shallots, stir together 2 Tbsp all-purpose flour, ½ tsp salt, and ¼ tsp pepper. Add 2 sliced shallots and toss to coat. Heat ½ cup (4 fl oz/125 ml) canola oil in a saucepan over medium-high heat until very hot. Shake off any excess flour from the shallots and fry until golden brown, 4 minutes. Drain on paper towels and season with salt.

STEAK & POTATO SOUP WITH FRIED SHALLOTS

serves 4–6

1 sweet potato, peeled and chopped

1 parsnip, peeled and chopped

5 Tbsp (3 fl oz/80 ml) olive oil

Salt and freshly ground pepper

¾ lb (375 g) flank steak

1 large yellow onion, finely chopped

2 cloves garlic, minced

2 celery ribs, finely chopped

2 Tbsp all-purpose flour

2 Tbsp tomato paste

3 cups (24 fl oz/750 g) beef broth

Fried Shallots (left)

Preheat the oven to 400°F (200°C). Line a baking sheet with parchment paper. In a bowl, toss the sweet potato and parsnip with 2 Tbsp of the oil. Season generously with salt and pepper. Spread the vegetables in an even layer on the prepared pan and roast, stirring once, until caramelized, about 25 minutes.

Warm a grill pan or frying pan over high heat. Brush both sides of the steak with 1 Tbsp of the oil and season with salt and pepper. Cook to medium-rare, 5–6 minutes per side. Let the steak rest for 10 minutes, then cut into ½-inch (12-mm) cubes.

In a large, heavy pot, warm the remaining 2 Tbsp oil over medium-high heat. Add the onion, garlic, and celery and sauté until softened, about 5 minutes. Add the flour and stir constantly for 1 minute. Add the tomato paste and broth, stir to combine, and cook for 10 minutes. Add the sweet potatoes, parsnips, and steak and cook for 5 minutes. Season with salt and pepper.

Serve, garnished with the shallots.

27

Serve this classic Southwestern soup with thick wedges of corn bread and cold Mexican beer.

TURKEY SOUP WITH CHIPOTLE & LIME

serves 4

1 small can chipotle chiles in adobo

1 Tbsp olive oil

1 red onion, minced

2 cloves garlic, minced

4 cups (32 fl oz/1 l) chicken broth

1 can (15 oz/470 g) crushed tomatoes

½ tsp ground cumin

2 cups (12 oz/375 g) shredded cooked turkey

3 Tbsp fresh lime juice

Corn tortilla chips, crumbled queso fresco, diced avocado, and cilantro leaves for serving

Purée the chipotles in a blender. Measure out ½–1 tsp of the purée. Refrigerate the remainder for another use (it will keep for 1 month).

In a large, heavy pot, warm the oil over medium heat. Add the onion and garlic and sauté until the onion is soft, about 6 minutes. Add the broth, tomatoes, and cumin and bring to a boil. Reduce the heat to low, cover, and simmer for 10 minutes. Stir in the turkey, lime juice, and chipotle purée to taste. Serve, garnished with tortilla chips, cheese, avocado, and cilantro.

28

A warming potato soup makes a satisfying meal on any cold day, and in summer is refreshing served chilled. Crumbled goat cheese, chopped chives or scallions, or a swirl of yogurt are other good options for toppings.

LEEK & POTATO SOUP WITH BLUE CHEESE

serves 4–6

3 Tbsp unsalted butter

6 cups (18 oz/560 g) thinly sliced leeks (white and pale green parts)

1 large yellow onion, sliced

5 cups (40 fl oz/1.25 l) chicken broth

1 lb (500 g) russet potatoes, peeled and cut into chunks

Salt

3 oz (90 g) blue cheese, crumbled (about ¾ cup), plus more for garnish

1 tsp dry mustard

Sweet paprika for garnish

In a large, heavy pot, melt the butter over medium-low heat. Add the leeks and onion and sauté until tender, about 15 minutes. Add 4 cups (32 fl oz/1 l) of the broth, the potatoes, and 1 tsp salt. Bring to a boil, reduce the heat to low, cover, and simmer until the potatoes are tender, about 15 minutes. Remove from the heat and let cool slightly.

Working in batches, purée the soup in a blender. Return to the pot and stir in the 3 oz cheese and the mustard. Heat over medium-low heat, then adjust the consistency with the remaining broth. Serve, garnished with cheese and a sprinkle of paprika.

29

There's nothing more satisfying than a hearty bowl of soup like this one, chock-full of bright vegetables and tender lentils. Unlike other dried legumes, lentils need no presoaking, and they cook relatively quickly. For a vegetarian version of this soup, use vegetable broth instead of chicken.

VEGETABLE-LENTIL SOUP WITH SHERRY

serves 6

2 Tbsp olive oil

1 yellow onion, chopped

1 clove garlic, minced

1 carrot, peeled and chopped

1 red bell pepper, seeded and chopped

6 cups (48 fl oz/1.5 l) chicken broth

2 cups (14 oz/440 g) lentils, picked over and rinsed

1 can (28 oz/875 g) diced tomatoes

1 tsp smoked paprika

1 tsp ground cumin

Salt and freshly ground pepper

4 oz (125 g) baby spinach leaves, coarsely chopped

2 Tbsp dry sherry

2-oz (60-g) piece Parmesan cheese

In a large, heavy pot, warm the oil over medium-high heat. Add the onion and sauté until soft, about 5 minutes. Add the garlic, carrot, and bell pepper and sauté for 3 minutes. Stir in the broth, lentils, tomatoes with their juices, paprika, and cumin. Season with ½ tsp salt and ¼ tsp pepper. Bring to a boil. Reduce the heat to maintain a simmer, cover, and cook until the lentils are very tender, about 20 minutes.

Stir in the spinach and cook, uncovered, just until it is wilted, about 2 minutes. Stir in the sherry. Season with salt and pepper and serve, using a vegetable peeler to garnish the soup with shavings of Parmesan.

30

Here's a fresh take on a classic chowder, made with flavorful smoked fish. For a lighter version, use whole milk in place of the cream.

SMOKED TROUT CHOWDER

serves 4–6

3 Tbsp unsalted butter

1 yellow onion, chopped

1 fennel bulb (¾ lb/375 g), stalks and fronds removed, quartered, cored, and thinly sliced

2 cups (16 fl oz/500 ml) chicken broth

1 cup (8 fl oz/250 ml) bottled clam juice

3 small red potatoes, cut into small dice

1 cup (8 fl oz/250 ml) heavy cream

8 oz (250 g) smoked trout, crumbled

2 tsp fresh lemon juice

1 Tbsp minced dill

Salt and freshly ground pepper

In a large, heavy pot, melt the butter over medium-high heat. Add the onion and fennel and sauté until soft, about 7 minutes. Add the broth and clam juice and bring to a boil. Add the potatoes, reduce the heat to medium-low, and simmer until the potatoes are tender, about 8 minutes. Add the cream, smoked trout, lemon juice, and dill and cook for 4 minutes. Season with salt and pepper and serve.

31

This classic soup, loved by both kids and adults, is a great way to use leftover rice. Serve with grilled Cheddar cheese and sliced apple sandwiches.

OLD-FASHIONED TOMATO & RICE SOUP

serves 6

3 Tbsp unsalted butter

1 small yellow onion, chopped

2 cloves garlic, minced

2 cans (28 oz/875 g each) diced tomatoes

¼ cup (2 fl oz/60 ml) heavy cream

1 cup (5 oz/155 g) steamed white rice

Salt and freshly ground pepper

In a large saucepan, melt the butter over medium-high heat. Add the onion and garlic and sauté until translucent, about 5 minutes. Add the tomatoes with their juices and bring to a boil. Reduce the heat to low and simmer for 20 minutes. Remove from the heat and let cool slightly.

Working in batches, purée the soup in a blender. Return to the saucepan. Stir in the cream and rice and return to a gentle boil. Season with salt and pepper and serve.

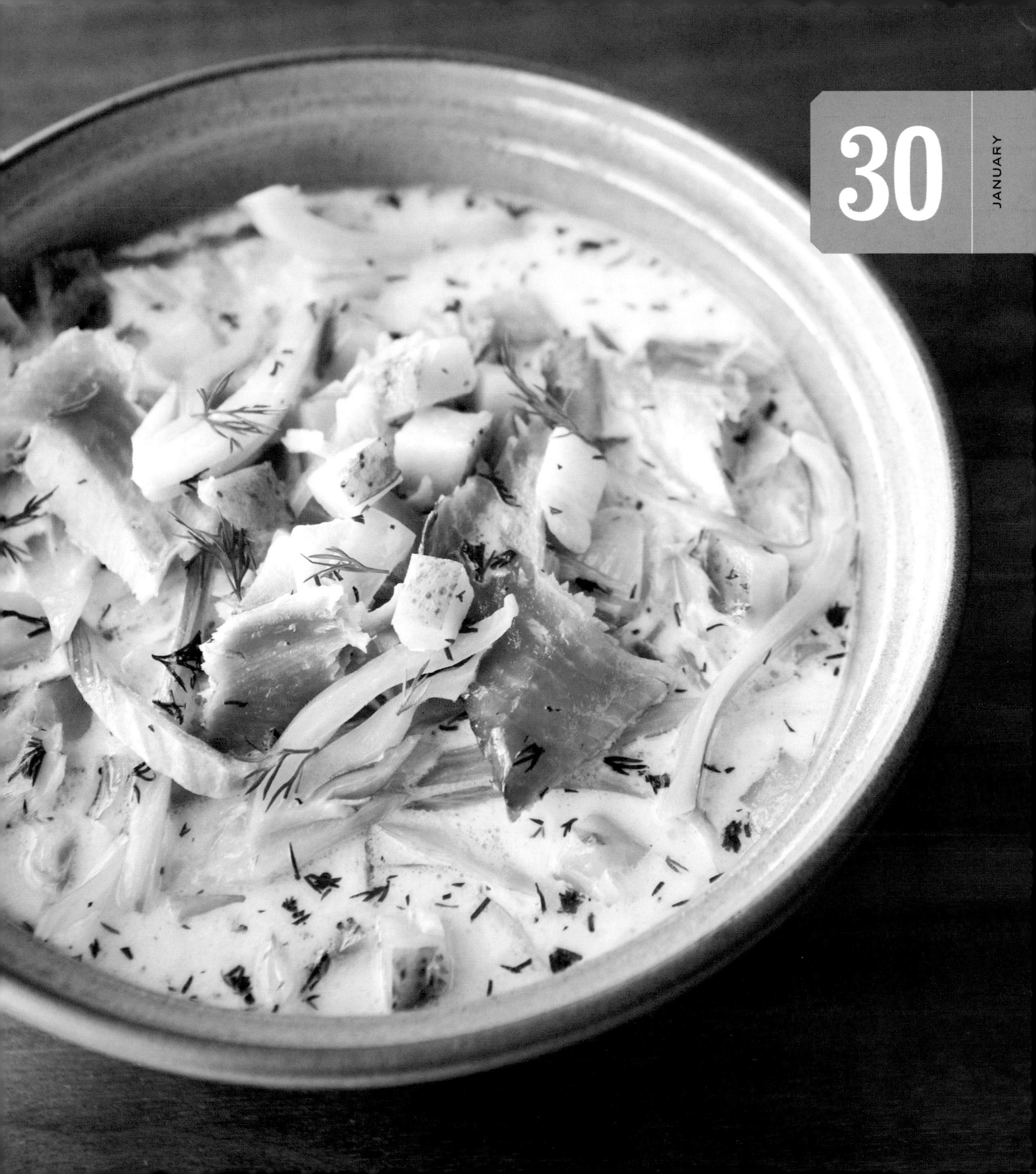

30 JANUARY

1
WINTER GREENS & SHIITAKE SOUP WITH POACHED EGGS
page 34

2
CHILI CON CARNE
page 34

3
SPANISH-STYLE PEAR, PUMPKIN & BEAN SOUP
page 36

4
ORECCHIETTE IN AROMATIC BROTH
page 36

8
SEARED DUCK & BEET GREENS SOUP
page 40

9
CHICKEN STEW WITH OLIVES & ALMONDS
page 40

10
NEW ENGLAND CLAM CHOWDER
page 41

11
LEMONGRASS SOUP WITH SHRIMP & CHILE
page 41

15
CREAMY CAULIFLOWER SOUP WITH CRISPY PROSCIUTTO
page 45

16
BLACK-EYED PEA SOUP WITH HERBS & GARLIC
page 46

17
STONE SOUP
page 46

18
BEEF PHO
page 47

22
THAI SQUASH & COCONUT MILK SOUP
page 51

23
BEEF STEW WITH ORANGE ZEST & RED WINE
page 52

24
YELLOW SPLIT PEA SOUP WITH HAM
page 52

25
LENTIL SOUP WITH PASTA & SAGE
page 53

5

ROASTED ROOT VEGETABLE
& BARLEY STEW
page 37

6

PASTA & BEAN SOUP WITH FONTINA
page 37

7

CHICKPEA, PORCINI & FARRO SOUP
page 39

12

CHICKEN STEW WITH
BUTTERMILK-CHIVE DUMPLINGS
page 42

13

SUN-DRIED TOMATO
SOUP WITH CRAB
page 42

14

CELERY, LEEK & OYSTER BISQUE
page 45

19

SEAFOOD STEW WITH SAFFRON,
SERRANO HAM & ALMONDS
page 48

20

PARMESAN STRACIATELLA WITH KALE
page 48

21

BLACK BEAN SOUP WITH
MEYER LEMON CRÈME FRAÎCHE
page 51

26

SAUSAGE & KALE SOUP
page 53

27

HAM, BEAN & ESCAROLE SOUP
page 54

28

TOMATO BROTH WITH
SHRIMP, FETA & OREGANO
page 54

Stews, chilis, and bisques—hearty, flavorful, and rich— are the favored soups of winter. These long-simmered concoctions can be made with virtually any type of meat, fish, or vegetable, making them easy to vary for palates and occasions. Draw on seasonal ingredients like winter greens such as kale, chard, and escarole, which need little more than seasoned broth, a bit of ham or sausage, and a sprinkle of cheese to shine.

february

1

WINTER GREENS & SHIITAKE SOUP WITH POACHED EGGS

serves 6

3 Tbsp olive oil

1 small yellow onion, chopped

4 cloves garlic, minced

1 lb (500 g) shiitake mushrooms, stemmed and sliced

2 bunches chard, chopped

5 cups (40 fl oz/1.25 l) chicken broth, plus more as needed

Salt and freshly ground pepper

½ tsp white vinegar

6 eggs

Rustic and homey in feel—yet polished in presentation with the addition of a poached egg— this becomes a complete meal with a side of crusty bread. Substitute any sturdy green for the chard.

In a large, heavy pot, warm the oil over medium-high heat. Add the onion, garlic, and mushrooms and sauté until the mushrooms begin to turn golden, 5–7 minutes. Add the chard, stir well, and cook for 3 minutes. Add the broth and bring to a boil. Reduce the heat to low and simmer until the chard is tender but not mushy, about 12 minutes, adding more broth if needed. Season with salt and pepper.

In a frying pan, heat 1 inch (2.5 cm) of water over medium heat. Add the vinegar and reduce the heat to bring the water to a gentle simmer. Break an egg into a small bowl and, using a large spoon, place it gently in the water. Using a tablespoon, occasionally spoon the hot water over the top of the exposed egg. Cook until the egg is set but the yolk is still runny, about 5 minutes. Remove the egg with a slotted spoon. Repeat to poach the remaining eggs.

Ladle the soup into bowls, top with the poached eggs, and serve.

2

CHILI CON CARNE

serves 4–6

2 lb (1 kg) boneless beef chuck, trimmed and cut into ½-inch (12-mm) cubes

Salt and freshly ground pepper

2 Tbsp canola oil

½ cup (2 oz/60 g) finely chopped mixed chiles, such as jalapeño, serrano, and poblano, seeded if desired

1 small red bell pepper, seeded and finely chopped

8 cloves garlic, minced

4 tsp chili powder

1 tsp ground cumin

½ tsp ground coriander

1 can (28 oz/875 g) diced tomatoes

1 tsp dried oregano

2 cups (16 fl oz/500 ml) beef broth or water

1 cup (8 oz/250 g) sour cream (optional)

Leaves from 12 cilantro sprigs

Long, slow simmering gives this Texas-style chili time to develop a complex, robust flavor and hearty texture. You can garnish the chili with just about anything you like, from sour cream to chopped onions to shredded cheese.

Sprinkle the meat evenly with salt and pepper. In a large, heavy frying pan, warm 1 Tbsp of the oil over medium heat. Working in batches, brown the beef cubes on all sides, about 5 minutes per batch. Transfer to a large, heavy pot.

Warm the remaining 1 Tbsp oil in the pan over medium heat. Add the chiles, bell pepper, and garlic and sauté until the vegetables are softened and beginning to turn golden, about 5 minutes. Stir in the chili powder, cumin, and coriander and cook for about 1 minute. Add the tomatoes with their juices and the oregano, season with salt and pepper, and stir well to scrape up any browned bits on the pan bottom.

Add the vegetable mixture to the pot with the beef. Place over medium heat, add the broth, and bring to a gentle boil, stirring occasionally. Reduce the heat to maintain a gentle simmer, cover, and cook until the meat is very tender and the liquid is slightly thickened, about 2½ hours. If the chili seems too soupy, uncover the pot for the last 30 minutes to evaporate some of the liquid.

Season the chili with salt and pepper and serve, garnished with sour cream, if desired, and cilantro leaves.

3

SPANISH-STYLE PEAR, PUMPKIN & BEAN SOUP

serves 6–8

This chunky soup can feature lentils in place of the chickpeas or white beans, and other vegetables, like braised greens, in place of the green beans. Garnish with chopped fresh flat-leaf parsley and a drizzle of extra-virgin olive oil.

1 cup (7 oz/220 g) dried chickpeas, picked over and rinsed

1 cup (7 oz/220 g) small dried white beans, picked over and rinsed

8 Tbsp (4 fl oz/125 ml) olive oil

1 large yellow onion, chopped

¼ cup (1½ oz/45 g) chopped serrano ham

1 Tbsp sweet paprika

1 cup (8 fl oz/250 ml) canned diced tomatoes, with juices

Pinch of saffron steeped in ¼ cup (2 fl oz/60 ml) hot chicken broth or water

12 almonds

1 slice country-style bread, cut in half

2 cloves garlic

2 Tbsp sherry vinegar

3 pears

1½ cups (8 oz/250 g) peeled and coarsely chopped pumpkin or butternut squash

½ lb (250 g) green beans, trimmed and cut into 2-inch (5-cm) lengths

Salt and freshly ground pepper

Put the chickpeas and beans in a bowl with plenty of water to cover and soak for at least 4 hours or up to overnight.

In a large, heavy pot, bring 8 cups (64 fl oz/250 l) water to a boil over high heat. When the water boils, drain the chickpeas and beans and add to the pot. Bring to a boil, reduce the heat to low, and simmer until tender, about 1 hour.

Meanwhile, in a frying pan, warm 2 Tbsp of the oil over medium heat. Add the onion and sauté until soft, 5–7 minutes. Stir in the ham and paprika and then the tomatoes. Cook, stirring occasionally, for 10 minutes to blend the flavors. Add the saffron and its soaking liquid, mix well, and remove from the heat.

In another frying pan, warm the remaining 6 Tbsp oil over medium heat. Add the almonds, bread, and garlic and cook, stirring occasionally, until golden, about 5 minutes. Using a slotted spoon, transfer the almonds, bread, and garlic to a mortar or a small food processor. Grind with a pestle or process to a paste. Stir in the vinegar. ⟶

After the beans have cooked for 1 hour, peel the pears, then halve them, core them, and cut them into chunks. Add the pears and pumpkin to the beans and simmer for 10 minutes. Stir in the onion mixture, green beans, and bread mixture and simmer until the green beans and squash are tender, 10–15 minutes. Season with salt and pepper and serve.

4

ORECCHIETTE IN AROMATIC BROTH

serves 6–8

Orecchiette (or "little ears") are perfectly shaped to trap the fragrant broth in their indentations, but you can substitute any small pasta shape you like. Use a good-quality aged balsamic vinegar for the best flavor.

1 Tbsp olive oil

4 oz (125 g) sliced pancetta, finely chopped

6 large yellow onions, thinly sliced

2 leeks, white and pale green parts, thinly sliced

7 cups (56 fl oz/1.75 l) chicken broth

6 oz (185 g) orecchiette pasta

6 slices country-style bread

2 cloves garlic

3 Tbsp balsamic vinegar

Salt and freshly ground pepper

In a large, heavy pot, warm the oil over medium heat. Add the pancetta, onions, and leeks and sauté until the onions and leeks are soft, about 15 minutes. Add the broth and simmer, covered, for 15 minutes. Add the orecchiette and continue to simmer, covered, until al dente, 12–15 minutes.

Meanwhile, in a toaster or under a broiler, toast the bread slices until golden. Rub one side of each slice with garlic.

Add the vinegar to the soup and season with salt and pepper. Stir to mix well and serve with the garlic toasts.

5

ROASTED ROOT VEGETABLE & BARLEY STEW

serves 6

If you have trouble finding Jerusalem artichokes, sometimes called sunchokes, add any other favorite root vegetable in their place. For a hit of flavor and crunch, garnish with crumbled cooked bacon or pancetta.

6 Tbsp (3 fl oz/90 ml) olive oil

1 yellow onion, finely chopped

1 carrot, peeled and finely chopped

1 celery rib, finely chopped

1 cup (8 fl oz/250 ml) dry white wine

5½ cups (44 fl oz/1.35 l) vegetable broth

½ cup (4 oz/125 g) pearl barley

¼ cup (⅓ oz/10 g) minced flat-leaf parsley

2 tsp minced thyme

1 celery root, peeled and diced

½ lb (250 g) Jerusalem artichokes, peeled and quartered

3 parsnips, peeled and thinly sliced

1 red onion, cut into 1-inch (2.5-cm) pieces

1 potato, peeled and cut into 1-inch (2.5-cm) pieces

Salt and freshly ground pepper

Preheat the oven to 400°F (200°C). Lightly oil a baking sheet.

In a large, heavy pot, warm 3 Tbsp of the oil over medium-high heat. Add the yellow onion, carrot, and celery and sauté until browned, 7–8 minutes. Raise the heat to high, add the wine, and stir to scrape up any browned bits on the bottom of the pot. Continue to cook until the wine is reduced by half, 5 minutes.

Add the broth and bring to a boil over high heat. Add the barley, parsley, and thyme, reduce the heat to medium-low, and cook, uncovered, for 35 minutes. Add the celery root, Jerusalem artichokes, and parsnips, cover, and cook over medium-low heat until tender, 15–20 minutes.

Meanwhile, in a large bowl, combine the red onion, potato, and remaining 3 Tbsp oil. Toss to coat well. Spread on the prepared baking sheet and sprinkle with 2 tsp salt. Roast until the vegetables are browned and tender, 40–45 minutes.

Add the roasted vegetables to the pot and stir well. Season with salt and pepper and serve.

6

PASTA & BEAN SOUP WITH FONTINA

serves 6

Be sure you have ovenproof bowls on hand for this filling soup, which is topped with slices of toasted bread covered in melted cheese. You can use any small tubular pasta, such as ditalini or even macaroni, in place of the pennette.

3 Tbsp olive oil

2 yellow onions, chopped

2 Tbsp minced garlic

4 oz (125 g) sliced pancetta, finely chopped

1 can (15 oz/470 g) white beans, drained

1 cup (8 fl oz/250 ml) canned diced tomatoes, with juices

6 cups (48 fl oz/1.5 l) beef broth

¼ cup (⅓ oz/10 g) minced flat-leaf parsley

2 Tbsp minced oregano

Salt and freshly ground pepper

8 oz (250 g) pennette pasta

6 slices country-style bread, toasted

3 cups (12 oz/375 g) shredded Fontina cheese

Preheat the oven to 350°F (180°C). In a large, heavy pot, warm the oil over low heat. Add the onions and sauté until very tender, 10–15 minutes. Add the garlic and sauté for about 2 minutes. Add the pancetta and sauté for about 5 minutes. Add the beans, tomatoes, broth, parsley, and oregano and simmer, stirring occasionally, for about 10 minutes.

Meanwhile, bring a large pot of water to a boil. Add 2 tsp salt and the pennette and cook until almost al dente, about 9 minutes or according to the package directions. Drain and add to the soup. Season with salt and pepper.

Ladle the soup into ovenproof bowls. Top each with a piece of toasted bread and sprinkle with cheese. Place on a baking sheet and bake until the cheese is completely melted, about 10 minutes. Serve.

FEBRUARY

7

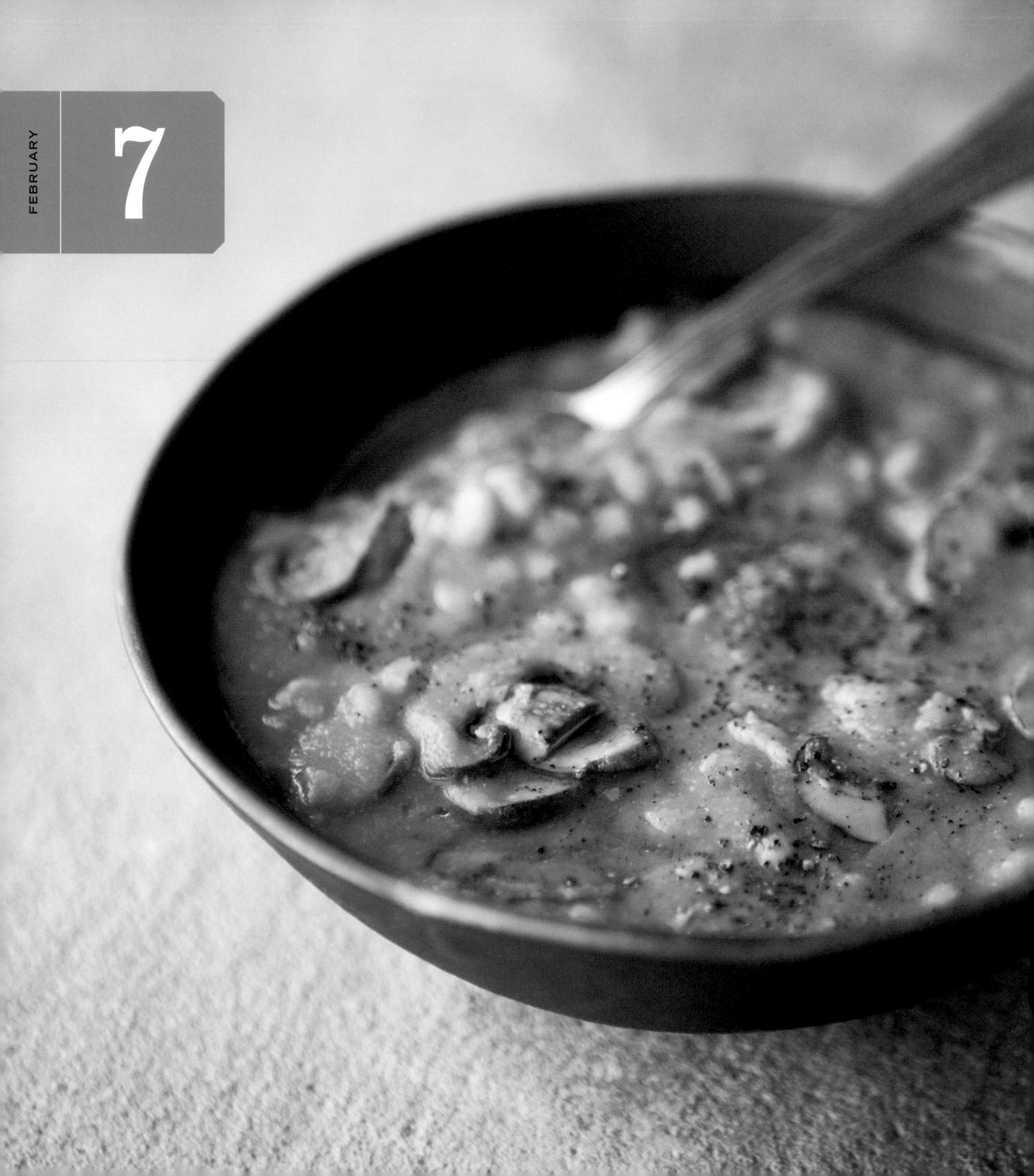

7

Every ingredient in this warming peasant-style soup, from the chickpeas and fresh herbs to the farro and porcini mushrooms, invokes Tuscany. For the most authentic pairing, serve with a Chianti Classico.

CHICKPEA, PORCINI & FARRO SOUP

serves 4–6

1½ cups (9½ oz/295 g) dried chickpeas, picked over and rinsed

⅓ cup (3 fl oz/80 ml) olive oil

1 yellow onion, finely chopped

2 cloves garlic, minced

1 small rosemary sprig

1 Tbsp tomato paste

Salt and freshly ground pepper

4 cups (32 fl oz/1 l) vegetable broth or water

⅓ cup (2 oz/60 g) farro

FOR THE MUSHROOMS

½ lb (250 g) porcini or cremini mushrooms

1½ Tbsp extra-virgin olive oil

1 clove garlic, minced

2 Tbsp dry white wine

1 thyme sprig

Salt and freshly ground pepper

1½ tsp unsalted butter

Extra-virgin olive oil for drizzling

Put the chickpeas in a large bowl with water to cover and soak for at least 4 hours or up to overnight. Drain the chickpeas, rinse well, and place in a large saucepan. Add 8 cups (64 fl oz/2 l) cold water and bring to a boil over high heat. Reduce the heat to low and simmer, uncovered, until the chickpeas are tender, about 2 hours.

In a large, heavy pot, warm the oil over medium-low heat. Add the onion, garlic, and rosemary and sauté until the onion is softened, 5–7 minutes. In a small bowl, dissolve the tomato paste in 1 cup (8 fl oz/ 250 ml) warm water, and add to the pot. Stir in the chickpeas and their cooking liquid and season with salt and pepper. Bring to a simmer over medium heat and cook for 3 minutes. Add the broth, return to a simmer, and cook, uncovered, until the flavors have blended, about 30 minutes. Remove from the heat and let cool slightly. Discard the rosemary sprig. ⤖

Working in batches, purée the soup in a blender. Return to the pot and bring to a simmer over medium heat. Add the farro and cook until tender yet still slightly chewy, about 25 minutes.

Meanwhile, to prepare the mushrooms, thinly slice them lengthwise. In a large frying pan, warm the oil over medium heat. Add the garlic and sauté until fragrant, about 1 minute. Add the mushrooms and cook, stirring, until they begin to soften, 3–4 minutes. Raise the heat to high, add the wine and thyme, and cook, stirring constantly, for about 3 minutes. Reduce the heat to low, season with salt and pepper, and continue to cook, stirring often, until the mushroom juices have evaporated, about 15 minutes. Remove from the heat and discard the thyme sprig. Stir in the butter.

Stir the mushrooms into the soup. Serve, drizzled with olive oil and garnished with a grinding of pepper.

8

Grocery stores will often cut the beet greens off of the bunches of beets, so if you don't see them at the market, ask the produce manager. Once cut from the stems, the greens wilt quickly, so use them the day you purchase them.

SEARED DUCK & BEET GREENS SOUP

serves 4

2 small duck breasts (¾ lb/375 g total weight), skin on

3 Tbsp olive oil

Salt and freshly ground pepper

1 small yellow onion, chopped

3 cloves garlic, minced

1 bunch beet greens, tough stems discarded, leaves chopped

4 cups (32 fl oz/1 l) chicken broth

10 drops Asian sesame oil

2 green onions, white and tender green parts, chopped

Brush the duck breasts with 1 Tbsp of the olive oil and season with salt and pepper. Heat a grill pan over high heat until it is very hot. Put the duck breasts in the pan, skin side down, and cook for 7 minutes. Turn the duck breasts over and cook to medium rare, 5–7 minutes more. Transfer to a cutting board and let rest for at least 10 minutes. Remove and discard the skin and shred the meat into bite-size pieces. Set aside.

In a large, heavy pot, warm the remaining 2 Tbsp olive oil over medium-high heat. Add the onion and garlic and cook the onions until translucent, about 5 minutes. Add the beet greens, stir, and sauté for 3 minutes. Add the broth, shredded duck, and sesame oil. Stir to combine and simmer for 5 minutes to blend the flavors. Stir in the green onions, season with salt and pepper, and serve.

9

This colorful and richly flavored dish is enlivened with green olives and toasted almonds. If you like, serve it atop couscous and garnish with thinly sliced lemons or minced preserved lemon peel.

CHICKEN STEW WITH OLIVES & ALMONDS

serves 4

½ cup (2½ oz/75 g) slivered almonds

2 Tbsp olive oil

4 skinless, boneless chicken breast halves, cut into bite-sized pieces

2 tsp peeled and minced fresh ginger

1 large sweet white onion, cut into bite-sized pieces

3 large carrots, peeled and cut into 1-inch (2.5-cm) pieces

1 large red bell pepper, seeded and cut lengthwise into strips ½ inch (12 mm) wide

2 tsp ground turmeric

½ cup (4 fl oz/125 ml) chicken broth

⅓ cup (2 oz/60 g) pitted green olives, sliced

Salt and freshly ground pepper

Preheat the oven to 350°F (180°C). Spread the almonds on a baking sheet and toast until fragrant, about 5 minutes. Pour into a bowl and set aside.

In a large, heavy pot, heat the olive oil over medium-high heat. Add the chicken pieces and sauté until golden brown, 8–10 minutes. Transfer to a dish. Add the ginger, onion, and carrots and sauté until the onion is softened, about 5 minutes.

Return the chicken and any accumulated juices to the pot and stir in the bell pepper and turmeric. Add the broth and bring to a simmer, stirring to scrape up any browned bits on the bottom of the pot. Reduce the heat to medium-low, cover, and simmer gently until the chicken is opaque throughout, about 15 minutes.

Stir in the olives and toasted almonds. Season with salt and pepper and serve.

10

NEW ENGLAND CLAM CHOWDER

serves 6–8

3 strips bacon, chopped

1 Tbsp unsalted butter

2 celery ribs, chopped

1 yellow onion, finely chopped

3 fresh thyme sprigs or ¼ tsp dried thyme

2 large russet potatoes, peeled and cut into ½-inch (12-mm) cubes

2 cans (6½ oz/200g each) clam meat, drained and chopped, clam juice reserved

1½ cups (12 fl oz/375 ml) milk

1 cup (8 fl oz/250 ml) heavy cream

Salt and freshly ground pepper

Chopped flat-leaf parsley for garnish

You can use the meat of 2 lb (1 kg) freshly steamed clams if you prefer. Littleneck or cherrystones are good varieties for chowder. Discard any clams that fail to close to the touch, then steam them in a wide, covered saucepan with 1 cup (8 fl oz/250 ml) water until they open, about 5 minutes. Discard any clams that do not open. Let cool, then remove the meat from the shells.

In a large saucepan over medium heat, cook the bacon, stirring often, until it starts to brown and has rendered some of its fat, about 3 minutes. Using a slotted spoon, transfer to paper towels to drain. Add the butter to the bacon drippings. When it melts, add the celery, onion, and thyme and sauté until the onion is translucent, about 3 minutes. Add the potatoes and stir well. Add the reserved clam liquor and 2 cups (16 fl oz/500 ml) water and bring to a boil. Reduce the heat to low, cover, and simmer until the potatoes are tender, about 20 minutes.

Add the milk and cream, stirring well to combine. Add the clam meat, heat through, and season to taste with salt and pepper. Discard the thyme sprigs and serve, sprinkled with the reserved bacon and parsley.

11

LEMONGRASS SOUP WITH SHRIMP & CHILE

serves 4

2 tsp canola oil

5 lemongrass stalks, center white parts only, thinly sliced

1 Tbsp peeled and minced fresh ginger

4 cups (32 fl oz/1 l) chicken broth

1 small red chile, seeded and thinly sliced

½ lb (250 g) medium shrimp, peeled and deveined

2 green onions, dark and light green parts, chopped

1 Tbsp minced cilantro

Add cubed chicken breast, tofu, or sliced vegetables in place of, or along with, the shrimp. If using chicken, add it to the broth before simmering it for 15 minutes. A squeeze of fresh lime juice just before serving will brighten the flavors.

In a large, heavy pot, warm the oil over medium-high heat. Add the lemongrass and the ginger and sauté for 3 minutes. Add the broth and 1 cup (8 fl oz/240 ml) water and bring to a boil. Reduce the heat to low and simmer, uncovered, for 15 minutes. Add the chile and shrimp and cook until the shrimp are bright pink, 2–3 minutes. Remove from the heat, stir in the green onions and cilantro, and serve.

12

CHICKEN STEW WITH BUTTERMILK-CHIVE DUMPLINGS

serves 4

This is a great way to use up leftover cooked chicken; just skip the first step, and substitute chicken broth for the poaching liquid. Feel free to change up the vegetables: add spinach, sweet potatoes, or peas.

2 skinless, boneless chicken breast halves

2 skinless, boneless chicken thighs

1 bay leaf

3 peppercorns

Salt and freshly ground pepper

4 Tbsp (2 oz/60 g) unsalted butter

2 leeks, white parts only, chopped

2 carrots, peeled and sliced

3 celery ribs, sliced

2 Tbsp all-purpose flour

4 cups (32 fl oz/1 l) chicken broth

1 russet potato, peeled and cut into ½-inch (12-mm) dice

2 Tbsp heavy cream

FOR THE DUMPLINGS

1¼ cups (5 oz/155 g) all-purpose flour

1 tsp baking soda

½ tsp salt

1 Tbsp chopped chives

Large pinch of cayenne

3 Tbsp cold unsalted butter, cut into bits

½ cup (4 fl oz/125 ml) buttermilk

Put the chicken breasts and thighs, bay leaf, peppercorns, and ¼ tsp salt in a saucepan and add cold water to cover by 1 inch (2.5 cm). Bring to a boil, then reduce the heat to medium-low. Simmer until the chicken is cooked through, 15–20 minutes, skimming off any foam on the surface. Remove the chicken, shred the meat, and set aside. Reserve 2 cups (16 fl oz/500 ml) of the poaching liquid.

In a large saucepan, melt the butter over medium-high heat. Add the leeks, carrots, and celery and sauté until they begin to soften, about 5 minutes. Add the flour and cook for 2 minutes, stirring. Add the broth and the reserved poaching liquid and bring to a boil. Add the potato and reduce the heat to medium-low. Cook until the potato begins to soften, about 10 minutes. »→

Add the chicken and cream and continue to cook until the soup thickens and the potatoes are very tender, 5 minutes. Season with salt and pepper.

To make the dumplings, sift together the flour, baking soda, and salt into a bowl. Stir in the chives and cayenne. With a pastry blender, cut in the cold butter until it resembles coarse cornmeal. Add the buttermilk and stir just to combine. Use your hands to form small dumplings and add them to the soup, cover, and let steam for 20 minutes. Serve.

13

SUN-DRIED TOMATO SOUP WITH CRAB

serves 4

Sun-dried tomatoes give this soup a stunning, deep red color and complex flavor. The crab garnish gives it a luxurious and indulgent feel, but you could easily substitute cooked shrimp or even herbed croutons.

2 Tbsp unsalted butter

2 shallots, minced

1 cup (5 oz/150 g) drained oil-packed sun-dried tomatoes, julienned

1 can (15 oz/470 g) diced tomatoes

1½ cups (12 fl oz/375 ml) chicken broth

3 Tbsp heavy cream

Salt and freshly ground pepper

¼ lb (125 g) fresh lump crabmeat, picked over for shell fragments

2 Tbsp chopped chives

In a large saucepan, melt the butter over medium-high heat. Add the shallots and sauté until soft, about 5 minutes. Add the sun-dried tomatoes, diced tomatoes, and broth and bring to a boil. Reduce the heat to low and simmer for 20 minutes. Remove from the heat and let cool slightly.

Working in batches, purée the soup in a blender or food processor. Return to the saucepan over low heat and add the cream. Stir to combine, season with salt and pepper, and serve, topped with the crabmeat and sprinkled with the chives.

14

CELERY, LEEK & OYSTER BISQUE

serves 6

18 small oysters in the shell
or bottled shucked oysters

2 Tbsp unsalted butter

1 yellow onion, coarsely chopped

5 large leeks, white and pale green parts,
coarsely chopped

5 celery ribs, coarsely chopped

3 bottles (8 fl oz/250 ml each) clam juice

½ cup (4 fl oz/125 ml) heavy cream

1–2 tsp fresh lemon juice

Salt and freshly ground pepper

Oysters have long been thought to have aphrodisiac qualities, so what better soup than this to serve on Valentine's Day? Spring for fresh oysters if you can, and do not overcook them, or they will become rubbery.

If using oysters in the shell, shuck them, reserving their liquor. If using bottled oysters, drain them, reserving the liquor. Refrigerate the oysters, then strain the liquor.

In a large, heavy pot, melt the butter over medium-low heat. Add the onion, leeks, and celery and sauté until soft, about 20 minutes. Add the clam juice, 3 cups (24 fl oz/750 ml) water, and the reserved oyster liquor. Bring to a boil over high heat. Reduce the heat to medium and simmer, uncovered, until the vegetables are very soft, about 30 minutes. Remove from the heat and let cool slightly.

Working in batches, purée the soup until very smooth, 3–4 minutes per batch. Strain the purée through a fine-mesh sieve into a large saucepan. Add the reserved oysters, cream, and lemon juice and bring to a gentle simmer over medium heat. Simmer, uncovered, until the oysters are slightly firm to the touch and opaque and their edges curl slightly, 1–2 minutes. Season with salt and pepper and serve.

15

CREAMY CAULIFLOWER SOUP WITH CRISPY PROSCIUTTO

serves 4–6

2 oz (60 g) thinly sliced prosciutto

2 Tbsp unsalted butter

1 yellow onion, chopped

2 celery ribs, chopped

2 cloves garlic, minced

1 head cauliflower (about 1¾ lb/875 g),
coarsely chopped (about 4 cups)

¼ tsp freshly grated nutmeg

4 cups (36 fl oz/1 l) chicken broth,
plus more as needed

¼ cup (2 fl oz/60 ml) heavy cream

Salt and ground white pepper

Be careful not to over-salt the soup, as the prosciutto garnish will add a good amount of salt. To make it vegetarian, use vegetable broth in place of the chicken broth and crispy fried shallots (page 28) for the prosciutto.

Preheat the oven to 375°F (190°C). Place the prosciutto slices in a single layer on a baking sheet. Bake until crispy, 15–18 minutes. Let cool, then crumble.

In a large, heavy pot, melt the butter over medium-high heat. Add the onion, celery, and garlic and sauté until soft, 5–7 minutes. Add the cauliflower and nutmeg, stir well to coat, and cook for 5 minutes. Add the 4 cups broth and bring to a boil. Reduce the heat to low and simmer until the cauliflower is very tender, 20–25 minutes. Remove from the heat and let cool slightly.

Working in batches, purée the soup in a blender. Return to the pot and add more broth if the soup is too thick. Stir in the cream. Return the soup just to a boil, season with salt and pepper, and serve, garnished with the prosciutto.

16

BLACK-EYED PEA SOUP WITH HERBS & GARLIC

serves 8–10

1 lb (500 g) black-eyed peas, picked over and rinsed

¼ cup (2 fl oz/60 ml) olive oil

1 large yellow onion, chopped

6 cloves garlic, thinly sliced

½ cup (4 fl oz/125 ml) dry white wine

4 cups (32 fl oz/1 l) chicken broth, plus more as needed

2 Tbsp tomato paste

Bouquet Garni (see left)

½ cup (¾ oz/20 g) chopped flat-leaf parsley

Salt and freshly ground pepper

A bouquet garni refers to a bundle of fresh herbs tied together with kitchen string. For this recipe, use 3 flat-leaf parsley sprigs, 2 thyme sprigs, and a bay leaf. Remember to remove and discard the bouquet garni prior to serving.

Put the black-eyed peas in a bowl with water to cover and soak for at least 4 hours or up to overnight. Drain.

In a large, heavy pot, warm the oil over medium-high heat. Add the onion and garlic and sauté until translucent, about 5 minutes. Add the wine and cook for 3 minutes. Add the black-eyed peas, 4 cups broth, and tomato paste and stir to combine. Bring the soup to a boil. Reduce the heat to low, add the bouquet garni, and simmer, uncovered, until the peas are tender, 45–55 minutes.

Remove the bouquet garni and add more broth if necessary. Stir in the chopped parsley, season with salt and pepper, and serve.

17

STONE SOUP

serves 6

3 Tbsp olive oil

2 yellow onions, chopped

2 cloves garlic, minced

¼ lb (125 g) bacon, in one piece

¼ lb (125 g) Mexican chorizo or fresh garlic sausage

4 boiling potatoes, peeled and chopped

4 carrots, peeled and chopped

2 turnips, peeled and chopped

1 small head savoy cabbage or 1 bunch kale, trimmed and shredded

2 cups (12 oz/375 g) canned diced plum tomatoes

1 bay leaf

8 cups (64 fl oz/2 l) chicken broth

1 can (15 oz/470 g) kidney beans, drained

½ cup (¾ oz/20 g) chopped cilantro

Salt and freshly ground pepper

This is the proverbial "stone" soup, created from the various ingredients given by curious villagers. In that vein, feel free to vary the ingredients depending on what you have available.

In a large, heavy pot, warm the oil over medium heat. Add the onions and garlic and sauté until tender, 7–10 minutes. Add the bacon, chorizo, potatoes, carrots, turnips, cabbage, tomatoes, bay leaf, and broth. Bring to a boil over high heat, reduce the heat to very low, and simmer until the vegetables are tender, about 30 minutes.

Skim off any foam from the surface and discard the bay leaf. Remove the meats and cut into bite-sized pieces. Return the meats to the pot and add the beans and cilantro. Simmer over medium heat for 5 minutes to warm through. Season with salt and pepper and serve.

18

Take the time to prepare this classic Vietnamese soup properly and you will not be disappointed. Set out sliced jalapeño chiles and/or chile sauce, such as Sriracha, for those who like a spicier broth.

BEEF PHO

serves 6

3 lb (1.5 kg) oxtails, cut into 2-inch (5-cm) pieces

2 lb (1 kg) beef brisket

4-inch (10-cm) piece fresh ginger, cut into 4 pieces and crushed

10 shallots, unpeeled

1 lb (500 g) daikon radish, cut into 2-inch (5-cm) chunks

2 carrots, cut into thirds

7 star anise

5 whole cloves

2 cinnamon sticks

3 Tbsp Asian fish sauce

2 tsp sugar, or to taste

½ lb (250 g) beef sirloin, wrapped in plastic wrap and frozen for 1 hour

Leaves from ½ bunch cilantro

½ bunch basil, preferably Thai

2 limes, cut into wedges

½ lb (250 g) flat rice noodles, ¼ inch (6 mm) wide, soaked in warm water for 20 minutes

1 white onion, thinly sliced

3 green onions, white and tender green parts, thinly sliced

1 lb (500 g) bean sprouts

Bring a large, heavy pot of water to a boil. Add the oxtails and brisket, return to a boil, and boil for 3 minutes. Pour off the water, then add 4 qt (4 l) fresh water to the pot and bring to a boil.

Meanwhile, place a dry frying pan over high heat and add the ginger and shallots. Cook, turning occasionally, until evenly colored, 2–3 minutes. Transfer to the pot and add the daikon, carrots, star anise, cloves, and cinnamon sticks. Return to a boil, reduce the heat to a gentle simmer, cover partially, and cook for 1½ hours.

Remove the brisket and let cool. Continue to simmer the stock until it is fragrant and light amber in color, about 1 hour longer. ⇥

Cut the brisket across the grain into thin slices. Strain the stock through a sieve into a heatproof bowl and skim off the fat. Discard the oxtails and vegetables. Return the stock to the pot and season with the fish sauce and sugar. Bring to a gentle simmer.

Cut the partially frozen beef on the diagonal into paper-thin slices. Arrange on a platter. On a separate platter, arrange the cilantro, basil, and lime wedges.

Bring a large saucepan of water to a boil. Slide the noodles into the boiling water, stir well, and cook until just tender, 1–2 minutes. Drain. Divide the noodles among bowls. Put a few brisket slices in each bowl. Top with white onion slices, green onions, and bean sprouts. Ladle the hot stock into the bowls. Serve with the platters of beef and herbs for adding to the bowls.

19

Inspired by Spain's beloved paella, this saffron-scented dish features an enticing combination of briny mussels, sweet shrimp, and salty Spanish ham. If you can't find Spanish serrano ham, prosciutto can be substituted. Clams can be substituted for the mussels.

SEAFOOD STEW WITH SAFFRON, SERRANO HAM & ALMONDS

serves 6

1 cup (5½ oz/170 g) blanched almonds

6 cups (48 fl oz/1.5 l) chicken broth

¼ cup (2 fl oz/60 ml) olive oil

2 yellow onions, chopped

1 red bell pepper, chopped

½ tsp ground cumin

3 cloves garlic, minced

1 cup (6 oz/185 g) chopped serrano ham

1 can (15 oz/470 g) diced tomatoes

½ cup (3½ oz/105 g) long-grain white rice

¼ tsp saffron threads

Salt and freshly ground pepper

1 lb (500 g) medium shrimp, peeled and deveined

12 mussels, scrubbed and debearded

1 cup (5 oz/155 g) frozen peas, thawed

¼ cup (⅓ oz/10 g) minced flat-leaf parsley

Process the almonds in a food processor until very finely ground. Add 1 cup (8 fl oz/250 ml) of the broth and process until the mixture looks milky. Strain through a fine-mesh sieve into a bowl, pressing hard on the solids. Discard the solids.

In a large, heavy pot, warm the oil over medium-high heat. Add the onions and sauté until just beginning to look translucent, about 2 minutes. Add the bell pepper, cumin, garlic, and ham and cook until the vegetables are tender, about 5 minutes. Add the tomatoes and remaining 5 cups (40 fl oz/1.25 l) broth and bring to a simmer. Reduce the heat and simmer for 10 minutes to blend the flavors.

Meanwhile, in a saucepan, bring 1 cup (8 fl oz/250 ml) water to a boil over medium heat. Rinse the rice under cold running water until the water runs clear. Add the rice, saffron, and ¼ tsp salt to the boiling water. Cover, reduce the heat to low, and cook the rice for 15 minutes. Remove from the heat and let stand undisturbed for 5 minutes. Fluff the rice. »→

Raise the heat under the soup to medium-high and add the reserved almond liquid, the shrimp, the mussels, discarding any that do not close to the touch, and the peas. Cook, stirring occasionally, until the shrimp are pink and the mussels have opened, about 5 minutes. Discard any unopened mussels. Season with salt and pepper.

Place a scoop of the rice in each bowl and top with the stew. Garnish with the parsley and serve.

20

Just a few elements make up this simple soup, so use only the finest-quality ingredients you can find, like rich chicken broth, farm-fresh eggs, and freshly grated Parmigiano-Reggiano cheese. Spinach can be substituted for the kale.

PARMESAN STRACIATELLA WITH KALE

serves 6–8

8 cups (64 fl oz/2 l) chicken broth

1 bunch kale, thick stems and ribs removed, roughly torn

1 tsp cornstarch

5 eggs

Salt and freshly ground pepper

1 cup (4 oz/125 g) grated Parmesan cheese

2 Tbsp extra-virgin olive oil

In a large saucepan, bring the broth to a simmer over medium-high heat. Divide the kale among bowls.

In a bowl, mix together the cornstarch and 2 tsp water. Add the eggs, season with salt and pepper, and whisk to blend.

Stir two-thirds of the cheese and the oil into the broth. Stir the egg mixture and drizzle into the broth in a circular motion. Stir gently so that the egg forms thin ribbons. Remove from the heat and let stand until the eggs are cooked through, about 1½ minutes. Ladle the broth over the kale and serve, passing the remaining cheese at the table.

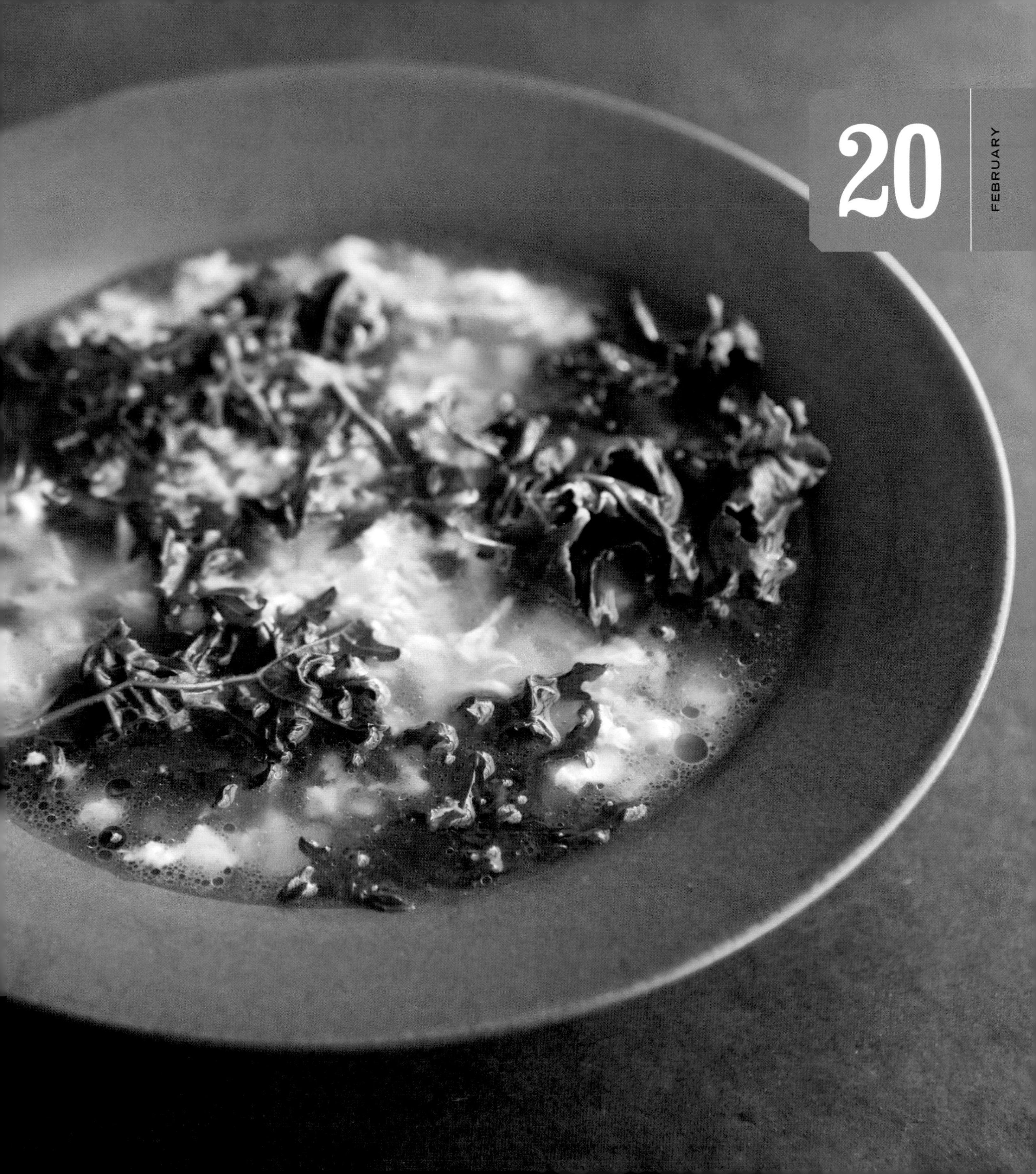

20 FEBRUARY

21

To make the meyer lemon crème fraîche, in a small bowl, combine ½ cup (4 oz/125 g) room-temperature crème fraîche or sour cream; the grated zest of 1 Meyer lemon; 1 Tbsp fresh Meyer lemon juice; and a pinch of salt.

BLACK BEAN SOUP WITH MEYER LEMON CRÈME FRAÎCHE

serves 4–6

½ lb (250 g) dried black beans, picked over and rinsed

1 Tbsp olive oil

1 small white onion, chopped

2 cloves garlic, minced

1 small jalapeño chile, seeded and minced

1 tsp ground cumin

¼ cup (2 fl oz/60 ml) dry sherry

4 cups (32 fl oz/1 l) chicken or vegetable broth

Salt and freshly ground pepper

Meyer Lemon Crème Fraîche (left)

2 green onions, dark and light green parts only, sliced (optional)

Place the dried beans in a bowl with cold water to cover and soak for at least 4 hours or up to overnight. Drain.

In a large, heavy pot, warm the oil over medium-high heat. Add the onion and garlic and sauté until softened, about 5 minutes. Add the jalapeño and cumin and cook, stirring constantly, for 2 minutes. Add the beans, sherry, and broth and bring to a boil. Reduce the heat to low and simmer, covered, until the beans are tender, about 1¼ hours.

For a smooth soup, remove the pot from the heat and let cool slightly. Working in batches, purée the soup in a blender. Return to the pot and warm over low heat. Season with salt and pepper.

Top the soup with the crème fraîche and green onions, if using, and serve.

22

Fresh Thai basil, which has a more assertive flavor than Italian sweet basil, is worth seeking out to garnish this soup. For a heartier meal, serve the soup over a bed of steamed jasmine rice.

THAI SQUASH & COCONUT MILK SOUP

serves 6

4 shallots, quartered

2 red or green serrano or jalapeño chiles, seeded

1 lemongrass stalk, center white part only, smashed and chopped

1 can (14 fl oz/430 ml) coconut milk

2 cups (16 fl oz/500 ml) chicken broth or water

6 kaffir lime leaves, spines removed

1 kabocha, acorn, or butternut squash (about 1 lb/500 g), peeled and cut into ¾-inch (2-cm) pieces

1½ Tbsp Asian fish sauce

1 Tbsp fresh lime juice

½ tsp sugar

½ cup (½ oz/15 g) basil leaves, preferably Thai

In a blender, combine the shallots, chiles, lemongrass, and ¼ cup (2 fl oz/60 ml) water. Process to form a smooth paste.

Open the can of coconut milk without shaking it. Scrape the thick cream from the top into a large, heavy pot. Stir in the spice paste and bring to a boil over medium-high heat. Reduce the heat to medium and cook uncovered, stirring occasionally, until fragrant, about 5 minutes. Add the remaining coconut milk, broth, lime leaves, and squash. Stir to combine, raise the heat to medium-high, and bring to a boil. Reduce the heat to low and simmer uncovered, stirring once or twice, until the squash is tender, about 15 minutes.

Stir in the fish sauce, lime juice, sugar, and basil, and serve.

23

Kalamata olives lend a strong briny flavor to this rich stew, although pitted green olives would be delicious as well. Buy an organic orange, if you can, or else be sure to wash the orange thoroughly before removing the zest.

BEEF STEW WITH ORANGE ZEST & RED WINE

serves 6–8

2 Tbsp all-purpose flour

Salt and freshly ground pepper

3 lb (1.5 kg) beef chuck roast, trimmed and cut into 1½-inch (4-cm) chunks

3 Tbsp olive oil

1 orange

2 yellow onions, chopped

3 cloves garlic, minced

2 tsp minced thyme

1½ Tbsp fennel seeds, crushed

¾ cup (6 fl oz/180 ml) dry red wine

¾ cup (6 fl oz/180 ml) chicken broth

1 cup (6 oz/185 g) canned diced tomatoes

4 carrots, peeled and sliced

1½ cups (7 oz/220 g) Kalamata olives, pitted and halved

¼ cup (⅓ oz/10 g) finely chopped flat-leaf parsley

In a resealable plastic bag, combine the flour, 2 tsp salt, and 1 tsp pepper. Add the beef, seal the bag, and shake to coat. In a large, heavy pot, warm 1 Tbsp of the oil over medium-high heat. Remove half the beef pieces from the bag, shaking off excess flour, and add to the pot in a single layer. Cook without stirring until deeply browned, about 4 minutes. Turn and cook without stirring until deeply browned on the second side, about 4 minutes. Transfer to a bowl. Repeat with 1 Tbsp of the oil and the remaining beef. Wipe the pot clean.

Using a vegetable peeler, remove the zest from half of the orange in wide strips. Finely grate the zest from the remaining orange half. Set aside.

Add the remaining 1 Tbsp oil to the pot and warm over medium heat. Add the onions and sauté until just starting to soften, about 2 minutes. Stir in the garlic, orange zest strips, thyme, and fennel seeds and sauté until fragrant, about 45 seconds. Add the wine, raise the heat to high, and bring to a boil, stirring to scrape up any browned ⋙

bits on the bottom of the pot. Cook until reduced by half, about 4 minutes. Stir in the broth and tomatoes with their juices, then add the browned beef and any accumulated juices. Bring to a boil, reduce the heat to low, cover, and simmer until the beef is tender, about 2½ hours.

Add the carrots and olives, pushing them down into the liquid. Raise the heat to medium, cover, and cook until the carrots are tender, about 8 minutes. Stir in the grated orange zest and the parsley, season with salt and pepper, and serve.

24

This recipe departs just a bit from the traditional split pea soup: instead of adding the ham during the cooking process, it is sautéed and served crispy as a garnish, adding flavor and texture at the same time.

YELLOW SPLIT PEA SOUP WITH HAM

serves 4

3 oz (90 g) ham, thinly sliced

1 Tbsp unsalted butter

1 Tbsp olive oil

1 yellow onion, chopped

1 celery rib, chopped

4 cups (32 fl oz/1 l) chicken broth

½ lb (250 g) yellow split peas, picked over and rinsed

Salt and freshly ground pepper

Heat a large, heavy pot over medium-high heat. Add the ham and cook, turning once, until crisp, 7–8 minutes. Let cool, then crumble into bite-sized pieces.

Add the butter and oil to the pot and heat over medium-high heat until the butter is melted. Add the onion and celery and sauté until soft, about 5 minutes. Add the broth and bring to a boil. Add the peas, reduce the heat to low, and cook, partially covered and stirring occasionally, until the peas are tender, 45–50 minutes. Season with salt and pepper and serve, garnished with ham.

25

Pick small pasta shapes to suit the petite size of the lentils; those with "ini" word endings are a good scale to aim for. To make a vegetarian version, omit the pancetta and use vegetable broth instead of chicken. Serve with a decadent dollop of mascarpone.

LENTIL SOUP WITH PASTA & SAGE

serves 4

3 Tbsp olive oil

2 oz (60 g) sliced pancetta or bacon, chopped

1 small yellow onion, chopped

2 large cloves garlic, minced

1 carrot, peeled finely chopped

1 celery rib, finely chopped

1 Tbsp minced sage

2 cups (14 oz/440 g) lentils, picked over and rinsed

1 cup (8 fl oz/250 ml) canned diced tomatoes, with juices

6 cups (48 fl oz/1.5 l) chicken broth, plus more as needed

Salt and freshly ground pepper

¼ lb (125 g) tubettini, ditalini, or other small soup pasta

In a large, heavy pot, warm the oil over medium-high heat. Add the pancetta and sauté until lightly browned, about 2 minutes. Add the onion, garlic, carrot, celery, and sage, and sauté until the vegetables are softened, about 3 minutes.

Stir in the lentils and tomatoes and cook, stirring occasionally, for 5 minutes. Raise the heat to high, add the 6 cups broth, and bring to a boil. Add 1 Tbsp salt, reduce the heat to medium-low, and simmer, partially covered, until the lentils are nearly tender, 30–40 minutes. Add more broth if the soup starts to dry out.

Add the pasta and cook, stirring occasionally, until not quite al dente, about 2 minutes less than the package directions. (The pasta will continue to cook in the heat of the soup.) Season with salt and pepper and serve.

26

In Portugal, where this dish is known as caldo verde (or "green broth"), kale is a staple ingredient. Linguiça or chorizo are the commonly used sausages, but any garlicky pork sausage, such as kielbasa, will do. Serve with warm corn bread.

SAUSAGE & KALE SOUP

serves 4–6

¼ cup (2 fl oz/60 ml) olive oil

2 yellow onions, finely chopped

4 cloves garlic, minced

3 large russet potatoes (about 2½ lb/1.25 kg), peeled and thinly sliced

6 cups (48 fl oz/1.5 l) chicken or vegetable broth

¾ lb (375 g) kielbasa or other cooked sausage, sliced

1 bunch kale, thick stems and ribs removed, thinly sliced

Salt and freshly ground pepper

Extra-virgin olive oil for drizzling

In a large, heavy pot, warm the olive oil over medium heat. Add the onions and garlic and sauté until golden, 5–7 minutes. Add the potatoes and sauté for about 2 minutes. Add the broth, cover, and bring to a boil. Reduce the heat to a simmer and cook until the potatoes are tender, about 20 minutes. Remove from the heat and let cool slightly.

Working in batches, coarsely purée the soup in a blender, leaving some potato slices intact. Return to the pot, add the sausage, cover, and simmer over medium heat until the sausage is heated through, about 5 minutes. Add the kale and cook, uncovered, until wilted but still bright green, 3–5 minutes. Season with salt and pepper and serve, drizzled with extra-virgin olive oil.

27

The flavor of this hearty soup is enhanced with the addition of savory ham and Parmesan. Pleasantly bitter escarole simmers in the broth just long enough to wilt and mellow; if you can't find escarole at the market, substitute Swiss chard or kale.

HAM, BEAN & ESCAROLE SOUP

serves 4–6

2–3 Tbsp olive oil

½ lb (250 g) thickly sliced ham, cut into cubes

1 yellow onion, finely chopped

4 cloves garlic, minced

7 cups (56 fl oz/1.75 l) chicken broth

1 head escarole, cored, leaves torn into pieces

2 cans (15 oz/470 g each) white beans, drained

2 Tbsp minced rosemary

¼ tsp red pepper flakes

½ cup (2 oz/60 g) grated Parmesan cheese

In a large, heavy pot, warm 2 Tbsp of the oil over medium-high heat. Add the ham and sauté until crisp, about 3 minutes. Transfer to a plate. Add more oil if necessary and sauté the onion and garlic over medium heat until softened, about 4 minutes. Add the broth and bring to a boil. Add the escarole and cook, stirring, until wilted, 2–3 minutes. Add the beans, rosemary, and red pepper flakes. Bring to a boil, reduce the heat to medium-low, and simmer for 5 minutes.

Stir in the ham. Mash some of the beans to thicken the soup slightly and simmer for 2 minutes. Season with salt and pepper and serve, garnished with some of the cheese. Pass the remaining cheese at the table.

28

This simple tomato soup, adorned with a trio of classic Greek ingredients— shrimp, feta cheese, and oregano—comes together in less than 30 minutes. Serve with sliced country bread that's been lightly toasted and rubbed with a cut garlic clove.

TOMATO BROTH WITH SHRIMP, FETA & OREGANO

serves 4–6

2 Tbsp olive oil

1 small yellow onion, chopped

4 cloves garlic, minced

3 cans (14½ oz/455 g each) diced tomatoes, drained

4 cups (32 fl oz/1 l) chicken broth

Salt and freshly ground pepper

½ lb (250 g) medium shrimp, peeled and deveined

½ lb (250 g) feta cheese, crumbled

2 Tbsp chopped oregano

In a large, heavy pot, warm the oil over medium-high heat. Add the onion and garlic and sauté until translucent, 5–7 minutes. Add the tomatoes and sauté for 4 minutes. Add the broth and bring to a boil. Reduce the heat to low and simmer for 20 minutes. Remove from the heat and let cool slightly.

Purée half of the soup in a blender. Return to the pot and season with salt and pepper. Keep warm over low heat while you prepare the shrimp.

Preheat the broiler to high. Pour ½ cup (4 fl oz/125 ml) of the tomato broth into a shallow oven-safe dish. Lay the shrimp in a single layer on top of the tomato broth and sprinkle with the feta. Put the shrimp under the broiler for 4 minutes. Remove the shrimp, sprinkle with the oregano, and put back under the broiler until cooked through, 1–2 minutes. Ladle the broth into bowls, top each serving with the shrimp and feta, and serve.

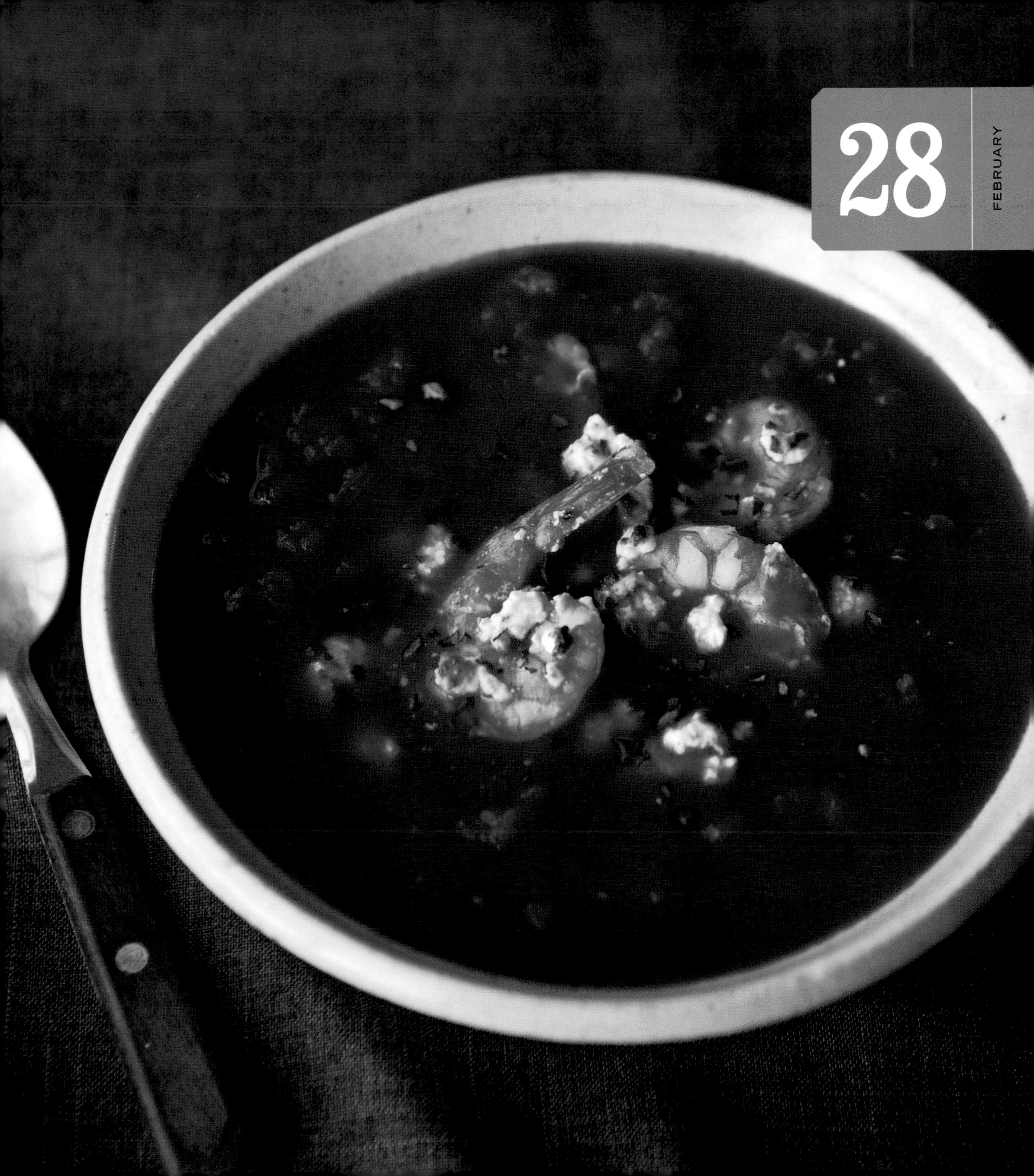

1
GREEN GARLIC &
NEW POTATO SOUP
page 58

2
CREAM OF ASPARAGUS SOUP
page 58

3
ARTICHOKE SOUP
WITH MOREL BUTTER
page 60

4
SHRIMP, MUSHROOM
& SORREL SOUP
page 60

8
CAULIFLOWER SOUP
WITH CHERVIL
page 63

9
MUSHROOM SOUP WITH
THYME & GREEN ONIONS
page 64

10
CREAMY PEA SOUP WITH
CITRUS OIL & CHIVES
page 64

11
THREE-ONION SOUP WITH
CAMBOZOLA GRILLED CHEESE
page 65

15
MISO SOUP WITH SHRIMP
& PEA SHOOTS
page 69

16
BEEF & MUSHROOM
SOUP WITH FARRO
page 69

17
IRISH LAMB STEW
page 70

18
CHICKEN & WILD RICE
SOUP WITH GINGER
page 70

22
MOROCCAN LAMB MEATBALL
& COUSCOUS SOUP
page 72

23
ARTICHOKE, SPRING
PEA & MINT SOUP
page 75

24
PORK STEW
WITH PRUNES & SWEET POTATOES
page 75

25
THREE-BEAN SOUP
WITH LINGUIÇA
page 76

29
PEA & ARBORIO RICE PURÉE
page 77

30
CHILLED POTATO & LEEK SOUP
page 78

31
CHICKPEA & ROASTED TOMATO
SOUP WITH FRIED ROSEMARY
page 78

5
BROCCOLI-LEEK SOUP
page 61

6
WILD RICE SOUP WITH BACON
page 61

7
**CRANBERRY BEAN &
PAPPARDELLE SOUP**
page 63

12
**LEMONY ASPARAGUS & RICE SOUP
WITH PARMESAN**
page 65

13
**BABY BOK CHOY &
BEEF NODDLE SOUP**
page 66

14
**PARMESAN BROTH WITH
LEMON, CHICKEN & SPINACH**
page 66

19
**NAPA CABBAGE SOUP WITH
PORK & BEAN SPROUTS**
page 71

20
PASTA IN BROTH WITH CHIVES
page 71

21
**CHICKEN & CHIPOTLE SOUP
WITH AVOCADO & LIME**
page 72

26
**FIVE-SPICE BROTH WITH SALMON
& ONION DUMPLINGS**
page 76

27
**FENNEL BROTH WITH
CHARD & CHORIZO**
page 77

28
BLACK-EYED PEA STEW
page 77

As the frost gives way to warmer weather, tender green vegetables begin to break ground, starting with baby spinach and arugula, asparagus, and artichokes. In soups, these young vegetables pair nicely with fresh herbs, citrus oils, poached eggs, and cheeses. Rainy days mixed with breaks of sun make for prime mushroom season, adding meaty flavor and texture to the soup pot.

march

1

Just as new potatoes are potatoes that haven't reached maturity, green garlic is simply immature garlic. Mild in flavor, it resembles a baby leek or green onion. Look for it at farmers' markets in early spring, or substitute 1 clove of mature garlic for every head of green garlic.

GREEN GARLIC & NEW POTATO SOUP

serves 6

1 Tbsp unsalted butter

20 heads green garlic (about 6 oz/185 g), ½–1 inch (12 mm–2.5 cm) in diameter at root end

8 cups (64 fl oz/2 l) chicken broth

1¼ lb (625 g) red new potatoes, peeled and quartered

FOR THE GARNISH

1½ Tbsp extra-virgin olive oil

3 heads green garlic, ½–1 inch (12 mm–2.5 cm) in diameter at root end, bulbs minced

2 Tbsp chopped flat-leaf parsley

Salt and freshly ground pepper

¼ cup (2 fl oz/60 ml) heavy cream

2 Tbsp white wine vinegar

In a large, heavy pot, melt the butter over low heat. Coarsely chop the green garlic bulbs. Add to the pot along with ½ cup (4 fl oz/125 ml) of the broth. Cover and cook until the garlic is soft, about 20 minutes. Add the potatoes and the remaining 7½ cups (60 fl oz/1.75 l) broth and raise the heat to medium-high. Simmer, covered, until the potatoes are soft, about 20 minutes.

Meanwhile, to make the garnish, in a small saucepan over low heat, warm the oil. Add the minced green garlic bulbs and sauté until soft, about 2 minutes. Do not let the garlic turn golden. Let cool for 10 minutes. Stir in the parsley and season with salt and pepper. Set aside.

Remove the soup from the heat and let cool slightly. Working in batches, purée the soup well in a blender. Strain through a fine-mesh sieve into a clean pot. Stir in the cream and vinegar. Season with salt and pepper and serve, topped with the garnish.

2

To trim a stalk of asparagus, gently bend it about 2 inches (5 cm) from the bottom and the stalk should snap naturally, right at the point where the tender and tough parts meet. Peel any thicker stems.

CREAM OF ASPARAGUS SOUP

serves 4–6

1 Tbsp unsalted butter

2 Tbsp olive oil

2 leeks, white and light green parts, finely chopped

1 lb (500 g) thick asparagus, trimmed, peeled, and cut into 2-inch (5-cm) pieces, tips reserved

1 russet potato, peeled and cut into 2-inch (5-cm) chunks

4 cups (32 fl oz/1 l) chicken broth

Salt and ground white pepper

Juice of ½ lemon

3 Tbsp crème fraîche or sour cream

1 Tbsp finely chopped chives

In a large, heavy pot, melt the butter with the oil over medium heat. Add the leeks and sauté until softened, about 5 minutes. Add the asparagus stalks and potato and sauté until beginning to soften, about 3 minutes. Add the broth and season with salt and pepper. Bring to a boil over medium-high heat. Reduce the heat to low, cover partially, and cook until the vegetables are very tender, about 15 minutes.

Meanwhile, bring a small saucepan of water to a boil. Add the lemon juice and reserved asparagus tips and cook until crisp-tender, about 3 minutes. Drain and let cool slightly.

Working in batches, purée the soup in a blender. Return to the pot and reheat over low heat. Serve, garnished with the crème fraîche, asparagus tips, and chives.

3

MARCH

*Dried morel
mushrooms create
a sumptuous
butter topping
for this soup,
which showcases
a favorite spring
vegetable. Trimming
artichokes takes
some technique,
but it's worth
learning how to
do it for the tender
hearts. This soup
is excellent served
with a roast chicken.*

ARTICHOKE SOUP WITH MOREL BUTTER

serves 4–6

FOR THE MOREL BUTTER

1 Tbsp small pieces dried morel mushrooms

Boiling water as needed

1 small clove garlic

Salt

4 Tbsp (2 oz/60 g) unsalted butter, at room temperature

1 Tbsp white wine vinegar, or juice of ½ lemon

4 large or 5–6 medium artichokes (about 2½ lb/1.25 kg)

1 Tbsp unsalted butter

3 Tbsp olive oil

4 shallots, chopped

2 cloves garlic, chopped

½ cup (4 fl oz/125 ml) dry white wine

2 cups (16 fl oz/500 ml) chicken broth

1 bay leaf, 3 thyme sprigs, and 4 large flat-leaf parsley sprigs tied together to make a bouquet garni

Salt and freshly ground pepper

To make the morel butter, in a small bowl, combine the mushrooms with boiling water to cover. Cover and soak for 30 minutes. Drain, rinsing if they are gritty, then squeeze out the excess moisture. In a small food processor, process the garlic with a pinch of salt until minced. Add the mushrooms and process until finely chopped. Add the butter and process until mixed. Transfer to a bowl and refrigerate.

Fill a large bowl with water and add the vinegar. Peel, then cut off the stem of each artichoke flush with the bottom. Slice the stems and add to the vinegar water. Snap off the outer leaves until you reach the tender inner leaves, placing the outer leaves in a saucepan. Cut off the top one-third of each artichoke and quarter the rest lengthwise. Cut out the choke from each quarter. As you work, add the quarters to the vinegar water.

Add 5 cups (40 fl oz/1.25 l) water to the saucepan holding the outer leaves. Bring to a boil over medium-high heat. Cook, uncovered, until the water takes on the mineral flavor of artichokes, 15 minutes. ↠

Strain through a fine-mesh sieve into a large measuring cup. Discard the leaves. You should have about 4 cups (32 fl oz/1 l) liquid.

Drain the artichokes and chop. In a large, heavy pot, melt the butter with the oil over medium-high heat. Add the shallots and garlic and sauté until softened, about 5 minutes. Add the chopped artichokes and sauté until half cooked, about 5 minutes. Add the wine and cook until reduced to 1–2 Tbsp. Add the artichoke liquid, the broth, and the bouquet garni. Bring to a boil, reduce the heat to medium, and cook, uncovered, until the artichokes are just tender, 10–15 minutes.

Remove from the heat and discard the bouquet. Using a slotted spoon, transfer the artichoke pieces to a food processor. Add a small amount of the cooking liquid, and purée. Return to the pot and stir to combine. Reheat over medium-high heat and season with salt and pepper. Serve, topped with some of the morel butter.

4

MARCH

*Sorrel has a slightly
sharp flavor and is a
wonderful addition
to light soups such
as this one. If you
can't find sorrel, add
a Latin twist with a
squeeze of fresh lime
juice and a sprinkle
of minced cilantro
and jalapeño chile
just before serving.*

SHRIMP, MUSHROOM & SORREL SOUP

serves 4–6

3 oz (90 g) sorrel or baby spinach

3 Tbsp olive oil

2 shallots, minced

4 cloves garlic, minced

½ lb (250 g) white mushrooms, sliced

5 cups (40 fl oz/1.25 l) chicken broth

1 lb (500 g) shrimp, peeled and deveined

Salt and freshly ground pepper

Remove any tough stems from the sorrel and cut the leaves crosswise into ribbons.

In a saucepan, warm the olive oil over medium-high heat. Add the shallots and garlic and sauté until soft, about 5 minutes. Add the mushrooms and sauté, stirring often, until they are soft and brown, 7–10 minutes. Add the broth and bring to a boil. Add the shrimp and cook until they are bright pink, 2–3 minutes. Remove the pan from the heat and stir in the sorrel. Season with salt and pepper and serve.

5

BROCCOLI-LEEK SOUP

serves 4

2 Tbsp olive oil

2 leeks, white and pale green parts, finely chopped

1½ lb (750 g) broccoli, tough stems peeled, florets and stems cut into 1-inch (2.5-cm) pieces

4 cups (32 fl oz/1 l) chicken broth

Salt and ground white pepper

¼ cup (2 oz/60 g) sour cream or plain yogurt

Garlic Croutons (left)

2 Tbsp finely chopped chives

To make the garlic croutons, cut 3 slices coarse country bread into bite-sized cubes. In a frying pan over medium-high heat, combine 3 Tbsp olive oil and 2 cloves garlic, thinly sliced. Fry until the garlic turns brown; do not let it burn. Scoop out and discard the garlic. Add the bread to the pan and fry, stirring often, until golden brown, about 5 minutes.

In a large, heavy pot, warm the oil over medium heat. Add the leeks and sauté until softened, 3–5 minutes. Add the broccoli and sauté until slightly softened, about 2 minutes. Add the broth and bring to a simmer over medium heat. Cover partially and cook until the vegetables are tender, 15–20 minutes. Remove from the heat and let cool.

Working in batches, purée the soup in a blender or food processor. Return to the pot and reheat over medium heat. Season with salt and pepper and serve, garnished with the sour cream, croutons, and chives.

6

WILD RICE SOUP WITH BACON

serves 4

8 slices thick-cut bacon

1 Tbsp unsalted butter

1 carrot, peeled and chopped

1 yellow onion, chopped

2 cloves garlic, minced

½ tsp dried thyme

¼ cup (2 fl oz/60 ml) dry white wine

4 cups (32 fl oz/1 l) chicken broth

1 cup (6 oz/185 g) wild rice

2 Tbsp heavy cream

Salt and freshly ground pepper

Wild rice brings chewy texture and a nutty, earthy flavor to soup. Here, a touch of cream and smoky bacon elevate a simple soup into a luxurious treat. Serve with a green salad dressed with a citrus vinaigrette.

Lay the bacon slices on the bottom of a large, heavy pot. Place over medium-high heat and cook, turning once, until crisp, about 8 minutes. Transfer to paper towels to drain. Let cool, then cut into 1-inch (2.5-cm) pieces. Set aside.

Add the butter, carrot, onion, and garlic to the pot and cook over medium-high heat, stirring occasionally, until the carrot begins to soften, 5–7 minutes. Stir in the thyme and cook for 1 minute. Add the wine and cook for about 3 minutes, stirring to scrape up any browned bits on the bottom of the pot. Add the broth and rice and bring to a boil. Reduce the heat to low, cover, and simmer until the rice is tender, about 1 hour.

Add the cream and bacon to the soup, return to a simmer, and cook, uncovered, until the soup thickens, about 5 minutes. Season with salt and pepper and serve.

7

MARCH

Many Italian soups feature a combination of beans and pasta. Red-speckled cranberry beans, an Italian favorite (also called borlotti beans), are worth seeking out if you've never tried them, although other types of cooked beans can be substituted here.

CRANBERRY BEAN & PAPPARDELLE SOUP

serves 8

1½ oz (45 g) dried porcini mushrooms, soaked in hot water to cover for 30 minutes

8 Tbsp (4 fl oz/125 ml) olive oil

1 clove garlic, minced

Small handful of sage leaves, finely chopped, plus torn whole leaves for garnish

1 cup (8 fl oz/250 ml) canned diced tomatoes, with juices

8 cups (64 fl oz/2 l) chicken broth

1 cup (3 oz/90 g) roughly broken pappardelle or tagliatelle

1 can (15 oz/470 g) cranberry (borlotti) beans, drained

Salt and freshly ground pepper

Drain the mushrooms, rinsing if they are gritty, then squeeze out the excess moisture. In a large, heavy pot, warm 3 Tbsp of the oil over medium heat. Add the garlic, chopped sage, and mushrooms and sauté for 3 minutes. Add the tomato and cook, stirring occasionally, until the flavors are well blended, about 5 minutes.

Pour in the broth and bring to a boil. Add the pasta and cook, uncovered, for 5 minutes. Reduce the heat to medium. Stir in the beans. Season with salt and pepper and serve, garnished with the torn sage leaves and drizzled with the remaining 5 Tbsp oil.

8

MARCH

A creamy vegetable soup is a hallmark of home cooking. Here, cauliflower is simmered with potato and milk and then puréed to a smooth, velvety texture. To make the soup even creamier, use a mixture of cream and milk.

CAULIFLOWER SOUP WITH CHERVIL

serves 6

1 small head cauliflower (about ¾ lb/375 g), coarsely chopped (including core)

1 boiling potato (about ½ lb/250 g), peeled and diced

3¼–3½ cups (26–28 fl oz/810–875 ml) milk

Salt and ground white pepper

2 Tbsp unsalted butter

⅛ tsp grated nutmeg

¼ cup (⅓ oz/10 g) chervil or flat-leaf parsley leaves

Bring a large saucepan of water to a boil over medium-high heat. Add the cauliflower and potato, reduce the heat to medium, and cook until the vegetables soften slightly, about 5 minutes. Drain well and return to the pan. Add 2½ cups (20 fl oz/625 ml) of the milk and ½ tsp salt and bring to a boil over medium-high heat. Reduce the heat to medium, cover, and cook until the cauliflower and potato are tender, 15–20 minutes. Remove from the heat and let cool slightly.

Working in batches, purée the soup in a blender or food processor, adding the remaining milk as needed to reach the desired creamy consistency. Transfer to a clean saucepan and bring to a simmer over medium heat. Stir in the butter, the nutmeg, and ¼ tsp pepper. Serve, garnished with the chervil.

9

Dried porcini mushrooms are a useful pantry item to have on hand for adding rich flavor to soups and sauces. To give this soup a creamy texture, purée half of it before you add the green onions.

MUSHROOM SOUP WITH THYME & GREEN ONIONS

serves 4

1 oz (30 g) dried porcini mushrooms

3 Tbsp unsalted butter

2 Tbsp olive oil

2 shallots, minced

5 cloves garlic, minced

1½ lb (750 g) white mushrooms, sliced

½ tsp dried thyme

½ cup (4 fl oz/125 ml) dry sherry

4 cups (32 fl oz/1 l) chicken broth

Salt and freshly ground pepper

1 bunch green onions, white and dark green parts, chopped

In a small bowl, combine the mushrooms with 1 cup (8 fl oz/250 ml) hot water. Cover and soak for 30 minutes. Lift out the mushrooms, reserving the soaking liquid. Rinse if they are gritty, then squeeze out the excess moisture. Coarsely chop the mushrooms, and pour the soaking liquid through a coffee filter into another bowl. Set aside.

In a medium saucepan, melt the butter with the olive oil over medium-high heat. Add the shallots and the garlic and sauté until soft, 4–5 minutes. Add the white mushrooms and cook, stirring often, until browned, 10–12 minutes. Add the porcini mushrooms and thyme and cook for 5 minutes. Add ½ cup (4 fl oz/125 ml) of the porcini soaking liquid and the sherry and cook until most of the liquid is absorbed, 7–8 minutes. Add the chicken broth and bring to boil. Reduce the heat to medium-low and let simmer, uncovered, for 25 minutes to blend the flavors.

Season with salt and pepper, stir in the green onions, and serve.

10

To make the citrus oil, in a small saucepan combine ½ cup (4 fl oz/ 125 ml) extra-virgin olive oil; ½ cup (4 fl oz/125 ml) grapeseed oil; and the grated zest of 1 Meyer lemon. Bring to a simmer over medium-low heat and cook for 10 minutes. Let cool to room temperature. Strain into a small bowl.

CREAMY PEA SOUP WITH CITRUS OIL & CHIVES

serves 4–6

1 Tbsp unsalted butter

1 Tbsp olive oil

1 small yellow onion, chopped

4 cups (32 fl oz/1 l) chicken or vegetable broth

5 cups (25 oz/780 g) fresh or frozen peas

⅓ cup (3 fl oz/80 ml) heavy cream

Salt and freshly ground pepper

Citrus Oil for topping (left)

Thinly sliced chives for garnish

In a large, heavy pot, melt the butter with the oil over medium-high heat. Add the onion and sauté until translucent, about 5 minutes. Add the broth and bring to a boil. Add the peas and cook for 5 minutes. Remove from the heat and let cool slightly.

Working in batches, purée the soup in a blender. Pass the soup through a fine-mesh sieve set over a bowl, pressing with a spoon to extract all the liquid. Return the soup to the pot and add the cream. Bring to a boil over medium-high heat and remove from the heat. Season with salt and pepper.

Serve the soup, drizzled with the citrus oil and garnished with the chives.

11

Onion soup is particularly tasty with cheese, whether grated or crusted atop. Here, a lighter version of the classic French onion soup finds the perfect match in a creamy, buttery grilled cheese sandwich.

THREE-ONION SOUP WITH CAMBOZOLA GRILLED CHEESE

serves 6

2 Tbsp unsalted butter

¼ cup (2 fl oz/60 ml) olive oil

3 large yellow onions, sliced

6 shallots, sliced

3 leeks, white and pale green parts, sliced

1 Tbsp light brown sugar

¼ cup (2 fl oz/60 ml) dry white wine

4 cups (32 fl oz/1 l) chicken broth

Salt and freshly ground pepper

FOR THE GRILLED CHEESE

12 thin slices cranberry-walnut or other fruit-and-nut bread

2 Tbsp unsalted butter, at room temperature

6 oz (185 g) Cambozola or Camembert cheese, at room temperature

In a large, heavy pot, melt the butter with the oil over high heat. Add the onions, shallots, and leeks and sauté until the onions soften, 8–10 minutes. Reduce the heat to low and continue to cook, stirring occasionally, for 30 minutes. Sprinkle the brown sugar over the onions, stir, and cook for 10 minutes. Add the white wine and bring to a simmer, stirring to scrape up any browned bits on the bottom of the pan. Cook until the wine is absorbed, 3–4 minutes. Add the broth and bring to a boil over medium-high heat. Reduce the heat to medium and simmer, uncovered, for 10 minutes. Remove from the heat and let cool slightly.

Purée half of the soup in a blender and return to the pot. Season with salt and pepper.

To make the grilled cheese, spread one side of each slice of bread with the butter. Spread 1 oz of the Cambozola on the unbuttered side of each of 6 bread slices and top with another slice of bread, with the buttered sides on the outside of the sandwich. In a frying pan, cook the sandwiches over medium-low heat until the bread is toasted and the cheese is melted, about 4 minutes per side. Cut each sandwich in half.

Ladle the soup into bowls and serve with the grilled cheese on the side.

12

This is a great way to use up leftover cooked white rice. The tough ends of the asparagus don't go to waste here: they infuse the flavor of the vegetable into the broth. Do not add the asparagus spears until you are ready to serve the soup, as they lose their beautiful green coloring quickly.

LEMONY ASPARAGUS & RICE SOUP WITH PARMESAN

serves 4

2 bunches asparagus

4 cups (32 fl oz/1 l) chicken broth

3 Tbsp unsalted butter

1 small yellow onion, finely chopped

3 cloves garlic, minced

1½ cups (7½ oz/235 g) cooked white rice

Grated zest of 1 lemon

3 Tbsp fresh lemon juice

Salt and freshly ground pepper

Grated Parmesan cheese for serving

Snap the tough ends from the asparagus spears and reserve them. Cut the spears into 1-inch (2.5-cm) pieces. In a saucepan, combine the broth and tough asparagus ends. Bring to a boil over medium-high heat, reduce the heat to low, and simmer for 10 minutes. Strain the broth into a bowl. Discard the solids.

In large, heavy pot, melt the butter over medium-high heat. Add the onion and garlic and sauté until translucent, about 5 minutes. Add the broth and bring to a boil. Reduce the heat to low, add the rice, asparagus pieces, lemon zest, and lemon juice, and simmer just until the asparagus is crisp-tender, about 3 minutes.

Season with salt and pepper and serve, topped with grated cheese.

13

BABY BOK CHOY & BEEF NOODLE SOUP

serves 6–8

4-inch (10-cm) piece fresh ginger

2 Tbsp canola oil

1 yellow onion, thinly sliced

4 cinnamon sticks

1 star anise

5 cloves garlic, crushed and thinly sliced

2 tsp Asian chile garlic paste

4 cups (32 fl oz/1 l) chicken broth

½ cup (4 fl oz/125 ml) soy sauce

2 lb (1 kg) beef blade steak, trimmed and cut into slices ¼-inch (6-mm) thick

Salt

1½ lb (750 g) fresh Chinese wheat noodles

5 heads baby bok choy (about 1½ lb/750 g), trimmed, each cut lengthwise into quarters

4 green onions, thinly sliced

Peppery and piquant, fresh ginger invigorates any dish. Here, cinnamon and star anise add flavor complexity, while chewy noodles and tender slices of beef add heartiness. Nearly any Asian-style noodles, including rice vermicelli, can be used; consult the package for cooking instructions.

Peel the ginger, cut into thin slices, and crush each slice with the flat side of a chef's knife.

In a large, heavy pot, warm the oil over medium-high heat. Add the onion and sauté until softened, about 3 minutes. Add the cinnamon sticks and star anise and cook, stirring, until the spices are fragrant and the cinnamon sticks begin to uncurl, about 2 minutes. Add the crushed ginger, the garlic, and the chile garlic paste and cook, stirring, until fragrant, about 45 seconds. Add the broth and soy sauce. Pour in 4½ cups (36 fl oz/1.1 l) water, raise the heat to high, cover, and bring to a boil. Stir in the beef and return to a boil. Reduce the heat to low, cover partially, and simmer until the beef is very tender, about 1½ hours.

In a large saucepan, bring 4 qt (4 l) water to a boil over high heat. Stir in 1 Tbsp salt and the noodles, return to a boil, and cook until the noodles are tender, about 3 minutes. Drain the noodles, rinse well under warm running water, and drain again. Divide the noodles among bowls. ⤳

Using a slotted spoon, remove and discard the cinnamon sticks, star anise, and ginger from the soup. Add the bok choy and cook just until crisp-tender, about 5 minutes. Stir in half of the green onions. Ladle the soup over the noodles, distributing the beef and bok choy evenly. Garnish with the remaining green onions and serve.

14

PARMESAN BROTH WITH LEMON, CHICKEN & SPINACH

serves 4–6

2 small skinless, boneless chicken breast halves (about ¾ lb/375 g)

2 Tbsp olive oil

1 small yellow onion, chopped

3 cloves garlic, minced

1-inch (2.5-cm) piece of Parmesan cheese rind, plus cheese shavings for garnish

6 cups (48 fl oz/1.5 l) chicken broth

Juice of 1 lemon

1 small bunch spinach, tough stems removed

Salt and freshly ground pepper

This simple recipe can be made even easier by using shredded rotisserie or grilled chicken. Adding the rind from a piece of Parmesan cheese during cooking adds depth of flavor to a soup.

In a small saucepan, combine the chicken breasts with cold water to cover by 1 inch (2.5 cm). Bring to a boil over medium-high heat. Reduce the heat to low and simmer until the chicken is opaque throughout, 15–18 minutes, skimming off any foam on the surface. Transfer to a plate and let cool. Shred the chicken.

In a large, heavy pot, warm the oil over medium-high heat. Add the onion and garlic and cook until translucent, about 5 minutes. Add the Parmesan rind, broth, and lemon juice and bring to a boil. Reduce the heat to low and simmer, uncovered, for 15 minutes. Add the spinach and chicken and continue to simmer, stirring constantly, just until the spinach is wilted. Remove and discard the Parmesan rind and season with salt and pepper. Serve, topped with Parmesan shavings.

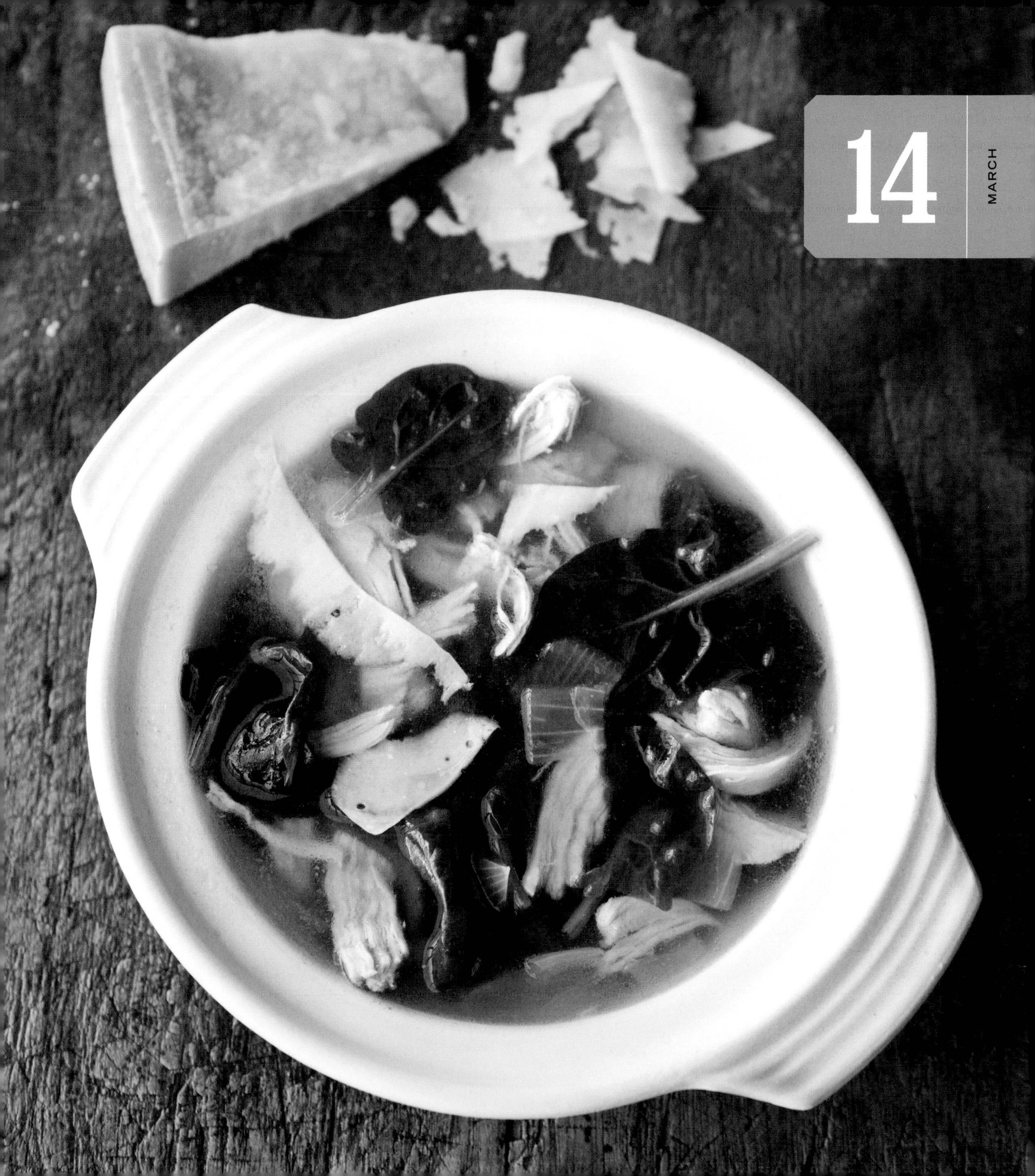

14

MARCH

MARCH

15

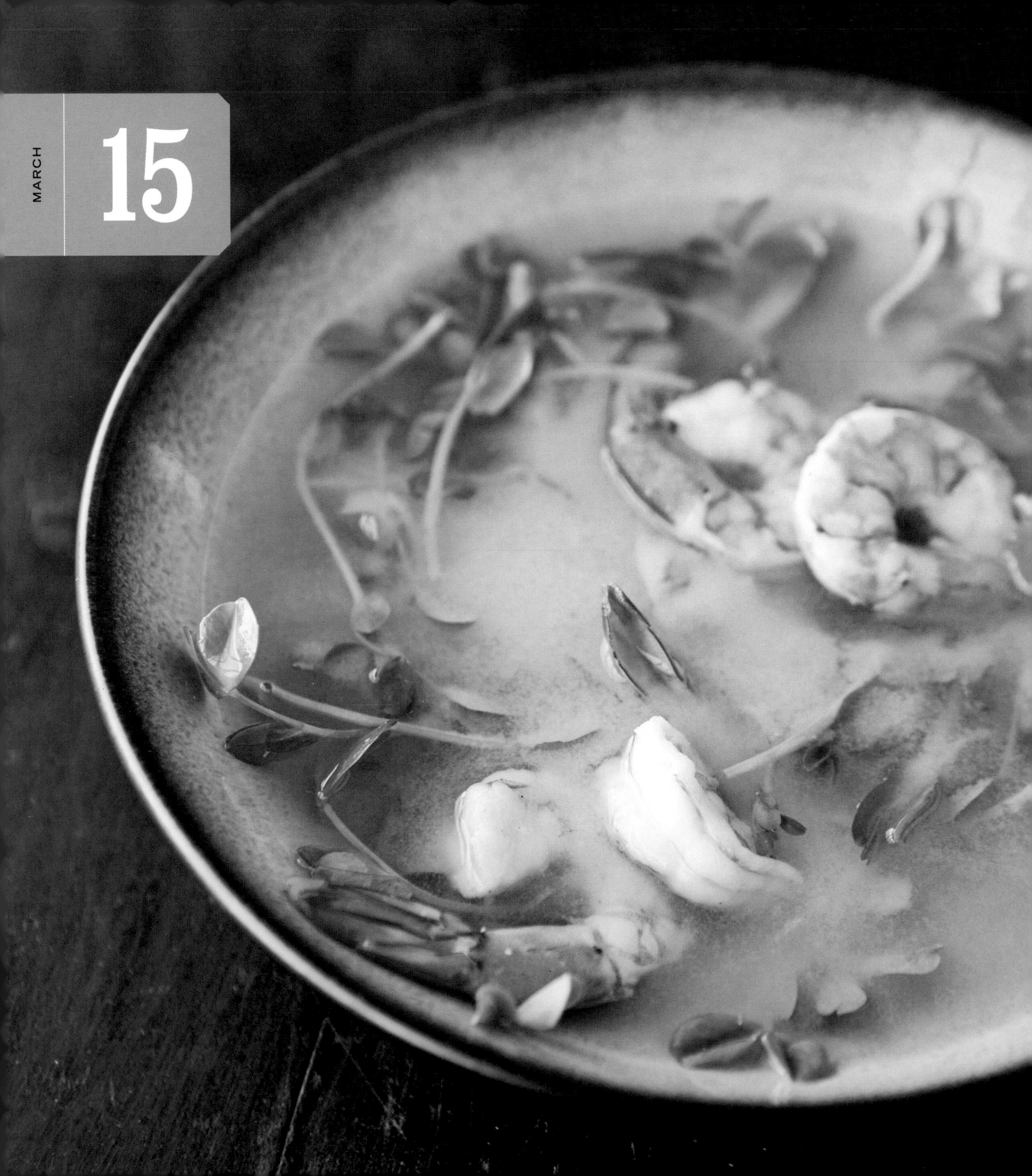

15

Traditional miso soup is served with dried shiitake mushrooms, sliced scallions, and tiny cubes of tofu; here it gets a springtime profile with shrimp and pea shoots.

MISO SOUP WITH SHRIMP & PEA SHOOTS

serves 2

3-inch (7.5-cm) piece kombu

½ cup (½ oz/15 g) bonito flakes

2 Tbsp light miso paste

¼ lb (4 oz/125 g) shrimp, peeled and deveined

⅓ cup (⅓ oz/10 g) pea shoots

In a large saucepan, combine the kombu and 3 cups (24 fl oz/750 ml) cold water. Bring to a boil over medium heat. Remove and discard the kombu. Remove from the heat, add the bonito flakes, and stir gently once. Let stand for 5 minutes. Strain the broth through a fine-mesh sieve, discarding the bonito flakes. Return the broth to the saucepan.

In a small bowl, combine the miso paste with ¼ cup (2 fl oz/60 ml) of the warm broth. Stir until the paste is softened and very smooth. Stir into the broth and warm gently over medium heat, taking care not to boil the soup.

Add the shrimp and simmer just until bright pink, about 4 minutes. Stir in the pea shoots and serve.

16

Dried porcini mushrooms have a woodsy flavor and an intense earthy aroma that easily matches the richness of beef. Farro, with its nutty taste and chewy texture, adds yet another hearty element to this soup.

BEEF & MUSHROOM SOUP WITH FARRO

serves 6–8

¾ oz (20 g) dried porcini mushrooms

1½ Tbsp olive oil

¾ lb (375 g) fresh cremini mushrooms, thinly sliced

1 yellow onion, finely chopped

3 carrots, peeled and cut into slices ¼ inch (6 mm) thick

3 cloves garlic, minced

1½ tsp minced thyme

¾ cup (4 oz/125 g) canned diced tomatoes

1½ cups (9 oz/280 g) farro, rinsed and drained

8 cups (64 fl oz/2 l) beef broth

2 cups (12 oz/375 g) shredded cooked beef

4 Tbsp (⅓ oz/10 g) chopped flat-leaf parsley

Salt and freshly ground pepper

In a heatproof bowl, combine the porcini with hot water to cover. Soak for 30 minutes. Lift out the mushrooms, reserving the soaking liquid. Rinse if they are gritty, then squeeze out the excess moisture. Slice thinly. Pour the soaking liquid through a coffee filter into another bowl. Set aside.

In a large, heavy pot, warm 1 Tbsp of the oil over medium heat. Add the cremini mushrooms and sauté until they release their liquid and the liquid evaporates, about 7 minutes. Add the remaining ½ Tbsp oil and then the onion, carrots, garlic, and thyme. Sauté until the vegetables are softened and beginning to brown, about 7 minutes. Add the porcini and their soaking liquid, the tomatoes with their juices, the farro, and the beef broth. Bring to a boil over high heat. Reduce the heat to low and simmer, stirring occasionally, until the farro is almost tender, about 20 minutes.

Add the shredded beef, half of the parsley, and 1½ tsp salt. Season with pepper and stir to mix well. Simmer until the meat is heated through and the farro is completely tender, about 10 minutes. Serve, garnished with the remaining parsley.

17

Nothing against corned beef and cabbage, but St. Patty's day might be even more delicious with this country-style lamb and vegetable stew. Simmering for 2 hours yields especially tender results. Serve thick slices of Irish soda bread alongside.

IRISH LAMB STEW

serves 4–6

2 lb (1 kg) boneless lamb shoulder, trimmed and cut into 1-inch (2.5-cm) cubes

4 white boiling potatoes, peeled and cut into slices ½ inch (12 mm) thick

2 yellow onions, cut in half lengthwise and then crosswise into slices ½ inch (12 mm) thick

1 large turnip, peeled and cut into slices ¼ inch (6 mm) thick

2 thyme sprigs, or 4 tsp dried thyme

3 flat-leaf parsley sprigs, plus more for garnish

Salt and freshly ground pepper

In a large, heavy pot, combine the lamb cubes with water to cover. Drain and add fresh water to cover by 1 inch (2.5 cm). Bring to a boil over high heat and boil for 5 minutes. Using a slotted spoon, transfer the lamb to a dish. Pour the broth into a bowl.

Layer half of the potato slices in the bottom of the same pot. Cover with half of the onion slices and then top with all of the turnip slices. Distribute the lamb evenly over the turnips and top with the thyme and the 3 parsley sprigs. Season with 1 tsp salt and 4 tsp pepper. Top with the remaining onions and then the remaining potatoes. Strain the lamb broth through a fine-mesh sieve over the potatoes. Bring to a low boil over high heat. Reduce the heat to medium-low, cover, and simmer until the lamb is tender, about 2 hours. Discard the thyme and parsley sprigs from the pot. Serve, garnished with parsley sprigs.

18

Two kinds of rice give texture and flavor to this fragrant soup. Full of aromatic cold-fighters like ginger, garlic, and cilantro, this soup makes a comforting dish to bring to a friend who is under the weather.

CHICKEN & WILD RICE SOUP WITH GINGER

serves 6

½ cup (3 oz/90 g) wild rice, rinsed

1 Tbsp Asian sesame oil

1 Tbsp canola oil

1 yellow onion, chopped

1 Tbsp peeled and grated fresh ginger

2 cloves garlic, minced

4 cups (32 fl oz/1 l) chicken broth

1 carrot, peeled and diced

3 skinless, bone-in chicken breast halves

2 skinless, bone-in chicken thighs

½ cup (3½ oz/105 g) long-grain white rice

¼ cup (¾ oz/20 g) thinly sliced green onions

¼ cup (⅓ oz/10 g) chopped cilantro

Salt and freshly ground pepper

In a small saucepan, bring 2 cups (16 fl oz/ 500 ml) water to a boil. Add the wild rice, reduce the heat to a simmer, cover, and cook until tender, 45–50 minutes. Drain.

Meanwhile, in a large, heavy pot, warm the sesame and canola oils over medium-high heat. Add the yellow onion and sauté until softened, 3–5 minutes. Add the ginger and garlic and sauté for 2 minutes. Add the broth, carrot, chicken pieces, and white rice. Pour in 2 cups (16 fl oz/500 ml) water and bring to a simmer. Reduce the heat to medium-low, cover, and cook until the chicken is opaque throughout, about 15 minutes.

Transfer the chicken to a plate to cool. Remove the meat from the bones and tear into bite-sized pieces. Stir the chicken back into the soup along with the green onions, cilantro, and wild rice. Season with salt and pepper and serve.

NAPA CABBAGE SOUP WITH PORK & BEAN SPROUTS

serves 6–8

4-inch (10-cm) piece fresh ginger

6 cups (48 fl oz/1.5 l) chicken broth

½ cup (4 fl oz/125 ml) plus 3 Tbsp Chinese rice wine or dry sherry

5 Tbsp (3 fl oz/80 ml) soy sauce

½ lb (250 g) boneless pork loin chop, cut into thin strips

10 dried shiitake mushrooms

1 head napa cabbage (about 2½ lb/1.25 kg)

4 tsp canola oil

6 cloves garlic, minced

2 tsp Asian sesame oil

Salt

1½ cups (4½ oz/140 g) mung bean sprouts

Asian chile oil for serving

6 green onions, dark green tops only, thinly sliced

Once rehydrated, dried shiitake mushrooms assume a chewy, almost meaty texture, and their soaking water is infused with smoky flavor. This liquid, added to the broth, creates a savory background for mild-tasting cabbage, hot chile oil, and crunchy bean sprouts.

Peel the ginger. Mince half. Cut the other half into 6 slices and crush each slice with the flat side of a chef's knife. In a large, heavy pot, combine the crushed ginger, broth, and the ½ cup (4 fl oz/125 ml) rice wine and bring to a boil over high heat. Remove from the heat, cover, and let stand for about 30 minutes to blend the flavors. Using a slotted spoon, remove and discard the crushed ginger.

Meanwhile, in a bowl, stir together the minced ginger, the 3 Tbsp rice wine, 2 Tbsp of the soy sauce, and the pork. Let stand at room temperature for 30 minutes.

In a small bowl, combine the mushrooms with 1 cup (8 fl oz/250 ml) hot water. Soak for 30 minutes. Lift out the mushrooms and cut off and discard the stems. Cut the caps into quarters. Pour the soaking liquid through a coffee filter into the pot of stock.

Separate the leaves from the cabbage and cut crosswise into 1-inch (2.5-cm) pieces. In a large nonstick frying pan, warm 2 tsp of the canola oil over high heat. Add the cabbage and stir-fry for 1 minute. Add the garlic and stir-fry until the cabbage is just crisp-tender, about 2 minutes. ⟩⟩→

Scrape into the pot. Add the remaining 2 tsp canola oil to the frying pan and warm over high heat. Add the mushrooms and the pork with its marinade and stir-fry until the pork is opaque, about 2 minutes. Transfer to the pot. Add the remaining 3 Tbsp soy sauce to the pot along with the sesame oil and 1 tsp salt. Bring to a boil over high heat, reduce the heat to low, cover partially, and simmer for 10–15 minutes to blend the flavors.

Serve, garnished with a handful of bean sprouts, a drizzle of chile oil, and a sprinkling of green onion tops.

PASTA IN BROTH WITH CHIVES

serves 6

2 lb (1 kg) chicken necks and backs, fat removed

1 small yellow onion, quartered

1 small carrot, peeled and coarsely chopped

⅛ tsp dried thyme

5 oz (155 g) stelline, ditalini, farfalline, or other small soup pasta

1 Tbsp minced chives

Salt and freshly ground pepper

½ cup (2 oz/60 g) grated Parmesan cheese

In Italy, this soup is called pasta en brodo. It makes a wonderful first course, or lends itself well to embellishments and improvisations. For extra color and flavor, try adding green beans, fresh herbs, peas, Swiss chard, or spinach.

In a large, heavy pot, combine the chicken, onion, carrot, and thyme. Pour in 8 cups (64 fl oz/2 l) water and bring to a boil. Reduce the heat to low and simmer, uncovered, for 3 hours, skimming off any foam on the surface. Periodically add water to the pot to maintain the original level. Strain the broth into a clean pot. Discard the bones. Skim the fat and discard. You should have 8 cups (64 fl oz/2 l); add more water if necessary.

Heat the broth over medium-high heat. Add the pasta and cook until al dente, 2–3 minutes or according to the package directions. Stir in the chives and season with salt and pepper. Serve sprinkled with the cheese.

21

CHICKEN & CHIPOTLE SOUP WITH AVOCADO & LIME

serves 6

The rambunctious flavor of the smoky chipotle chile in this classic soup is tamed by the addition of earthy chickpeas. Garnish with minced fresh cilantro and/or crumbled queso fresco, if you like.

6 cups (48 fl oz/1.5 l) chicken broth

1 skinless, bone-in whole chicken breast

1 mint sprig

1 Tbsp canola oil

½ large white onion, chopped

1 large carrot, peeled and chopped

2 cloves garlic, chopped

1 chipotle chile in adobo, finely chopped

1 cilantro sprig

Salt and freshly ground pepper

1 can (15 oz/470 g) chickpeas, drained

1 avocado, pitted, peeled, and diced

1 lime, cut into 6 wedges

In a large saucepan, bring the broth, chicken, and mint to a simmer over medium heat. Cook, partially covered, until the chicken is opaque throughout, about 15 minutes, skimming off any foam on the surface. Lift out the chicken and mint. Discard the mint. Let the chicken cool, then remove the meat from the bones and shred. Reserve the broth.

In a large, heavy pot, warm the oil over medium heat. Add the onion, carrot, and garlic and sauté until translucent, about 5 minutes. Pour in the broth and add the chile, cilantro, ½ tsp salt, and ½ tsp pepper. Bring to a simmer, cover, and cook for 20 minutes. Stir in the chickpeas and simmer, uncovered, for 10 minutes. Add the chicken and heat through.

Serve, topped with the avocado. Pass lime wedges at the table.

22

MOROCCAN LAMB MEATBALL & COUSCOUS SOUP

serves 4–6

Israeli couscous has much bigger pearls than Moroccan couscous, but it is still very quick-cooking. The meatballs also make a delicious dinner on their own over a bed of couscous.

FOR THE MEATBALLS

1 tsp ground coriander

1 tsp ground cumin

¼ tsp curry powder

¼ teaspon dried oregano

¼ tsp dried thyme

⅛ tsp dry mustard

⅛ tsp chili powder

Pinch of ground cinnamon

Salt and freshly ground pepper

1 lb (500 g) ground lamb

2 Tbsp tomato paste

1 cup (6 oz/185 g) Israeli couscous

3 Tbsp olive oil

2 shallots, minced

5 cloves garlic, minced

3 cups (24 fl oz/750 ml) chicken broth

1 Tbsp chopped mint

To make the meatballs, preheat the oven to 375°F (190°C). Oil a baking sheet. In a small bowl, combine the coriander, cumin, curry powder, oregano, thyme, mustard, chili powder, and cinnamon. Stir in ½ tsp salt. Add the lamb and tomato paste and mix to combine with your hands. For each meatball, scoop up 1 tsp of the lamb mixture, form into a meatball, and place on the prepared pan. Bake until the meatballs are cooked through, about 10 minutes.

In a small saucepan, bring 1¼ cups (10 fl oz/310 ml) water to a boil over high heat. Add the couscous, reduce the heat to low, cover, and cook until all the liquid is absorbed, 8–10 minutes.

Meanwhile, in a large, heavy pot, warm the oil over medium-high heat. Add the shallots and garlic and sauté for 1 minute. Add the broth and bring to a boil. Reduce the heat to low and add the meatballs and couscous and simmer for 10 minutes. Remove from the heat. Stir in the mint, season with salt and pepper, and serve.

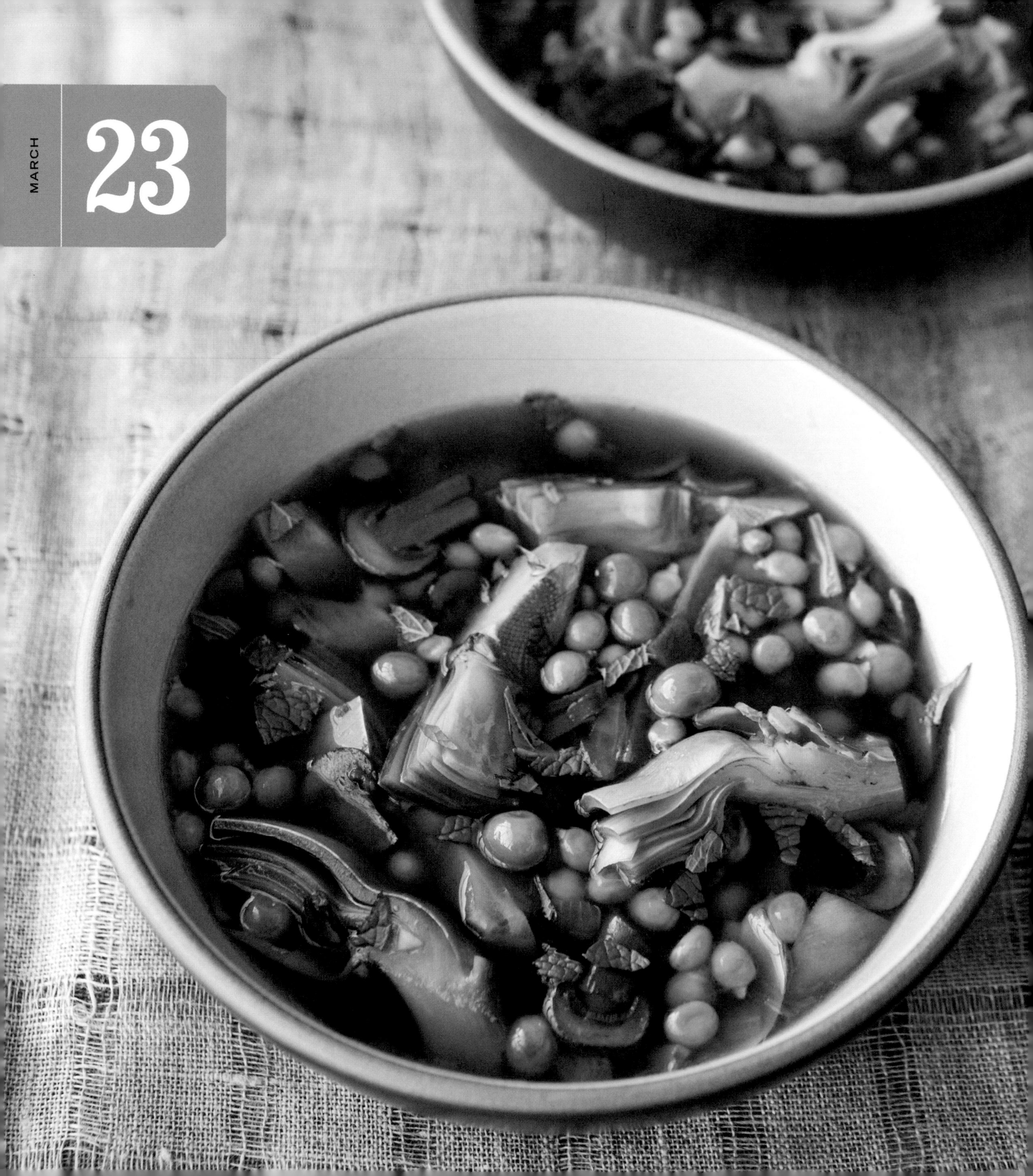

23

ARTICHOKE, SPRING PEA & MINT SOUP

serves 4–6

The clear broth of this soup allows the green hues from the artichokes and peas to really shine. Use a shallow bowl to present the soup so that you can see all the elements.

Juice of ½ lemon

12 small artichokes

2 Tbsp unsalted butter

1 yellow onion, finely chopped

2 cloves garlic, minced

½ lb (250 g) cremini mushrooms, thinly sliced

5 cups (40 fl oz/1.25 l) chicken broth

1 cup (5 oz/155 g) fresh peas

2 Tbsp chopped mint

Salt and freshly ground pepper

Fill a bowl with water and add the lemon juice. Cut off the stem of each artichoke flush with the bottom. Snap off the outer leaves until you reach the tender inner leaves. Cut off the top one-third of each artichoke to remove the pointed tips. Quarter the artichoke lengthwise. Cut out the choke from each quarter. As you work, add the quarters to the lemon water.

In a large, heavy pot, melt the butter over medium heat. Add the onion and garlic and cook until translucent, about 5 minutes. Drain the artichoke quarters and add to the pan with the mushrooms. Stir to coat, and cook for 4 minutes. Add the broth and bring to a boil. Reduce the heat to low and simmer, uncovered, until the artichokes are tender but not mushy, about 10 minutes. Add the peas and cook for 3 minutes. Stir in the mint, season with salt and pepper, and serve.

24

PORK STEW WITH PRUNES & SWEET POTATOES

serves 6

This sweet stew would be delicious served over steamed basmati rice. It will taste even better the next day, as the flavors will continue to blend.

4 Tbsp (2 fl oz/60 ml) olive oil

1½ lb (750 g) pork tenderloin, trimmed and cut into 1½-inch (4-cm) cubes

Salt and freshly ground pepper

1 large white onion, cut in half lengthwise and then crosswise into slices ¼ inch (6 mm) thick

4 cloves garlic, minced

1 large sweet potato (¾ lb/375 g), peeled and cut into ½-inch (12-mm) dice

1½ cups (12 fl oz/375 ml) apple cider

2 cups (16 fl oz/500 ml) chicken broth

1 cup (6 oz/185 g) pitted prunes

2 Tbsp minced flat-leaf parsley

Preheat the oven to 350°F (180°C). In a large, heavy pot, warm 2 Tbsp of the oil over high heat. Season the pork generously with salt and pepper. In batches, sauté the pork until browned on all sides, 7–8 minutes total. Transfer to a bowl and set aside.

Reduce the heat to medium-high and warm the remaining 2 Tbsp oil. Add the onion, garlic, and sweet potato and cook, stirring often, until the vegetables soften, 7–8 minutes. Add the cider and bring to a simmer, stirring to scrape up any browned bits on the bottom of the pot. Add the pork and any accumulated juices, the broth, and prunes and stir to combine.

Cover the pot tightly and transfer to the oven. Cook for 1½ hours. Remove from the oven, season with salt and pepper, stir in the parsley, and serve.

THREE-BEAN SOUP WITH LINGUIÇA

serves 4–6

*This soup features
a trio of beans
and linguiça, a
Portuguese sausage
that's laden with
garlic and paprika.
Choose either mild
or hot sausage to suit
your palate. Puréeing
a portion of the beans
helps thicken the
consistency.*

¾ cup (5 oz/155 g) *each* dried pink beans,
cannellini beans, and chickpeas, rinsed

2 Tbsp olive oil

1 yellow onion, chopped

2 celery ribs, chopped

3 cloves garlic, minced

1 small red bell pepper, seeded and chopped

5 cups (40 fl oz/1.25 l) chicken broth

1 bay leaf

1 carrot, peeled

5 oz (155 g) linguiça sausage, cut into ¼-inch
(6-mm) pieces

1 cup (6 oz/185 g) canned diced tomatoes

1 tsp dried marjoram

½ tsp smoked paprika

Salt and freshly ground pepper

Place the dried beans and chickpeas in a
bowl with cold water to cover and soak for
at least 4 hours or up to overnight. Drain.

In a large, heavy pot, warm the oil over
medium-low heat. Add the onion, celery,
garlic, and bell pepper and sauté until
softened, about 5 minutes. Add the beans,
broth, bay leaf, carrot, and 5 cups (40 fl oz/
1.25 l) water, and bring to a boil. Reduce
the heat to low and simmer, uncovered,
stirring occasionally, until the beans are
tender, 1½–2 hours.

Remove the carrot and chop it. Remove
and discard the bay leaf. In a blender, purée
3 cups (21 oz/655 g) of the beans with ½ cup
(4 fl oz/125 ml) of the cooking liquid. Return
to the pot. Add the sausage, tomatoes with
their juices, marjoram, paprika, and chopped
carrot. Season with ½ tsp salt and ¼ tsp
pepper, and heat through. Serve.

FIVE-SPICE BROTH WITH SALMON & ONION DUMPLINGS

serves 4

*This aromatic
soup is best served
right away as the
dumplings do not
reheat well. You
can make the broth
and assemble the
dumplings ahead of
time, but don't cook
the dumplings until
just before you are
ready to serve.*

2 Tbsp canola oil

1 large shallot, minced

1½ tsp peeled and minced fresh ginger

¼ tsp Chinese five-spice powder

4 cups (32 fl oz/1 l) chicken broth

Salt

FOR THE DUMPLINGS

¼ lb (125 g) salmon fillet, skin and pin bones
removed, finely chopped

2 green onions, white and pale green parts,
finely chopped

½ tsp canola oil

Salt and freshly ground pepper

20 wonton wrappers

2 green onions, dark green parts only, sliced

In a large saucepan, warm the 2 Tbsp oil over
medium-high heat. Add the shallot and ginger
and sauté for 3 minutes. Add the five-spice
powder, the broth, 2 cups (16 fl oz/500 ml)
water, and 2 tsp salt. Bring to a boil. Reduce
the heat to low and simmer, uncovered, for
about 15 minutes to blend the flavors. Remove
from the heat and season with salt.

To make the dumplings, in a bowl, stir
together the salmon, chopped green onions,
and ½ tsp oil. Stir in ¼ tsp salt and ⅛ tsp
pepper. Place 1 tsp of the salmon mixture in
the middle of each wonton wrapper. Using
your fingers, apply a small amount of water
on all edges of the wrapper. Fold the wrapper
diagonally, forcing out any air bubbles as you
press to seal. Take the 2 points on the longest
side of the triangle and fold so that the tips
meet. Apply a small amount of water on the
tips and firmly press to stick them together.

Return the soup to a simmer. Carefully add
the dumplings and cook until just tender,
about 3 minutes. Ladle the soup into bowls,
garnish with the sliced green onions,
and serve.

27

This fennel broth tastes light, but it is packed with flavor. The chard gives texture, and the spicy chorizo adds a taste explosion. You can substitute Parmesan cheese for the pecorino romano.

FENNEL BROTH WITH CHARD & CHORIZO

serves 4

¾ lb (375 g) cured Spanish chorizo, halved lengthwise then cut into ¼-inch (6-mm) slices

1 Tbsp olive oil

2 shallots, minced

3 cloves garlic, minced

1 fennel bulb, stalks and fronds removed, quartered and thinly sliced

⅓ cup (3 fl oz/80 ml) dry white wine

4 cups (32 fl oz/1 l) chicken broth

1 bunch chard, ribs removed, leaves coarsely chopped

Salt and freshly ground pepper

Grated pecorino romano cheese for serving

In a large, heavy pot, sauté the chorizo over medium-high heat until browned on both sides, about 7 minutes. Transfer to a bowl and set aside.

In the same pot, combine the olive oil, shallots, garlic, and fennel. Sauté until the fennel softens and begins to caramelize, about 10 minutes. Add the white wine and bring to a simmer, stirring to scrape up any browned bits on the bottom of the pot. Add the broth, stir to combine, bring to a simmer, and cook for 5 minutes. Add the chard and chorizo, stir to combine, and simmer for 5 minutes. Season with salt and pepper and serve, topped with the cheese.

28

Here is a shortened and slightly healthier version of the traditional Southern stew. Garnish with chopped onion and serve with warm jalapeno-corn bread.

BLACK-EYED PEA STEW

serves 4–6

2 Tbsp olive oil

1 large yellow onion, chopped

4 cloves garlic, minced

1 bunch collard greens, chopped

5 oz (155 g) cooked ham steak, cubed

3 cups (24 fl oz/750 ml) chicken broth, plus more as needed

2 cans (15 oz/470 g each) black-eyed peas, drained

2 Tbsp tomato paste

Salt and freshly ground pepper

In a large, heavy pot, warm the oil over medium-high heat. Add the onion and garlic and sauté until soft, 5–7 minutes. Add the collard greens and ham and cook, stirring often, for 5 minutes. Add the broth and bring to a boil. Reduce the heat to low, add the black-eyed peas and tomato paste, stir well, and simmer for 30 minutes. Add more chicken broth if necessary. Season with salt and pepper and serve.

29

Fresh peas have a short season, but when available, they are well worth the added step of shucking. For the sweetest results, try to use them the day of purchase. Arborio rice adds body and creaminess to the soup without dulling the flavor of the peas. Garnish with minced fresh mint.

PEA & ARBORIO RICE PURÉE

serves 4

1 Tbsp canola oil

1 leek, white part only, chopped

1 white onion, chopped

1 small zucchini, trimmed and chopped

1 Tbsp Arborio rice

2 cups (10 oz/315 g) fresh or frozen peas

Salt

In a large saucepan, warm the oil over medium-high heat. Add the leek, onion, and zucchini and stir to coat with the oil. Reduce the heat to low, cover tightly, and cook until the vegetables are soft, about 10 minutes. Add the rice and 3 cups (24 fl oz/750 ml) water, raise the heat to medium, and bring to a boil, then reduce to a simmer, cover, and cook for 10 minutes. Add the peas, cover, and cook until tender, 5–10 minutes. Remove from the heat and let cool slightly. Working in batches, purée the soup in a blender. Season with salt and serve.

30

CHILLED POTATO & LEEK SOUP

serves 4

4 leeks, white part only, chopped

4 large green onions, white part only, chopped

3 cups (24 fl oz/750 ml) chicken broth

1 lb (500 g) Yukon gold potatoes, peeled and chopped

1½ Tbsp unsalted butter

Salt and ground white pepper

2 Tbsp minced chives

This is a lighter version of the classic vichyssoise. It delivers the buttery flavor of the original by using yellow-fleshed potatoes and just a modest amount of butter.

In a large, heavy pot over medium-high heat, combine the leeks, the green onions, and ½ cup (4 fl oz/125 ml) of the broth. Bring to a boil, reduce the heat to low, cover, and cook until the vegetables have wilted and begin to soften, about 8 minutes. Add the potatoes and remaining 2½ cups (20 fl oz/625 ml) broth, cover, and cook until the vegetables are very soft, 25–30 minutes. Let cool for 15 minutes. Stir in the butter.

Working in batches, purée the soup in a blender. Return to the pot. Stir in ¼ tsp salt and season with pepper. Cover and refrigerate until well chilled, 3–4 hours or up to overnight. The soup will thicken and become very creamy. Serve, garnished with the chives.

31

CHICKPEA & ROASTED TOMATO SOUP WITH FRIED ROSEMARY

serves 4–6

1 lb (500 g) Roma (plum) tomatoes

4 Tbsp olive oil

Salt and freshly ground pepper

1 large yellow onion, chopped

4 cloves garlic, minced

1 tsp ground cumin

½ tsp paprika

1 cinnamon stick

3 cans (15 oz/470 g each) chickpeas, drained

4 cups (32 fl oz/1 l) chicken broth

1 Tbsp sour cream

Fried Rosemary for garnish (left)

To make the fried rosemary, in a small frying pan, warm 2 Tbsp olive oil over high heat. Add 4 sprigs rosemary, 2 at a time, and fry for 1 minute on each side. Transfer to paper towels to drain. Once they are cool enough to handle, remove the leaves and chop, if desired.

Preheat the oven to 450°F (230°C). Slice the tomatoes in half and place in a single layer on a baking sheet. Drizzle with 2 Tbsp of the oil and season with salt and pepper. Roast the tomatoes until they are soft and caramelized, 25–30 minutes. Set aside.

In a large, heavy pot, warm 2 Tbsp oil over medium-high heat. Add the onion and the garlic and sauté until soft, about 5 minutes. Add the cumin, paprika, and cinnamon stick and toast the spices, stirring often, for 2 minutes. Add the chickpeas, roasted tomatoes, and broth, stir to combine, and bring to a boil. Reduce the heat to low and simmer until the chickpeas are very tender, about 45 minutes. Remove from the heat and let cool slightly.

Transfer about two-thirds of the chickpeas and broth to a blender and purée. Return to the pot and stir in the sour cream.

Season the soup with salt and pepper and serve, garnished with fried rosemary.

1
SPRING VEGETABLE SOUP
page 82

2
LAMB & DRIED APRICOT STEW
page 82

3
CARAMELIZED ONION SOUP WITH GORGONZOLA CROUTONS
page 84

4
VENETIAN RICE & PEA SOUP
page 84

8
MATZOH BALL SOUP
page 87

9
UDON NOODLE SOUP WITH CHICKEN & SPINACH
page 88

10
ASPARAGUS-CHERVIL PURÉE WITH LEMON MASCARPONE
page 88

11
VEAL STEW WITH TARRAGON
page 89

15
ASPARAGUS SOUP WITH POACHED EGGS & CRISPY PROSCIUTTO
page 93

16
THAI HOT & SOUR SOUP
page 93

17
THREE-MUSHROOM PURÉE WITH SHERRY
page 94

18
BALSAMIC BEEF STEW
page 94

22
CARROT & COCONUT PURÉE WITH CURRIED ALMONDS
page 96

23
CHICKEN-LEMONGRASS SOUP
page 99

24
CLAMS IN FENNEL BROTH WITH PARSLEY VINAIGRETTE
page 99

25
LENTIL & ANDOUILLE SOUP
page 100

29
SPINACH SOUP WITH SUMAC & FETA
page 102

30
KIELBASA & SAUERKRAUT SOUP
page 102

5
SORREL PURÉE WITH TORN CROUTONS
page 85

6
LEEK SOUP WITH PANCETTA & BREAD CRUMBS
page 85

7
DASHI WITH SCALLOPS, WATERCRESS & SOBA NOODLES
page 87

12
FAVA BEAN SOUP
page 89

13
SHRIMP & SPINACH NOODLE SOUP
page 90

14
ARTICHOKE & QUINOA SOUP WITH GREEN GARLIC
page 90

19
MANHATTAN CLAM CHOWDER
page 95

20
FAVA BEAN & FARFALLE SOUP
page 95

21
CREAM OF BROCCOLI SOUP
page 96

26
BLACK BEAN CHILI
page 100

27
VEGETABLE-TORTELLINI SOUP
page 101

28
CREAMY MUSHROOM SOUP WITH HAM & PEAS
page 101

Lengthening daylight hours nurture an expanding array of fresh ingredients to enhance spring soups. Young onions, chives, green garlic, and watercress appear, delivering bold and grassy flavors. With their short season, fava beans and English peas join the farmers' market bounty this month. In soups and stews, these pair well with tender meats like lamb and ham.

april

1

In Italy, this soup is known as vignole, which loosely means "a celebration of spring," so feel free to throw in any spring vegetable you can find. Swirl a spoonful of pesto on top, and serve with rustic bread and a bright Italian white wine such as Vermentino.

SPRING VEGETABLE SOUP
serves 6–8

Juice of ½ lemon

8 baby artichokes

4 thyme sprigs

Salt and freshly ground pepper

3 lb (1.5 kg) fava beans in the pods, shelled

2 Tbsp olive oil

8 small leeks, white and pale green parts, cut into 1-inch (2.5-cm) slices

1 bunch green onions, chopped

6 slices prosciutto, torn into strips ½ inch (12 mm) wide

6 cups (48 fl oz/1.5 l) chicken broth

1 cup (2 oz/60 g) shredded chard

1 cup (2 oz/60 g) shredded sorrel

1 cup (1 oz/30 g) baby spinach leaves

1 cup (5 oz/155 g) fresh or frozen peas

½ cup (½ oz/15 g) packed mint leaves

Fill a bowl with water and add the lemon juice. Cut off the stem of each artichoke flush with the bottom. Snap off the outer leaves until you reach the tender inner leaves. Cut off the top one-third of each artichoke to remove the pointed tips. As you work, add the artichokes to the lemon water. Fill a saucepan with water and add the thyme and a large pinch of salt. Drain the artichokes and add to the pan. Bring to a boil over medium-high heat and cook until the artichokes are tender, about 10 minutes. Let cool in the water. Drain the artichokes and halve lengthwise. Cut out the chokes.

Bring a saucepan of water to a boil over high heat. Add the fava beans and cook for 1 minute. Drain, rinse under cold running water, and drain again. Split open the skin of each bean along its edge and slip the bean from the skin. Discard the skins.

In a large, heavy pot, warm the oil over medium heat. Add the leeks, green onions, and prosciutto and sauté until the prosciutto is lightly browned, about 3 minutes. Add the broth and bring to a boil. Add the chard, sorrel, spinach, peas, artichokes, and fava beans. Simmer until the vegetables are bright green and the peas float to the top, 3–4 minutes. Season with salt and pepper, stir in the mint, and serve.

2

This aromatic stew is even better the next day, once the spices have had time to really infuse the meat with flavor. Serve with a simple green salad dressed with a lemony vinaigrette.

LAMB & DRIED APRICOT STEW
serves 6–8

2 Tbsp olive oil

1½ lb (750 g) boneless lamb shoulder, trimmed and cut into 1-inch (2.5-cm) cubes

1 large yellow onion, chopped

3 cloves garlic, minced

2 tsp ground cumin

½ tsp ground coriander

¼ tsp cayenne pepper

Salt and freshly ground black pepper

2 cups (16 fl oz/500 ml) chicken broth

1 can (14½ oz/455 g) diced tomatoes

1 can (8¾ oz/270 g) chickpeas, rinsed

¼ cup (2 oz/60 g) dried apricots, halved

1 cinnamon stick

3 Tbsp chopped flat-leaf parsley

In a large, heavy pot, warm the oil over medium-high heat. Cook the lamb in 2 batches until browned on all sides, 6–8 minutes per batch. Transfer to a bowl.

Add the onion and garlic and sauté until soft, 5–7 minutes. Add the cumin, coriander, and cayenne, season with ¼ tsp black pepper, and cook, stirring constantly, for 2 minutes. Add the broth and bring to a simmer, stirring to scrape up any browned bits on the bottom of the pot. Add the tomatoes, chickpeas, apricots, cinnamon stick, and lamb and bring to a boil. Reduce the heat to low, cover partially, and simmer, stirring occasionally, until the lamb is tender and the stew thickens, about 1¼ hours.

Stir in the parsley, season with salt and pepper, and serve.

3

This soup, sweet with caramelized onions and savory with beef broth and blue cheese, gets a touch of acidity and brightness from the addition of dry vermouth.

CARAMELIZED ONION SOUP WITH GORGONZOLA CROUTONS

serves 6

7 Tbsp (3½ oz/105 g) unsalted butter, at room temperature

2 lb (1 kg) yellow onions, thinly sliced

2 lb (1 kg) sweet onions, such as Vidalia, thinly sliced

Salt and freshly ground pepper

¾ cup (6 fl oz/180 ml) dry vermouth

4 cups (32 fl oz/1 l) chicken broth

2 cups (16 fl oz/500 ml) beef broth

3 flat-leaf parsley sprigs, 2 thyme sprigs, and 2 small bay leaves, tied together to make a bouquet garni

1 baguette, cut on the diagonal into slices 1 inch (2.5 cm) thick

6 oz (185 g) tangy blue cheese, such as Gorgonzola or Roquefort

In a large, heavy pot, melt 3 Tbsp of the butter over medium heat. Add all the onions and 1 tsp salt. Cook, stirring often, until the onions release their moisture, the moisture evaporates, and browned bits form on the bottom of the pot, about 45 minutes. Raise the heat to medium-high, add ⅓ cup (3 fl oz/80 ml) water, bring to a simmer, and stir to scrape up the browned bits from the bottom of the pot. Cook until the water evaporates and browned bits form again, about 5 minutes. Repeat four times, adding ⅓ cup water at a time.

Add the vermouth, stir to scrape up the browned bits, and cook until the liquid has almost evaporated, about 4 minutes. Add the chicken and beef broths, the bouquet garni, and 1½ tsp salt. Bring to a boil over high heat. Reduce the heat to low, cover, and simmer for about 30 minutes to blend the flavors.

Meanwhile, preheat the oven to 425°F (220°C). Arrange the baguette slices on a baking sheet and toast until lightly browned, about 5 minutes. Remove from the oven and preheat the broiler. Crumble the blue cheese into a bowl. Add 2 Tbsp of the butter and, using a fork, mash to form a fairly smooth paste. ⟫⟶

Spread each baguette slice with a scant tablespoon of the blue cheese mixture and return to the baking sheet. Broil until the cheese is golden brown in spots, about 1½ minutes.

Add the remaining 2 Tbsp butter to the soup and stir vigorously to blend. Remove and discard the bouquet. Season with salt and pepper and serve, topping each bowl with 2 baguette slices.

4

Risotto rice lends its creamy consistency to this surprisingly quick and easy soup, punctuated with a handful of verdant green peas—substitute fresh, if available. Finish with a sprinkle of grated lemon zest.

VENETIAN RICE & PEA SOUP

serves 4

2 Tbsp unsalted butter

1 shallot, minced

1 celery rib, chopped

½ cup (3½ oz/105 g) medium-grain white rice, such as Arborio

3 cups (24 fl oz/750 ml) chicken broth

2 cups (10 oz/315 g) fresh or frozen peas

½ cup (2 oz/60 g) grated Parmesan cheese

1 Tbsp minced flat-leaf parsley

Salt and freshly ground pepper

In a large, heavy pot, melt the butter over medium heat. Add the shallot and celery and sauté until the shallot is translucent, about 2 minutes. Add the rice and cook, stirring, until the grains are translucent with a white dot in the center, about 1 minute.

Raise the heat to medium-high, add the broth and 2 cups (16 fl oz/500 ml) water, and bring to a boil. Reduce the heat to low, cover, and simmer until the rice is tender, about 15 minutes. Add the peas and cook, stirring occasionally, for 5 minutes. Stir in the Parmesan and parsley, season with salt and pepper, and serve.

SORREL PURÉE WITH TORN CROUTONS

serves 6

Sorrel leaves resemble those of spinach and arugula and, like the latter, are often classified as herbs. The plant thrives in the coolness of early spring, when its young leaves have their most delicate taste and texture.

FOR THE TORN CROUTONS

¼ lb (125 g) day-old country-style sourdough bread, crusts removed

3 Tbsp unsalted butter, melted

Salt and freshly ground pepper

2 Tbsp unsalted butter

2 yellow onions, chopped

9 oz (280 g) sorrel leaves, stemmed, or baby spinach

1¼ lb (625 g) small red or new potatoes, peeled and thinly sliced

2 cups (16 fl oz/500 ml) chicken or vegetable broth

½ cup (4 fl oz/125 ml) heavy cream

To make the croutons, preheat the oven to 400°F (200°C). Tear the bread into ½-inch (12-mm) pieces and place on a baking sheet. Drizzle the 3 Tbsp butter over the bread, sprinkle with salt and pepper, and toss to coat evenly. Bake until golden and crisp, 10–15 minutes. Let cool.

In a large, heavy pot, melt the 2 Tbsp butter over medium heat. Add the onions and sauté until softened, about 2 minutes. Raise the heat to high, and add the sorrel, potatoes, and broth. Pour in 4 cups (32 fl oz/1 l) water and bring to a boil. Reduce the heat to medium-low, cover, and simmer until the potatoes are soft, 15–20 minutes. Remove from the heat and let cool slightly.

Working in batches, purée the soup well in a blender. Strain through a fine-mesh sieve into a clean pot. Stir in the cream and season with salt and pepper. Reheat over medium heat. Serve, garnished with the croutons.

LEEK SOUP WITH PANCETTA & BREAD CRUMBS

serves 8

Dressed up with a topping of crispy pancetta and buttered bread crumbs, this simple leek soup is suitable for a special occasion. To clean leeks, halve them lengthwise and rinse under cold water, separating the layers to expose any dirt hidden inside.

3 oz (90 g) thinly sliced pancetta, cut into ½-inch (12-mm) pieces

4 Tbsp (2 oz/60 g) unsalted butter

1 cup (2 oz/60 g) fresh bread crumbs

4 leeks, white and pale green parts, finely chopped

2 Tbsp chopped yellow onion

1 celery rib, chopped

1 small potato, peeled and chopped

6 cups (48 fl oz/1.5 l) chicken broth

1 cup (8 fl oz/250 ml) heavy cream

In a frying pan, sauté the pancetta over medium heat until crispy, 4–5 minutes. Transfer to paper towels to drain. In a saucepan, melt 2 Tbsp of the butter over medium-high heat. Add the bread crumbs and cook, stirring, until golden brown, about 5 minutes. Transfer to a plate and set aside.

In a large, heavy pot, melt the remaining 2 Tbsp butter over medium-high heat. Add the leeks, onion, celery, and potato and sauté until the leeks and onion are translucent, 3–4 minutes. Add the broth, reduce the heat to low, cover, and simmer until the potato is tender, about 15 minutes. Remove from the heat and let cool slightly.

Working in batches, purée the soup in a blender. Return to the pot, add the cream, and bring to just under a boil over medium-high heat. Let cool, then strain through a fine-mesh sieve lined with cheesecloth into a clean pot. Bring to a simmer over low heat and cook, uncovered, for about 5 minutes to blend the flavors. Serve, sprinkled with the pancetta and garnished with the bread crumbs.

7

DASHI WITH SCALLOPS, WATERCRESS & SOBA NOODLES

serves 6–8

1 lb (500 g) large sea scallops,
tough muscles removed

2 pieces kombu, about 4 inches (10 cm) each

1½ cups (1½ oz/45 g) lightly
packed bonito flakes

½ lb (250 g) buckwheat soba noodles

5 Tbsp (3 fl oz/80 ml) soy sauce

3 Tbsp mirin

Salt

1 bunch watercress, tough stems removed

Feathery bonito flakes, a staple in the Japanese pantry, infuse their savory, smoky flavor into a broth called dashi. Mild-tasting kombu, or dried sea kelp, is also a key ingredient in dashi. You can find both at well-stocked markets and Asian groceries.

Cut each scallop crosswise into thirds. Cover and refrigerate until needed.

In a large saucepan, combine the kombu and 8 cups (64 fl oz/2 l) water and bring to a simmer over medium heat; do not let it boil. As soon as the liquid reaches a simmer, remove and discard the kombu. Stir in the bonito flakes. Remove from the heat and let stand, covered, until the flakes sink to the bottom of the pot and the dashi, or stock, is fragrant, about 5 minutes.

Meanwhile, in another large saucepan, bring another 8 cups water to a boil over high heat. Add the noodles, reduce the heat to medium, and simmer until tender, about 3 minutes. Drain the noodles, rinse well with warm water, drain again, and divide among bowls.

Strain the dashi through a fine-mesh sieve into a large bowl and discard the bonito flakes. Return the dashi to the pan. Add the soy sauce and mirin and bring to a simmer over medium heat. Add the scallops, reduce the heat to low, and simmer gently until the scallops are opaque throughout, about 3 minutes.

Taste the dashi and adjust the seasoning with salt. Add the watercress to the bowls with the noodles. Ladle the dashi and scallops into the bowls and serve.

8

MATZOH BALL SOUP

serves 6

4 eggs

3 Tbsp canola oil

1 cup (5 oz/155 g) matzoh meal

2 Tbsp chopped flat-leaf parsley

¼ cup (⅓ oz/10 g) chopped cilantro

Salt and freshly ground pepper

2–4 Tbsp seltzer water

6 cups (48 fl oz/1.5 l) chicken broth

8 slices peeled ginger

1 leek, white and pale green parts, chopped

2 Tbsp minced chives

There are countless family recipes for this classic comfort food, often served during the Passover festivities in spring. Here, herb-flecked matzoh balls are simmered in a flavorful chicken broth infused with leek and ginger.

In a bowl, whisk together the eggs and oil. Stir in the matzo meal, parsley, cilantro, ½ tsp salt, and ⅛ tsp pepper. Add 2 Tbsp seltzer and stir to form a slightly sticky mixture. If it is too dry, add 1–2 additional Tbsp seltzer. Cover the bowl with plastic wrap and refrigerate until cold, about 2 hours.

Fill a large, heavy pot three-fourths full with water and add 1 Tbsp salt. Bring to a boil over high heat, then reduce to a simmer. Form the matzo mixture into balls 1 inch (2.5 cm) in diameter. You should have 12 balls in all. Drop the balls into the simmering water and cook, uncovered, until they rise to the top and are cooked all the way through, 30–40 minutes. Using a slotted spoon, transfer the matzo balls to a baking sheet. Set aside.

Add the chicken broth and ginger to a saucepan and bring to a simmer over medium-high heat. Reduce the heat to medium-low, add the leek, and simmer, uncovered, until tender, about 10 minutes. Discard the ginger.

Add the matzo balls to the simmering broth and reheat for 3 minutes. Ladle the broth into bowls and place 2 matzo balls in each bowl. Serve, garnished with the chives.

9

Japanese udon noodles are often served chilled in the summer and hot in the winter, and toppings are chosen to reflect the seasons. Here, they are paired with spinach and green onions and topped, just before serving, with an egg that cooks gently in the hot broth.

UDON NOODLE SOUP WITH CHICKEN & SPINACH

serves 4

⅛ tsp granulated dashi mixed with 1 cup (8 fl oz/250 ml) hot water

1 Tbsp mirin

1 Tbsp dark soy sauce

1 tsp sugar

½ tsp cornstarch

Ground white pepper

¾ lb (375 g) skinless, boneless chicken breast halves, cut into 1-inch (2.5-cm) pieces

FOR THE BROTH

¾ tsp granulated dashi mixed with 6 cups (48 fl oz/1.5 l) hot water

3 Tbsp dark soy sauce

2 Tbsp light soy sauce

2 Tbsp rice vinegar

1 Tbsp sugar

1 lb (500 g) udon noodles or thick rice noodles

Salt and freshly ground black pepper

3 cups (3 oz/90 g) loosely packed spinach leaves, cut into 2-inch (5-cm) strips, immersed in boiling water for 1 minute, drained, and squeezed dry

4 eggs

4 green onions, white and pale green parts, thinly sliced

1 tsp chili powder

In a saucepan, combine the dashi mixture, mirin, soy sauce, sugar, and cornstarch. Add ⅛ tsp pepper and bring to a boil over high heat. Add the chicken pieces, reduce the heat to medium, and simmer, uncovered, until the chicken is opaque throughout, 10–12 minutes. Remove from the heat.

To make the broth, in a large saucepan, combine the dashi mixture, soy sauces, vinegar, and sugar. Add ⅛ tsp pepper and bring to a boil over medium-high heat. Reduce the heat to medium-low and simmer for 5 minutes. Keep warm.

Bring a saucepan of water to a boil over high heat. Stir in the noodles and 1 tsp salt. Cook until the noodles are just tender, 2–3 minutes. Drain and divide among bowls. ⇥

Top each serving of noodles with the chicken mixture and spinach. Crack an egg into each bowl and gently pour the hot broth over the top. Serve, garnished with the green onions and a dusting of chili powder.

10

To make the lemon mascarpone, in a small bowl, stir together 4 oz (125 g) room-temperature mascarpone; 1 Tbsp grated lemon zest; 2 tsp lemon juice; and a pinch of salt.

ASPARAGUS-CHERVIL PURÉE WITH LEMON MASCARPONE

serves 4–6

1 Tbsp olive oil

1 small yellow onion, finely chopped

2 cloves garlic, minced

3 cups (24 fl oz/750 ml) chicken or vegetable broth

2 lb (1 kg) asparagus, trimmed and chopped

2 Tbsp minced chervil or flat-leaf parsley

Salt and freshly ground pepper

Lemon Mascarpone (left)

In a large, heavy pot, warm the oil over medium-high heat. Add the onion and garlic and sauté until translucent, about 5 minutes. Add the broth and bring to a boil. Add the asparagus and chervil, reduce the heat to medium-low, and simmer until the asparagus is tender, about 10 minutes. Remove from the heat and let cool slightly.

Working in batches, purée the soup in a blender. Return to the pot and season with salt and pepper. Reheat over low heat.

Serve the soup, garnished with a dollop of the mascarpone.

11

Tender springtime veal stars in this twist on a classic French stew, brightened with grassy herbs and a pinch of golden saffron. Pair with a dry French rosé; or, choose a good-quality white wine for cooking and simply pour the rest at the table.

VEAL STEW WITH TARRAGON

serves 4–6

3½ lb (1.75 kg) boneless veal stew meat, trimmed and cut into 2-inch (5-cm) pieces

3 cups (24 fl oz/750 ml) chicken broth

1 cup (8 fl oz/250 ml) dry white wine

3–4 Tbsp chopped tarragon

2–3 Tbsp chopped flat-leaf parsley

1 large clove garlic

2 shallots, chopped

2 green onions, white part only, thinly sliced

½ carrot, peeled and diced

½ celery rib, diced

2 bay leaves

¼ tsp grated lemon zest

1 cup (6 oz/185 g) canned diced tomatoes

Large pinch of saffron threads

Salt and freshly ground pepper

¾ cup (6 fl oz/180 ml) heavy cream

2 egg yolks

Juice of 1 lemon

In a large, heavy pot, combine the veal, broth, and wine. Add enough water to cover the meat with liquid. Bring to a boil, then reduce the heat to low and skim off the foam that rises to the surface. Add 1 Tbsp of the tarragon and 1 Tbsp of the parsley. Add the garlic, shallots, green onions, carrot, celery, bay leaves, lemon zest, and tomatoes with their juices. In a mortar using a pestle, crush the saffron and add half of it to the pot. Season with salt and pepper. Cover and simmer over low heat until the meat is very tender but not falling apart, 2½–3 hours. Using a slotted spoon, transfer the meat to a bowl.

Spoon off any fat from the cooking liquid. Set the pot over high heat and boil until the liquid is reduced by half and intensely flavored, about 10 minutes. Remove and discard the bay leaves. Add the remaining saffron and return the meat to the pot. Reduce the heat to medium.

In a small bowl, whisk together the cream and egg yolks. Whisk in a ladleful of the hot liquid, then pour into the pot and stir well. Cook over medium heat until »→

the stew thickens slightly, taking care not to scramble the eggs, 3–4 minutes. Stir in the lemon juice. Season with salt and pepper. Sprinkle with the remaining tarragon and parsley and serve.

12

Fava beans are a favorite in France and Italy, where the esteemed seasonal vegetable is eaten in as many ways as possible throughout its short growing season. If you find some at your market, snatch them up and let them shine in this simple, creamy soup.

FAVA BEAN SOUP

serves 6

3 lb (1.5 kg) fava beans in the pods, shelled

2 mint sprigs

1 thyme sprig, plus more for garnish

Salt and freshly ground pepper

1½ cups (12 fl oz/375 ml) milk

¼ cup (2 oz/60 g) crème fraîche or sour cream

2 Tbsp unsalted butter

In a large saucepan, bring 4 cups (32 fl oz/1 l) water to a boil over medium-high heat. Add the fava beans and cook for 1–2 minutes. Using a slotted spoon, transfer the beans to a colander, reserving the cooking liquid, and rinse the beans under cold running water. Drain. Split open the skin of each bean along its edge and slip the bean from the skin. Discard the skins.

Pour the cooking liquid into a large measuring cup. Return 1 cup (8 fl oz/250 ml) to the pan and reserve the remainder. Add the beans, mint, the thyme sprig, and 1 tsp salt to the pan and bring to a boil over medium-high heat. Reduce the heat to medium, partially cover, and cook until the beans are tender, about 15 minutes. Remove from the heat and let cool slightly.

Working in batches, purée the soup in a blender or food processor. Return to the pan over medium heat. Slowly whisk in 1¼ cups (10 fl oz/310 ml) of the milk. The soup will be creamy but somewhat stiff. Whisk in the crème fraîche and butter. Whisk in more milk or some of the reserved cooking liquid until the soup reaches the desired consistency. Serve, garnished with thyme sprigs and pepper.

13

SHRIMP & SPINACH NOODLE SOUP

serves 4–6

2 Tbsp olive oil

1 yellow onion, thinly sliced

2 cloves garlic, minced

¼ lb (125 g) white mushrooms, thinly sliced

5 cups (40 fl oz/1.25 l) chicken broth

½ lb (250 g) udon noodles

½ lb (250 g) shrimp, peeled and deveined

1 small bunch spinach, tough stems removed

3 green onions, white and tender green parts, thinly sliced

Salt and freshly ground pepper

This quick-cooking soup is perfect for a busy weeknight. You can substitute nearly any similar green for the spinach; tender pea shoots, available at many farmers' markets in the springtime, would be delicious.

In a large, heavy pot, warm the oil over medium-high heat. Add the onion, garlic, and mushrooms and sauté until the mushrooms release their liquid and begin to turn golden brown, 5–7 minutes. Add the broth and bring to a boil. Add the udon noodles and cook for 4 minutes. Add the shrimp and cook until they turn bright pink, 2–3 minutes. Stir in the spinach and cook just until wilted. Stir in the green onions, season with salt and pepper, and serve.

14

ARTICHOKE & QUINOA SOUP WITH GREEN GARLIC

serves 6–8

Juice of ½ lemon

12 artichokes

2 Tbsp unsalted butter

1 yellow onion, finely diced

4 heads green garlic, white and pale green bottoms finely chopped, tender green tops thinly sliced

½ tsp minced thyme

6 cups (48 fl oz/1.5 l) chicken broth

¾ cup (8 oz/250 g) quinoa, cooked

Salt and freshly ground pepper

Extra-virgin olive oil for serving

The fresh, mellow flavor of green garlic adds a welcome springtime accent in this earthy soup that combines nutty quinoa and sweet, mild-tasting artichokes. You can substitute cooked barley or farro for the quinoa.

Fill a large bowl with water and add the lemon juice. Cut off the stem of each artichoke flush with the bottom. Snap off the outer leaves until you reach the tender inner leaves. Cut off the top one-third of the artichoke. As you work, add the artichokes to the lemon water.

In a large pot fitted with a steamer basket, bring 2–3 inches (5–7.5 cm) of water to a boil over medium-high heat. Place the artichokes in the steamer. Cover and cook until the bottoms are tender when pierced with a knife, 35–40 minutes. Drain upside down on paper towels until cool. Pull off the leaves from each artichoke and cut out the chokes. Finely chop the hearts.

In a large, heavy pot, melt the butter over medium heat. Add the onion and sauté until softened, about 5 minutes. Add the chopped green garlic bottoms and cook until fragrant, 3–4 minutes. Add the thyme, broth, and chopped artichokes, raise the heat to high, and bring to a boil. Reduce the heat to low, cover, and simmer for about 10 minutes to blend the flavors.

Purée half of the mixture in a blender and return to the pot. Add the quinoa and 1½ tsp salt, and season with pepper. Cook gently over medium-low heat until heated through, about 10 minutes. Ladle the soup into bowls and drizzle with olive oil. Sprinkle with pepper and the green garlic tops and serve.

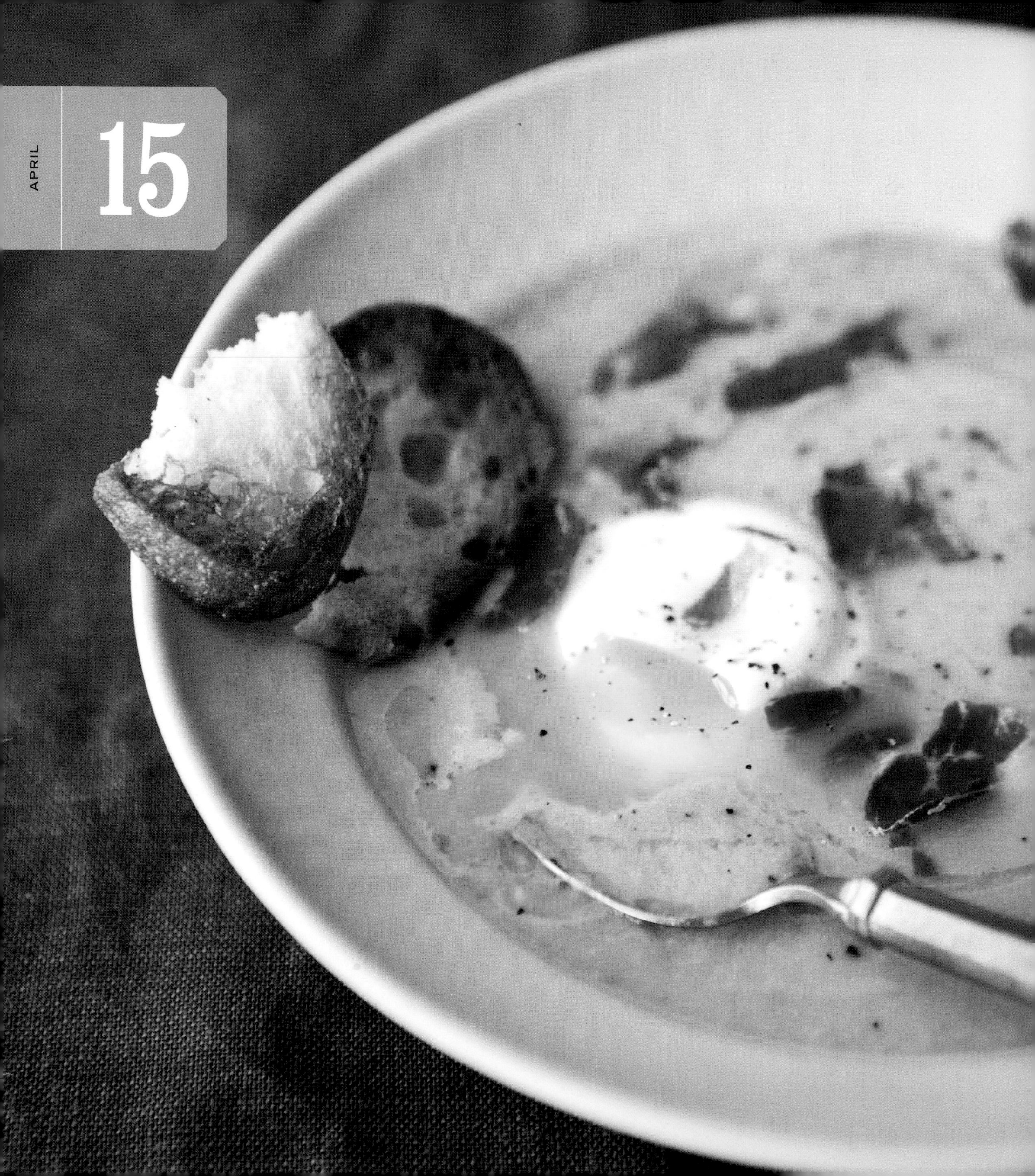
APRIL
15

15

ASPARAGUS SOUP WITH POACHED EGGS & CRISPY PROSCIUTTO

serves 4

A perfect spring luncheon soup, this is wonderful served with a glass of dry white wine or even Champagne. You can make the soup a day ahead and reheat it gently while you fry the prosciutto and poach the eggs. Serve with toasted baguette slices.

2 oz (60 g) prosciutto, thinly sliced

2 Tbsp unsalted butter

1 yellow onion, chopped

2 cloves garlic, minced

¼ cup (2 fl oz/60 ml) dry white wine

3 cups (24 fl oz/750 ml) chicken broth

2 bunches asparagus, trimmed and cut into ½-inch (12-mm) pieces

2 Tbsp heavy cream

Salt and freshly ground pepper

1 tsp white vinegar

4 eggs

Lay the prosciutto slices in the bottom of a large, heavy pot. Cook over medium-high heat, turning with tongs, until the prosciutto is crispy, about 7 minutes. Transfer to paper towels. Let cool, then crumble.

Add the butter, onion, and garlic to the same pot and sauté until translucent, 5 minutes. Add the wine, bring to a simmer, stir to scrape up any browned bits on the bottom of the pot, and cook for 3 minutes. Add the broth and bring to a boil. Add the asparagus and cook, uncovered, until tender, 8–10 minutes. Remove from the heat and let cool slightly.

Working in batches, purée the soup in a blender. Return to the pot, add the cream, and bring to a boil over medium heat. Season with salt and pepper and keep warm over low heat.

In a frying pan, heat 1 inch (2.5 cm) of water over medium heat. Add the vinegar and reduce the heat to keep the water at a gentle simmer. Break an egg into a small bowl and, using a large spoon, place the egg gently in the water. Using a tablespoon, occasionally spoon the hot water over the top of the exposed egg. Cook until the egg is set but the yolk is still runny, about 5 minutes. Remove the egg with a slotted spoon. Repeat to poach the remaining eggs.

Ladle the soup into bowls, top with the poached eggs and prosciutto, and serve.

16

THAI HOT & SOUR SOUP

serves 6

You may need to take a trip to an Asian market to source the classic Thai ingredients in this fragrant soup. If you can't find kaffir lime leaves, substitute the grated zest of 1 lime. Adjust the amount of chiles and lime juice according to your taste.

¾ lb (375 g) large shrimp, peeled and deveined, tail segments intact and shells reserved

3 lemongrass stalks, center white part only, smashed and cut into 1-inch (2.5-cm) lengths

5 thin slices galangal, about ¼ inch (6 mm) thick

3 fresh or dried kaffir lime leaves

2 Tbsp Asian fish sauce

5 oz (155 g) white mushrooms, stem ends trimmed and caps quartered

1 tomato, peeled (page 172) and cut into thin wedges

¼ small yellow onion, cut lengthwise into thin slivers

4 tsp Thai red or green chile paste

2 small red or green chiles such as Thai or serrano

¼ cup (2 fl oz/60 ml) fresh lime juice, or to taste

¼ cup (⅓ oz/10 g) chopped cilantro

In a large saucepan, combine the shrimp shells with 5 cups (40 fl oz/1.25 l) water. Add the lemongrass to the pan. Bring to a simmer over medium heat, cover partially, and simmer gently for 15 minutes to blend the flavors. Strain the broth through a fine-mesh sieve into a clean saucepan.

Add the galangal, lime leaves, fish sauce, mushrooms, tomato, onion, and chile paste. Remove the stems from the chiles, then quarter the chiles lengthwise. Add as many of the quarters to the broth as you like; you may want to start with just a few.

Bring the soup to a simmer over medium heat, cover partially, and simmer gently until the mushrooms are barely tender, about 2 minutes. Taste halfway through and add more chile quarters if the soup is not spicy enough. Stir in the shrimp and simmer just until they turn pink, about 2 minutes. Remove from the heat.

Stir in the ¼ cup lime juice and the cilantro. Taste and adjust the seasoning with more lime juice, if desired, and serve.

17

THREE-MUSHROOM PURÉE WITH SHERRY

serves 4–6

1½ oz (45 g) dried mushrooms such as porcini or shiitake

3 Tbsp olive oil

1 yellow onion, finely chopped

1 lb (500 g) fresh white mushrooms, thinly sliced

½ lb (250 g) shiitake mushrooms, stemmed and thinly sliced

3 Tbsp all-purpose flour

Salt and freshly ground pepper

4 cups (32 fl oz/1 l) beef, chicken, or vegetable broth

½ cup (4 fl oz/125 ml) half-and-half

¼ cup (2 fl oz/60 ml) dry sherry

2 Tbsp finely chopped flat-leaf parsley

A trio of earthy mushrooms, dried and fresh, creates deep flavor and a variety of textures. Sherry lends a touch of acidity to brighten the palate. Dry to very dry sherries, like golden fino or the slightly darker manzanilla, are best for soups.

In a heatproof bowl, combine the dried mushrooms and 3 cups (24 fl oz/750 ml) very hot water. Soak for 30 minutes. Drain well, reserving 2 cups (16 fl oz/500 ml) of the soaking liquid. Strain the soaking liquid through a coffee filter into another bowl and set aside.

In a large, heavy pot, warm the oil over medium heat. Add the onion and sauté until softened, 5–7 minutes. Add the fresh mushrooms and cook, stirring, until slightly softened, about 3 minutes. Sprinkle with the flour and season with salt and pepper. Stir to coat the mushrooms and to cook the flour, about 1 minute. Add the broth and the reserved mushroom soaking liquid. Add the drained dried mushrooms and reduce the heat to medium-low. Simmer until all the mushrooms are completely softened, about 15 minutes. Remove from the heat and let cool slightly.

Working in batches, purée the soup in a blender or food processor, making sure to leave a little texture. Return to the pot and place over medium heat. Add the half-and-half and sherry and cook for about 3 minutes to blend the flavors. Serve, garnished with the parsley.

18

BALSAMIC BEEF STEW

serves 6

3 Tbsp all-purpose flour

Salt and freshly ground pepper

2 lb (1 kg) boneless beef chuck, trimmed and cut into 1½-inch (4-cm) pieces

3 Tbsp canola oil

1 large red onion, sliced

2 bay leaves

1 cup (8 fl oz/250 ml) full-bodied red wine

2 cups (16 fl oz/500 ml) beef broth

1 lb (500 g) red or Yukon gold potatoes, unpeeled, cut into 1½-inch (4-cm) chunks

3 large carrots, peeled and cut into 1-inch (2.5-cm) chunks

2 Tbsp balsamic vinegar

This beef-and-potato stew will warm you up—and also fill you up—on a chilly spring evening. It goes perfectly with a glass of red wine or bottle of dark ale. Use good-quality balsamic vinegar for drizzling.

In a resealable plastic bag, combine the flour, ½ tsp salt, and ½ tsp pepper. Add the beef, seal the bag, and shake to coat the beef. In a large, heavy pot, warm the oil over medium-high heat. Working in batches, remove the beef from the bag, shaking off the excess flour, and add to the pot in a single layer. Cook, turning as needed, until the meat is browned on all sides, 6–8 minutes. Transfer to a plate. Add the onion, reduce the heat to medium, and sauté until golden, about 5 minutes. Stir in the bay leaves, wine, and broth.

Return the meat and any accumulated juices to the pot. Bring to a simmer, then reduce the heat to low. Cover and cook until the meat is nearly fork-tender, 1½–2 hours. Add the potatoes and carrots, cover, and cook until the vegetables are tender, about 30 minutes. Remove and discard the bay leaves.

Season the stew with salt and pepper, stir in the vinegar, and serve.

19

APRIL

Among the various seafood chowders, Manhattan clam chowder stands out because it includes tomatoes in its clear broth instead of the more typical base of milk or cream. The result is a bright, fresh flavor that supports the briny taste of the clams.

MANHATTAN CLAM CHOWDER

serves 4

FOR THE CLAM BROTH

1 thick slice yellow onion

½ celery rib with leaves

1 bay leaf

1 clove garlic, lightly crushed

Salt

3 lb (1.5 kg) cherrystone or littleneck clams, scrubbed

1 slice thick-cut lightly smoked bacon, cut into ¼-inch (6-mm) dice

1 Tbsp olive oil

1 small onion, finely chopped

1 celery rib, finely chopped

1 large clove garlic, minced

1 can (15½ oz/485 g) crushed tomatoes

1 Tbsp minced flat-leaf parsley, plus whole leaves for garnish

1 tsp thyme leaves

3 Tbsp pearl barley

To make the broth, in a large saucepan over high heat, combine the onion, celery, bay leaf, and garlic. Add 3 cups (24 fl oz/750 ml) water and 1 tsp salt and bring to a boil over high heat. Reduce the heat to low, cover, and cook for 20 minutes to blend the flavors.

Add the clams to the broth, discarding any that do not close to the touch. Raise the heat to medium-high, cover, and cook until the clams open, 3–4 minutes for littlenecks, 4–5 minutes for cherrystones. Transfer the opened clams to a large bowl. Discard any unopened clams.

Strain the broth through a fine-mesh sieve lined with cheesecloth into a heatproof bowl. Working over the sieve to capture any juices, pull the clam meats from the shells and return to the bowl. Cut the clams into ½-inch (12-mm) pieces and refrigerate. Measure the broth; you will need 4 cups (32 fl oz/1 l). Add water if necessary.

In a large, heavy pot, combine the bacon and oil. Warm over medium-low heat until they sizzle. Add the onion, celery, and garlic and sauté until soft, about 12 minutes. Add the strained broth, tomatoes, minced parsley, and thyme. Season with ½ tsp salt and ⤖

⅛ tsp pepper. Bring to a boil over medium-high heat. Stir in the barley, reduce the heat to low, cover, and cook until the barley is very soft, about 50 minutes.

Add in the clams and cook, stirring often, until heated through, about 3 minutes. Serve, garnished with parsley leaves.

20

APRIL

Celebrate spring— and the arrival of fava beans—with this Italian-inspired soup. You can substitute any small- to medium-sized pasta shape for the farfalle. Serve immediately, so the pasta doesn't overcook.

FAVA BEAN & FARFALLE SOUP

serves 6

2½ lb (1.25 kg) fava beans in the pods, shelled

9 cups (72 fl oz/2.1 l) chicken broth

6 oz (185 g) farfalle

1 Tbsp fresh lemon juice

Salt and freshly ground pepper

½ cup (2 oz/60 g) grated Parmesan cheese

Bring a pot of water to a boil. Add the fava beans and cook for 20 seconds. Drain, rinse under cold running water, and drain again. Split open the skin of each bean along its edge and slip the bean from the skin. Discard the skins.

In a large, heavy pot, bring the broth to a boil. Add the farfalle and cook until al dente, 10–12 minutes or according to the package directions. Add the fava beans and lemon juice. Season with salt and pepper.

Serve the soup, passing the Parmesan at the table.

21

Broccoli, which is at its best from fall through spring, gives this cream soup a full flavor and a warm, pleasing color. Garnish with chunky croutons or crumbled cooked bacon.

CREAM OF BROCCOLI SOUP

serves 4

1 bunch broccoli (about 1¼ lb/625 g), tough stems peeled, florets and stems coarsely chopped

2 cups (16 fl oz/500 ml) milk, plus 1 cup (8 fl oz/250 ml) if needed

2 cups (16 fl oz/500 ml) chicken broth

3 Tbsp unsalted butter

3 Tbsp all-purpose flour

Salt and freshly ground pepper

½ cup (4 fl oz/125 ml) heavy cream

In a wide-bottomed saucepan, bring ½ inch (12 mm) of water to a boil. Place a steamer basket in the pan, add the broccoli, cover, and cook until tender, about 5 minutes. Remove the broccoli from the pan and let cool. Transfer the broccoli to a food processor and process until finely chopped.

In separate saucepans, warm the 2 cups milk and the broth over low heat. In a large, heavy pot, melt the butter over medium-low heat. Stir in the flour until blended. Whisking constantly, gradually add the hot milk. Cook, stirring often, until the mixture is bubbling and has thickened, about 3 minutes. Gradually whisk in the hot stock and cook, stirring slowly, for about 3 minutes. Stir in the broccoli. Add 1 tsp salt and ⅛ tsp pepper. Reduce the heat to low, cover, and cook, stirring occasionally, for 10 minutes. Remove from the heat and let cool slightly.

Working in batches, purée the soup in a food processor or a blender. Return to the pot and stir in the cream. Reheat over low heat, stirring constantly, for about 5 minutes. If the soup seems too thick, thin it with a little milk, adding it ¼ cup (2 fl oz/60 ml) at a time. Season with salt and pepper and serve.

22

Bright coriander harmonizes with two kinds of sweetness in this soup—a familiar, earthy sweetness from the carrots and a more exotic, tropical sweetness from the coconut. Serve as a first course preceding a simple roast chicken or rack of lamb.

CARROT & COCONUT PURÉE WITH CURRIED ALMONDS

serves 6–8

1½ tsp sugar

Salt and freshly ground pepper

¼ tsp ground coriander, plus 1 Tbsp

½ tsp curry powder

1½ tsp unsalted butter, plus 3 Tbsp

½ cup (2 oz/60 g) sliced almonds, toasted (page 207)

1 yellow onion, chopped

2 lb (1 kg) carrots, peeled and thinly sliced

¼ cup (1 oz/30 g) unsweetened shredded coconut, toasted

½ tsp ground ginger

4 cups (32 fl oz/1 l) chicken broth

2 cans (14 oz/440 g each) coconut milk

2 tsp rice vinegar

Stir together ½ tsp of the sugar, ¼ tsp salt, the ¼ tsp coriander, and the curry powder.

In a nonstick frying pan, melt the 1½ tsp butter with 1 Tbsp water and the remaining 1 tsp sugar over medium-high heat. Bring to a boil, swirling the pan to blend. Add the almonds, stir to coat, and cook until the liquid is almost evaporated, about 45 seconds. Transfer to the bowl with the spice mixture and toss to coat the almonds evenly. Pour onto a piece of parchment paper, spread in a single layer, and let cool.

In a large, heavy pot, melt the 3 Tbsp butter over medium-high heat. Add the onion, carrots, coconut, ginger, and the 1 Tbsp coriander and stir to combine. Reduce the heat to low, cover, and cook until the vegetables give off some of their liquid, about 10 minutes. Add the broth, raise the heat to high, and bring to a boil. Reduce the heat to low, cover, and simmer until the carrots are tender, about 20 minutes. Remove from the heat and let cool slightly.

Working in batches, purée the soup in a blender. Pour into a clean pot. Add the coconut milk (reserve some for serving), the vinegar, and 1 tsp salt. Cook gently over medium-low heat, stirring occasionally, until heated through, about 10 minutes. Serve, sprinkled with the spiced almonds and swirled with coconut milk.

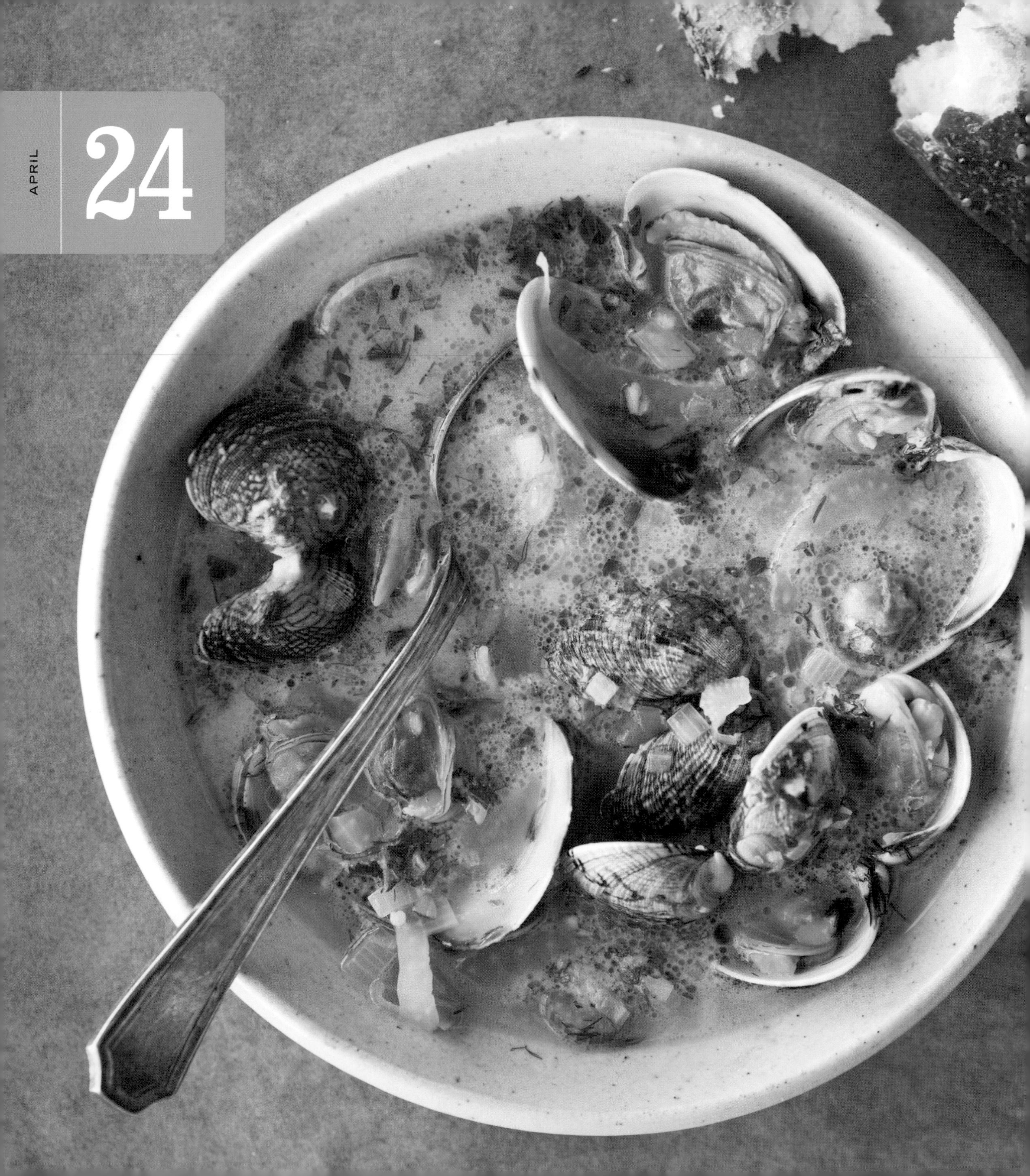

23

This soup, filled with the flavors of Thailand, is easy to make and very addictive. Do not eat the galangal, lemongrass, and lime leaves; they deliver flavor, but are too tough to consume.

CHICKEN-LEMONGRASS SOUP

serves 6

1 lb (500 g) skinless, boneless chicken breasts, cut into 1-inch (2.5-cm) pieces

2 cups (16 fl oz/500 ml) chicken broth

3 cups (24 fl oz/750 ml) coconut milk

10 slices galangal

4 lemongrass stalks, center white part only, smashed and cut into 2-inch (5-cm) lengths

6 green Thai chiles or 8 green serrano chiles, cut in half crosswise

8 kaffir lime leaves, spines removed

½ cup (3½ oz/105 g) drained canned straw mushrooms

½ cup (2 oz/60 g) sliced bamboo shoots

3 Tbsp Asian fish sauce

¼ cup (2 fl oz/60 ml) fresh lime juice

¼ cup (¼ oz/7 g) cilantro leaves

In a large saucepan, combine the chicken pieces, broth, coconut milk, galangal, lemongrass, chiles, and lime leaves. Bring to a boil over high heat, reduce the heat to maintain a gentle boil, and cook, uncovered, until the chicken is opaque, about 20 minutes.

Stir in the mushrooms and bamboo shoots, raise the heat to high, and bring to a boil. Add the fish sauce and lime juice, then taste and adjust the seasonings. Serve, garnished with the cilantro.

24

You can use cockles or mussels in place of the clams in this recipe. Serve with crusty country-style bread to soak up the broth. The parsley vinaigrette is also delicious drizzled on sliced grilled chicken or fish.

CLAMS IN FENNEL BROTH WITH PARSLEY VINAIGRETTE

serves 4

FOR THE VINAIGRETTE

⅓ cup (½ oz/15 g) minced flat-leaf parsley

Grated zest and juice of 1 lemon

1 Tbsp extra-virgin olive oil

1 Tbsp Dijon mustard

1 clove garlic, minced

Salt and freshly ground pepper

1 Tbsp unsalted butter

1 Tbsp olive oil

2 cloves garlic, sliced

2 small fennel bulbs, including stalks and fronds, sliced

2 shallots, minced

½ cup (4 fl oz/125 ml) dry white wine

1 cup (8 fl oz/250 ml) chicken broth

2 lb (1 kg) manila clams, scrubbed

To make the vinaigrette, in a small bowl, stir together the parsley, lemon zest and juice, oil, mustard, and garlic. Season with salt and pepper and let stand at room temperature.

In a large, heavy pot, melt the butter with the oil over medium-high heat. Add the garlic, fennel, and shallots and sauté until soft, about 5 minutes. Add the wine and cook for 2 minutes. Add the broth and bring to a boil. Add the clams to the pot, discarding any that do not close to the touch. Cover and cook until the clams open, 6–8 minutes. Discard any unopened clams.

Ladle the clams and broth into bowls, drizzle with the vinaigrette, and serve.

25

LENTIL & ANDOUILLE SOUP

serves 8–10

1 lb (500 g) andouille sausage, cut into
¼-inch-thick (6-mm-thick) slices

2 Tbsp olive oil

2 carrots, peeled and chopped

1 large yellow onion, chopped

4 large cloves garlic, minced

1 lb (500 g) lentils, picked over and rinsed

8 cups (64 fl oz/2 l) chicken broth,
plus more as needed

1 Tbsp heavy cream

¼ cup (⅓ oz/10 g) chopped flat-leaf parsley

Salt and freshly ground pepper

You can make this soup ahead and refrigerate it, but you will need to add more broth when you rewarm it as the lentils will have absorbed most of the liquid. Kielbasa can be substituted for the andouille.

In a large, heavy pot, cook the sausage slices over medium-high heat until browned on both sides, about 8 minutes. Transfer to a plate and set aside.

Add the oil, carrots, onion, and garlic to the same pot and sauté until the vegetables are softened, about 8 minutes. Add the lentils and broth and bring to a boil. Reduce the heat to low and simmer, uncovered, stirring occasionally, until the lentils are tender, about 1 hour. Remove from the heat and let cool slightly.

Purée half of the soup in a food processor. Return to the pot and stir to combine. Stir in the sausage, cream, and parsley, and reheat over low heat. Season with salt and pepper and serve.

26

BLACK BEAN CHILI

serves 6–8

2 cups (14 oz/440 g) dried black beans,
picked over and rinsed

3 Tbsp canola oil

3 yellow onions, finely chopped

5 cloves garlic, minced

¼ cup (2 oz/60 g) chili powder

4 tsp dried oregano

4 tsp ground cumin

1 tsp ground coriander

1 Tbsp paprika

¼ tsp cayenne pepper

3 cups (24 fl oz/750 ml) vegetable broth

1½ cups (9 oz/280 g) canned diced tomatoes

½–1 canned chipotle chile in adobo or
1 small jalapeño chile, seeded and minced

1 Tbsp rice vinegar or white wine vinegar

3 Tbsp finely chopped cilantro,
plus 6–8 sprigs for garnish

Salt

½ cup (2 oz/60 g) diced Muenster cheese

½ cup (4 oz/125 g) sour cream

Starting with dried black beans, and allowing the ingredients to simmer and the flavors to meld, will yield the tastiest chili. Add a dollop of fresh tomato salsa, if you like, and serve with corn bread or warm corn tortillas.

Place the dried beans in a bowl with cold water to cover and soak for at least 4 hours or up to overnight. Drain.

In a large, heavy pot, warm the oil over medium heat. Add the onions and sauté until softened, about 5 minutes. Stir in the garlic, chili powder, oregano, cumin, coriander, paprika, and cayenne. Cook, stirring occasionally, for about 5 minutes.

Add the broth, tomatoes with their juices, chile, and beans. Pour in 3 cups (24 fl oz/ 750 ml) water and bring to a boil. Reduce the heat to low, cover partially, and cook for 45 minutes. Uncover and continue to cook until the beans are tender, about 45 minutes. If the chili is too soupy, use a potato masher to mash some of the beans to help thicken the mixture. Stir in the vinegar and chopped cilantro. Season with salt.

Divide the cheese among bowls and ladle in the chili. Serve, garnished with the sour cream and cilantro sprigs.

27

VEGETABLE-TORTELLINI SOUP

serves 4–6

3 Tbsp olive oil

1 yellow onion, chopped

2 cloves garlic, minced

3 carrots, peeled and chopped

6 oz (185 g) white mushrooms, sliced

1 russet potato, peeled
and cut into small cubes

1 tsp dried thyme

1 can (14½ oz/455 g) diced tomatoes

4 cups (32 fl oz/1 l) chicken broth

9 oz (280 g) cheese tortellini

2 cups (2 oz/60 g) packed spinach leaves

Salt and freshly ground pepper

*Few kids can say
no to this soup,
especially if you use
red and/or green
tortellini and serve it
with warm, buttery
garlic bread. It's a
great way to use up
surplus vegetables,
so feel free to toss in
whatever you find in
the vegetable drawer.*

In a large, heavy pot, warm the oil over
medium-high heat. Add the onion and garlic
and sauté until translucent, about 5 minutes.
Add the carrots, mushrooms, and potato
and cook, stirring often, until the vegetables
begin to soften, 8–10 minutes. Add the
thyme and cook, stirring, for 1 minute.
Add the tomatoes and broth and bring to
a boil. Reduce the heat to low and simmer,
uncovered, until the carrots and potatoes
are tender, 15–20 minutes.

Add the tortellini and cook for about
8 minutes. Add the spinach and cook,
stirring, just until wilted. Season with
salt and pepper and serve.

28

CREAMY MUSHROOM SOUP WITH HAM & PEAS

serves 4

3 Tbsp unsalted butter

2 Tbsp olive oil

1 lb (500 g) white mushrooms, sliced

1 small yellow onion, chopped

2 cloves garlic, chopped

2 Tbsp all-purpose flour

¼ cup (2 fl oz/60 ml) dry white wine

2 cups (16 fl oz/500 ml) chicken broth

6 oz (185 g) cooked ham, cubed

¼ cup (2 oz/30 g) fresh or frozen peas

3 Tbsp heavy cream

Salt and freshly ground pepper

*Everyday cream of
mushroom soup gets
a boost from savory
ham cubes and green
peas. For an earthier
flavor, substitute
cremini mushrooms.*

In a large, heavy pot, melt the butter with
the oil over medium-high heat. Add the
mushrooms, onion, and garlic and cook,
stirring often, until the mushrooms are very
soft, 12–15 minutes. Stir in the flour and
cook, stirring constantly, for 1 minute. Add
the wine and cook for 3 minutes. Add the
broth and bring to a boil. Reduce the heat to
low and simmer, uncovered, until the soup
thickens, about 20 minutes. Remove from
the heat and let cool slightly.

Purée half of the soup in a blender and
return to the pot. Add the ham, peas, and
cream, and return to a boil. Remove from the
heat, season with salt and pepper, and serve.

29

SPINACH SOUP WITH SUMAC & FETA

serves 6–8

Sumac, a tart Middle Eastern spice, brightens up this spinach soup, as does a sprinkle of feta cheese. This is a great recipe to have in your arsenal because it calls for frozen spinach, but you can substitute fresh spinach if you have some on hand.

2 Tbsp unsalted butter

1 Tbsp olive oil

1 large yellow onion, finely chopped

4 cloves garlic, minced

2 tsp sumac

1½ tsp ground cumin

1 tsp ground coriander

¼ tsp cayenne pepper

2 bags (1 lb/500 g each) frozen chopped spinach, thawed

4½ cups (36 fl oz/1.1 l) chicken broth, plus more as needed

Grated zest and juice of 1 lemon

3 Tbsp heavy cream

Salt and freshly ground black pepper

6 oz (185 g) feta cheese, crumbled

In a large, heavy pot, melt the butter with the oil over medium-high heat. Add the onion and garlic and sauté until translucent, about 5 minutes. Add the sumac, cumin, coriander, and cayenne, and cook for 2 minutes. Stir in the spinach, broth, and lemon zest and juice. Bring to a boil. Reduce the heat to low and simmer, stirring frequently, for 10 minutes. Remove from the heat and let cool slightly.

Purée half of the soup in a blender. Return to the pot, thin with additional chicken broth, if desired, then stir in the cream. Season with salt and pepper, and reheat over low heat. Serve, topped with the crumbled feta.

30

KIELBASA & SAUERKRAUT SOUP

serves 8–10

Germany is to thank for this genius combination of sausages and pickled cabbage, a sour-savory comfort food. This soup feeds a crowd, but it also freezes well if you have any left over. Serve with hunks of freshly baked rye or pumpernickel bread.

1 lb (500 g) kielbasa sausage, sliced

2 Tbsp olive oil

2 yellow onions, thinly sliced

4 cloves garlic, minced

1 sweet potato (about 10 oz/315 g), peeled and shredded

6 cups (48 fl oz/1.5 l) chicken broth

1 lb (500 g) sauerkraut, drained

2 Tbsp tomato paste

Salt and freshly ground pepper

Warm a large, heavy pot over medium-high heat. Add the kielbasa slices and sauté until browned on both sides, about 8 minutes. Transfer to a bowl and set aside.

Put the oil in the same pot. Add the onions and garlic and cook, stirring often and scraping up the brown bits on the bottom of the pot, until softened, 5–7 minutes. Add the sweet potato, the broth, and 1 cup (8 fl oz/250 ml) water and bring to a boil. Reduce the heat to low and simmer, uncovered, for 10 minutes. Add the sauerkraut, tomato paste, and kielbasa, stir well to combine, and simmer, uncovered, for 10 minutes. Season with salt and pepper and serve.

1
CHILLED CARROT SOUP WITH GINGER & ORANGE ZEST
page 106

2
POTATO-LEEK PURÉE WITH SMOKED SALMON & DILL
page 106

3
MUSHROOM & MADEIRA SOUP WITH BRIE CHEESE
page 108

4
MOROCCAN-SPICED VEGETARIAN CHILI
page 108

8
PEA & MINT PURÉE WITH LEMON
page 111

9
FIVE-SPICE CHICKEN NOODLE SOUP
page 112

10
RED BEAN & ANDOUILLE SOUP
page 112

11
LEEK & ASPARAGUS VICHYSSOISE
page 113

15
CURRIED CARROT PURÉE
page 117

16
PEA SHOOT & PASTA SOUP
page 117

17
ARTICHOKE SOUP WITH CAMEMBERT CROSTINI
page 118

18
BEAN & ELBOW PASTA SOUP WITH BASIL PESTO
page 118

22
CHILLED SOUR CHERRY SOUP WITH TARRAGON
page 120

23
SWEET ONION SOUP WITH BLUE CHEESE TOASTS
page 123

24
CRAB & ASPARAGUS EGG FLOWER SOUP
page 123

25
FENNEL VICHYSSOISE
page 124

29
SIMPLE ASPARAGUS SOUP
page 125

30
GINGERY BROTH WITH PRAWNS & GREEN ONIONS
page 126

31
SPINACH & VERMICELLI SOUP WITH FRIED EGG
page 126

5
WONTON SOUP
page 109

6
MUSHROOM-QUINOA SOUP
page 109

7
TURKEY MEATBALL
SOUP WITH ARUGULA
page 111

12
GREEN LENTIL SOUP
page 113

13
SPICY COCONUT CURRY
SEAFOOD SOUP
page 114

14
RAMEN NOODLE SOUP
WITH SUGAR SNAP PEAS
page 114

19
ISRAELI COUSCOUS SOUP WITH
CURRY, CHICKEN & SPINACH
page 119

20
WATERCRESS SOUP
page 119

21
COLD ZUCCHINI & AVOCADO SOUP
page 120

26
EGG-LEMON SOUP WITH FAVA
BEANS & FRIED GARLIC CHIPS
page 124

27
STRAWBERRY-LEMON SOUP
page 125

28
CREAMY SPINACH-LEEK SOUP
page 125

May heralds high spring, when brisk but ever-sunnier days welcome bowls full of tender shoots and leaves. Enjoy the season's last asparagus, artichokes, and fava beans, and if a few residual rain showers linger, take comfort in a creamy wild mushroom soup while you still can. As the weather continues to warm, stone fruit and berries, starting with cherries and strawberries, steadily sneak into markets, welcoming the cold soups of the summer season.

may

1

CHILLED CARROT SOUP WITH GINGER & ORANGE ZEST

serves 4–6

2 Tbsp olive oil

1 yellow onion, chopped

2 cloves garlic, minced

2-inch (5-cm) piece fresh ginger, peeled and minced

2 lb (1 kg) carrots, thinly sliced

4 cups (32 fl oz/1 l) vegetable broth

Salt and freshly ground pepper

Grated zest of 1 orange

This light and bright soup, which can be served cold or hot, is a fitting welcome to spring. Try replacing the ginger with 2 tsp cumin seed or coriander seed and the orange zest with lime zest or lemon zest. Use chicken broth in place of the vegetable broth for a richer taste.

In a large, heavy pot, warm the oil over medium-high heat. Add the onion, garlic, and ginger and sauté until soft, about 5 minutes. Add the carrots, stir, and cook for 5 minutes. Add the broth and bring to a boil. Reduce the heat to low and simmer until the carrots are very tender, about 35 minutes. Remove from the heat and let cool slightly.

Working in batches, purée the soup in a blender or food processor and return to the pot. Season with salt and pepper.

Stir in the orange zest and let the soup cool to room temperature. Cover and refrigerate until well chilled, at least 3 hours or up to overnight. Serve.

2

POTATO-LEEK PURÉE WITH SMOKED SALMON & DILL

serves 6

2 Tbsp olive oil

2 leeks, white and pale green parts, chopped

2 russet potatoes, peeled and finely diced

4 cups (32 fl oz/1 l) chicken broth

½ cup (4 fl oz/125 ml) heavy cream

1 Tbsp chopped dill

Salt and freshly ground pepper

¼ lb (125 g) smoked salmon, chopped

For a stunning presentation, serve this soup in shallow bowls so the salmon doesn't sink to the bottom. The dill can be replaced by chopped chervil or chives, if you prefer.

In a large, heavy pot, warm the oil over medium-high heat. Add the leeks and sauté until soft, about 5 minutes. Add the potatoes and the broth and bring to a boil. Reduce the heat to low and simmer until the potatoes are very soft, about 20 minutes. Remove from the heat and let cool slightly.

Working in batches, purée the soup in a blender. Return to the pot and stir in the cream and dill. Return the soup to a gentle boil, turn off the heat, and season with salt and pepper.

Serve, garnished with the smoked salmon.

3

MUSHROOM & MADEIRA SOUP WITH BRIE CHEESE

serves 4

¼ cup (2 oz/60 g) unsalted butter

2 small shallots, chopped

1 small white sweet onion, chopped

1 lb (500 g) cremini mushrooms, coarsely chopped

1 russet potato, peeled and cut into ½-inch (12-mm) dice

2 cups (16 fl oz/500 ml) chicken broth

Salt and freshly ground pepper

1 cup (8 fl oz/250 ml) heavy cream

2–3 Tbsp good-quality Madeira wine

Pinch of grated nutmeg

2 oz (60 g) Brie cheese, rind removed and cheese sliced into 8–12 thin pieces

Chopped basil for garnish

Any ripe, soft cheese is tasty with this soup. Be sure to have it at room temperature when ready to serve so that it melts into the soup on impact.

In a large, heavy pot, melt the butter over medium-low heat. Add the shallots and onion and sauté until translucent, 5–6 minutes. Add the mushrooms, increase the heat to medium, and sauté until the mushrooms begin to release their liquid, 8–10 minutes; do not allow the onions to brown. Add the potato and broth and season with salt. Cover partially, and simmer until the mushrooms and potato are soft, 15–20 minutes, adjusting the heat if necessary to maintain a simmer. Remove from the heat and let cool slightly.

Working in batches, purée the soup in a blender or food processor. Return to the pot and add the cream. Place over medium-low heat and bring almost to a simmer; do not allow to boil. Add Madeira to taste, the nutmeg, and pepper to taste.

Ladle the soup into bowls and float 2 or 3 pieces of the cheese on the surface of each serving. Sprinkle with the basil and serve.

4

MOROCCAN-SPICED VEGETARIAN CHILI

serves 6

4 large ancho chiles

4 large whole cloves garlic, plus 6 large cloves, sliced

1 yellow onion, chopped

1½ tsp ground turmeric

1½ tsp ground cinnamon

1½ tsp ground cumin

1½ tsp ground coriander

1 can (28 oz/875 g) diced tomatoes

1 butternut squash (about 1¼ lb/625 g), halved, seeded, peeled, and cut into ½-inch (12-mm) cubes

2 cans (15½ oz/485 g each) chickpeas

2 zucchini, cut into ½-inch (12-mm) dice

⅓ cup (2 oz/60 g) sliced dried apricots

⅓ cup (2 oz/60 g) sliced pitted prunes

Serve this richly spiced vegetarian chili with toasted pita bread or on a bed of steamed couscous or rice. Hubbard or acorn may be used in place of the butternut squash.

In a saucepan, combine the chiles and 3 cups (24 fl oz/750 ml) water and bring to a boil. Remove from the heat. Cover and let stand for 15 minutes. Using tongs or a slotted spoon, transfer the chiles to a work surface; reserve the liquid. Discard the stems and seeds from the chiles. In a blender or food processor, combine the chiles with the 4 whole cloves garlic and ½ cup (4 fl oz/125 ml) of the chile soaking liquid. Process until smooth and set aside.

Heat a large, heavy pot over medium heat. Coat the pan with nonstick cooking spray. Add the onion, the sliced garlic cloves, turmeric, cinnamon, cumin, and coriander and sauté until the onion and garlic have softened, about 5 minutes. Stir in the tomatoes and their juices, the butternut squash, and chile purée. Cover and simmer, stirring occasionally, until the butternut squash is just tender, about 25 minutes.

Stir in the chickpeas with their liquid, the zucchini, and the dried apricots and prunes. Simmer, uncovered, until the zucchini is tender, about 15 minutes. Serve.

WONTON SOUP

serves 4–6

FOR THE WONTONS

¼ lb (125 g) diced pork, chicken, or shrimp

1½ tsp peeled and grated fresh ginger

2 Tbsp chopped water chestnuts

1½ Tbsp chopped green onion, white part only

1 Tbsp chopped cilantro

1 Tbsp light soy sauce

1 tsp rice wine (optional)

1 small egg

Salt and ground white pepper

24 wonton wrappers

2–3 dried black mushrooms, soaked in hot water to cover for 30 minutes and drained

6 cups (48 fl oz/1.5 l) chicken broth

¾ cup (1¾ oz/50 g) small bok choy leaves

1½-inch (4-cm) piece carrot, peeled and cut into thin matchsticks

1 green onion, tender green part only, cut into thin matchsticks

Simmered in broth, stuffed wontons plump and tenderize for a satisfying soup. Triangles are easy to fold, but also try little bundles or half moons, as you like.

To make the wontons, in a food processor, combine the pork, chicken, or shrimp and the ginger and process to a smooth paste. Add the water chestnuts, green onion, cilantro, soy sauce, rice wine (if using), and egg. Season with salt and pepper and process again until a smooth paste forms.

Working with 1 wonton wrapper at a time, place it on a work surface and moisten any 2 edges with cold water. Place 2–3 tsp of the filling in the center and fold in half into a triangle. Press the edges firmly to seal, then fold the two outer points across the top of the mound and pinch the edges together. If they do not stick, moisten with a little water. Repeat until all the dumplings are filled.

To prepare the soup, remove and discard the stems from the mushrooms if necessary and slice the caps. In a saucepan, bring the broth to a boil over medium heat. Add the bok choy leaves, carrot, and mushrooms and simmer for 2 minutes.

Meanwhile, bring a saucepan three-fourths full of water to a boil over high heat. Add the wontons, reduce the heat to medium, and simmer gently until they float to the ≫

surface and the skins are tender, about 3 minutes. Using a wire skimmer, carefully lift out the wontons and divide evenly among individual bowls.

Ladle the soup over the wontons, garnish with the green onion tops, and serve.

MUSHROOM-QUINOA SOUP

serves 4

2 Tbsp unsalted butter

2 Tbsp all-purpose flour

Salt and freshly ground pepper

1 leek, white part only, halved and thinly sliced

1 carrot, peeled and finely chopped

1 celery rib, finely chopped

1 cup (8 fl oz/250 ml) dry red wine

4 cups (32 fl oz/1 l) vegetable or chicken broth

1 lb (500 g) cremini mushrooms, quartered

⅓ cup (2 oz/60 g) quinoa, well rinsed

A good choice for spring soups, quinoa is lighter than some other grains and has a nuttiness that pairs well with young vegetables like asparagus, artichokes, new potatoes, and the mushrooms used in this recipe.

In a large, heavy pot, melt the butter over medium heat. Remove from the heat and slowly add the flour, whisking out any lumps. Add ½ tsp salt and ¼ tsp pepper. Return the pan to medium heat and cook the roux, stirring constantly, until it begins to brown, about 3 minutes. Add the leek, carrot, and celery and stir. Slowly add the wine while whisking constantly. Reduce the heat to low and let simmer, stirring occasionally, until the flavors have blended and the mixture has thickened, about 20 minutes.

Meanwhile, in a saucepan, bring the broth to a simmer over medium heat. Add the mushrooms and cook, uncovered, for 10 minutes. When the wine mixture is ready, add the broth and mushrooms and stir well. Bring to a boil, then reduce the heat to medium-low. Add the quinoa and simmer, uncovered, until tender, about 20 minutes. Season with salt and pepper and serve.

7

*Double the recipe
for the meatballs
and freeze half
for another meal.
They are especially
delicious served
over buttered
noodles with
shaved Parmesan.*

TURKEY MEATBALL
SOUP WITH ARUGULA

serves 6

FOR THE MEATBALLS

1 lb (500 g) ground turkey

¼ lb (125 g) prosciutto, finely chopped

1 clove garlic, minced

½ cup (2 oz/60 g) seasoned
dried bread crumbs

1 egg, lightly beaten

2 Tbsp minced flat-leaf parsley

Grated zest of 1 lemon

Salt and freshly ground pepper

2 Tbsp olive oil

1 yellow onion, chopped

3 cloves garlic, minced

6 cups (48 fl oz/1.5 l) chicken broth

3 ripe plum tomatoes, seeded and chopped

3 cups (3 oz/90 g) arugula

Salt and freshly ground pepper

Grated pecorino romano cheese for garnish

To make the meatballs, preheat the oven
to 375°F (190°C). In a large bowl, combine
the ground turkey, prosciutto, garlic, bread
crumbs, egg, parsley, lemon zest, ½ tsp salt,
and ¼ tsp pepper and mix well. Scoop out
a teaspoonful of the turkey mixture, form a
meatball, and place on an oiled baking sheet.
Repeat until all the meatballs are formed.
Bake the meatballs until cooked through,
10–15 minutes. Set aside.

In a large, heavy pot, warm the oil over
medium-high heat. Add the onion and the
garlic and sauté until soft, about 5 minutes.
Add the broth and bring to a boil. Reduce the
heat to low, add the tomatoes, and simmer
for 10 minutes. Add the arugula and the
meatballs and stir just until the arugula is
wilted, about 1 minute. Season with salt and
pepper. Serve, topped with the pecorino.

8

*This quintessential
spring soup is
simply divine,
showcasing tender
fresh peas. You can
substitute frozen
peas if necessary,
or to enjoy this dish
throughout the year.
For an elegant and
flavorful garnish,
swirl crème fraîche
or olive oil on top.*

PEA & MINT PURÉE
WITH LEMON

serves 4–6

2 Tbsp unsalted butter

2 shallots, minced

3 cups (24 fl oz/750 ml) chicken broth

3 cups (15 oz/470 g) fresh or frozen peas,
plus more for garnish

½ cup (¾ oz/20 g) chopped mint,
plus small leaves for garnish

1 Tbsp sour cream

Grated zest of 1 lemon

Salt and freshly ground pepper

Extra-virgin olive oil for drizzling

In a large, heavy pot, melt the butter over
medium-high heat. Add the shallots and
cook until soft, 5 minutes. Add the broth
and bring to a boil. Add the peas, reserving
a few for the garnish, and cook until tender,
3–5 minutes. Stir in the chopped mint.
Remove from the heat and let cool slightly.

Working in batches, purée the soup in a
blender or food processor. Return to the
pot, stir in the sour cream, and warm over
medium heat. Turn off the heat and stir in
the lemon zest. Season with salt and pepper
and serve, garnished with mint leaves and
peas and drizzled with oil.

9

FIVE-SPICE CHICKEN NOODLE SOUP

serves 4

6 cups (48 fl oz/1.5 l) chicken broth

3 shallots, thinly sliced

2 Tbsp peeled and minced fresh ginger

1 tsp Chinese five-spice powder

3 limes

¼ cup (2 fl oz/60 ml) Asian fish sauce

2 tsp sugar

1 cup (1 oz/30 g) slivered basil, preferably Thai

1 jalapeño chile, thinly sliced

2 cups (12 oz/375 g) shredded cooked chicken

6 oz (185 g) dried rice stick noodles, soaked in hot water for 15 minutes and drained

2 green onions, white and tender green parts, thinly sliced

This is a simple version of a classic Asian soup, with the warming flavors of ginger and chile. Rice noodles are a quick and easy choice; requiring only a brief soak in hot water, they are added just before serving.

In a large saucepan, combine the broth, shallots, ginger, and five-spice powder and bring to a boil over high heat. Reduce the heat to low and simmer for 10 minutes.

Squeeze the juice from 2 of the limes (about 3 Tbsp juice). In a small bowl, combine the lime juice, fish sauce, and sugar and stir to dissolve the sugar. Cut the remaining lime into wedges and place on a plate with the basil and chile.

Pour the lime juice mixture into the broth and stir in the chicken to heat through. Add the noodles to heat for about 5 seconds. Serve, garnished with the green onions and passing the lime wedges, basil, and chile at the table.

10

RED BEAN & ANDOUILLE SOUP

serves 6–8

4 cups (28 oz/875 g) dried red kidney beans, picked over and rinsed

1 meaty ham bone, about 1 lb (500 g), trimmed of excess fat

1 yellow onion, chopped

1 celery rib, chopped

2 cloves garlic, chopped

1 large bay leaf

½ tsp dried thyme

Hot sauce, such as Tabasco

Salt and freshly ground pepper

½ lb (250 g) andouille or other lean smoked sausage, cut into slices ¼ inch (6 mm) thick

Chopped green onions, white and tender green parts, for garnish

This New Orleans–style soup is easy to vary; use a different kind of bean, chicken or vegetable broth, or another lean sausage. Serve with a side of corn bread and hot sauce for dousing.

Soak the dried beans in cold water to cover for at least 4 hours or overnight.

In a large, heavy pot, combine the ham bone and 6 cups (48 fl oz/1.5 l) water and bring to a boil over high heat. Reduce the heat to medium-low and simmer briskly for 1 hour, skimming frequently to remove any foam that rises to the surface.

Remove from the heat. Using tongs, carefully lift the bone from the pot and set aside. When cool enough to handle, remove the meat from the bone, discarding any fat. Skim any fat from the surface of the broth and return the bone to the broth.

Drain the beans and add to the broth along with the yellow onion, celery, garlic, bay leaf, and thyme. Return to high heat and bring to a boil. Reduce the heat to low, cover, and simmer, stirring frequently, until the beans are tender, about 2 hours.

Remove and discard the ham bone and bay leaf and let the soup cool slightly. Scoop out 3 cups (21 oz/655 g) of the beans with a little liquid and purée in a blender or food processor. Return to the pot. Cut the reserved ham into bite-sized pieces and add to the pot. Season with a few drops of hot-pepper sauce, salt, and pepper.

In a large frying pan, brown the andouille over medium-high heat, 2 minutes per side.

Serve, topped with sausage and green onions.

11

LEEK & ASPARAGUS VICHYSSOISE

serves 6–8

5 leeks (about 2½ lb/1.25 kg total), white and pale green parts

2 Tbsp unsalted butter

2 Tbsp canola oil

1 tsp minced thyme

5 cups (40 fl oz/1.25 l) chicken broth

1 small russet potato, peeled and coarsely chopped

2 lb (1 kg) asparagus, trimmed and coarsely chopped

1 cup (1 oz/30 g) packed baby spinach leaves

1 cup (8 fl oz/250 ml) half-and-half, plus 3 Tbsp

Salt and freshly ground pepper

Vichyssoise is usually served chilled, but if you prefer it warm, reheat slightly after blending and serve. For a healthier, brighter green soup, omit the half-and-half or use yogurt instead.

Cut the leeks in half lengthwise and then cut each half crosswise into pieces ¼ inch (6 mm) thick. Rinse well and drain.

In a large, heavy pot, melt 1 Tbsp of the butter with 1 Tbsp of the oil over medium-high heat. Set aside 1 cup (4 oz/125 g) of the leeks and add the rest to the pot along with the thyme. Reduce the heat to low, cover, and cook, stirring occasionally, until the leeks are softened, about 10 minutes. Add the broth and potato, raise the heat to medium-high, cover, and bring to a boil. Reduce the heat to medium-low and simmer until the potato is tender, about 10 minutes.

When the potato is tender, add the asparagus, cover the pot, and cook until the asparagus is bright green and just tender, about 3 minutes. Stir in the spinach and cook just until it wilts, about 45 seconds. Remove from the heat and let cool slightly.

Working in batches, purée the soup in a blender. Pour the purée into a bowl, add the 1 cup (8 fl oz/250 ml) half-and-half, 1 tsp salt, and pepper to taste. Stir to blend and let cool to room temperature. Transfer to a covered container and refrigerate until well chilled, at least 3 hours or up to overnight.

When ready to serve, in a frying pan, melt the remaining 1 Tbsp butter with the remaining 1 Tbsp oil over medium heat. Add the reserved 1 cup (4 oz/125 g) leeks ⟫→

and ¼ tsp salt and sauté until the leeks are crisp, about 8 minutes. Transfer to paper towels to drain.

Taste the soup and season with salt and pepper. Serve, drizzled with the remaining 3 Tbsp half-and-half and topped with the fried leeks.

12

GREEN LENTIL SOUP

serves 4

2 slices thick-cut bacon, cut into ¼-inch (6-mm) pieces

1 clove garlic, minced

½ small yellow onion, finely chopped

2 carrots, peeled and finely chopped

1 celery rib, finely chopped

1½ cups (10½ oz/330 g) small green (du Puy) lentils

2 tsp thyme leaves

Salt and freshly ground pepper

1 bay leaf

2 drained oil-packed sun-dried tomatoes, chopped

Of all the lentils, the French du Puy variety hold their shape best when cooked, so don't be tempted to purée this soup. The speckled blue-green lentils look beautiful in a brothy mix with sun-dried tomatoes and carrots.

In a large, heavy pot, cook the bacon over medium heat, stirring occasionally, until lightly crisp, about 5 minutes. Add the garlic, onion, carrots, and celery and sauté until the onion is translucent and the vegetables are soft, about 3 minutes. Add the lentils and stir well. Add 4 cups (32 fl oz/1 l) water, the thyme, 1 tsp salt, ½ tsp pepper, and the bay leaf. Reduce the heat to low and simmer, adding more water if needed, until the lentils are tender but firm, 30–40 minutes.

Serve, garnished with the sun-dried tomatoes.

13

SPICY COCONUT CURRY SEAFOOD SOUP

serves 4–6

A rich coconut curry, fresh egg noodles, and briny-sweet shellfish blend into citrus and spice notes. Substitute thinly sliced cooked chicken or beef for the seafood, stirring them into the soup toward the end of cooking to warm through.

2 Tbsp canola oil

½ cup (5 oz/155g) Asian chile paste

3 cups (24 fl oz/750 ml) coconut milk

¼ cup (2 fl oz/60 ml) Asian fish sauce

2 Tbsp fresh lime juice

2 Tbsp brown sugar

1 Tbsp tamarind paste

Salt

1 lb (500 g) fresh Asian egg noodles

½ lb (250 g) large shrimp, peeled and deveined

½ lb (250 g) cleaned squid bodies, cut into rings ½ inch (12 mm) wide

1 lb (500 g) mussels, scrubbed and debearded

2 green onions, white and tender green parts

Mung bean sprouts, cilantro sprigs, Thai basil sprigs, and sliced serrano chile for garnish

1 lime, cut into wedges

In a large, heavy pot, warm the oil over medium-high heat. Add the chile paste and sauté until fragrant, about 2 minutes. Add the coconut milk, fish sauce, lime juice, sugar, tamarind paste, and 2 cups (16 fl oz/ 500 ml) water and bring to a boil. Cook for 2 minutes, then reduce the heat to low and simmer the soup for 10 minutes to blend the flavors.

Meanwhile, bring a large saucepan three-fourths full of water to a boil over high heat. Stir in 1 tsp salt. Add the noodles and cook until just tender, 2–3 minutes. Drain and divide them among bowls.

In the same pan, bring 4 cups (32 fl oz/1 l) water to a boil. Reduce the heat to low, add the shrimp, and cook until they just turn pink, about 1 minute. Using a slotted spoon, transfer the shrimp to a large bowl. Add the squid to the same simmering water and cook until they turn opaque, about 1 minute. Transfer to the bowl with the shrimp. Add the mussels to the simmering water, discarding any that do not close to the touch. ↠

Cook just until the shells open, 2–3 minutes. Transfer the cooked mussels to the bowl of seafood, discarding any unopened mussels. Discard the cooking liquid.

Just before serving, ready all of the garnishes: thinly slice the green onions on the diagonal. Add all of the seafood to the simmering soup and cook just to heat through, about 3 minutes. Use tongs to top each bowl of noodles with a variety of seafood, and then ladle the hot soup over the seafood. Generously top each bowl with the garnishes and serve. Pass lime wedges at the table.

14

RAMEN NOODLE SOUP WITH SUGAR SNAP PEAS

serves 4–6

Ramen noodles are a fast, easy, and inexpensive staple to keep on hand. Sugar snap peas and diced tomatoes add depth, flavor, and nutritional value to this perfect weeknight soup.

2 Tbsp olive oil

2 shallots, chopped

4 cloves garlic, minced

6 cups (48 fl oz/1.5 l) chicken broth

3 oz (90 g) dried ramen noodles

1 can (14½ oz/455 g) diced tomatoes

1½ cups (5 oz/155 g) sugar snap peas, trimmed and halved diagonally

4 green onions, white and tender green parts, thinly sliced

Salt and freshly ground pepper

Hot sauce, such as Sriracha, for serving

In a large, heavy pot, warm the oil over medium-high heat. Add the shallots and garlic and sauté for 3 minutes. Add the broth and bring to a boil. Add the ramen noodles and tomatoes and cook, stirring occasionally, for 5 minutes. Add the sugar snap peas and green onions and cook for 2 minutes. Season with salt and pepper and serve, passing the hot sauce at the table.

15

Here, curry powder and orange juice add flavor and vibrancy to this earthy carrot soup. To mix it up, try a touch of ground cinnamon or ginger in place of or in addition to the curry powder.

CURRIED CARROT PURÉE

serves 4

1 Tbsp olive oil, plus more for drizzling

1 large shallot, minced

1½ lb (750 g) carrots, peeled and coarsely chopped

1 tsp curry powder

6 cups (48 fl oz/1.5 l) chicken broth

2 Tbsp fresh orange juice

Salt and freshly ground pepper

In a large, heavy pot, warm the 1 Tbsp oil over medium heat. Add the shallot and sauté until translucent, about 2 minutes. Add the carrots, curry powder, and broth. Raise the heat to medium-high and bring to a boil. Reduce the heat to low, cover, and cook until the carrots are tender, about 20 minutes. Remove from the heat and add the orange juice. Let cool slightly.

Working in batches, purée the soup in a blender or food processor. Season with salt and pepper.

The soup can be served warm or chilled. To serve warm, return to the pot and gently warm over medium heat. To serve chilled, let cool, transfer to a covered container, and refrigerate for at least 3 hours or up to overnight. Serve, drizzled with oil.

16

Look for fresh pea shoots at farmers' markets in early spring, or at Asian markets year-round. Tender and sweet, they deliver the flavor of fresh peas without the effort of shelling. If pea shoots are unavailable, baby spinach can substitute.

PEA SHOOT & PASTA SOUP

serves 4

Salt and freshly ground pepper

½ cup (3½ oz/105 g) stelline or other small soup pasta

2 eggs

4 cups (32 fl oz/1 l) chicken broth

1 small carrot, peeled and chopped

2 cups (2 oz/60 g) chopped pea shoots

¼ cup (1 oz/30 g) grated Parmesan cheese

Bring a small saucepan of salted water to a boil. Add the pasta and cook until al dente, about 8 minutes or according to the package directions. Drain and rinse under cold running water. In a small bowl, beat the eggs lightly and season with salt and pepper.

In a large saucepan, combine the broth with 1 cup (8 fl oz/250 ml) water. Bring to a simmer over medium-high heat. Add the carrot and simmer, uncovered, until crisp-tender, 5–6 minutes. Add the pea shoots and simmer until tender, 2–3 minutes. Remove from the heat. Slowly drizzle in the beaten egg, stirring the soup gently in one direction to form even threads of cooked egg. Gently stir in the pasta and cheese. Season with salt and pepper and serve.

17

Try Brie, St. André, or a soft goat cheese in place of the Camembert. Serve extra crostini and a bottle of Pinot Gris at the table for a light spring dinner. If you prefer to use fresh artichokes, prep the hearts according to the method on page 75.

ARTICHOKE SOUP WITH CAMEMBERT CROSTINI

serves 6

2 Tbsp olive oil

1 small yellow onion, chopped

2 cloves garlic, minced

¼ cup (2 fl oz/60 ml) dry white wine

1 small russet potato, peeled and finely diced

8 oz (250 g) frozen artichoke hearts

2 cups (16 fl oz/500 ml) chicken broth

Salt and freshly ground pepper

FOR THE CROSTINI

12 thin baguette slices

2 oz (60 g) Camembert cheese, at room temperature

In a large saucepan, warm the oil over medium-high heat. Add the onion and the garlic and sauté until translucent, about 5 minutes. Add the white wine and potato and cook for 5 minutes. Add the artichoke hearts and broth and bring to a boil. Reduce the heat to low and simmer until the potato is very tender, about 20 minutes. Remove from the heat and let cool slightly.

Working in batches, purée the soup in a blender or food processor. Return to the saucepan and season with salt and pepper.

To make the crostini, preheat the broiler to high. Top each baguette slice with a thin slice of Camembert. Place on a baking sheet and broil until the cheese melts slightly, 1–2 minutes.

Serve, topping each bowl with 2 crostini.

18

To make the pesto, finely grind ⅓ cup (2 oz/60 g) pine nuts and 3 cloves garlic in a food processor. Add 2 cups (2 oz/ 60 g) packed basil leaves and purée. With the motor running, add ½ cup (4 fl oz/125 ml) extra-virgin olive oil in a steady stream. Stop and add ½ cup (2 oz/60 g) grated Parmesan and purée. Season with salt and pepper.

BEAN & ELBOW PASTA SOUP WITH BASIL PESTO

serves 6–8

Salt and freshly ground pepper

1 cup (3½ oz/105 g) elbow pasta

2 Tbsp olive oil

1 yellow onion, chopped

4 cloves garlic, minced

2 Tbsp tomato paste

5 cups (40 fl oz/1.25 l) chicken broth

1 can (14½ oz/455 g) diced tomatoes, drained

1 can (15 oz/470 g) butter beans, drained

1 can (15 oz/470 g) cannellini beans, drained

¼ cup (⅓ oz/10 g) chopped basil

Basil Pesto (left)

In a saucepan, bring 4 cups (32 fl oz/1 l) water to a boil. Add ¼ tsp salt and the pasta and cook until al dente, about 8 minutes, or according to the package directions. Drain and set aside.

In a large, heavy pot, warm the oil over medium-high heat. Add the onion and the garlic and sauté for 5 minutes. Add the tomato paste and stir to combine. Add the broth and tomatoes and bring to a boil. Reduce the heat to low and simmer for 20 minutes. Add the pasta, butter beans, and cannellini beans and simmer for 5 minutes. Stir in the basil and season with salt and pepper.

Serve, topping each bowl with a dollop or swirl of pesto.

19

ISRAELI COUSCOUS SOUP WITH CURRY, CHICKEN & SPINACH

serves 4–6

1 cup (6 oz/185 g) Israeli couscous

2 small skinless, boneless chicken breast halves (about ¾ lb/375 g total)

3 Tbsp olive oil

Salt and freshly ground pepper

1 small yellow onion, chopped

2 cloves garlic, minced

½ tsp curry powder

¼ tsp ground turmeric

6 cups (48 fl oz/1.5 l) chicken broth

2 cups (2 oz/60 g) baby spinach leaves

This soup is a great way to use leftover rotisserie or grilled chicken. When reheating, you may need to add more broth or water, as the couscous will absorb the liquid as it sits.

Preheat the oven to 375°F (190°C).

In a small saucepan, bring 1¼ cups (10 fl oz/310 ml) water to a boil. Add the couscous, stir once, and cover. Reduce the heat to low and cook until all the water is absorbed, 8–10 minutes. Set aside.

Place the chicken breasts on a baking sheet, brush with 1 Tbsp of the oil, and season with salt and pepper. Bake the chicken until it is cooked all the way through, 18–20 minutes. When it is cool enough to handle, shred the chicken and set aside.

In a large, heavy pot, warm the remaining 2 Tbsp oil over medium-high heat. Add the onion and the garlic and sauté until soft, about 5 minutes. Add the curry powder and turmeric, stir to combine, and cook for 2 minutes. Add the broth and bring to a boil. Reduce the heat to low, add the couscous and chicken and simmer, stirring occasionally, until the couscous is al dente, about 10 minutes. Stir in the spinach and cook just until it wilts, about 45 seconds. Season with salt and pepper and serve.

20

WATERCRESS SOUP

serves 4

¼ cup (2 fl oz/60 ml) olive oil

1 yellow onion, coarsely chopped

2 large Yukon gold potatoes, peeled and diced

1 lb (500 g) leeks, white and pale green parts, thinly sliced

4 cups (32 fl oz/1 l) chicken broth or water

Salt and freshly ground pepper

2 bunches watercress

1 cup (8 fl oz/250 ml) heavy cream

Watercress may bring visions of delectable finger sandwiches, but this favorite salad ingredient also has a tradition in British soups. The peppery green leaves are popular in creamy soups that can be eaten hot or chilled; hot watercress soup is often topped with crisp croutons, while cold soup is given a swirl of cream.

In a large saucepan, warm the oil over medium heat. Add the onion and sauté until softened, 5–7 minutes. Stir in the potatoes and cook for 2 minutes. Add the leeks, raise the heat to medium-high, and cook, stirring occasionally, until the leeks begin to soften and wilt, about 4 minutes. Add the broth and season with salt and pepper. Raise the heat to high, bring to a boil, then reduce the heat to medium-low and simmer, uncovered, until the vegetables are very soft, about 25 minutes.

Strip the watercress leaves from the stems and discard the stems. Add the leaves to the saucepan and cook just until they are tender, about 3 minutes. Remove from the heat and let cool slightly.

Working in batches, purée the soup in a blender or food processor. Stir in the cream. Taste and adjust the seasoning.

To serve the soup hot, gently reheat over medium heat. To serve the soup cold, transfer to a covered container and refrigerate until well chilled, at least 2 hours. Ladle the soup into bowls and serve.

21

COLD ZUCCHINI & AVOCADO SOUP

serves 4

Good-quality olive oil and ripe avocados are imperative to the success of this dish. Serve with a shredded carrot, feta, and pine nut salad. This soup can also be served at room temperature.

⅔ cup (3½ oz/105 g) whole raw almonds

4 zucchini, trimmed and chopped

4 celery ribs, chopped

¼ cup (2 fl oz/60 ml) extra-virgin olive oil

¼ cup (2 fl oz/60 ml) fresh lemon juice

2 ripe avocados, pitted, peeled, and diced

A few dashes of Tabasco sauce

Salt and freshly ground pepper

3 Tbsp chopped basil

Put the almonds into a food processor and pulse until finely ground. Add the zucchini, celery, oil, and lemon juice and purée until very smooth. Add the avocados and 1½ cups (12 fl oz/375 ml) water and continue to purée. If needed, add 1 Tbsp of water at a time to achieve the desired consistency. Add the Tabasco and combine. Season with salt and pepper.

Serve, topped with chopped basil.

22

CHILLED SOUR CHERRY SOUP WITH TARRAGON

serves 6–8

For a less sweet and more festive soup, replace the fruity red wine with a dry Prosecco or a sparkling rosé stirred in after chilling to preserve the bubbles. Save a little bubbly for serving alongside.

3 lb (1.5 kg) fresh sour cherries, stemmed and pitted

3 Tbsp unsalted butter

4 shallots, minced

2 tsp grated lemon zest

2 cups (16 fl oz/500 ml) fruity red wine

2 Tbsp cornstarch

⅔ cup (5 oz/155 g) sugar, plus more as needed

Salt

1 lb (500 g) fresh sweet cherries, stemmed, pitted, and quartered

¼ cup (2 fl oz/60 ml) heavy cream (optional)

¼ cup (⅓ oz/10 g) chopped tarragon

Using a food processor, process the sour cherries to a smooth purée. Pour the purée through a fine-mesh sieve set over a bowl and, using a wooden spoon, press hard on the solids to extract as much liquid as possible. Discard the solids in the sieve.

In a large, heavy pot, melt the butter over medium heat. Add the shallots and sauté until softened, about 3 minutes. Stir in the lemon zest and cook until fragrant, about 45 seconds. Add the sour-cherry purée, the wine, and 1½ cups (12 fl oz/375 ml) water and stir to blend. Raise the heat to medium-high and bring to a simmer.

In a small bowl, whisk together the cornstarch with ¼ cup (2 fl oz/60 ml) water and stir it into the simmering cherry mixture along with the ⅔ cup sugar and a pinch of salt. Reduce the heat to medium-low and simmer, stirring often, until thickened to the consistency of light cream, about 4 minutes. Remove from the heat and stir in the sweet cherries. Transfer the soup to a nonaluminum bowl and let cool completely. Cover and refrigerate until well chilled, at least 4 hours or up to overnight.

When ready to serve, taste the soup and adjust the seasoning with salt and sugar. Serve, drizzled with cream, if using, and sprinkled with tarragon.

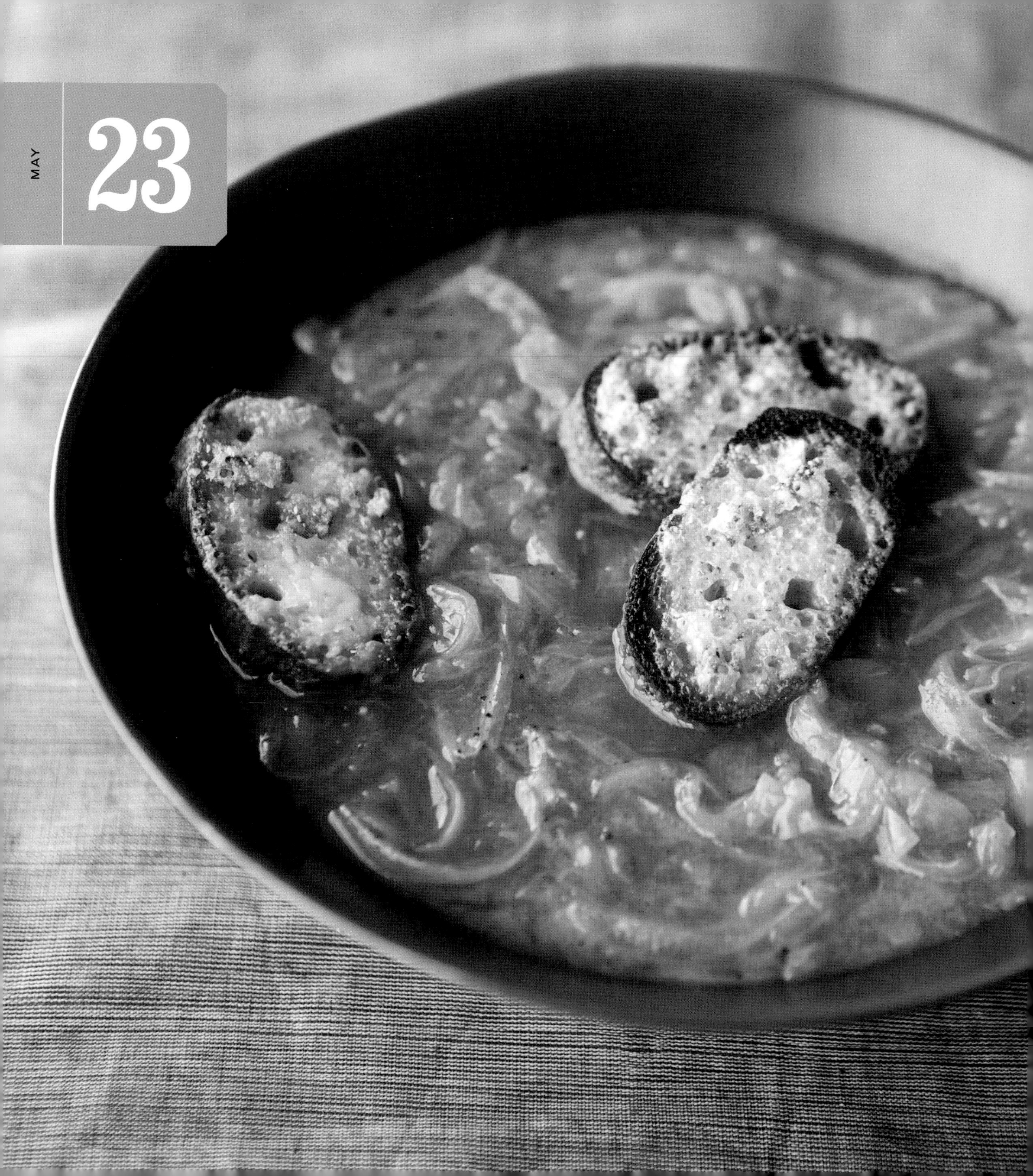

23

Vidalia onions have a high sugar content and caramelize beautifully. But they really do take 30 minutes to reach their optimal flavor, so be patient at the stove.

SWEET ONION SOUP WITH BLUE CHEESE TOASTS

serves 4–6

3 Tbsp unsalted butter

2 Tbsp olive oil

4 sweet onions, such as Vidalia, thinly sliced

1 Tbsp balsamic vinegar

3 cloves garlic, minced

¼ cup (2 fl oz/60 ml) dry white wine

3 cups (24 fl oz/750 ml) chicken broth

Salt and freshly ground pepper

FOR THE BLUE CHEESE TOASTS

1 baguette, cut into 8–12 thin slices

3 oz (90 g) blue cheese, crumbled

In a large, heavy pot, melt the butter with the oil over high heat. Add the onions and sauté until they begin to soften, 5–7 minutes. Reduce the heat to low and continue to cook, stirring occasionally, for 30 minutes. Add the vinegar, stir to combine, and cook, stirring occasionally, for 30 minutes. Stir in the garlic and cook for 5 minutes. Add the wine and cook for 2 minutes. Add the broth, raise the heat to medium-high, and bring to a boil. Remove from the heat and let cool slightly.

Purée half of the soup in a blender. Return to the pot and season with salt and pepper.

Meanwhile, to make the blue cheese croutons, preheat the broiler to high. Place the bread slices on a baking sheet and cover each with blue cheese. Place under the broiler until the cheese is melted and the croutons are toasted, 1–2 minutes.

Serve, topping each bowl with 2 or 3 toasts.

24

For this soup, try to catch the moment when your local crab haul overlaps with the spring asparagus harvest. Either lump crabmeat or flake will work, but avoid vacuum-packed, frozen, or imitation—with so few ingredients, freshness is key.

CRAB & ASPARAGUS EGG FLOWER SOUP

serves 4

4 cups (32 fl oz/1 l) chicken broth

1 tsp peeled and minced fresh ginger

½ lb (250 g) asparagus, trimmed and cut on the diagonal into 1-inch (2.5-cm) pieces

1 Tbsp cornstarch

1 egg, well beaten

2 tsp dry sherry

1 tsp Asian sesame oil

1 tsp soy sauce

1 cup (6 oz/185 g) fresh lump or flake crabmeat, picked over for shell fragments

In a large saucepan, combine the broth and ginger over medium-high heat and bring to a rolling boil. Add the asparagus, reduce the heat to medium, cover, and simmer until the asparagus is crisp-tender, about 3 minutes.

Meanwhile, in a bowl, mix together the cornstarch and 2 Tbsp water. Set aside.

Reduce the heat to medium-low. Stir 2 Tbsp of the hot broth into the beaten egg. Slowly pour the egg mixture into the broth, stirring constantly to form even threads of cooked egg. Add the cornstarch mixture, sherry, sesame oil, and soy sauce to the broth. Cook, stirring, until the soup thickens slightly, about 1 minute.

Stir in the crabmeat and cook just until it is warmed through, 2–3 minutes. Taste and adjust the seasoning, then serve.

25
MAY

Traditional vichyssoise is a cold potato and leek soup. In this version, fennel takes center stage. This soup is just as good warm as it is cold, so you can make that decision based on the weather.

FENNEL VICHYSSOISE
serves 4–6

2 Tbsp unsalted butter

1 Tbsp olive oil

½ yellow onion, chopped

2 fennel bulbs (1½ lb/750 g total), stalks and fronds removed, quartered, cored, and thinly sliced

¼ cup (2 fl oz/60 ml) dry white wine

3 cups (24 fl oz/750 ml) vegetable broth

1 russet potato (¾ lb/375 g), peeled and diced

½ cup (4 fl oz/125 ml) heavy cream

Salt and ground white pepper

In a large, heavy pot, melt the butter with the oil over medium-high heat. Add the onion and fennel and sauté until the fennel is very soft, 7–9 minutes. Add the wine and cook, stirring often, for 2 minutes. Add the broth, bring to a boil, then add the potato. Reduce the heat to medium-low and simmer until the potato is very soft, 30–35 minutes. Remove from the heat and let cool slightly.

Working in batches, purée the soup in a blender. Return to the pot, stir in the cream, and bring to a gentle boil. Remove from the heat and season to taste with salt and pepper.

If serving cold, let the soup cool to room temperature. Transfer to a covered container and refrigerate until well chilled, at least 3 hours or up to overnight. Serve.

26
MAY

To make fried garlic chips, thinly slice 8 cloves of garlic. Warm 2 Tbsp oil in a small frying pan over medium heat. Add the garlic and cook, stirring often, until golden brown, about 3 minutes. Transfer to paper towels to drain.

EGG-LEMON SOUP WITH FAVA BEANS & FRIED GARLIC CHIPS
serves 6–8

Salt

3 lb (1.5 kg) fava beans in the pods, shelled

1 large lemon

8 cups (64 fl oz/2 l) chicken broth

⅔ cup (4½ oz/145 g) long-grain white rice, such as basmati

1 bay leaf

2 eggs, at room temperature

2 egg yolks, at room temperature

Fried Garlic Chips (left)

Bring a large saucepan of water to a boil. Add 1 Tbsp salt and the fava beans and cook for 2 minutes. Drain and rinse under cold water. Pinch open the skin of each bean along its edge and slip the bean from the skin. Discard the skins.

With a vegetable peeler, remove the zest from the lemon in wide strips, then squeeze ¼ cup (2 fl oz/60 ml) juice and set aside.

In a large, heavy pot, bring the broth to a boil over high heat. Stir in the rice, lemon zest, bay leaf, and 1½ tsp salt. Reduce the heat to medium, cover, and simmer until the rice is tender, 15–20 minutes.

Remove the bay leaf and lemon zest from the broth. In a bowl, whisk together the eggs, egg yolks, and lemon juice. Whisking constantly, ladle about one-fourth of the hot broth mixture into the egg mixture and whisk until blended. Stir back into the pot. Add the fava beans, reduce the heat to low, and cook, stirring, until the soup thickens and wisps of steam appear, about 5 minutes. Do not allow the soup to come to a simmer, and remove it from the heat as soon as it has thickened.

Taste and adjust the seasoning. Serve, garnished with the garlic chips.

27
MAY

STRAWBERRY-LEMON SOUP
serves 4–6

1 lb (500 g) fresh or frozen strawberries

¼ cup (2 oz/60 g) sugar

2 lemons

¼ cup (2 fl oz/60 g) dry white wine

4–6 tsp crème fraîche or sour cream for serving

For a special garnish, roll the bottom half of whole strawberries in crème fraîche and sprinkle with lemon zest. Fresh mint also pairs nicely with this summery soup.

If you are using frozen strawberries, let them defrost in a bowl, reserving all their juices. Put the strawberries, sugar, the grated zest and juice of 1 lemon, and the wine into a blender and purée.

Transfer the soup to a nonreactive bowl, cover, and refrigerate until well chilled, at least 3 hours.

Serve, garnished with a dollop of the crème fraîche and the grated zest of the remaining lemon.

28
MAY

CREAMY SPINACH-LEEK SOUP
serves 4–6

1 Tbsp unsalted butter

1 Tbsp olive oil

2 leeks, white and pale green parts, chopped

½ tsp grated nutmeg

1½ cups (12 fl oz/375 ml) vegetable broth

2 large bunches spinach, tough stems removed

¼ cup (2 fl oz/60 ml) heavy cream

Salt and freshly ground pepper

Here, nutmeg is the secret ingredient that laces this simple spinach soup, mellowing the earthy dark greens.

In a large, heavy pot, melt the butter with the oil over medium-high heat. Add the leeks and nutmeg and sauté until the leeks are softened, 5–7 minutes. Add the broth and bring to a boil. Add the spinach and cook, stirring often, for 10 minutes. Remove from the heat and let cool slightly.

Working in batches, purée the soup in a blender. Return to the pot, add the cream, and bring just to a boil. Season with salt and pepper. Serve.

29
MAY

SIMPLE ASPARAGUS SOUP
serves 4–6

2 Tbsp olive oil

1 yellow onion, chopped

2 cloves garlic, minced

3 cups (24 fl oz/750 ml) chicken broth

2 lb (1 kg) asparagus, trimmed and cut into ½-inch (12-mm) pieces

2 Tbsp heavy cream

Grated zest and juice of 1 lemon

Salt and freshly ground pepper

Spring asparagus is gorgeous, but overcook it and it will turn a dingy brown color. If you buy fat asparagus spears, cut them into smaller pieces so they will cook faster in the broth.

In a large, heavy pot, warm the oil over medium-high heat. Add the onion and garlic and sauté until translucent, about 5 minutes. Add the broth and bring to a boil. Add the asparagus and cook until tender, 8–10 minutes. Remove from the heat and let cool slightly.

Working in batches, purée the soup in a blender. Return to the pot, add the cream, and bring just to a boil. Turn the heat off and stir in the lemon zest and juice. Season with salt and pepper and serve.

30

GINGERY BROTH WITH PRAWNS & GREEN ONIONS

serves 4

The aromatic broth can be made ahead and stored in the refrigerator for up to 3 days. Cook the shrimp and green onions in the broth just before serving.

3 green onions

2 tsp canola oil

3-inch (7.5-cm) piece of fresh ginger, peeled and grated

1 clove garlic, minced

⅛ tsp Chinese five-spice powder

¼ lb (125 g) cremini mushrooms, thinly sliced

½ red bell pepper, seeded and thinly sliced

4 cups (32 fl oz/1 l) chicken broth

2 Tbsp soy sauce

½ lb (250 g) medium shrimp, peeled and deveined

Thinly slice the green onions on the diagonal, reserving the white and pale green parts in one bowl and the dark green parts in a separate bowl.

In a large, heavy pot, warm the oil over medium-high heat. Add the ginger and garlic and cook until fragrant, about 4 minutes. Add the five-spice powder, mushrooms, red pepper, and the white and light green parts of the green onions and cook, stirring often, for 3–4 minutes. Add the broth, 2 cups (16 fl oz/500 ml) water, and the soy sauce and simmer for 20 minutes. Raise the heat to high and return the broth to a boil. Add the shrimp and cook until bright pink, about 3 minutes. Serve, sprinkled with the dark green parts of the green onions.

31

SPINACH & VERMICELLI SOUP WITH FRIED EGG

serves 4

Both kid and adult friendly, this soup uses ingredients that you probably already have in your pantry. Substitute chard, kale, or other sturdy cooking greens for the spinach.

1 Tbsp olive oil

½ small yellow onion, thinly sliced

1 clove garlic, minced

5 cups (40 fl oz/1.25 l) chicken broth

½ lb (250 g) vermicelli, broken into 2-inch (5-cm) pieces

1 bunch spinach, stemmed

1 Tbsp unsalted butter

4 eggs

Hot sauce, such as Sriracha, for serving (optional)

In a large saucepan, warm the oil over medium-high heat. Add the onion and garlic and sauté until translucent, about 5 minutes. Add the broth and bring to a boil. Add the vermicelli, return to a boil, and cook, stirring occasionally, for 4 minutes. Add the spinach and stir through just until it is wilted, about 2 minutes. Reduce the heat to low to keep the soup warm while you prepare the eggs.

In a nonstick frying pan, melt the butter over medium heat. Fry each egg until it is set but the yolk is still runny, 5–6 minutes.

Ladle the soup into bowls and top each with a fried egg. Serve, passing the hot sauce at the table, if using.

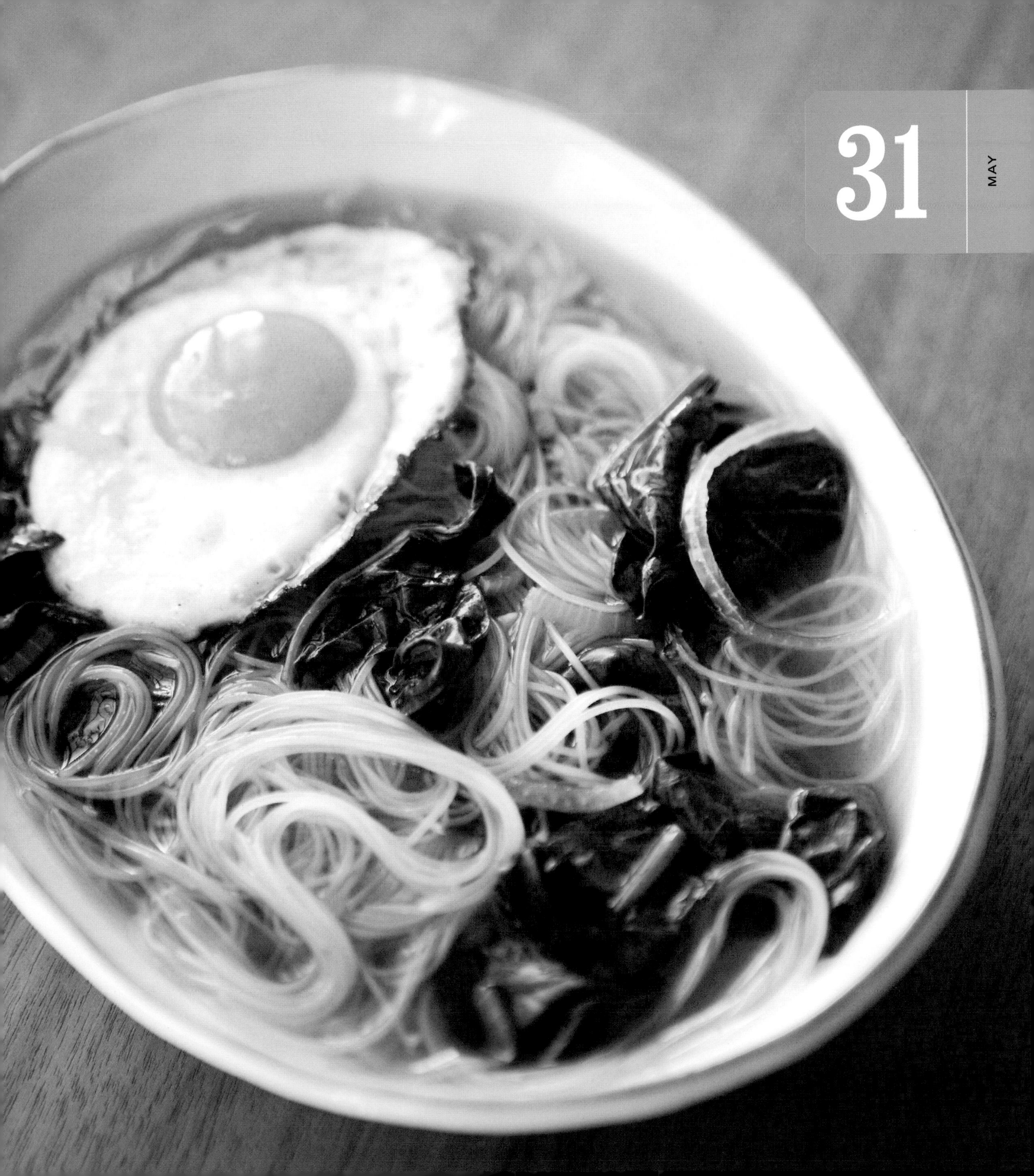

1
**SWEET CORN CHOWDER
WITH BACON**
page 130

2
**GOLDEN BEET SOUP WITH
DILLED GOAT CHEESE**
page 130

3
CUCUMBER-DILL SOUP
page 132

4
CHILLED SUMMER SQUASH SOUP
page 132

8
**LIMA BEAN, PEA & ZUCCHINI
PURÉE WITH PESTO**
page 135

9
VEGETABLE SOUP WITH ANELLINI
page 136

10
**QUINOA IN LEMON BROTH
WITH GREENS & PARMESAN**
page 136

11
SOUR CHERRY–RIESLING SOUP
page 137

15
**ROASTED RED PEPPER PURÉE
WITH SPICY CORN SALSA**
page 141

16
**ZUCCHINI SOUP
WITH PASTA & MINT**
page 141

17
ROASTED BEET PURÉE WITH FETA
page 142

18
CURRIED CHICKPEA STEW
page 142

22
CHEESE & ARUGULA RAVIOLI SOUP
page 144

23
BRAZILIAN FISH STEW
page 147

24
**THREE-POTATO CHOWDER WITH
CORN, CILANTRO & LIME**
page 147

25
**RAMEN NOODLES WITH
EDAMAME & MUSHROOMS**
page 148

29
**AVOCADO SOUP WITH
SHRIMP & SALSA**
page 150

30
PROVENÇAL MINESTRONE
page 150

5

ROASTED TOMATO SOUP WITH SERRANO HAM & BURRATA
page 133

6

COLD ALMOND SOUP WITH GRAPES
page 133

7

LUMP CRAB IN TOMATO-ROSEMARY BROTH
page 135

12

SPICY COCONUT BROTH WITH UDON NOODLES & SHRIMP
page 137

13

ROMAN CHICKPEA SOUP
page 138

14

SOBA NOODLES & SEARED SALMON IN GINGER–GREEN ONION BROTH
page 138

19

CREAMY POBLANO CHILE SOUP
page 143

20

COOL HONEYDEW-MINT SOUP
page 143

21

STRAWBERRY-RHUBARB SOUP WITH PROSECCO
page 144

26

CUBAN BLACK BEAN SOUP
page 148

27

CHILLED YELLOW PEPPER SOUP WITH CHIVES
page 149

28

MELON & PROSCIUTTO SOUP WITH MASCARPONE CHEESE
page 149

Warmer weather solicits bumper crops of melons, sweet corn, and summer squash, in all shapes and sizes. These are perfect for light soups fit for the season. As the temperature steadily climbs, chilled soups from classic cool cucumber to fruit purées such as tart-sweet rhubarb and strawberries are refreshing choices. And for a taste of sand and sun, chowders offer an ideal vehicle for kernels of corn, hunks of potato, and flakes of tender fish.

june

1

SWEET CORN CHOWDER WITH BACON

serves 4–6

8–10 large ears of corn, husks and silk removed

4 slices thick-cut bacon, cut into ½-inch (12-mm) pieces

1 yellow onion, chopped

½ lb (250 g) red or white boiling potatoes, peeled and chopped

4 cups (32 fl oz/1 l) vegetable or chicken broth

1 bay leaf

2 Tbsp chopped fresh thyme, or 2 tsp dried

1½–2 cups (12–16 fl oz/375–500 ml) milk

1 red bell pepper, seeded and diced

1–3 Tbsp whiskey (optional)

Generous pinch of red pepper flakes

Salt and freshly ground pepper

¼ cup (⅓ oz/10 g) chopped flat-leaf parsley

In high summer, just-harvested sweet corn hardly needs to be cooked. A splash of Canadian whiskey, made of distilled corn and other grains, gives this sweet, smooth chowder a nice rough edge. Simmer the cobs in the stock for extra flavor.

Working with one ear of corn at a time, hold it stem end down on a cutting board. Carefully cut off the kernels, rotating the ear after each cut until all the kernels are stripped from the cob. Set the kernels and the cobs aside separately. You should have about 4 cups (1½ lb/750 g) corn kernels.

In a heavy soup pot, fry the bacon over medium heat until crisp, about 5 minutes. Using a slotted spoon, transfer the bacon to paper towels to drain. Add the onion to the bacon drippings in the pot and sauté until translucent, about 10 minutes.

Add the potatoes, broth, bay leaf, thyme, 2 cups (12 oz/375 g) of the corn kernels, and the cobs to the pot. Simmer, uncovered, until the potatoes are tender, 12–15 minutes.

Remove from the heat and remove and discard the bay leaf and the cobs. Let cool slightly. Working in batches, purée the soup in a blender or food processor. Return to the pot.

Set the pot over low heat and stir in the remaining corn kernels, enough of the milk to achieve a nice consistency, the bell pepper, whiskey (if using), and the red pepper flakes. Season with salt and pepper. Serve, sprinkled with crumbled bacon and parsley.

2

GOLDEN BEET SOUP WITH DILLED GOAT CHEESE

serves 6–8

5 golden beets (about 2½ lb/ 1.25 kg total), trimmed

1 Yukon gold potato

¼ lb (125 g) fresh goat cheese, crumbled

¾ cup (6 fl oz/180 ml) half-and-half

½ tsp fresh lemon juice

3 Tbsp minced dill, plus leaves for garnish

Salt and freshly ground pepper

2 Tbsp unsalted butter

1 yellow onion, chopped

2 cloves garlic, minced

6 cups (48 fl oz/1.5 l) chicken broth

1 tsp white wine vinegar

With its distinct caraway nuances and celery-like flavor, feathery dill complements both earthy beets and tangy fresh goat cheese. Golden beets are as sweet as red, but they have a finer, milder taste that lightens this silky, summery soup.

Preheat the oven to 400°F (200°C). Wrap the beets and potato in foil and place on a baking sheet. Roast until tender when pierced with a knife, about 1 hour. Open the foil and let cool, then peel and chop the beets and potato.

Meanwhile, in a small bowl, combine the goat cheese, ¼ cup (2 fl oz/60 ml) of the half-and-half, the lemon juice, minced dill, ¼ tsp salt, and pepper to taste. Using a fork, vigorously beat until blended and pourable but still thick. Set aside.

In a large, heavy pot, melt the butter over medium heat. Add the onion and garlic and sauté until softened, about 5 minutes. Add the broth and bring to a boil over medium-high heat. Add the beets and potato, reduce the heat to low, cover partially, and cook for 15 minutes. Remove from the heat and let cool slightly.

Working in batches, purée the soup in a blender. Return to the pot and add the vinegar, 1½ tsp salt, pepper to taste, and the remaining ½ cup (4 fl oz/125 ml) half-and-half and stir. Place over medium-low heat and cook gently, stirring occasionally, until heated through, about 10 minutes.

Season with salt and pepper. Serve, garnished with a dollop of the goat cheese mixture and the dill leaves.

3

CUCUMBER-DILL SOUP

serves 6

3 English cucumbers, peeled, halved lengthwise, and seeded

1 cup (8 oz/250 g) Greek-style or other thick, whole-milk plain yogurt

1 Tbsp fresh lemon juice

3 green onions, white and tender green parts, chopped

3 Tbsp chopped dill

1 clove garlic, chopped

1 tsp caraway seeds, crushed

Salt and ground white pepper

1 cup (8 fl oz/250 ml) vegetable broth

2 Tbsp extra-virgin olive oil

A chilled soup is a welcome start to the summer, and easy to pack for outdoor day trips. Select a container with a tight-fitting lid that permits easy pouring. Pack over ice, and to serve, pour the soup into widemouthed glasses or cups for sipping.

Coarsely chop 5 of the cucumber halves and transfer to a large bowl. Add the yogurt, lemon juice, green onions, dill, garlic, caraway seeds, 1 tsp salt, and ¼ tsp white pepper. Stir to combine, cover, and set aside at room temperature for 1 hour to blend the flavors. Dice the remaining cucumber half and set aside.

Working in batches, purée the cucumber-yogurt mixture in a blender. With the machine running, slowly add the broth and purée until fully incorporated. Transfer to a covered container and refrigerate until well chilled, about 2 hours.

Just before serving, stir in the diced cucumber and oil. Pour the soup into wide-mouthed glasses and serve.

4

CHILLED SUMMER SQUASH SOUP

serves 6

6 summer squash, trimmed, halved, and sliced

3 Tbsp olive oil

Salt and freshly ground pepper

2 leeks, white and pale green parts, finely chopped

3 Yukon gold or other boiling potatoes, peeled and chopped

2 cloves garlic, minced

4 cups (32 fl oz/1 l) chicken broth, plus more as needed

4 Tbsp (½ oz/15 g) finely chopped basil

2 Tbsp finely chopped chives

1 Tbsp fresh lemon juice

Roasting summer squash in a hot oven banishes all trace of bitterness and brings out this vegetable's delicate, sweet flavor. The sunny-hued vegetable creates a pretty soup, but its close cousins zucchini, crookneck, and pattypan are interchangeable.

Preheat the oven to 400°F (200°C). Toss the squash with 1 Tbsp of the oil and season with salt and pepper. Spread on a baking sheet and roast for 20 minutes. Set aside.

In a large, heavy pot, warm the remaining 2 Tbsp oil over medium heat. Add the leeks and sauté until softened, 5–7 minutes. Add the potatoes and sauté until lightly browned, 5 minutes. Add the garlic and cook for 1 minute. Add the broth, cover, and cook until the potatoes are tender, about 15 minutes. Remove from the heat and let cool slightly. Add the roasted squash.

Working in batches, purée the soup in a blender. Add more broth as needed to give the soup the desired consistency. Transfer to a bowl and refrigerate until well chilled, at least 3 hours.

Stir in 2 Tbsp of the basil, the chives, and the lemon juice. Season with salt and pepper. Serve, garnished with the remaining basil.

5

ROASTED TOMATO SOUP WITH SERRANO HAM & BURRATA

serves 4

4 thin slices serrano ham

2½ lb (1.25 kg) small tomatoes, such as plum or campari, halved

4 Tbsp (2 fl oz/60 ml) olive oil

Salt and freshly ground pepper

1 yellow onion, chopped

4 cloves garlic, minced

2 cups (16 fl oz/500 ml) chicken broth

6 oz (185 g) burrata or fresh mozzarella cheese, sliced

1 Tbsp finely chopped chives

Tomatoes and mozzarella are a classic combination that only gets better with Spain's signature cured ham. Make sure the serrano dries out completely in the oven for the best grinding. Burrata is an especially soft and creamy pulled cheese; slice it just before you are ready to serve, but even if it falls apart, torn pieces will taste delicious melting into the soup.

Preheat the oven to 200°F (95°C). Place the ham in a single layer on a baking sheet and bake until completely dried, about 1 hour and 45 minutes. Transfer the ham to paper towels and blot it to remove any excess oil. Tear the ham into small pieces, transfer to a spice grinder, and grind into a fine dust. Set aside.

Raise the oven temperature to 450°F (230°C). Arrange the tomatoes in a single layer on a baking sheet, drizzle with 2 Tbsp of the oil, and season with salt and pepper. Roast the tomatoes until very soft and caramelized, 25–30 minutes. Set aside.

In a large, heavy pot, warm the remaining 2 Tbsp oil over medium-high heat. Add the onion and garlic and sauté until translucent, about 5 minutes. Add the tomatoes with all their juices and stir to combine. Using a wooden spoon, break up the tomatoes a bit and sauté for 3 minutes. Add the broth and bring to a boil. Reduce the heat to low and simmer for 20 minutes. Remove from the heat and let cool slightly.

Purée half of the soup in a blender. Return to the pot, stir in the ham dust, and season with salt and pepper.

Ladle the soup into bowls. Garnish each bowl with a slice of burrata and let it sit for a minute or two so that the cheese begins to melt into the soup. Top each bowl with chopped chives and serve.

6

COLD ALMOND SOUP WITH GRAPES

serves 4

1 cup (5½ oz/170 g) blanched almonds

4 small slices day-old rustic-style bread, crusts removed, soaked in water to cover, and squeezed dry

2 cloves garlic

Salt and freshly ground pepper

6 Tbsp (3 fl oz/90 ml) extra-virgin olive oil

3 Tbsp white wine vinegar

3 cups (24 fl oz/750 ml) ice water, or as needed

36 green seedless grapes, peeled and halved

This light-hued gazpacho, as opposed to the familiar tomato-based one, is probably closest to the original version, which was simply bread, water, oil, and vinegar. In southern Spain, the milky almond base is given a refreshing finish with the addition of peeled grapes.

In a food processor or blender, combine the almonds, soaked bread, garlic, and 1 tsp salt and pulse until the almonds are very finely ground. With the motor running, slowly add the oil, vinegar, and 1 cup (8 fl oz/250 ml) of the ice water and process until you have a creamy white liquid. Transfer to a bowl.

Stir in as much of the remaining 2 cups (16 fl oz/500 ml) ice water as needed to achieve the consistency you prefer. Season with salt and pepper. Transfer to a covered container and refrigerate until well chilled, at least 2 hours.

Just before serving, stir in the grapes. Serve.

7 LUMP CRAB IN TOMATO-ROSEMARY BROTH

serves 4

2 lb (1 kg) ripe plum tomatoes, halved

4 Tbsp olive oil

Salt and freshly ground pepper

2 shallots, minced

5 cloves garlic, minced

½ tsp red pepper flakes

½ cup (4 fl oz/125 ml) dry white wine

4 tsp rosemary leaves, chopped

2 cups (16 fl oz/500 ml) chicken broth

1 Tbsp unsalted butter

¼ lb (125 g) fresh lump crabmeat, picked over for shell fragments

Bruschetta (left)

To make bruschetta, brush both sides of 4 thick slices of crusty Italian bread with olive oil and rub with the cut side of a garlic clove. Warm a grill pan over high heat until very hot. Add the bread and grill until toasted with grill marks, about 3 minutes per side.

Preheat the oven to 450°F (230°C). Arrange the tomatoes, cut side up, in a single layer on a baking sheet, drizzle with 2 Tbsp of the oil, and season with salt and pepper. Roast the tomatoes until very soft and caramelized, 25–30 minutes. Set aside.

In a large, heavy pot, warm the remaining 2 Tbsp oil over medium heat. Add the shallots and garlic and sauté for 2 minutes. Add the red pepper flakes and cook for 1 minute. Add the tomatoes with all their juices and the white wine and simmer for 3 minutes. Add the rosemary and broth and bring to a boil. Reduce the heat to low and simmer for 15 minutes. Season with salt and pepper. For a clear broth, strain through a fine-mesh sieve into a medium saucepan set over low heat.

In a small frying pan, melt the butter over high heat until sizzling. Add the crabmeat, stir gently to coat, and heat for 30 seconds.

Ladle the soup into bowls, pile the crabmeat in the middle of each bowl, and serve with pieces of bruschetta alongside.

8 LIMA BEAN, PEA & ZUCCHINI PURÉE WITH PESTO

serves 4

2 Tbsp olive oil

2 small yellow onions, thinly sliced

4 zucchini, thinly sliced

4 cups (32 fl oz/1 l) chicken broth

2 cups (12 oz/375 g) fresh or frozen lima beans

1 cup (5 oz/155 g) fresh or frozen peas

Salt and freshly ground pepper

2 Tbsp sour cream

¼ cup (2 fl oz/60 ml) Basil Pesto (page 118)

The combination of fresh vegetables gives this soup an intense green color as well as a sweet flavor and satisfying texture—all of which becomes even more pleasing with a swirl of sour cream and a dollop of pesto at serving time.

In a large, heavy pot, warm the oil over medium-high heat. Add the onions and zucchini and sauté until they are just turning golden, 6–7 minutes. Add the broth and bring to a boil. Add the lima beans and peas. When the soup returns to a boil, reduce the heat to medium-low and simmer until the vegetables are soft, 20–25 minutes. Stir in ¼ tsp salt and ⅛ tsp pepper. Remove from the heat and let cool slightly.

Working in batches, purée the soup in a blender or food processor until completely smooth. Transfer to a clean pan and reheat gently. Stir in the sour cream.

Serve, topped with pesto.

9

VEGETABLE SOUP WITH ANELLINI

serves 4–6

Anellini, or "little rings" in Italian, resemble just that. Choosing pasta shapes is no exact science, but one way is to match the other elements in the dish: here, the anellini are a good size relative to the diced veggies, and easy to scoop up with an eager soupspoon.

Salt and freshly ground pepper

½ cup (3½ oz/105 g) anellini or other small soup pasta such as tubetti, pastina, orzo, or stelline

6 Tbsp (3 fl oz/90 ml) olive oil

3 leeks, white part only, thinly sliced

1 fennel bulb, stalks and fronds removed, finely diced, plus a handful of feathery fronds, chopped

1 bay leaf

1 Tbsp chopped thyme

2 cloves garlic, crushed

1 cup (6 oz/185 g) fresh corn kernels (from about 2 ears)

2 small zucchini, finely diced

3 large tomatoes, peeled (page 172), seeded, and finely diced

5 drained oil-packed sun-dried tomatoes, finely diced

6 cups (48 fl oz/1.5 l) vegetable broth

Basil Pesto (page 118) for serving

Bring a saucepan of water to a boil. Generously salt the boiling water, add the pasta, and cook until not quite al dente, 6–8 minutes. (It will cook further in the soup.) Drain and toss with 2 Tbsp of the oil. Set aside.

In a large, heavy pot, heat the remaining 4 Tbsp (2 fl oz/60 ml) oil over medium heat. Add the leeks, fennel bulb and fronds, bay leaf, and thyme. Season with salt and pepper and sauté until all the vegetables are fragrant and just starting to soften, about 5 minutes. Add the garlic and sauté for 1 minute. Add the corn and zucchini, season with a bit more salt, and sauté for 2–3 minutes. Add the fresh and sun-dried tomatoes and the broth. Raise the heat to high and bring to a boil. Reduce the heat to medium and cook, uncovered, at a lively simmer until all the vegetables are tender, 15–20 minutes. Skim the surface if necessary to remove any foam. Add the cooked pasta. Taste and adjust the seasoning. Cook briefly just to reheat the pasta.

Serve, garnished with pesto.

10

QUINOA IN LEMON BROTH WITH GREENS & PARMESAN

serves 4

A lemony broth is the perfect base for soups in the spring and summer. The broth brightens the flavor of garden-fresh vegetables and also tastes great with the grains and cheese and bread toppings in this recipe.

6 cups (48 fl oz/1.5 l) chicken or vegetable broth

1 cup (8 oz/250 g) quinoa

1 small bunch lacinato (dinosaur) kale or swiss chard, stems and tough ribs removed, leaves cut crosswise into ribbons

1 bunch green onions, white and green parts, chopped

Salt and freshly ground pepper

½ cup (4 fl oz/125 ml) fresh lemon juice, plus more to taste

Extra-virgin olive oil for drizzling

Parmesan cheese shavings for garnish

Garlic Croutons (page 61)

In a large, heavy pot, bring the broth to a boil over high heat. Stir in the quinoa, reduce the heat to medium-high, and boil, uncovered, until tender, about 15 minutes or according to the package directions.

Stir in the kale, green onions, 1 tsp salt, and a grinding of pepper, and cook until the kale is crisp-tender, about 5 minutes. Stir in the lemon juice and cook for 5 minutes to blend the flavors and warm through.

Season to taste with salt and pepper and more lemon juice, if desired. Serve, drizzled with olive oil and garnished with the cheese shavings and garlic croutons.

11

This German-inspired soup makes a light, pretty first or last course on a hot summer evening. If sour cherries are unavailable, use fresh or frozen Bing cherries and dried cranberries and reduce the amount of honey to 1 tablespoon, or to taste. If you like, garnish with a splash of cream.

SOUR CHERRY–RIESLING SOUP

serves 6

2 cups (16 fl oz/500 ml) dry Riesling wine

2 cups (16 fl oz/500 ml) cherry juice

2¼ lb (1.1 kg) fresh sour cherries, pitted, or 2 lb (1 kg) pitted frozen sour cherries

½ cup (3 oz/90 g) dried sour cherries

1 cinnamon stick, about 2 inches (5 cm) long

¼ cup (3 oz/90 g) honey

¼ cup (2 fl oz/60 ml) fresh orange juice

2 Tbsp cornstarch

1 Tbsp grated orange zest

½ cup (4 oz/125 g) sour cream or plain yogurt

¼ tsp ground cardamom

In a large, heavy pot, combine the wine, cherry juice, half of the fresh or frozen cherries, the dried cherries, and the cinnamon stick and bring to a simmer over medium heat. Reduce the heat to low and cook, uncovered, until the cherries are soft, about 15 minutes. Remove from the heat and remove the cinnamon stick and discard. Let cool slightly.

Working in batches, purée the soup in a blender or food processor until the cherries are finely chopped but retain their texture. Return to the pot.

In a small bowl, stir together the honey, orange juice, cornstarch, and orange zest to make a paste. Whisk the paste into the soup and place over low heat. Cook, stirring occasionally, until thickened, about 5 minutes. Stir in the remaining cherries. Transfer to a covered container and refrigerate until well chilled, at least 2 hours.

In a small bowl, stir together the sour cream and cardamom. Serve, topped with a dollop of the cardamom-spiced cream.

12

For a spicier soup, add another sliced fresh chile and some more red curry paste. Substitute cubes of firm tofu and use vegetable broth for a vegetarian version.

SPICY COCONUT BROTH WITH UDON NOODLES & SHRIMP

serves 4

Salt

5 oz (155 g) udon noodles

1 Tbsp canola oil

2-inch (5-cm) piece fresh ginger, peeled and minced

2 lemongrass stalks, center white part only, smashed and thinly sliced

1 small red chile, seeded and sliced

2 Tbsp red curry paste

2 cans (14 fl oz/440 ml each) light coconut milk

2 cups (16 fl oz/500 ml) chicken broth

½ lb (250 g) medium shrimp, peeled and deveined

2 green onions, white and tender green parts, thinly sliced on the diagonal

Bring a pot of water to a boil. Add ¼ tsp salt and the udon noodles. Cook for 4 minutes, drain, and rinse under cold water. Set aside.

In a large, heavy pot, warm the oil over medium-high heat. Add the ginger, lemongrass, and chile and sauté until soft, about 5 minutes. Add the red curry paste, coconut milk, and broth and whisk to combine. Bring to a boil, reduce the heat to low, and simmer for 10 minutes. Return the soup to a boil, add the shrimp, and cook until bright pink, about 2 minutes. Add the noodles and stir to combine.

Using tongs, divide the noodles among 4 bowls. Ladle the soup over the noodles and serve, garnished with the green onions.

13

The combination of pasta and legumes is perennial throughout Italy, but a steaming pot of Roman pasta e ceci proves the popularity deserved. Chickpeas muddle happily with broken-up pieces of long, flat tagliatelle or fettuccine noodles, but ditalini (thimbles), maltagliati (egg pasta scraps), or quadrucci (pasta squares) would be equally authentic and delicious.

ROMAN CHICKPEA SOUP

serves 4

1½ cups (10½ oz/330 g) dried chickpeas, picked over and rinsed

½ tsp baking soda

1 large clove garlic, unpeeled, plus 2 cloves garlic, minced

1 celery rib with leaves

1 small rosemary sprig

Salt and freshly ground pepper

3 Tbsp extra-virgin olive oil

2 oz (60 g) sliced pancetta, finely diced

2 Tbsp tomato paste

½ lb (250 g) tagliatelle or fettuccine pasta, broken into 2-inch (5-cm) pieces

Place the chickpeas in a bowl with cold water to cover by 3 inches (7.5 cm), and stir in the baking soda. Let stand for 24 hours. Drain and rinse well.

In a large saucepan, combine the rehydrated chickpeas, the unpeeled garlic clove, the celery rib, rosemary sprig, and 7 cups (56 fl oz/1.75 l) water. Bring to a gentle boil over medium-high heat. Adjust the heat to maintain a steady simmer, cover partially, and cook until the chickpeas are tender, about 1½ hours.

When the chickpeas are ready, remove the pan from the heat. Measure out ½ cup (4 fl oz/125 ml) of the broth and set aside. Stir in 2 tsp salt and let the chickpeas stand for 5 minutes. Remove and discard the garlic, celery, and rosemary. Remove 1 cup (7 oz/220 g) of the chickpeas and mash them with a fork or potato masher. Return them to the pot and stir to combine.

In a frying pan, warm the olive oil over medium-low heat. Add the pancetta and sauté until golden brown, about 3 minutes. Stir in the minced garlic, reduce the heat to low, and sauté until the garlic is softened, about 1 minute. Add the tomato paste and the reserved chickpea broth and stir well.

Add the pancetta mixture and pasta to the pot and bring to a gently boil over medium heat. Cook for 10 minutes, or until the pasta is just al dente. Season with salt and pepper and serve.

14

Even kids (and adults) who are suspicious of fish tend to make an exception for firm-fleshed salmon fillets, especially when served over a bowl of tempting buckwheat noodles and broth. Accompany with an Asian-inspired salad, such as cucumbers dressed in sesame.

SOBA NOODLES & SEARED SALMON IN GINGER–GREEN ONION BROTH

serves 4

4 green onions

4 cups (32 fl oz/1 l) chicken broth

2-inch (5-cm) piece fresh ginger, peeled and minced

1 star anise

2 Tbsp soy sauce

1 tsp mirin

A few drops of Asian sesame oil

6 oz (185 g) soba noodles, broken in half

¾ lb (375 g) center-cut salmon, cut into 4 equal pieces, skin and pinbones removed

2 Tbsp olive oil

Salt and freshly ground pepper

Thinly slice the green onions, reserving the white and pale green parts in one bowl and the dark green parts in a separate bowl.

In a large, heavy pot, combine the broth, ginger, the white and pale green slices of the green onions, the star anise, soy sauce, mirin, and sesame oil over medium-high heat. Bring the broth to a boil, reduce the heat to low, and simmer for 10 minutes. Turn the heat off, cover the pan, and let steep for 10 minutes.

Strain the soup, discard the solids, and return the broth to the pot. Bring the broth to a boil. Add the soba noodles and cook, stirring once or twice, for 4 minutes. Keep warm over low heat.

Place a small frying pan over high heat until it is very hot. Brush the salmon with the oil and season with salt and pepper. Sear the salmon to medium-rare, 4–5 minutes per side.

To serve, use tongs to divide the soba noodles among 4 shallow bowls. Ladle the hot broth into each bowl and top with a piece of seared salmon. Garnish with the sliced dark green onions and serve.

15

ROASTED RED PEPPER PURÉE WITH SPICY CORN SALSA

serves 4–6

2 Tbsp olive oil

1 small yellow onion, chopped

2 cloves garlic, minced

1 jar (24 oz/750 g) roasted
red bell peppers, drained

1 russet potato, peeled and diced

4 cups (32 fl oz/1 l) chicken broth

1 Tbsp sour cream

Salt and freshly ground pepper

FOR THE SPICY CORN SALSA

1 Tbsp unsalted butter

1 Tbsp minced jalapeño chile

1 Tbsp thinly sliced green onion,
white and tender green parts

1 cup (6 oz/185 g) fresh corn kernels
(from about 2 ears), or 1 cup frozen corn

Salt and freshly ground pepper

Guests will be stunned by this outrageously colorful soup. The recipe calls for jarred peppers, for convenience, but you can roast your own, substituting 3 fresh peppers. Serve the soup with a simple cheese quesadilla or tortilla chips.

In a large, heavy pot, warm the oil over medium-high heat. Add the onion and garlic and sauté until translucent, about 5 minutes. Add the roasted peppers and potato, stir to coat, and cook for 3 minutes. Add the broth and bring to a boil. Reduce the heat to low and simmer until the potatoes are very tender, 25–30 minutes. Remove from the heat and let cool slightly.

Working in batches, purée the soup in a blender or food processor. Return to the pot, stir in the sour cream, and season with salt and pepper.

Meanwhile, to make the salsa, melt the butter in a small frying pan over high heat. Add the jalapeño and green onion and cook, stirring constantly, until the butter begins to brown, about 2 minutes. Add the corn kernels, stir to combine, and cook for 2 minutes. Season with salt and pepper.

Serve the soup, topped with the corn salsa.

16

ZUCCHINI SOUP WITH PASTA & MINT

serves 6

3 Tbsp olive oil

1 yellow onion, chopped

8 cups (64 fl oz/2 l) chicken broth

3 russet potatoes, peeled and diced

Salt and freshly ground pepper

3 small zucchini, thinly sliced

1 cup (3 oz/90 g) ditalini, tubetti,
or other small soup pasta

2 Tbsp chopped mint

⅓ cup (1½ oz/45 g) grated
pecorino romano cheese

This simple summertime soup contains a few fresh gratings of nutmeg, which brings out the flavor of most green vegetables. It's worth it to salt and drain the shredded zucchini, as the step removes a light edge of bitterness. Don't worry about the salt: most of it washes away in the squeezing and rinsing.

In a large, heavy pot, warm the oil over medium heat. Add the onion and sauté until tender, about 5 minutes. Add the broth and potatoes and season with salt and pepper. Bring to a simmer, add the zucchini, and cook until the vegetables soften, about 10 minutes. Add the pasta and cook, stirring frequently, until al dente, 8–10 minutes or according to the package directions. Stir in the mint.

Serve, sprinkled with the cheese.

17

ROASTED BEET PURÉE WITH FETA

serves 4

This soup couldn't be simpler, but it delivers big color and flavor. Roasting beets concentrates their natural sweetness, and salty feta is a perfect complement.

3 large red or yellow beets, trimmed, leaving 1 inch (2.5 cm) of stem

1½ Tbsp olive oil

1 Tbsp unsalted butter

¼ yellow onion, chopped

4 cups (32 fl oz/1 l) chicken, beef, or vegetable broth

Salt and freshly ground pepper

½ cup (2½ oz/75 g) crumbled feta cheese

2 Tbsp coarsely chopped dill

Preheat the oven to 350°F (180°C). Put the beets in a baking dish and drizzle with the oil, turning to coat. Roast until the beets are easily pierced with a fork, about 1 hour. Remove from the oven. When the beets are cool enough to handle, peel and coarsely chop them.

In a large, heavy pot, melt the butter over medium heat. Add the onion and sauté until translucent, about 2 minutes. Add the beets and broth, bring to a simmer, reduce the heat to low, and cook, uncovered, for 10 minutes. Remove from the heat and let cool slightly.

Working in batches, purée the soup in a blender or food processor. Serve warm or let cool to room temperature, transfer to a covered container, and refrigerate until chilled, at least 2 hours or up to overnight. Season with salt and pepper and serve, garnished with the feta and dill.

18

CURRIED CHICKPEA STEW

serves 4

Grinding garlic, ginger, and chile together is the first step in many Indian recipes. The resulting paste should be sautéed in a little oil to release maximum flavor before more liquids are added into the mix. Here, hearty chickpeas and potatoes form a flavorful vegetarian stew, thick enough to be served over steamed rice.

1 yellow onion, coarsely chopped

2 Tbsp peeled and minced fresh ginger

4 cloves garlic, chopped

1 small red or green jalapeño chile, seeded and chopped

1½ Tbsp curry powder

Salt and freshly ground pepper

4 Tbsp (2 fl oz/60 ml) corn or peanut oil

2 large boiling potatoes, peeled and cut into small cubes

½ lb (250 g) fresh or frozen okra, trimmed and thickly sliced (optional)

1½ cups (12 fl oz/375 ml) chicken or vegetable broth

1 can (14½ oz/455 g) chickpeas, drained

Steamed rice for serving

In a blender, combine 1 Tbsp water with the onion, ginger, garlic, and chile and process until a paste forms. In a small bowl, stir together the curry powder and ½ tsp salt.

Heat a large frying pan over high heat until very hot and add 2 Tbsp of the oil. Add the potatoes and sauté until lightly browned, about 5 minutes. Season with ¼ tsp salt and, using a slotted spoon, transfer to a bowl. Return the pan to high heat and add 1 Tbsp of the oil. Add the okra, if using, and sauté until slightly crisp, about 5 minutes. Using the slotted spoon, transfer the okra to the bowl with the potatoes.

Return the pan to medium-high heat and add the remaining 1 Tbsp oil. Add the onion-garlic paste and fry until fragrant, about 2 minutes. Stir in the curry powder mixture and broth, mix well, and bring to a boil. Return the vegetables to the pan and add the chickpeas. Reduce the heat to low and cook, uncovered, until the potatoes are tender, 15–20 minutes. Season with salt and pepper and serve, ladled over the steamed rice.

19

The large poblano chile is extremely versatile. It can be stuffed, cut into rajas (strips), which are used in a variety of ways, or made into this simple, yet elegant traditional soup. The cream sweetens the rich spice of the chiles, and the peas lend a brighter green hue.

CREAMY POBLANO CHILE SOUP

serves 4–6

¼ cup (2 oz/60 g) unsalted butter

1 tsp canola oil

4 poblano chiles, roasted, peeled, seeded, and chopped

1 white onion, chopped

3 cloves garlic, chopped

6 cups (48 fl oz/1.5 l) chicken broth

1 cup (5 oz/155 g) fresh or frozen peas

Salt and freshly ground pepper

½ cup (2½ oz/75 g) blanched almonds, finely ground

5 Tbsp (2½ fl oz/75 ml) crema or sour cream

In a large, heavy pot, melt the butter with the oil over medium heat. Stir in the chiles, onion, and garlic and sauté, stirring, until well softened, about 3 minutes. Add the broth and peas and season with salt and pepper. Simmer, uncovered, for about 10 minutes to blend the flavors. Remove from the heat and let cool slightly.

Working in batches, purée the soup with the ground almonds in a blender. Taste and adjust the seasoning. Return to the pot and reheat the soup gently over medium heat.

Serve, garnished with the crema.

20

Long summer days coax the sweetest flavor from melons. Green-fleshed honeydew makes a pretty purée, but Casaba, Crenshaw, Persian, or other cantaloupe melons can be substituted with equally pleasing results. With a squeeze of lime and a lift from mint, this makes a simple and refreshing starter for a grilled dinner.

COOL HONEYDEW-MINT SOUP

serves 6

½ large honeydew melon (about 2 lb/1 kg), seeded, peeled, and chopped

¼ cup (¼ oz/7 g) loosely packed mint leaves, plus mint sprigs for garnish

3 Tbsp fresh lime juice, plus more as needed

1 Tbsp honey

Salt

Paper-thin lime slices for garnish

Working in batches, place the melon, mint leaves, 3 Tbsp lime juice, and honey in a blender. Purée on high speed until smooth and light, about 2 minutes for each batch. Transfer to a covered container and refrigerate until chilled, at least 2 hours.

Before serving, season with more lime juice, if needed, and salt. Serve, garnished with lime slices and mint sprigs.

21

STRAWBERRY-RHUBARB SOUP WITH PROSECCO

serves 4

¾ lb (375 g) rhubarb, thinly sliced

1 lb (500 g) strawberries, hulled and halved

2 Tbsp fresh orange juice

½ cup (4 oz/125 g) sugar

½ cup Prosecco or other dry, sparkling wine

Sweet strawberries and tart rhubarb combine in this party-friendly starter. When using sparkling wine in soups, add it at the last moment to prevent the bubbles from going flat. You can serve this garnished with tiny diced strawberries, or a sprig of mint.

Put the rhubarb and ½ cup (4 fl oz/125 ml) water in a large saucepan over medium heat. Cook, stirring often, for 10 minutes. Add the strawberries, orange juice, and sugar. Stir to combine and cook for 5 minutes. Remove from the heat and let cool slightly.

Purée the soup in blender. Allow to cool to room temperature. Transfer to a covered container and refrigerate until chilled, at least 3 hours or up to overnight. Just before serving, stir in the Prosecco and serve.

22

CHEESE & ARUGULA RAVIOLI SOUP

serves 4

FOR THE RAVIOLI

1 tsp olive oil

½ cup (½ oz/15 g) arugula

⅓ cup (3 oz/90 g) ricotta cheese

2 Tbsp grated Parmesan cheese

Pinch of grated nutmeg

Salt and freshly ground pepper

20 wonton wrappers

2 Tbsp olive oil

2 shallots, thinly sliced

4 cloves garlic, thinly sliced

4 cups (32 fl oz/1 l) chicken broth

1 can (14½ oz/455 g) diced tomatoes

1 Tbsp tomato paste

Salt and freshly ground pepper

1 cup (1 oz/30 g) arugula

¼ cup (⅓ oz/10 g) chopped basil

Grated Parmesan cheese for garnish

This soup is best eaten fresh, as the delicate ravioli may threaten to come apart with reheating. Feel free to vary the ravioli filling according to your likes; goat cheese and pancetta, or artichoke, garlic, and ricotta, for instance, could be equally delicious.

To make the ravioli, warm the oil in a small frying pan over medium heat. Add the arugula and sauté until wilted, 1 minute. Transfer the arugula to a cutting board, let cool slightly, and finely chop.

In a small bowl, combine the ricotta, Parmesan, nutmeg, and chopped arugula and season with salt and pepper. Place 1 tsp of the cheese mixture in the middle of each wonton wrapper. Moisten all sides of a wrapper with water and fold the wrapper diagonally, forcing out air bubbles as you press to seal. Repeat for all the ravioli.

To make the soup, in a large, heavy pot, warm the oil over medium-high heat. Add the shallots and garlic and cook until soft, about 4 minutes. Add the broth, tomatoes, and tomato paste and bring to a boil. Reduce the heat to low and simmer for 10 minutes. Season with salt and pepper.

Return the soup to a gentle boil. Carefully add the ravioli and cook for about 2 minutes. Add the arugula and basil and cook just until the greens are wilted, about 1 minute. Serve, passing Parmesan at the table.

JUNE

23

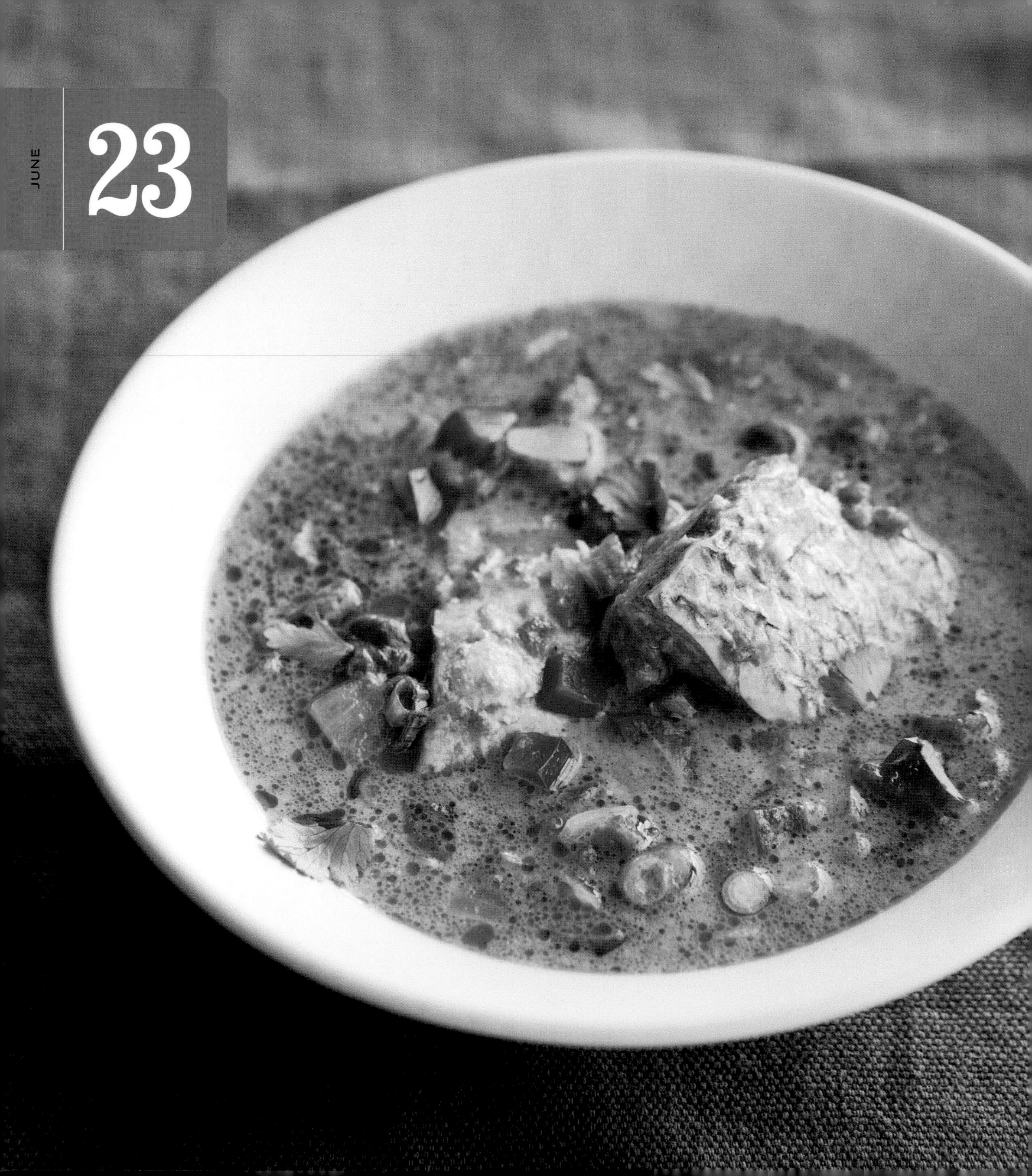

23

BRAZILIAN FISH STEW

serves 4

1 can (14½ oz/455 g) diced tomatoes

1 white onion, chopped

2 cloves garlic, minced

1 bay leaf

2 limes, 1 juiced and 1 cut into wedges

1 lb (500 g) red snapper, cut into 2-inch (5-cm) pieces

2 Tbsp olive oil

1 small red bell pepper, seeded and diced

1 can (14 fl oz/440 ml) coconut milk

1 cup (8 fl oz/250 ml) chicken broth

1 cup (8 fl oz/250 ml) bottled clam juice

3 green onions, white and tender green parts, chopped

2 Tbsp cilantro, minced

Hot sauce, such as Tabasco

Salt and freshly ground pepper

Moqueca is a traditional Brazilian fish stew that varies from region to region. This version includes tomatoes, peppers, plenty of seasoning, and a dose of creamy coconut milk. Feel free to replace the red snapper with whichever firm white fish looks freshest that day at the market.

In a bowl, combine the tomatoes, onion, garlic, bay leaf, and the juice of 1 lime. Add the fish to the bowl and gently spoon the marinade over to cover the fish. Cover the bowl and refrigerate for 1 hour.

Remove the fish from the bowl, brushing off the marinade, and set aside. In a large, heavy pot, warm the oil over medium-high heat. Add all of the marinade and the bell pepper to the pot and sauté until the vegetables are very soft, 8–10 minutes. Add the coconut milk, broth, and clam juice and bring to a boil. Reduce the heat to low and add the fish. Cook until the fish begins to flake, 4–5 minutes. Gently stir in the green onions and cilantro. Season with a few drops of hot sauce and salt and pepper. Serve, passing the lime wedges at the table.

24

THREE-POTATO CHOWDER WITH CORN, CILANTRO & LIME

serves 4–6

2 Tbsp canola oil

1 yellow onion, chopped

6 green onions, white and tender green parts, chopped

2 cloves garlic, minced

2 russet potatoes, about 1 lb (500 g) total, peeled and cubed

1 garnet yam or sweet potato, about ½ lb (250 g), peeled and cubed

2 Yellow Finn potatoes, about 1 lb (500 g) total, peeled and cubed

8 cups (64 fl oz/2 l) chicken broth

½ cup (¾ oz/20 g) chopped cilantro

Salt and freshly ground pepper

1½ cups (9 oz/280 g) corn kernels (from about 3 ears)

1 cup (8 fl oz/250 ml) milk or heavy cream

1 avocado

2 Tbsp fresh lime juice

Who says chowder only means clams? Inspired by Colombian ajiaco, this filling soup has an appealing variety of textures. Three types of potatoes— waxy Finns, starchy russets, and garnet yams—join sweet summer corn in this satisfying and memorable chowder.

In a large, heavy pot, warm the oil over medium-high heat. Add the yellow and green onions and sauté until softened, about 5 minutes. Stir in the garlic and the russet potatoes, yam, and Yellow Finn potatoes. Pour in the broth and add half of the cilantro. Bring to a boil, reduce the heat to low, and simmer, uncovered, until the potatoes are soft and the flavors are blended, about 20 minutes. Season with salt and pepper.

Add the corn and the milk to the pot. Simmer until the corn is tender, about 5 minutes; do not allow to boil. If you like, mash some of the potatoes with a fork to thicken the soup.

Meanwhile pit, peel, and chop the avocado. Toss the avocado pieces with the lime juice.

Stir the remaining cilantro into the soup and serve, topped with the avocado.

25

RAMEN NOODLES WITH EDAMAME & MUSHROOMS

serves 6

4 cups (32 fl oz/1 l) chicken broth

¼ cup (2 fl oz/60 ml) soy sauce

3 Tbsp ketchup

⅛ tsp hot chile oil

9 oz (280 g) ramen noodles

½ lb (250 g) Chinese mushrooms, thinly sliced

½ cup (2½ oz/75 g) cooked and shelled edamame

4 green onions, white and tender green parts, chopped

Hot sauce, such as Sriracha, for serving (optional)

Packaged versions can't compare with the freshness of this simple noodle soup, which really couldn't be easier to assemble. You can use any vegetables you have on hand. Chinese mushrooms include shiitake, enoki, and straw varieties, but even white mushrooms will be delicious.

In a large, heavy pot, bring the broth, 2 cups (16 fl oz/500 ml) water, the soy sauce, ketchup, and chile oil to a boil over medium-high heat. Add the ramen noodles, mushrooms, and edamame. Reduce the heat to medium-low and simmer for 5 minutes. Stir in the green onions.

Serve, passing the hot sauce, if using, at the table.

26

CUBAN BLACK BEAN SOUP

serves 6

2 cups (14 oz/440 g) dried black beans, picked over and rinsed

2 bay leaves

FOR THE SOFRITO

¾ cup (6 fl oz/180 ml) olive oil

2 red bell peppers, seeded and chopped

2 large white onions, chopped

8 cloves garlic, chopped

2 Tbsp dried oregano

1½ Tbsp ground cumin

Salt

1 Tbsp sugar

1 Tbsp sherry vinegar, plus more as needed

2 Tbsp dry sherry, plus more as needed

1 red onion, finely diced for garnish

½ cup (½ oz/15 g) cilantro leaves for garnish

Cuban restaurants have long been ladling out bowls of thick, rich black bean soup. Integral to the soup is the sofrito, a flavorful mixture of onions, garlic, bell peppers, chiles, herbs, and spices. Here, it is puréed and stirred directly into the beans.

Put the dried beans in a bowl with cold water to cover and soak for at least 4 hours or up to overnight. Drain the beans and put them in a large, heavy pot. Add the bay leaves and 4 quarts (4 l) water. Bring to a boil over high heat, reduce the heat to low, and simmer, stirring occasionally and adding more water as needed to cover, until the beans are tender, about 2 hours.

Meanwhile, to make the sofrito, in a large frying pan, warm the oil over medium heat. Add the bell peppers and sauté until they begin to soften, about 5 minutes. Add the white onions and sauté until tender and translucent, 10–12 minutes. Add the garlic, oregano, cumin, and 1½ Tbsp salt and sauté until the garlic is fragrant, about 2 minutes. Remove from the heat, let cool slightly, and discard the bay leaves. Working in batches, purée the mixture in a blender or food processor, 2–3 minutes per batch.

Stir the sofrito and sugar into the beans and simmer for 20–30 minutes to blend the flavors. Stir in the 1 Tbsp vinegar and 2 Tbsp sherry. Taste the soup and adjust the seasoning with vinegar, sherry, and salt. Serve, garnished with the red onion and cilantro.

27

This soup is sweet from the yellow bell peppers and carrots, but packed with a spicy punch from fresh ginger. Serve with toasted peasant bread topped with melted cheese and thinly sliced prosciutto.

CHILLED YELLOW PEPPER SOUP WITH CHIVES

serves 4

2 Tbsp olive oil

2 cloves garlic, minced

½ yellow onion, chopped

1 small carrot, peeled and thinly sliced

1 Tbsp peeled and minced fresh ginger

3 yellow bell peppers, roasted, peeled, seeded, and chopped

1 cup (8 fl oz/250 ml) chicken broth

1 Tbsp heavy cream

Salt and freshly ground pepper

2 Tbsp chopped chives

In a large, heavy pot, warm the oil over medium-high heat. Add the garlic, onion, and carrot and sauté until the carrot begins to soften, 5–7 minutes. Add the ginger and bell pepper and cook for 3 minutes, stirring often. Add the broth and bring to a boil. Reduce the heat to low and simmer for 25 minutes. Remove from the heat and let cool slightly.

Working in batches, purée the soup in a blender. Return to the saucepan, add the cream, and bring just to a boil. Remove from the heat, season with salt and pepper, and let the soup cool completely.

Transfer to a covered container and refrigerate until well chilled, at least 3 hours or up to overnight. Serve, garnished with chives.

28

This is a very sweet soup, but the intensity of summer melons is cut with salty crumbled prosciutto, their well-loved sidekick on the antipasti plate. The ham adds a savory note, and a dollop of creamy mascarpone rounds out the flavors.

MELON & PROSCIUTTO SOUP WITH MASCARPONE CHEESE

serves 4–6

2 oz (60 g) prosciutto, thinly sliced

1 very ripe cantaloupe, peeled and cut into chunks

2 Tbsp Champagne vinegar

Salt and freshly ground pepper

¼ cup (2 oz/60 g) mascarpone cheese

1 lime, cut into wedges, for serving

In a small frying pan, cook the prosciutto over medium-high heat, turning once, until very crisp, about 10 minutes. Transfer to paper towels to drain. Let cool, then crumble.

Put the cantaloupe chunks in a food processor and pulse until puréed. Add the vinegar and pulse 3 more times. Season with salt and pepper. Transfer to a covered container and refrigerate until well chilled, at least 3 hours.

Serve, topped with a dollop of the mascarpone, the crumbled prosciutto, and a squeeze of lime.

29

Usually served chilled, this Latin American soup is also delicious at room temperature. The zesty tomato salsa provides a lively contrast to the rich and creamy flavor of the avocado. Chopped grapefruit segments or tropical fruits could substitute for the tomatoes.

AVOCADO SOUP WITH SHRIMP & SALSA

serves 6–8

3 large avocados, peeled, pitted, and coarsely chopped

3 cups (24 fl oz/750 ml) chicken broth

1 cup (8 fl oz/250 ml) heavy cream

2 Tbsp fresh lemon juice

Salt and freshly ground pepper

FOR THE SALSA

3 tomatoes (about 1 lb/500 g), finely chopped

1 small red onion, minced

2 or 3 jalapeño chiles, minced

2 cloves garlic, minced

3 Tbsp fresh lemon or lime juice

¼ cup (⅓ oz/10 g) chopped cilantro

¼ cup (2 fl oz/60 ml) olive oil

12–16 cooked shrimp, peeled and diced

Working in batches, purée the avocados, broth, and cream in a blender. Transfer to a bowl. Add the lemon juice and season with salt and pepper. Cover and refrigerate until cold but not overly chilled, about 1 hour.

Meanwhile, to make the salsa, stir together the tomatoes, onion, chiles, garlic, lemon juice, cilantro, and oil. Season with salt and pepper.

Serve the soup, topped with the shrimp and garnished with the salsa.

30

To make pistou, in a blender, combine 3–4 cloves garlic, ¼ teaspoon coarse sea salt, 1 cup (1 oz/ 30 g) basil leaves and process until a paste forms. With the motor running, add ⅓ cup (3 fl oz/ 80 ml) extra-virgin olive oil in a slow, steady stream, processing until the mixture is thick and green. Refrigerate in an airtight container for up to 5 days. Makes ½ cup (4 fl oz/125 ml).

PROVENÇAL MINESTRONE

serves 4–6

2 cups (16 fl oz/500 ml) chicken broth

3 small boiling potatoes, peeled and diced

2 carrots, peeled and diced

1 tsp fresh thyme leaves, or ½ tsp dried

1 tsp minced fresh winter savory, or ½ tsp dried

Salt and freshly ground pepper

1 large zucchini, diced

1 small yellow onion, diced

½ lb (250 g) young, slender green beans, trimmed and cut into 1-inch (2.5-cm) pieces

1 lb (500 g) fresh cranberry beans in the pod, shelled, or 1 cup (7 oz/220 g) canned butter beans

½ cup (3 oz/90 g) spaghetti broken into 2-inch (5-cm) pieces

Pistou (left)

In a large, heavy pot, bring the broth and 6 cups (48 fl oz/1.5 l) water to a boil over medium-high heat. Add the potatoes, carrots, thyme, winter savory, 2 tsp salt, and ½ tsp pepper. Reduce the heat to medium and cook until the carrots are tender when pierced with a fork, about 20 minutes.

Add the zucchini, onion, green beans, and shelling beans and cook until the shelling beans are tender to the bite, 15–20 minutes.

Add the spaghetti and cook until al dente, 10–11 minutes, or according to the package directions. Taste and adjust the seasoning. Stir 2 Tbsp of the pistou into the soup.

Ladle the soup into bowls and serve, passing the remaining pistou at the table.

1
CHILLED CUCUMBER-YOGURT
SOUP WITH LEMON & MINT
page 154

2
SIMPLE ZUCCHINI SOUP
page 154

3
SPICY CORN SOUP
page 156

4
MEDITERRANEAN FISH STEW
page 156

8
CHILLED RED PEPPER & FENNEL
SOUP WITH INDIAN SPICES
page 159

9
CUCUMBER & GREEN
GRAPE GAZPACHO
page 160

10
SILKEN LIMA BEAN SOUP
WITH HAM CROÔTES
page 160

11
CORN & ZUCCHINI SOUP
WITH CRUMBLED BACON
page 161

15
MUSSEL CHOWDER
page 165

16
CHUNKY HEIRLOOM
TOMATO & BASIL SOUP
page 165

17
TOM YUM WITH SHRIMP
page 166

18
MEXICAN LIME SOUP WITH CHICKEN
page 166

22
TWO MELON SOUPS
page 168

23
SUMMER PANZANELLA
SOUP WITH TINY PASTA
page 171

24
CHICKEN SOUP WITH GNOCCHI,
BASIL & PARMESAN
page 171

25
GAZPACHO
page 172

29
NOODLE SOUP WITH
LEMONGRASS & TOFU
page 173

30
SWEET PEA DUMPLINGS IN
GINGERY GREEN ONION BROTH
page 174

31
VIETNAMESE TURKEY MEATBALLS
IN BROTH WITH RED ONION & HERBS
page 174

5
SOBA NOODLE SOUP
page 157

6
ROASTED EGGPLANT
SOUP WITH MINT
page 157

7
PINTO BEAN SOUP WITH
TOASTED JALAPEÑOS
page 159

12
CALAMARI STEW
page 161

13
ROASTED RED PEPPER SOUP
WITH GOAT CHEESE & HARISSA
page 162

14
MISO SOUP WITH BLACK COD
& GREEN ONIONS
page 162

19
BURMESE CHICKEN CURRY SOUP
page 167

20
TORTELLINI IN BROTH
page 167

21
CHIPOTLE-CORN PURÉE WITH
BAY SHRIMP & AVOCADO SALSA
page 168

26
ROASTED CHILE & CORN SOUP
WITH FARMER'S CHEESE
page 172

27
ROASTED NECTARINE
SOUP WITH MINT
page 173

28
CRAB & AVOCADO SOUP
page 173

July's warming sun ripens tomatoes on the vine, whose sweet flavor is showcased in light, brothy soups with herbs and pastina, grains, or meats added for heartiness. Toasted chiles enliven summer corn and beans, offering fire that mimics the summer heat. Chilled soups made from fresh fruits and vegetables, enhanced with sparkling wine, vibrant mint, or bracing vinegar, are perfect to begin an alfresco brunch or a backyard barbecue.

july

1

CHILLED CUCUMBER-YOGURT SOUP WITH LEMON & MINT

serves 8–10

6 large English cucumbers (about 5 lb/2.5 kg), peeled and seeded

8 Tbsp (¾ oz/20 g) minced mint

4 Tbsp (2 fl oz/60 ml) extra-virgin olive oil

Zest and juice of 1 large lemon

4 cups (32 fl oz/1 l) chicken broth

4 cups (2 lb/1 kg) plain yogurt

2 small cloves garlic, minced

Salt and freshly ground pepper

Serve this soup as a refreshing starter before a Mediterranean-inspired dinner of grilled cumin-spiced lamb and herbed couscous.

Finely chop 1 cucumber. Place half of the pieces between layers of paper towels, pressing to absorb excess moisture. Transfer to a small bowl, add 2 Tbsp of the mint and 1 Tbsp of the oil, and toss to combine. Cover and refrigerate. Cut the remaining 5 cucumbers into large chunks.

Working in batches, coarsely purée the cucumber chunks, the remaining mint, the lemon zest, and 2 cups (16 fl oz/500 ml) of the broth in a food processor or blender. Transfer to a large nonreactive bowl. Add the remaining 2 cups broth along with the finely chopped cucumber and mint mixture, the remaining 3 Tbsp oil, the lemon juice, the yogurt, and the garlic. Add 1½ tsp salt and season with pepper. Stir to blend well, cover, and refrigerate until well chilled, at least 4 hours or up to 12 hours. Serve.

2

SIMPLE ZUCCHINI SOUP

serves 4

1½–2 lb (750 g–1 kg) small zucchini, shredded

Salt and freshly ground pepper

2 Tbsp unsalted butter

2 yellow onions, chopped

2 cups (16 fl oz/500 ml) chicken broth

Grated nutmeg

2 tsp finely chopped mint

3 cups (24 fl oz/750 ml) milk

½ tsp fresh lemon juice

4 thin lemon slices

It's worth it to salt and drain the shredded zucchini to remove a light edge of bitterness. Don't worry about the salt: most of it washes away in the squeezing and rinsing.

Layer half of the zucchini in a colander set over a bowl. Sprinkle with salt, then top with the remaining zucchini and again sprinkle with salt. Let drain for 25–30 minutes. Pick up the drained zucchini by small handfuls and squeeze out the released juice. Return the zucchini to the colander and rinse quickly under cold running water to remove the salt. Again squeeze out the moisture, then set aside.

In a large, heavy pot, melt the butter over medium-low heat. Add the onions and sauté until translucent, 3–4 minutes. Add the broth, cover, and simmer until the onions are tender, 15–20 minutes. Remove from the heat and let cool slightly.

Working in batches, purée the mixture in a blender. Return to the pot. Add the zucchini, a pinch of nutmeg, and 1 tsp of the mint. Bring to a simmer, cover, and simmer for 6–8 minutes. Add the milk and lemon juice, and season with salt and pepper. Heat until the soup is very hot, but do not let boil. Serve, sprinkled with the remaining mint and garnished with the lemon slices.

SPICY CORN SOUP

serves 4

3 slices bacon, chopped

1 small yellow onion, chopped

1 celery rib, chopped

1 poblano chile, seeded and chopped

2 cloves garlic, minced

4 cups (32 fl oz/1 l) milk

1 cup (8 fl oz/250 ml) heavy cream

2 boiling potatoes, peeled and cut into bite-sized cubes

3 cups (18 oz/560 g) fresh corn kernels from about 6 ears) or 3 cups frozen

½ tsp red pepper flakes

Salt and freshly ground black pepper

Sweet meets heat in this reinvented chowder. The traditional creamy base gets a kick with the addition of both fresh and dried chile. Make it in high summer, when fresh corn kernels need only a brief simmer in the pot, emerging sweet and tender.

In a large, heavy pot, sauté the bacon over medium heat until it begins to crisp, about 5 minutes. Transfer to paper towels to drain. Add the onion, celery, chile, and garlic and sauté just until lightly browned, 6–7 minutes.

Raise the heat to medium-high, add the milk, cream, and potatoes, and bring to a boil. Reduce the heat to low and simmer, uncovered, until the potatoes are tender, about 15 minutes. Stir in the corn and red pepper flakes and simmer until the corn is tender, about 5 minutes. Remove from the heat and let cool slightly.

Purée about 2 cups (16 fl oz/500 ml) of the solids in a blender or food processor. Return to the pot and reheat. Season with salt and pepper and serve, garnished with the bacon.

MEDITERRANEAN FISH STEW

serves 6

¼ cup (2 fl oz/60 ml) olive oil

½ small yellow onion, finely chopped

1 celery rib including leaves, chopped

1 carrot, peeled and chopped

3 cloves garlic, minced

1 tsp dried thyme

½ tsp red pepper flakes

2 oil-packed anchovies

1 cup (8 fl oz/250 ml) dry white wine

1 can (14½ oz/455 g) diced tomatoes

4 cups (32 fl oz/1 l) fish broth

Pinch of saffron threads dissolved in 1 Tbsp hot water

1 bay leaf

1 rosemary sprig

2 lb (1 kg) firm white-fleshed fish fillets, cut into bite-sized pieces

12 littleneck or Manila clams, scrubbed

12 mussels, scrubbed and debearded

¾ lb (375 g) large shrimp, peeled and deveined

Salt

3 Tbsp minced flat-leaf parsley

Pungent garlic and sunny saffron define the Mediterranean mood of this shellfish-rich stew, which features a trio of clams, mussels, and prawns. Serve with warm, crusty bread, and lemon wedges for squeezing into the broth.

In a large, heavy pot, warm the oil over medium heat. Add the onion, celery, and carrot and sauté until the onion is translucent, 3–5 minutes. Add the garlic, thyme, red pepper flakes, and anchovies and sauté until the mixture is fragrant and the anchovies have melted, about 3 minutes. Add the wine and simmer until reduced by half, about 10 minutes. Add the tomatoes with their juices, broth, saffron mixture, bay leaf, and rosemary sprig. Pour in 1 cup (8 fl oz/250 ml) water. Reduce the heat to medium-low and simmer for 15 minutes.

Add the fish, cover, and simmer just until opaque, about 2 minutes. Add the clams, cover, and simmer until most of them open, about 6 minutes. Add the mussels, cover, and cook until they open, 3–4 minutes. Discard any unopened clams or mussels. Add the shrimp and cook, uncovered, just until pink, about 2 minutes. Remove from the heat and season with salt. Discard the bay leaf. Serve, garnished with the parsley.

5

This simple soup features wheat noodles and slices of pork, seasoned with the classic Asian trio of garlic, ginger, and soy. To slice the pork, place the chops in the freezer for half an hour. Firmed, the meat will be much easier to slice very thinly.

SOBA NOODLE SOUP

serves 4

2 Tbsp canola oil

2 boneless pork loin chops, cut into slices ¼ inch (6 mm) thick

1 Tbsp peeled and grated ginger

2 cloves garlic, thinly sliced

¼ yellow onion, finely chopped

1 Tbsp soy sauce

6 cups (48 fl oz/1.5 l) chicken broth

½ lb (250 g) soba noodles

4 white mushrooms, sliced

4 green onions, white and tender pale green parts, sliced

Salt and freshly ground pepper

In a small frying pan, warm the oil over medium heat. Add the pork and sauté until golden brown, about 4 minutes. Add the ginger, garlic, yellow onion, and soy sauce and sauté until the onion is translucent, about 2 minutes. Remove from the heat.

In a large, heavy pot, bring the broth to a boil over medium-high heat. Add the soba, stir to separate the noodles, and cook just until tender, about 5 minutes. Add the pork mixture, mushrooms, and green onions and cook for 1 minute to heat through. Season with salt and pepper and serve.

6

Roasted eggplant has an earthy, slightly smoky flavor that this simple soup highlights. For an edge of sweetness, swirl some roasted red bell pepper purée into each serving. The soup may also be served chilled.

ROASTED EGGPLANT SOUP WITH MINT

serves 4–6

1½ lb (750 g) small or medium eggplants

2 Tbsp unsalted butter

1 small yellow onion, finely chopped

1 clove garlic, finely chopped

2½ cups (20 fl oz/625 ml) vegetable broth

½ Tbsp finely chopped mint

1 cup (8 fl oz/250 ml) heavy cream

Salt and ground white pepper

Mint sprigs for garnish

Preheat the oven to 375°F (190°C).

Put the eggplants in a baking dish and pierce several times with a fork. Roast, turning occasionally, until the skins are evenly browned and deeply wrinkled, 1–1½ hours. Let cool, then peel.

In a large, heavy pot, melt the butter over medium heat. Add the onion and garlic and sauté until golden, 3–5 minutes. Add the eggplants, breaking them up with a wooden spoon, and sauté for 2–3 minutes. Add the broth and chopped mint, and bring to a boil. Reduce the heat to low, cover, and simmer for about 20 minutes. Remove from the heat and let cool slightly.

Working in batches, purée the soup in a blender. Return to the pot, stir in the cream, and reheat gently over medium-low heat. Season with salt and pepper. Serve, garnished with the mint sprigs.

JULY

7

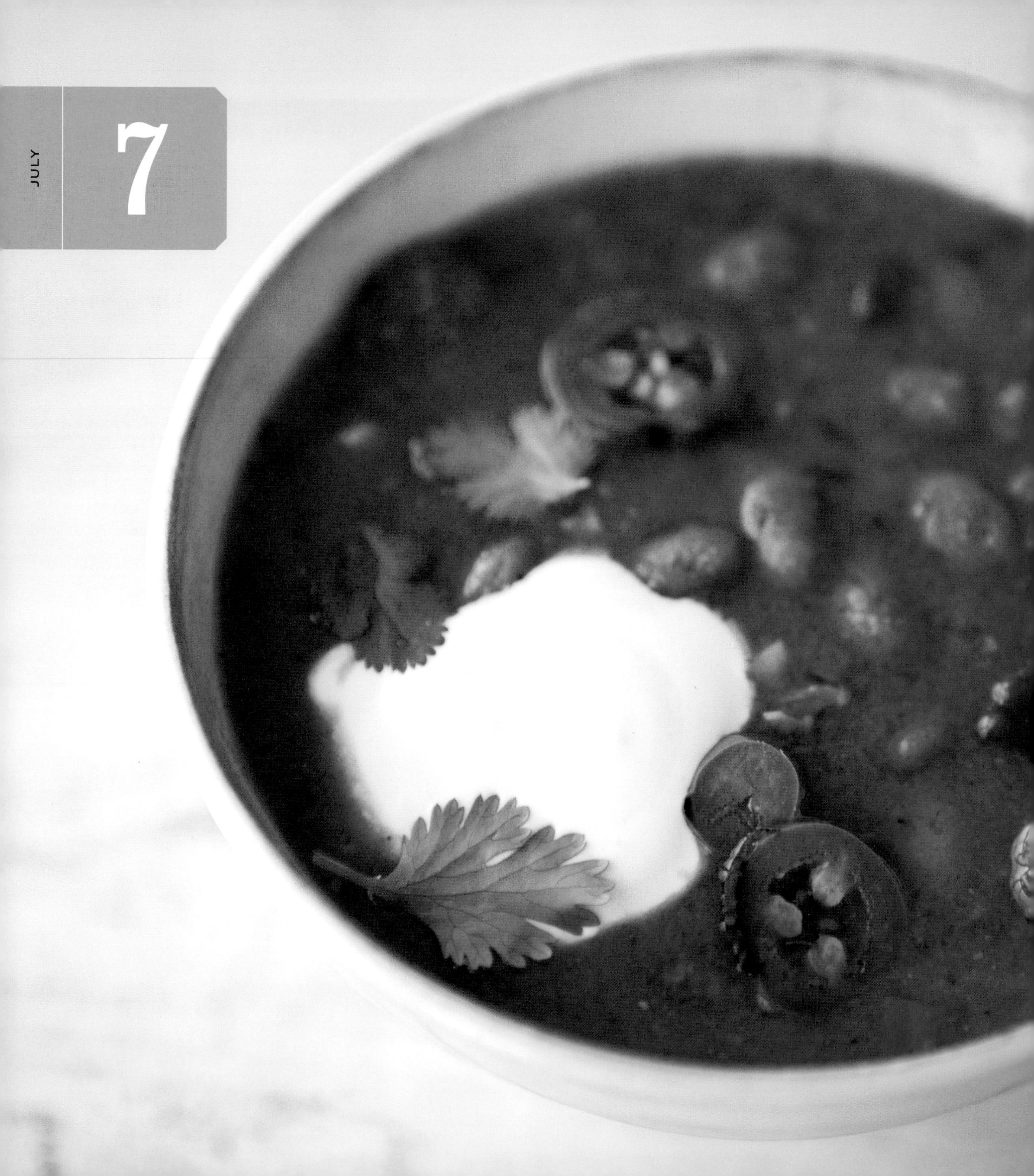

7

PINTO BEAN SOUP WITH TOASTED JALAPEÑOS

serves 6–8

6 cups (48 fl oz/1.5 l) chicken broth

1 smoked ham hock

6 jalapeño chiles

4 cloves garlic

2 Tbsp olive oil

2 yellow onions, finely chopped

2 carrots, peeled and finely chopped

1½ tsp dried oregano

1½ tsp ground cumin

¾ tsp ground coriander

¾ tsp chili powder

1 can (14½ oz/455 g) diced tomatoes

2 cans (14½ oz/455 g each) pinto beans, drained

¼ cup (2 fl oz/60 ml) fresh lime juice

Salt and freshly ground pepper

1 cup (8 oz/250 g) sour cream

⅓ cup (⅓ oz/10 g) cilantro leaves

Toasting fresh chiles and garlic on the stove top until they're charred and blistered deepens and mellows their strong flavors, coaxing out a subtle sweetness and adding a suggestion of smokiness to dishes like this soup.

In a large saucepan, bring the broth and ham hock to a boil over medium-high heat. Reduce the heat to low, cover, and simmer until fragrant, 1 hour. Discard the ham hock.

Meanwhile, in a small frying pan, toast the jalapeños and garlic over medium heat, tossing occasionally, until lightly charred, about 15 minutes. Let cool. Seed and mince 4 of the chiles. Cut the remaining 2 chiles into thin rings. Mince the garlic.

In a large, heavy pot, warm the oil over medium heat. Add the onions and carrots and sauté until softened, about 6 minutes. Stir in the minced chiles, garlic, oregano, cumin, coriander, and chili powder and sauté until fragrant, about 2 minutes. Add the ham broth, tomatoes with their juices, and beans. Bring to a boil, reduce the heat to low, and simmer for 20 minutes to blend the flavors. Remove from the heat and let cool slightly.

Working in batches, purée half of the soup in a blender. Return to the pot. Add the lime juice, 2½ tsp salt, and pepper to taste. Reheat over medium-low heat, stirring occasionally, for 10 minutes. Serve, garnished with the sour cream, toasted jalapeño rings, and cilantro.

8

CHILLED RED PEPPER & FENNEL SOUP WITH INDIAN SPICES

serves 6

3 Tbsp unsalted butter

1 yellow onion, chopped

2 cloves garlic, minced

3 red bell peppers, seeded and chopped

1 fennel bulbs, stalks and fronds removed, chopped

2 carrots, peeled and thinly sliced

1½ tsp garam masala

4 cups (32 fl oz/1 l) chicken broth

2 Tbsp sour cream

Salt and freshly ground pepper

This soup is great hot or cold. Serve with grilled ready-made naan: brush the naan with olive oil, cook in a very hot grill pan, and sprinkle with sea salt.

In a large, heavy pot, melt the butter over medium-high heat. Add the onion and garlic and sauté until translucent, about 5 minutes. Add the red peppers, fennel, and carrots and cook, stirring often, until the vegetables soften, 10–12 minutes. Stir in the garam masala and cook for 1 minute. Add the broth and bring to a boil. Reduce the heat to low and simmer for 30 minutes. Remove from the heat and let cool slightly.

Working in batches, purée the soup in a blender. Return to the pot, stir in the sour cream, and bring to a gentle boil. Remove from the heat and season with salt and pepper. Let cool completely, cover, and chill in the refrigerator for at least 3 hours. Serve.

9

CUCUMBER & GREEN GRAPE GAZPACHO

serves 4–6

1 cup sweet baguette pieces

1 Tbsp fresh lemon juice

2 tsp white wine vinegar, plus more to taste

½ cup (3 oz/90 g) raw almonds

3 small English cucumbers, peeled, seeded, and chopped

2 cups (12 oz/375 g) green grapes

1 clove garlic, coarsely chopped

¼ cup (2 fl oz/60 ml) extra-virgin olive oil

Salt and freshly ground pepper

A good-quality olive oil, green and peppery, will really make a difference in a soup that isn't cooked, such as this one. Salted crispy croutons add a nice counterpoint to this sweet, smooth soup.

Put the baguette pieces, lemon juice, and 2 tsp white wine vinegar in a bowl and stir to combine.

Put the almonds into a food processor and pulse until finely ground. Add the cucumbers, grapes, and garlic and pulse to purée. Add the bread mixture, oil, and ⅓ cup (3 fl oz/80 ml) water. Purée. Season to taste with salt, pepper, and additional white wine vinegar, if needed. Transfer to a covered container and refrigerate until chilled, at least 2 hours. Serve.

10

SILKEN LIMA BEAN SOUP WITH HAM CROÛTES

serves 6

4 lb (2 kg) fresh lima beans in the pod, shelled (about 4 cups), or 2 bags (1 lb/500 g each) frozen lima beans, thawed

8 cups (64 fl oz/2 l) chicken broth

1 russet potato, peeled and cut into ½-inch (12-mm) pieces

1 yellow onion, chopped

2 cloves garlic, chopped

1 carrot, peeled and chopped

Salt and freshly ground pepper

6 slices French bread, each 1 inch (2.5 cm) thick

½ cup (4 fl oz/125 ml) heavy cream

½ cup (3 oz/90 g) chopped country ham

⅓ cup (1½ oz/45 g) shredded Cheddar cheese

2 Tbsp cream cheese, at room temperature

1 Tbsp mayonnaise

1 Tbsp thyme leaves

Classic pork and beans is even better when made with garden-fresh beans and bubbling ham-and-cheese toasts. Lima beans are available fresh from June to September. Choose pods that are firm, plump, and dark green.

In a large, heavy pot, combine the beans, broth, potato, onion, garlic, and carrot. Add ½ tsp salt and ½ tsp pepper. Bring to a boil over high heat, then reduce the heat to low, cover partially, and cook, stirring occasionally, until the vegetables are very soft, about 1 hour.

Meanwhile, preheat the oven to 400°F (200°C). Arrange the bread slices on a baking sheet and toast until golden brown, about 10 minutes. Remove from the oven and turn on the broiler. Position a rack 6 inches (15 cm) from the heat source.

Remove the soup from the heat and let cool slightly. Working in batches, purée in a blender. Return to the saucepan and stir in the cream. Reheat the soup over low heat.

In a small bowl, stir together the ham, Cheddar cheese, cream cheese, and mayonnaise. Season with pepper. Spread evenly on the toasted bread. Broil until the topping is bubbly and golden, about 2 minutes.

Serve the soup sprinkled with the thyme, and pass the croûtes at the table.

11

The texture of the fried corn, bacon, and thyme garnish elevates this humble dish. You can make the soup ahead of time, but prepare the garnish just before serving. Serve with buttermilk biscuits.

CORN & ZUCCHINI SOUP WITH CRUMBLED BACON

serves 4–6

6 slices thick-cut bacon

1 Tbsp olive oil

1 yellow onion, chopped

3 cloves garlic, minced

2 zucchini, trimmed, halved lengthwise, and thinly sliced

4 cups (32 fl oz/1 l) chicken broth

3 cups (18 oz/560 g) fresh corn kernels (from about 6 ears) or 3 cups frozen

Salt and ground white pepper

1 Tbsp unsalted butter

¼ tsp minced thyme leaves

In a large, heavy pot, cook the bacon over medium heat, turning once, until crispy, about 8 minutes. Transfer to paper towels to drain. Let cool, then cut into bite-sized pieces. Set aside.

Discard all but 1 Tbsp of the bacon fat from the pot. Add the oil, onion, and garlic and sauté over medium-high heat until translucent, about 5 minutes. Add the zucchini and sauté for 5 minutes. Add the broth and bring to a boil. Add 2½ cups (15 oz/470 g) of the corn kernels and cook for 5 minutes. Remove from the heat and let cool slightly.

Working in batches, purée the soup in a blender. Return to the pot and season with salt and pepper.

In a small frying pan, melt the butter over high heat. Add the remaining ½ cup (3 oz/90 g) corn kernels, the bacon, and the thyme. Fry, stirring constantly, for 2 minutes and remove from the heat.

Serve the soup topped with the corn and bacon mixture.

12

The soup can be made ahead and frozen, but add the calamari just before serving as it only takes a few minutes to cook and it will become rubbery if overdone. It's fine to use frozen calamari for this recipe.

CALAMARI STEW

serves 6

2 Tbsp olive oil

1 yellow onion, chopped

4 cloves garlic, minced

½ tsp red pepper flakes

1 can (28 oz/875 g) crushed tomatoes

2 cups (16 fl oz/500 ml) chicken broth

1 red bell pepper, roasted (page 191), peeled, seeded, and chopped

¼ cup (⅓ oz/10 g) chopped basil

2 Tbsp chopped oregano

Salt and freshly ground pepper

1 lb (2 kg) calamari, cleaned and bodies thinly sliced, tentacles left whole

In a large, heavy pot, warm the olive oil over medium-high heat. Add the onion and garlic and sauté until translucent, about 5 minutes. Add the red pepper flakes and cook, stirring constantly, for 2 minutes. Add the tomatoes, broth, and bell pepper and bring to a boil. Reduce the heat to low and simmer for 30 minutes.

Stir in the basil and oregano and cook for 5 minutes. Season with salt and pepper. Raise the heat to medium-high and add the calamari, stirring to combine. Cook just until the calamari is opaque and cooked through, 3–5 minutes. Serve.

13

ROASTED RED PEPPER SOUP WITH GOAT CHEESE & HARISSA

serves 4

Roasting brings out the mellow sweetness of bell peppers, while fiery harissa and tangy goat cheese add dimension to this vibrant North African soup. Harissa can be found in well-stocked grocery stores and specialty markets.

4 red bell peppers (about 1½ lb/750 g)

3 Tbsp olive oil

1 yellow onion, chopped

1 clove garlic, minced

4 cups (32 fl oz/1 l) chicken broth

1 can (14½ oz/455 g) chickpeas, drained

¾ tsp smoked paprika

½ tsp ground cumin

Salt

1 tsp sherry vinegar

½–1 tsp harissa

2 oz (60 g) fresh goat cheese, crumbled

Preheat the oven to 375°F (190°C). Put the bell peppers on a baking sheet and rub with 1 Tbsp of the oil. Roast until the skins are blistered and the peppers are soft, 35–45 minutes. Let cool, then peel and remove the cores and seeds. Cut the peppers into 1½-inch (4-cm) pieces.

In a large, heavy pot, warm the remaining 2 Tbsp oil over medium-high heat. Add the onion and garlic and sauté until the onion is soft, 4–5 minutes. Add the bell peppers, broth, chickpeas, paprika, and cumin. Season with ¼ tsp salt. Cover, reduce the heat to medium, and simmer for 15 minutes to blend the flavors. Remove from the heat and let cool slightly.

Working in batches, purée the soup in a blender or food processor. Return to the pot and stir in the vinegar and harissa. Serve, garnished with the goat cheese.

14

MISO SOUP WITH BLACK COD & GREEN ONIONS

serves 2

This beautiful soup makes a perfect light dinner on a warm summer evening. Serve it in shallow bowls to showcase the caramelized black cod. A cold seaweed or sesame-spinach salad would pair well.

1 piece kombu, about 3 inches (7.5 cm)

½ cup (½ oz/15 g) bonito flakes

2 Tbsp white miso paste

5 oz (155 g) black cod, cut into 2–4 pieces

1 Tbsp olive oil

Salt and freshly ground pepper

1 green onion, white and tender green parts, thinly sliced

Put 3 cups (24 fl oz/750 ml) cold water and the kombu in a saucepan over medium heat. Bring to a boil and then remove and discard the kombu. Turn off the heat, add the bonito flakes, stir gently once, and let sit for 5 minutes. Strain the soup through a fine-mesh sieve and return the broth to the saucepan.

Put the miso paste in a small bowl and add ¼ cup (2 fl oz/60 ml) of the warm broth. Stir until the mixture is very smooth. Add the miso mixture to the saucepan and warm gently, taking care not to let the soup come to a boil.

Place a small frying pan over high heat until it is very hot. Season the cod with the oil, salt, and pepper and sear until just cooked through, 4 minutes per side.

To serve, ladle the soup into bowls, top with one or two pieces of fish, and sprinkle with green onions.

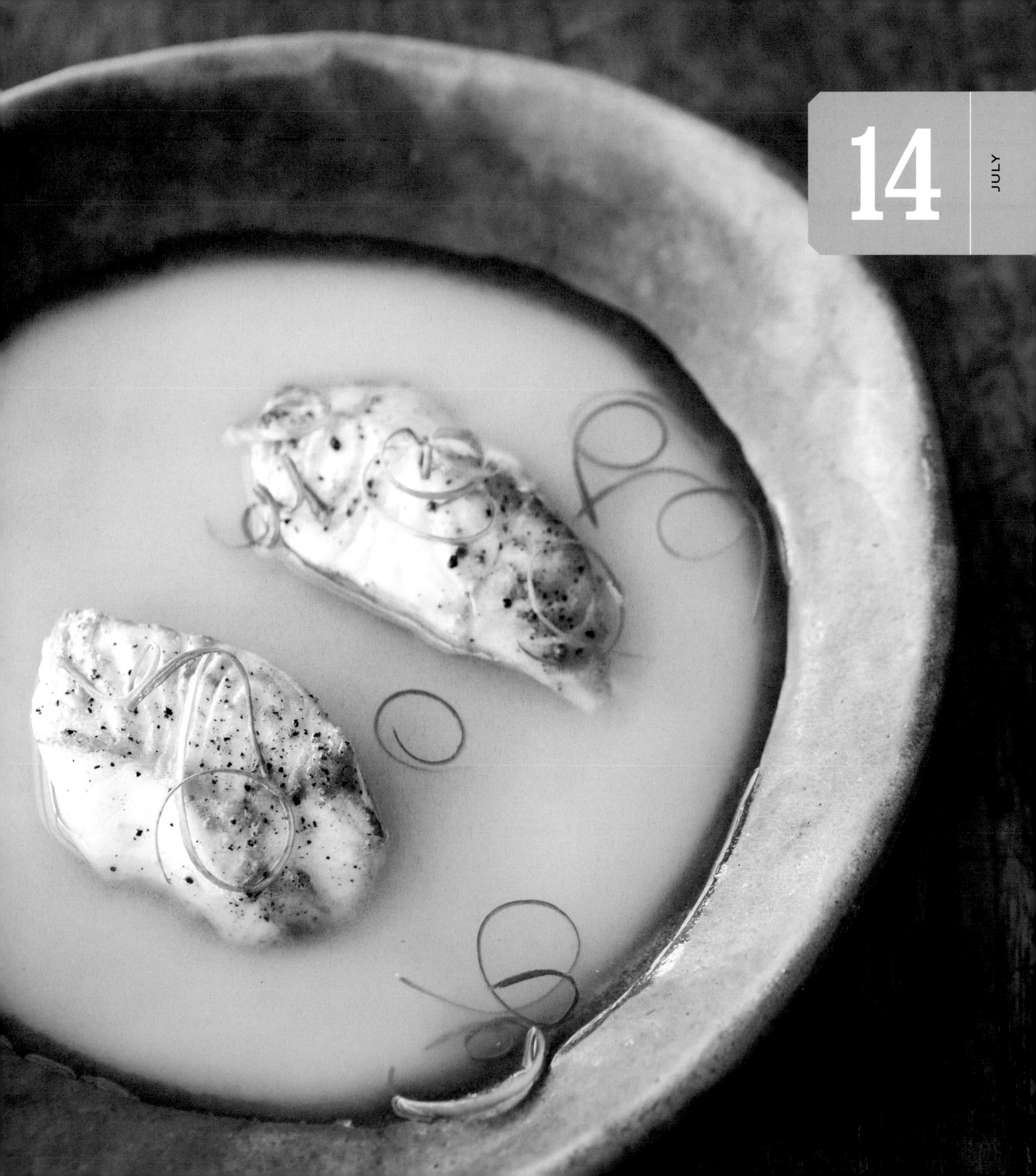
14
JULY

15

MUSSEL CHOWDER
serves 4–6

1 Tbsp olive oil

1 shallot, thinly sliced

½ cup (4 fl oz/125 ml) dry white wine

2½ cups (20 fl oz/625 ml) chicken broth

2 lb (1 kg) mussels, scrubbed and debearded

6 slices thick-cut bacon

1 small yellow onion, chopped

1 small fennel bulb (about ½ lb/250 g), stalks and fronds removed, quartered and thinly sliced

1 russet potato, peeled and diced

1 cup (8 fl oz/250 ml) heavy cream

1 Tbsp minced flat-leaf parsley

Salt and freshly ground pepper

You can adjust the thickness (and therefore the richness) of this soup by adjusting the broth-to-cream ratio. Serve with a simple green salad and plenty of crusty bread for dipping.

In a large saucepan over medium-high heat, warm the olive oil. Add the shallot and sauté until soft, 2 minutes. Add the wine and ½ cup (4 fl oz/125 ml) of the broth and bring to a boil. Add the mussels, discarding any that do not close to the touch, cover tightly, and steam until the mussels open, 5–7 minutes. Transfer the mussels to a bowl, discarding any unopened ones. When cool enough to handle, remove them from their shells, coarsely chop, and then refrigerate. Transfer the mussel cooking liquid to a bowl and reserve.

In a large, heavy pot, cook the bacon over medium heat, turning once, until it is crisp, about 8 minutes. Transfer to paper towels to drain. When cool enough to handle, cut into ½-inch (12-mm) pieces. Discard all but 1 Tbsp of the bacon fat from the pot and add the onion and fennel. Sauté until the vegetables are soft, about 7 minutes. Add the reserved mussel cooking liquid and the remaining 2 cups (16 fl oz/500 ml) broth and bring to a boil. Add the potato, reduce the heat to medium-low, and cook until the potato is tender, about 20 minutes. Add the bacon, mussels, and cream and simmer for 5 minutes. Stir in the parsley, season to taste with salt and pepper, and serve.

16

CHUNKY HEIRLOOM TOMATO & BASIL SOUP
serves 6

3 Tbsp olive oil

1 large yellow onion, chopped

4 cloves garlic, minced

2 carrots, peeled and finely chopped

3 red heirloom tomatoes (about 2 lb/1 kg total), coarsely chopped

3 yellow heirloom tomatoes (about 2 lb/1 kg total), coarsely chopped

2 cups (16 fl oz/500 ml) chicken broth

2 tsp sugar

1 Tbsp heavy cream

⅓ cup (⅓ oz/10 g) chopped basil

Salt and freshly ground pepper

Combining red and yellow tomatoes gives this soup a beautiful color. Keep the soup chunky, because when tomatoes are in season you really want to let their texture shine. Serve with bread sticks and butter or garlic croutons (page 61).

In a large, heavy pot, warm the oil over medium-high heat. Add the onion, garlic, and carrots and sauté until very soft, about 5 minutes. Add the tomatoes, broth, and sugar, stirring to combine, and bring to a boil. Reduce the heat to low and simmer for 30 minutes. Remove from the heat and let cool slightly.

Transfer half of the soup to a food processor and purée. Return to the pot and add the cream. Stir in the basil, season to taste with salt and pepper, and serve.

17

Lemongrass carries a wonderful citrusy scent that gives Thai dishes their signature aromatic quality. Along with the kaffir lime leaves, it beautifully balances the heat of the roasted chile paste in this classic preparation.

TOM YUM WITH SHRIMP

serves 6

¾ lb (375 g) large shrimp in the shell

2 Tbsp canola oil

4 lemongrass stalks, center white part only, smashed and cut into 2-inch (5-cm) lengths

6 slices fresh galangal or
3 slices dried galangal

6 green Thai chiles or 8 green serrano chiles, seeded and cut in half crosswise

6 cups (48 fl oz/1.5 l) chicken broth

8 kaffir lime leaves, spines removed

1–2 Tbsp roasted chile paste

1 cup (7 oz/220 g) drained
canned straw mushrooms

4-inch (10-cm) piece bamboo shoot,
thinly sliced

3 Tbsp Asian fish sauce

¼ cup (2 fl oz/60 ml) fresh lime juice

1 fresh red chile, sliced

¼ cup (¼ oz/7 g) cilantro leaves

Peel and devein the shrimp, reserving the shells. Rinse the shrimp. In a large, heavy pot, warm the oil over medium-high heat. Add the shrimp shells and fry, stirring, until they turn bright orange, about 1 minute. Add the lemongrass, galangal, green chiles, broth, and 4 of the lime leaves. Raise the heat to high and bring to a boil. Reduce the heat to medium and simmer, uncovered, for 15 minutes to blend the flavors. Pour the broth through a sieve placed over a clean pot. Discard the contents of the sieve.

Add the chile paste to taste, the mushrooms, and bamboo shoot, stir well, and bring to a boil over medium heat. Add the shrimp and the remaining 4 lime leaves. Cook until the shrimp turn pink and opaque, 1–2 minutes. Season with the fish sauce and lime juice.

Serve, garnished with the red chile slices and cilantro leaves.

18

This Mexican-inspired version of good old chicken soup gets its zip from lots of puckery lime juice. The uniquely bright, bracing sharpness of the fresh limes is countered by fragrant garlic, herbal oregano, and spicy jalapeño.

MEXICAN LIME SOUP WITH CHICKEN

serves 6

8–10 small limes

2 skin-on, bone-in chicken breast halves (about 10 oz/315 g each)

Salt and freshly ground pepper

1 Tbsp olive oil

1 large white onion, chopped

5 cloves garlic, minced

1 jalapeño chile, seeded and minced

3 cups (24 fl oz/750 ml) chicken broth

1½ tsp dried oregano

1 avocado, pitted, peeled, and diced

2 oz (60 g) queso fresco or ricotta salata cheese, crumbled

Tortilla chips for serving

Cut 2 of the limes into wedges and reserve. Juice as many of the remaining limes as needed to measure out ¼ cup (2 fl oz/60 ml) juice.

Season the chicken breasts with 1 tsp salt and ½ tsp pepper. In a large, heavy pot, warm the oil over medium heat. Add the chicken, skin side down, and cook, turning once, until browned, about 5 minutes. Transfer to a plate. Add the onion and sauté until translucent, about 4 minutes. Stir in the garlic and chile and sauté until fragrant, about 1 minute. Stir in the broth, 3 cups (24 fl oz/750 ml) water, the lime juice, and the oregano. Return the chicken to the pot. Raise the heat to high and bring the liquid to a boil, skimming off any foam on the surface. Reduce the heat to medium-low, cover partially, and simmer gently until the chicken is opaque throughout, about 40 minutes.

Keeping the soup at a simmer, remove the chicken. When it is cool enough to handle, remove and discard the skin and bones and shred the meat into bite-sized pieces. Stir the chicken into the soup. Serve, passing the avocado, cheese, tortilla chips, and lime wedges at the table.

19

BURMESE CHICKEN CURRY SOUP

serves 6

2 Tbsp peanut oil, plus more for frying

1⅛ lb (560 g) fresh thin Chinese egg noodles

3 cloves garlic, minced

2 Tbsp Thai red curry paste

2 tsp Madras curry powder

½ tsp ground turmeric

½ cup (4 fl oz/125 ml) coconut cream

¾ lb (375 g) skinless, boneless chicken thighs, cut into ¼-inch (6-mm) chunks

4 cups (32 fl oz/1 l) chicken broth

3 cups (24 fl oz/750 ml) coconut milk

2 Tbsp Asian fish sauce, or to taste

1 tsp brown sugar

2 Tbsp fresh lemon juice

3 Tbsp chopped pickled Chinese cabbage, rinsed with cold water and drained

3 green onions, white and tender green parts, chopped

½ English cucumber, peeled and thinly sliced

Fried Shallots (page 28)

2 lemons, cut into wedges

This dish calls for both Madras curry powder, a familiar Indian ingredient, and Thai red curry paste. Although the soup itself has plenty of flavor and texture, the traditional toppings heighten the enjoyment.

Pour 2 inches (5 cm) of peanut oil into a saucepan and heat to 375°F (190°C) on a deep-frying thermometer. Separate out a handful of the noodles and drop them into the hot oil. Fry until golden brown, about 1 minute. Using a wire skimmer, transfer to paper towels to drain.

Bring a large saucepan of water to a boil. Add the remaining noodles, stir well, and return to a boil. Cook for 1 minute. Drain, rinse with cold running water until cool, and drain thoroughly.

In a large, heavy pot, warm the 2 Tbsp oil over medium heat. Add the garlic and sauté until light golden brown, about 2 minutes. Add the curry paste, curry powder, and turmeric and sauté until the oil is fragrant and has a rich yellow hue, about 2 minutes. Add the coconut cream, raise the heat to medium-high, and cook, stirring frequently, until the cream boils gently and oil beads appear on the surface, 5–8 minutes. Add the chicken and stir to coat with the paste. ↳

Raise the heat to high, add the broth, coconut milk, fish sauce, and sugar, and bring to a boil. Reduce the heat to medium-low and simmer, uncovered, for 10 minutes to blend the flavors. Stir in the lemon juice and remove from the heat.

Divide the boiled noodles among bowls. Ladle the soup over the noodles. Top with the pickled cabbage, green onion, cucumber, shallots, and fried noodles. Serve with the lemon wedges for squeezing over the soup.

20

TORTELLINI IN BROTH

serves 4

6 cups (48 fl oz/1.5 l) beef broth

12 oz (375 g) fresh cheese tortellini

Salt and freshly ground pepper

⅓ cup (1½ oz/45 g) grated Parmesan cheese

¼ cup (⅓ oz/10 g) slivered basil

Ridiculously easy to make and always delicious, tortellini in broth makes a satisfying and comforting meal any day of the year. Try different filled pastas to vary the flavors, and add a handful of spinach if you'd like more greens.

In a saucepan, bring the broth to a boil over medium-high heat. Add the tortellini and cook for about 5 minutes, or according to package directions. Season with salt and pepper. Serve, garnished with the Parmesan and basil.

21

JULY

*No recipe ever seems
to call for an entire
can of chipotle chiles
in adobo. Store
unused chipotles in
the freezer, separated
out in an ice cube
tray until frozen,
and then put in
a ziplock bag
for easy access.*

CHIPOTLE-CORN PURÉE WITH BAY SHRIMP & AVOCADO SALSA

serves 4

2 Tbsp olive oil

1 small yellow onion, chopped

2 cloves garlic, minced

½ small chipotle chile in adobo, chopped

3½ cups (28 fl oz/875 ml) chicken broth

4 cups (24 oz/750 g) fresh corn kernels
(from about 8 ears)

Salt and freshly ground pepper

FOR THE SALSA

5 oz (155 g) cooked bay shrimp,
coarsely chopped

1 ripe avocado, pitted, peeled,
and finely diced

1 Tbsp fresh lime juice

2 tsp chopped cilantro

Salt and freshly ground pepper

In a large, heavy pot, warm the olive oil over
medium-high heat. Add the onion and garlic
and sauté until translucent, about 5 minutes.
Add the chipotle, stir to combine, and sauté
for 2 minutes. Add the broth and bring to a
boil. Add the corn and cook for 5 minutes.
Remove from the heat and let cool slightly.
Working in batches, purée the soup in a
blender or food processor. Return to the
pot and season with salt and pepper.

To make the salsa, put the shrimp
and avocado in a small bowl and stir
to combine. Stir in the lime juice and
cilantro and season with salt and pepper.
Serve the soup topped with the salsa.

22

JULY

*This soup is all
about presentation.
It'll look like it came
out of a restaurant
kitchen, but is
surprisingly easy to
pull off. To make the
melon strips, draw
a vegetable peeler
over a wedge of
peeled melon.*

TWO MELON SOUPS

serves 4–6

FOR THE CANTALOUPE SOUP

1 very ripe cantaloupe (about 2 lb/1 kg),
halved, seeded, peeled, and chopped

2 Tbsp sour cream

2 Tbsp fresh orange juice

Salt

FOR THE HONEYDEW SOUP

1 very ripe honeydew melon (about 2 lb/1 kg),
halved, seeded, peeled, and chopped

2 Tbsp sour cream

2 Tbsp fresh white grape juice

Salt

Melon strips for garnish (left)

Lime wedges for serving

To make the cantaloupe soup, purée
the cantaloupe in a food processor.
Add the sour cream, orange juice,
and a pinch of salt and pulse several
times to combine. Transfer to a covered
container and refrigerate until well
chilled, at least 2 hours.

Wash and dry the food processor.

To make the honeydew soup, purée
the honeydew in the food processor.
Add the sour cream, white grape juice,
and a pinch of salt and pulse several
times to combine. Transfer to a covered
container and refrigerate until well
chilled, at least 2 hours.

Ladle the soup into individual bowls or, to
serve the soups together, put a 3-inch (7.5-cm)
round cookie cutter in the center of a shallow
bowl. Hold the cookie cutter in place with
one hand, and with the other pour the
cantaloupe soup into the center of the cookie
cutter, filling it three-quarters of the way to
the top. Keeping your hand on the cookie
cutter, pour the honeydew soup around the
outside of the cookie cutter until the bottom
of the bowl is covered. Carefully lift the
cookie cutter out of the bowl. Repeat for each
serving. Serve, garnished with melon strips.
Pass lime wedges at the table.

23

SUMMER PANZANELLA SOUP WITH TINY PASTA

serves 4–6

1 loaf crusty Italian bread

3 Tbsp olive oil

Salt and freshly ground pepper

8 oz (250 g) tiny pasta, such as conchigliette or ditalini

2 shallots, minced

3 cloves garlic, minced

2 lb (1 kg) ripe tomatoes, diced

2 cups (16 fl oz/500 ml) chicken broth

⅓ cup (⅓ oz/10 g) chopped basil

Grated Parmesan cheese for serving

Make this at the height of summer, when tomatoes are their most flavorful. Serve with a simple endive salad with a light buttermilk dressing.

Preheat the oven to 375°F (190°C). Cut enough of the bread up into cubes to measure out 2 cups (2 oz/60 g). Place the bread cubes on a baking sheet, toss with 1 Tbsp of the oil, and season with salt and pepper. Toast in the oven, stirring once, until browned, about 12 minutes. Set aside.

Bring a saucepan of salted water to a boil. Add the pasta and cook until al dente, about 8 minutes or according to the package directions. Drain and set aside.

In a large, heavy pot, warm the remaining 2 Tbsp oil over medium-high heat. Add the shallots and garlic and sauté until translucent, about 5 minutes. Add the tomatoes and sauté until they soften, about 5 minutes. Add the broth and bring to a boil. Reduce the heat to low and simmer for 15 minutes to blend the flavors. Remove from the heat and let cool slightly.

Purée half of the soup in a blender or food processor. Return to the pot and add the toasted bread. Continue to cook for 10 minutes. Stir in the pasta and basil and season with salt and pepper.

Serve, sprinkled with the Parmesan.

24

CHICKEN SOUP WITH GNOCCHI, BASIL & PARMESAN

serves 4–6

2 small skinless, boneless chicken breast halves

3 Tbsp olive oil

Salt and freshly ground pepper

½ small yellow onion, chopped

2 garlic cloves, minced

4 cups chicken broth

1 can (14½ oz/455 g) oz) diced tomatoes

1 package (17½ oz/545 g) potato gnocchi

1 cup (1 oz/30 g) baby spinach

¼ cup (⅓ oz/10 g) chopped basil

Grated Parmesan cheese for serving

This is a great family weekday meal. The base is light and brothy, but the chicken and the gnocchi add substance. Use leftover rotisserie or grilled chicken to save time.

Preheat the oven to 375°F (190°). Place the chicken breasts on a baking sheet, brush with 1 Tbsp of the oil, and season with salt and pepper. Roast the chicken until opaque throughout, 18–20 minutes. Let the chicken cool to the touch, then shred into bite-sized pieces.

In a large, heavy pot, warm the remaining 2 Tbsp oil over medium-high heat. Add the onion and garlic and sauté until translucent, about 5 minutes. Add the broth and tomatoes with their juices and bring to a boil. Add the chicken and gnocchi and cook for 5 minutes. Remove from the heat, add the spinach and basil, and stir just until wilted. Season with salt and pepper.

Serve, passing the Parmesan at the table.

GAZPACHO

serves 6–8

2 tsp anchovy paste

4 cups (32 fl oz/1 l) tomato juice

3 lb (1.5 kg) tomatoes, peeled (left), seeded, and finely chopped

2 cups (16 fl oz/500 ml) chicken or vegetable broth

2 Tbsp olive oil

2 Tbsp red wine vinegar

3 cloves garlic, minced

Salt and freshly ground pepper

3 English cucumbers, peeled, seeded, and finely chopped

½ red onion, finely chopped

⅓ cup (½ oz/15 g) finely chopped basil, plus 2 Tbsp

1 red bell pepper, seeded and finely chopped

1 yellow bell pepper, seeded and finely chopped

Garlic Croutons (page 61) for garnish

To peel tomatoes, bring a pot of water to a boil. Using a sharp knife, cut a shallow X in the bottom end of each tomato. Have ready a bowl of ice water. Immerse the tomatoes in the boiling water for 15 seconds, then, using a slotted spoon, transfer them to the ice water to stop the cooking. Peel the tomatoes with your fingers or a small knife.

In a large nonreactive bowl, combine the anchovy paste and tomato juice and whisk until the anchovy paste is dissolved. Add the tomatoes, broth, oil, vinegar, and garlic and whisk until blended. Season with salt and pepper. Stir in the cucumbers, onion, and the ⅓ cup basil and mix well. Add the red and yellow bell peppers, reserving 2 Tbsp for garnish.

Purée 3 cups (24 fl oz/750 ml) of the soup in a blender. Return to the bowl. Cover and refrigerate until the soup is well chilled and the flavors have married, at least 3 hours.

Serve, garnished with the reserved bell peppers, the croutons, and the 2 Tbsp basil.

ROASTED CHILE & CORN SOUP WITH FARMER'S CHEESE

serves 4–6

3 ears fresh corn, husks intact

2 Tbsp unsalted butter

1 small yellow onion, chopped

3 cloves garlic, minced

1 tsp ground cumin

½ tsp ground coriander

1 poblano chile, roasted (page 191), seeded, and chopped

1 russet potato, peeled and finely diced

4 cups (32 fl oz/1 l) chicken broth, plus more as needed

1 Tbsp sour cream

Salt and freshly ground pepper

½ lb (250 g) farmer's cheese, crumbled

Farmer's cheese is a crumbly white fresh cheese—basically cottage cheese that has had the whey pressed out of it. Serve this soup with cut-up jicama and carrots and guacamole.

Preheat the oven to 400°F (200°C). Put the corn on a baking sheet and roast for 35 minutes. Remove from the oven and let cool to the touch. Remove and discard the husks and cut the kernels off the cobs. Set aside.

In a large, heavy pot, melt the butter over medium-high heat. Add the onion and garlic and sauté until translucent, about 5 minutes. Add the cumin and coriander and cook, stirring often, for 2 minutes to toast the spices. Add the poblano, potato, corn, and broth, stir to combine, and bring to a boil. Reduce the heat to low and simmer until the potatoes are very tender, about 25 minutes. Remove from the heat and let cool slightly.

Working in batches, purée the soup in a blender or food processor. Return to the pot and add more broth if necessary to achieve the desired consistency. Stir in the sour cream and season to taste with salt and pepper.

Serve, topped with the farmer's cheese.

27
JULY

ROASTED NECTARINE SOUP WITH MINT

serves 4

1 lb (500 g) nectarines, pitted and sliced

2 tsp balsamic vinegar

1 tsp olive oil

Salt and freshly ground pepper

½ cup (4 fl oz/125 ml) dry white wine

3 Tbsp fresh lemon juice

2 Tbsp honey

Chopped mint for garnish

You will have an easy time removing the skins from the nectarines once they've been roasted. Serve for brunch with lemon scones. This soup is also delicious served warm and garnished with a wedge of burrata cheese.

Preheat the oven to 400°F (200°C). Toss the nectarine slices with the balsamic vinegar and oil and season with salt and pepper. Spread the nectarines in a single layer on a baking sheet and roast in the oven until caramelized, about 25 minutes. Slip off and discard the peels from the nectarine slices.

Purée the nectarines in a food processor. Add the wine, lemon juice, and honey and pulse several times to combine. Transfer to a covered container and refrigerate until chilled, at least 3 hours. Serve, garnished with the mint.

28
JULY

CRAB & AVOCADO SOUP

serves 4

3 avocados, peeled, pitted, and coarsely chopped

2 serrano chiles, seeded and chopped

1 cup (8 fl oz/250 ml) coconut milk

Juice from 1 lime, or more as needed

Salt and ground white pepper

½ lb (250 g) fresh lump crabmeat, picked over for shell fragments

A touch of exotic coconut milk joins buttery avocado in this cool, smooth purée. Choose the freshest lump crabmeat you can find. A sprinkling of chives will be all the embellishment it requires.

In a food processor or blender, combine the avocados, chiles, coconut milk, and lime juice. Add ¾ cup (6 fl oz/180 ml) water and process to a smooth purée. Season with salt, pepper, and additional lime juice to taste.

Transfer to an airtight container and refrigerate for at least 2 and up to 8 hours. Serve, garnished with the crabmeat.

29
JULY

NOODLE SOUP WITH LEMONGRASS & TOFU

serves 4–6

3 oz (90 g) rice noodles

½ lb (250 g) firm tofu

1 tsp canola oil

2 lemongrass stalks, center white part only, smashed and thinly sliced

2 cloves garlic, minced

6 cups (48 fl z/1.5 l) chicken broth

1 Tbsp fresh lime juice

1 tsp Asian fish sauce

2 green onions, white and tender green parts, chopped

2 Tbsp minced cilantro

Because tofu is stored in liquid, you want to drain it really well before adding it to any dish. This will enhance the flavor of the tofu, and also ensure that it won't dilute the flavor of the broth.

In a bowl, combine the rice noodles with hot water to cover. Soak for 10 minutes, then drain.

Cut the tofu in half crosswise. Place both pieces on a plate and top with a second plate. Weigh down the top plate with a can. Let stand for 20 minutes to let the tofu drain. Pour off any water from the plate and cut the tofu into very small cubes.

In a large, heavy pot, warm the oil over medium heat. Add the lemongrass and garlic and sauté until softened, 5–6 minutes. Add the broth and bring to a boil. Reduce the heat and simmer, uncovered, for 20 minutes. Add the tofu, lime juice, and fish sauce and cook for 5 minutes. Stir in the green onions and cilantro. Serve.

30

SWEET PEA DUMPLINGS IN GINGERY GREEN ONION BROTH

serves 4–6

Because these dumplings are very delicate and fall apart if overcooked, do not cook them until you are just about ready to serve this soup. If you have leftover dumpling filling it makes a lovely spread on crostini.

4 cups (32 fl oz/1 l) chicken broth

2-inch (5-cm) piece fresh ginger, peeled and minced

2 green onions, white and tender green parts, thinly sliced, green tops reserved

1 star anise

2 Tbsp soy sauce

1 tsp mirin

A few drops Asian sesame oil

FOR THE DUMPLINGS

1 cup (5 oz/155 g) fresh or thawed frozen peas

2 Tbsp ricotta cheese

1 Tbsp grated Parmesan cheese

2 tsp canola oil

Salt and freshly ground pepper

24 wonton wrappers

In a large saucepan, combine the broth, ginger, sliced green onions, star anise, soy sauce, mirin, and sesame oil. Bring to a boil over medium-high heat, reduce the heat to low, and simmer for 10 minutes. Remove from the heat, cover the pan, and steep for 10 minutes. Strain the broth, discarding the solids, and return to the saucepan.

Meanwhile, to make the dumplings, combine the peas, ricotta, Parmesan, and oil in a food processor. Add ½ tsp salt and ¼ tsp pepper. Pulse several times to coarsely chop the peas and combine the ingredients. Do not purée. Place 1 tsp of the pea mixture in the middle of each wonton wrapper. Using your fingers, apply a small amount of water on all sides of the wrapper. Fold the wrapper diagonally, forcing out any air bubbles as you press to seal. Take the 2 points on the longest side of the triangle and fold so that the tips meet. Apply a small amount of water on the tips and press firmly to stick together.

Return the broth to a boil, carefully add the dumplings, and cook for 3 minutes. Slice the onion tops. Serve, topped with the sliced onion tops.

31

VIETNAMESE TURKEY MEATBALLS IN BROTH WITH RED ONION & HERBS

serves 6

Meatballs can be heavy and bland, but not when they are made with bright Southeast Asian flavors, as in this recipe, and handled with a light touch.

FOR THE MEATBALLS

1 lb (500 g) ground turkey

1 shallot, minced

2 cloves garlic, minced

2 Tbsp Asian fish sauce

1 Tbsp minced cilantro

Salt and freshly ground pepper

Grated zest of 1 lime

2 Tbsp olive oil

2-inch (5-cm) piece of fresh ginger, peeled and grated

2 lemongrass stalks, center white part only, smashed and thinly sliced

6 cups (48 fl oz/1.5 l) chicken broth

Juice of 1 lime

¼ small red onion, thinly sliced

1 Tbsp minced cilantro

2 tsp minced mint

To make the meatballs, preheat the oven to 375°F (190°C). Oil a baking sheet. In a bowl, combine the ground turkey, shallot, garlic, fish sauce, cilantro, 1 tsp salt, ½ tsp pepper, and the lime zest. Using your hands, combine well. For each meatball, scoop up a heaping teaspoonful of the mixture, form into a meatball, and place on the prepared pan. Bake until the meatballs are cooked through, 10–12 minutes.

In a large, heavy pot, warm the oil over medium-high heat. Add the ginger and lemongrass and sauté, stirring constantly, for 4 minutes. Add the broth and lime juice and bring to a boil. Reduce the heat to low and simmer for 10 minutes to blend the flavors. Add the meatballs, red onion, cilantro, and mint and continue to simmer for 5 minutes. Serve.

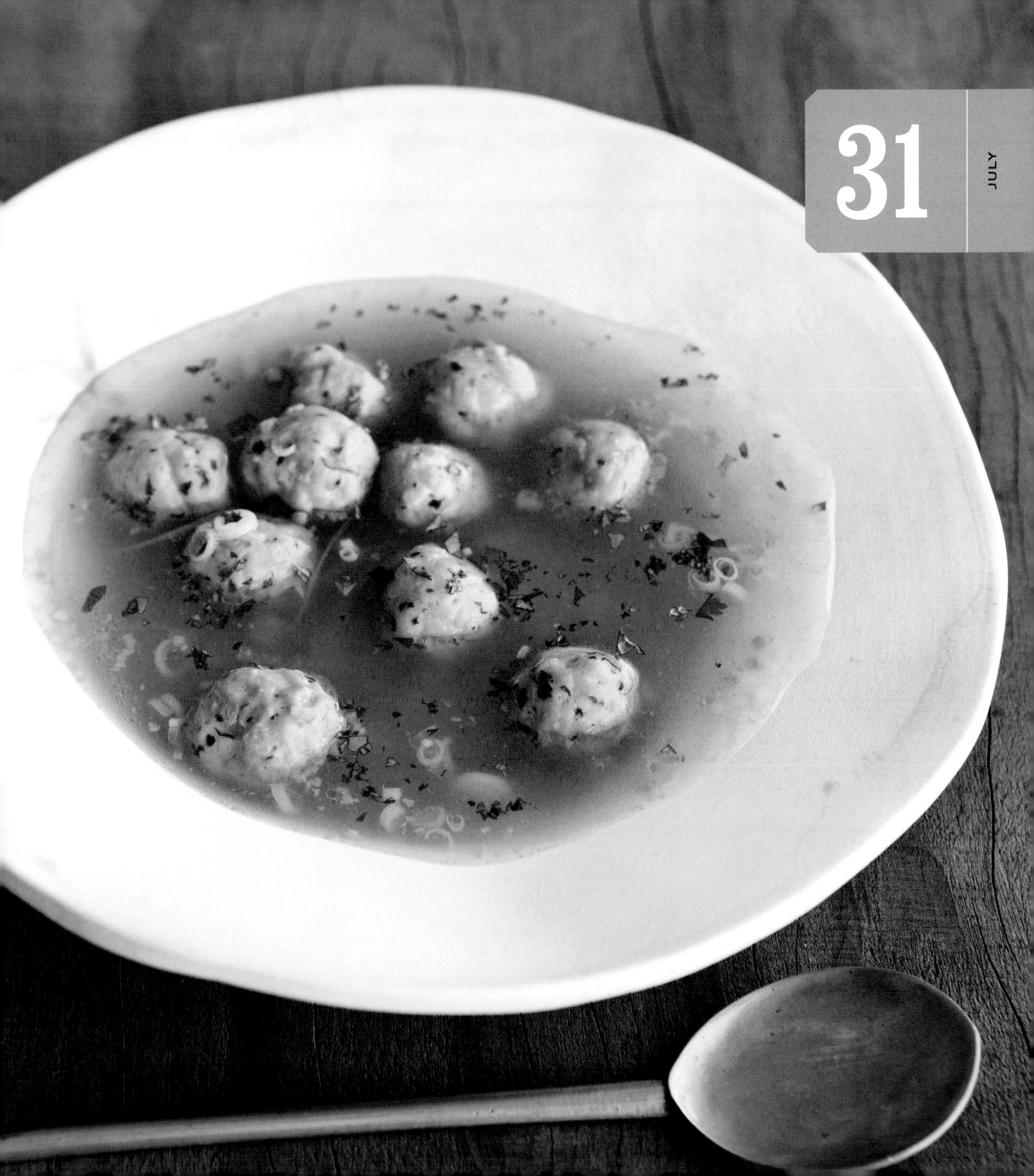

1
RATATOUILLE SOUP
page 178

2
WATERMELON GAZPACHO
WITH GOAT CHEESE CROÛTES
page 178

3
ACQUACOTTA
page 180

4
POACHED CHICKEN
SOUP WITH SPINACH
page 180

8
CHILLED CURRIED CORN SOUP
page 183

9
CAJUN SHRIMP SOUP
page 184

10
FRESH GREEN BEAN SOUP
page 184

11
GARLICKY PORK & CHILE SOUP
page 185

15
CHARRED EGGPLANT SOUP
WITH CUMIN & GREEK YOGURT
page 189

16
CREAMY CORN SOUP
WITH BACON & SAGE
page 189

17
AVOCADO SOUP WITH
LIME JUICE & RUM
page 190

18
SNAP PEA & SUCCOTASH SOUP
WITH PARSLEY-MINT PISTOU
page 190

22
TOMATO, ZUCCHINI
& FRESH CORN SOUP
page 192

23
ROASTED SUMMER VEGETABLE
SOUP WITH PESTO
page 195

24
SPICED BERRY SOUP
page 195

25
MUSSELS IN SAFFRON BROTH
page 196

29
LENTIL SOUP WITH SORREL
page 197

30
ROMANO BEAN, ZUCCHINI
& PARMESAN SOUP
page 198

31
PORK PHO
page 198

5
SMOKY RED PEPPER SOUP
page 181

6
TOMATO SOUP WITH WHITE WINE & SHALLOTS
page 181

7
FIDEO & CHICKEN SOUP WITH QUESO FRESCO
page 183

12
PEACH & RIESLING SOUP
page 185

13
YELLOW GAZPACHO WITH LEMON-BASIL RICOTTA
page 186

14
CHILLED CUCUMBER-BUTTERMILK SOUP WITH DILLED SHRIMP
page 186

19
ICED MELON SOUP WITH CHAMPAGNE & GINGER
page 191

20
SPICY POBLANO SOUP WITH TORTILLA STRIPS
page 191

21
BOUILLABAISSE
page 192

26
ROASTED TOMATO SOUP WITH CITRUS CRÈME FRAÎCHE
page 196

27
MISO SOUP WITH TOFU AND LONG BEANS
page 197

28
ANGEL HAIR IN CHICKEN BROTH WITH TOMATOES & BASIL
page 197

During the dog days of summer, heat-hungry vegetables flourish: tomatoes and peppers blush deeply red; cucumbers and green beans thrive; and deep-purple eggplant has its moment in the sun. Toss them together with the season's sweetest garlic and freshest herbs—basil, cilantro, dill, and mint. Chilled soups still reign, whether in inventive gazpachos or sweet fruit soups.

august

1

RATATOUILLE SOUP

serves 4

3 Tbsp olive oil

2 cloves garlic, minced

1 eggplant, peeled and cut into small cubes

1 zucchini, trimmed and chopped

1 yellow onion, quartered

1 red bell pepper, seeded and chopped

4 large tomatoes, peeled (page 172) and quartered

2–3 cups (16–24 fl oz/500–750 ml) chicken broth

Salt and freshly ground pepper

¼ cup (⅓ oz/10 g) minced basil

Inspired by France's most beloved peasant dish, this soup features a marriage of hot-weather produce: deep purple eggplants, summer squash, the season's sweetest red peppers and tomatoes, and a handful of basil leaves. It's summer in a bowl.

In a large, heavy pot, warm 2 Tbsp of the oil over medium heat. Add the garlic and sauté until fragrant, about 1 minute. Add the eggplant, zucchini, onion, and bell pepper and cook, stirring occasionally, until the vegetables have softened, 10–15 minutes. Add the tomatoes and the remaining 1 Tbsp oil. Cook, stirring occasionally, until the tomatoes begin to break down, about 15 minutes. Reduce the heat to low and simmer for 15 minutes.

Add 1 cup (8 oz/250 ml) of the broth to the vegetables. Purée the soup in a blender or food processor. Return to the pot and place over medium heat. Add enough broth to make a thick soup. Simmer until heated through, about 5 minutes. Season with salt and pepper and serve, garnished with the basil.

2

WATERMELON GAZPACHO WITH GOAT CHEESE CROÛTES

serves 6

4 cups (1½ lb/750 g) peeled and diced ripe watermelon

1 small English cucumber, peeled, seeded, and chopped

1 small ripe tomato, chopped

2 green onions, white and green parts, chopped

½ small jalapeño chile, seeded and chopped

1 tsp white wine vinegar

2 tsp extra-virgin olive oil

Salt and freshly ground pepper

FOR THE GOAT CHEESE CROÛTES

3 oz (90 g) goat cheese, at room temperature

2 Tbsp heavy cream

1 small and thin sweet baguette, thinly sliced

What a summertime treat to turn watermelon into a delicious and unexpected soup with a bit of a jalapeño kick. Make plenty of goat cheese croûtes and watch them vanish, as the salty cheese pairs beautifully with the sweet watermelon.

Put 3 cups (18 oz/560 g) of the watermelon into a food processor and pulse several times to coarsely chop, but not purée, the watermelon. Transfer to a bowl. Using a chef's knife, finely dice the remaining 1 cup (6 oz/185 g) watermelon and add to the bowl with the processed watermelon. The mixture should be very chunky.

Put the cucumber, tomato, green onions, and jalapeño into the food processor and purée. Transfer the purée to the bowl with the watermelon. Stir in the vinegar and oil. Season with salt and pepper. Cover the bowl and refrigerate for 1 hour.

To make the goat cheese croûtes, preheat the broiler to high. Put the goat cheese and cream into a bowl and stir to combine. Season with salt and pepper. Spread a thick layer of the goat cheese onto the baguette slices. Transfer to a baking sheet and put under the broiler until the cheese melts and turns golden, 2–3 minutes.

Serve the soup, and pass the goat cheese croûtes at the table.

3

There is no single recipe for this Tuscan classic, though it usually includes eggs, bread, and vegetables such as peppers and tomatoes.

ACQUACOTTA

serves 8

½ cup (4 fl oz/125 ml) olive oil

2 red onions, chopped

¾ lb (375 g) mixed red and yellow bell peppers, seeded and chopped

3 celery ribs, chopped

1 lb (500 g) tomatoes, peeled (page 172), seeded, and chopped

Salt and freshly ground pepper

3 eggs

½ cup (2 oz/60 g) grated Parmesan cheese

8 slices day-old country-style bread, toasted

1 clove garlic

In a large, heavy pot, warm the oil over medium heat. Add the onions and sauté until fragrant, about 4 minutes. Add the bell peppers and celery and sauté until soft, about 10 minutes. Stir in the tomatoes. Season with salt and pepper. Reduce the heat to low, cover, and simmer gently, stirring occasionally, until thick, about 1 hour.

Pour in 8 cups (64 fl oz/2 l) water, return to a simmer, and cook for 10 minutes. In a small bowl, beat together the eggs and cheese and pour into the soup. Stir briskly for a minute, then remove from the heat. Season with salt and pepper.

Rub the toasts with the garlic clove and divide among bowls. Ladle the soup over the toasts and serve.

4

You can use a peppery green like arugula or watercress in place of the spinach, or fresh pea shoots in spring. Squeeze in a fresh lemon wedge right before eating, and serve with a loaf of bread and a zippy white wine.

POACHED CHICKEN SOUP WITH SPINACH

serves 6–8

1 chicken (3½ lb/1.75 kg)

1-inch (2.5-cm) piece fresh ginger, plus 2-inch (5-cm) piece, peeled and finely julienned (optional)

1 onion, unpeeled, root end removed and halved

2 celery ribs, quartered

2 large carrots, peeled and quartered

Handful of flat-leaf parsley stems

2 thyme sprigs

1 tsp black peppercorns

1 small bay leaf

Salt

1 cup (2 oz/60 g) baby spinach leaves, coarsely chopped

Lemon wedges for serving

Hot sauce, such as Sriracha

Place the chicken in a large, heavy pot. Add the 1-inch (2.5-cm) piece of ginger, the onion, celery, carrots, parsley, thyme, peppercorns, bay leaf, and 1 tsp salt. Fill the pot with cold water to cover all the ingredients by 2 inches (5 cm). Bring to a boil over high heat and immediately reduce to a gentle simmer. Simmer, occasionally skimming any foam on the surface, until the juices run clear when you pierce the thickest part of the chicken's thigh, about 1½ hours.

Remove the chicken from the pot and transfer to a plate. Strain the broth through a colander into a bowl, discarding the solids. Line a fine-mesh strainer with two layers of cheesecloth. Strain the broth through the strainer to remove the fat. Rinse the pot and return the strained broth to it.

Once the chicken is cool enough to handle, use your fingers to remove and shred the meat, discarding the skin and bones. Add the shredded meat to the pot with the broth and pour in any juices that have collected on the plate. Season with salt. Bring to a boil, add the spinach, and stir just until wilted.

Serve, garnished with the julienned ginger, if using. Pass the lemon wedges and Sriracha sauce at the table.

5

SMOKY RED PEPPER SOUP

serves 8

1 large yellow onion, sliced

4 large cloves garlic, sliced

1 Tbsp chopped marjoram

1 Tbsp paprika, preferably
Spanish smoked paprika

Salt and freshly ground pepper

3 Tbsp olive oil

4 red bell peppers, roasted (page 191), peeled,
seeded, and chopped, any juices reserved

1 cup (2 oz/60 g) coarse fresh bread crumbs

4 anchovy fillets in olive oil

4 cups (32 fl oz/1 l) chicken or vegetable broth

4 tsp capers

*Thickened with
bread crumbs
and garnished
with capers and
anchovies, this
coarsely textured
puréed soup has a
distinctly Spanish
leaning. Serve hot
or chilled, as desired.*

Preheat the oven to 450°F (230°C). Place
the onion slices on a rimmed baking
sheet. Sprinkle with the garlic, marjoram,
and paprika. Season lightly with salt and
generously with pepper. Drizzle with the oil,
then stir to coat the onions completely and
spread them out on the baking sheet. Roast,
stirring often, until the onions are golden
and soft, 15–20 minutes.

Working in batches if necessary, combine
the roasted peppers and their juices and the
roasted onion mixture in a food processor
and process until a coarse purée forms. Add
the bread crumbs and 2 of the anchovies,
then process again just to a coarse purée.
Add 2 cups (16 fl oz/500 ml) of the broth and
purée again. Pour into a large, heavy pot
along with the remaining 2 cups broth and
bring to a simmer over medium heat, stirring
often. Taste and adjust the seasoning with
salt and pepper and simmer for 1–2 minutes
to blend the flavors.

Ladle the soup into bowls. Cut the remaining
2 anchovies lengthwise into 4 pieces each
and float 1 slice in each bowl. Sprinkle with
the capers and serve.

6

TOMATO SOUP WITH WHITE WINE & SHALLOTS

serves 4

10 plum tomatoes, halved

2 cloves garlic, minced

4 Tbsp (⅓ oz/10 g) chopped basil

5 Tbsp (2½ fl oz/75 ml) olive oil

4 shallots, halved

1½ cups (12 fl oz/375 ml) dry white wine

Salt and freshly ground pepper

*Plum, or Roma,
tomatoes can be
purchased year-
round, but blush
deepest in the
summer months
for incomparable
color and flavor.
A little wine, a
little garlic, and
a few leaves of
sweet-scented
basil showcase
the season's finest.*

Preheat the oven to 400°F (200°C). Arrange
the tomato halves, cut side up, in a roasting
pan. Sprinkle with the garlic and 1 Tbsp of
the basil and drizzle with 4 Tbsp (2 fl oz/
60 ml) of the oil. Roast until the tomatoes
are soft when pierced with a fork, about
40 minutes. Peel and discard the skins.

In a large, heavy pot, warm the remaining
1 Tbsp oil over medium-high heat. Add the
shallots and sauté for about 2 minutes. Add
the roasted tomatoes and garlic, wine, and
½ cup (4 fl oz/125 ml) water and bring to
a boil. Reduce the heat to medium-low and
simmer, uncovered, until the mixture has
thickened, about 20 minutes. Season with
salt and pepper. Remove from the heat and
let cool slightly.

Working in batches, purée the soup in a
blender or food processor to the desired
consistency. Return to the pot and reheat
to serving temperature. Serve, garnished
with the remaining 3 Tbsp basil.

AUGUST

7

7

Fideo is a thin Spanish pasta similar to vermicelli. Serve with grilled corn tortillas cut into triangles for dipping.

FIDEO & CHICKEN SOUP WITH QUESO FRESCO

serves 6

2 small skinless, boneless chicken breast halves

3 Tbsp olive oil

Salt and freshly ground pepper

1 white onion, chopped

4 cloves garlic, minced

1 tsp dried oregano

2 Tbsp tomato paste

½ chipotle chile in adobo, minced

6 cups (48 fl oz/1.5 l) chicken broth

1½ cups (4 oz/125 g) fideo noodles or vermicelli pasta broken into 2-inch (5-cm) pieces

2 Tbsp chopped cilantro

1 avocado, pitted, peeled, and diced

3 oz (90 g) queso fresco, crumbled

Preheat the oven to 375°F (190°C) and put the chicken breasts on a baking sheet. Brush the chicken with 1 Tbsp of oil and season with salt and pepper. Roast the chicken in the oven until it is cooked all the way through, about 20 minutes. When the chicken is cool enough to handle, shred it and set aside.

In a large, heavy pot, warm the remaining 2 Tbsp oil over medium-high heat. Add the onion and garlic and sauté until translucent, about 5 minutes. Add the oregano, tomato paste, and chipotle and stir well to combine. Add the broth and bring to a boil. Add the fideo and cook for 8 minutes. Add the shredded chicken and cilantro and stir to combine. Season to taste with salt and pepper.

Serve, topped with diced avocado and crumbled queso fresco.

8

This is a smooth chilled soup, seasoned simply with lemon juice and mellow spices. Curry powders vary in quality and lose their flavor relatively quickly, so sample different varieties until you find one you love, and then buy it in small quantities.

CHILLED CURRIED CORN SOUP

serves 6

2 Tbsp olive oil

2 leeks, white and pale green parts, finely chopped

2 small red potatoes, peeled and coarsely chopped

5 cups (30 oz/940 g) fresh corn kernels (from about 10 ears) or 5 cups frozen

2 tsp Madras curry powder

6 cups (48 fl oz/1.5 l) chicken broth

2 Tbsp fresh lemon juice

Salt and ground white pepper

6 thin lemon slices

½ cup (4 oz/125 g) sour cream

3 Tbsp finely chopped flat-leaf parsley

In a large, heavy pot, warm the oil over medium heat. Add the leeks and sauté until softened, 5 minutes. Add the potatoes and 4½ cups (27 oz/845 g) of the corn kernels and continue to cook for 2 minutes. Add the curry powder and cook for 1 minute. Add the broth and lemon juice and bring to a boil. Reduce the heat to medium-low, cover partially, and simmer until the potatoes are soft, about 20 minutes. Remove from the heat and let cool slightly.

Working in batches, purée the soup in a blender. Pass the purée through a fine-mesh sieve or food mill set over a bowl, pressing on the pulp. Discard any solids left in the sieve. Season to taste with salt and pepper. Let cool to room temperature. Transfer to a covered container and refrigerate until well chilled, at least 3 hours. Just before serving, bring a small saucepan three-fourths full of water to a boil. Add the remaining ½ cup (3 oz/90 g) corn kernels and blanch for 1 minute. Drain and let cool.

Serve the soup garnished with the corn kernels, lemon slices, sour cream, and chopped parsley.

9

Filé is the olive-green powder made from the dried and pulverized leaves of the sassafras plant. Like okra, it is frequently used as a thickener in Cajun gumbos. Look for it in the spice aisle of well-stocked markets.

CAJUN SHRIMP SOUP

serves 4

2 Tbsp olive oil

¼ cup (1½ oz/45 g) finely chopped yellow onion

2 cloves garlic, minced

½ green bell pepper, seeded and finely chopped

1 serrano chile, seeded and finely chopped

1 can (14½ oz/455 g) diced tomatoes

2 cups (16 fl oz/500 ml) chicken broth

½ tsp minced thyme

¼ tsp cayenne pepper

1 lb (500 g) shrimp, peeled and deveined

½ tsp filé powder

Salt and freshly ground black pepper

In a large, heavy pot, warm the oil over medium-high heat. Add the onion and sauté until translucent, about 2 minutes. Stir in the garlic and bell pepper, then add the chile, tomatoes with their juices, broth, thyme, and cayenne. Bring to a boil, reduce the heat to low, and simmer, uncovered, for 15 minutes to blend the flavors.

Add the shrimp and filé powder and cook just until the shrimp turn pink and opaque, about 3 minutes. Season with salt and pepper and serve.

10

Fresh summer beans star in this Portuguese peasant soup. If possible, use vegetable stock, as it allows the flavors of the vegetables to shine more distinctly than if you use poultry stock.

FRESH GREEN BEAN SOUP

serves 4–6

5 Tbsp (2½ fl oz/75 ml) olive oil

2 yellow onions, chopped

1 lb (500 g) tomatoes, peeled (page 172), seeded, and chopped

1 lb (500 g) boiling potatoes, peeled and diced

4 cups (32 fl oz/1 l) vegetable or chicken broth

1 lb (500 g) green beans, trimmed and cut on the diagonal into 1-inch (2.5-cm) pieces

Salt and freshly ground pepper

3 Tbsp chopped mint (optional)

In a large, heavy pot, warm the oil over medium heat. Add the onions and sauté until tender, 8–10 minutes. Add the tomatoes and potatoes and sauté for 3–5 minutes. Add the broth, raise the heat to high, and bring to a boil. Reduce the heat to low and simmer, uncovered, until the potatoes are very tender, about 20 minutes. Remove from the heat and let cool slightly.

Working in batches, purée the soup in a blender or food processor. Return to the pot.

Bring a saucepan three-fourths full of salted water to a boil. Add the green beans and cook until crisp-tender, about 5 minutes. Drain, reserving a bit of the cooking water to add to the purée if it is too thick.

Reheat the purée and season with salt and pepper. Add the green beans and simmer over medium heat until heated through, about 5 minutes. Thin with the reserved cooking water if needed.

Serve, garnished with the chopped mint, if using.

11

Lean pork loin melds with garlic and serrano chiles in this quintessentially Latin soup. Substitute cubed pork shoulder for even more succulent results. Serve with warmed tortillas, lime wedges, and a crisp Mexican beer.

GARLICKY PORK & CHILE SOUP

serves 4–6

1 lb (500 g) boneless pork loin, cut into cubes

Salt and freshly ground pepper

2 Tbsp olive oil

1 small yellow onion, chopped

2 cloves garlic, minced

3 serrano chiles, seeded and chopped

¼ cup (2 oz/60 g) long-grain rice

5 cups (40 fl oz/1.25 l) chicken broth

¼ cup (⅓ oz/10 g) minced cilantro

Juice of 1 lime

Season the pork cubes with salt and pepper. In a large, heavy pot, warm 1 Tbsp of the oil over medium-high heat. Working in batches if necessary to avoid crowding, add the pork and cook, turning as needed, until golden brown on all sides, about 6 minutes. Using a slotted spoon, transfer to a plate.

Reduce the heat to medium and add the remaining 1 Tbsp oil. Add the onion, garlic, chiles, and rice and stir to coat with the oil. Pour in the broth and bring to a boil. Reduce the heat to low, cover, and simmer until the rice is tender, about 15 minutes.

Return the pork to the pan, stir in the cilantro and lime juice, and cook until the pork is cooked through, about 5 minutes. Season with salt and pepper and serve.

12

Any variety of peach or nectarine works for this lightly boozy, Bellini-inspired soup. It makes a particularly good starter for an outdoor lunch, but you could also serve it as a refreshing finish to a warm-weather grilled dinner.

PEACH & RIESLING SOUP

serves 4

2 lb (1 kg) ripe peaches, peeled

1½ cups (12 oz/375 g) plain yogurt

2 Tbsp tawny port

⅓ cup (3 fl oz/80 ml) Riesling

¼ tsp ground ginger

Pinch of grated nutmeg

Honey for sweetening (optional)

Mint leaves for garnish

Cut the peaches in half and remove the pits. Cut one peach half into small cubes to use for garnishing and place in a bowl. Cover and refrigerate until ready to use.

Coarsely chop the remaining peach halves and purée in a food processor until smooth. Pour the purée into a bowl and stir in the yogurt, port, Riesling, ginger, and nutmeg. Whisk to blend well. Taste and add honey to sweeten, if desired. Cover and refrigerate until well chilled, at least 4 hours.

Serve, garnished with the reserved peach cubes and mint leaves.

13

YELLOW GAZPACHO WITH LEMON-BASIL RICOTTA

serves 6–8

2 yellow bell peppers, seeded and chopped

1 English cucumber, peeled, seeded and chopped

4 yellow tomatoes (about 2 lb/1 kg total), chopped, with all their juices

1 small yellow onion, chopped

2 cloves garlic, finely minced

2 Tbsp white wine vinegar

¼ cup (2 fl oz/60 ml) olive oil

Salt and freshly ground pepper

Tabasco sauce

FOR THE LEMON-BASIL RICOTTA

1 cup ricotta (8 oz/250 g), at room temperature

Grated zest of 1 lemon

¼ cup (⅓ oz/10 g) chopped basil

Salt

Adjust the spiciness as you like: add more hot sauce or even a fresh jalapeño. Serve the lemon-basil ricotta at room temperature so it incorporates easily. Leftover lemon-basil ricotta is a delicious spread for a vegetable sandwich wrap.

In a food processor, separately pulse the bell peppers, cucumber, tomatoes, and onion until finely chopped but not puréed. After each vegetable, transfer the contents of the food processor to a large bowl. Add the garlic, white wine vinegar, and oil and stir to combine. Season to taste with salt, pepper, and Tabasco.

To make the lemon-basil ricotta, combine the ricotta, lemon zest, basil, and a pinch of salt in a bowl and stir to mix well.

Serve the gazpacho, topped with a dollop of lemon-basil ricotta.

14

CHILLED CUCUMBER-BUTTERMILK SOUP WITH DILLED SHRIMP

serves 4

5 English cucumbers, peeled, seeded, and chopped

4 green onions, white and tender green parts, chopped

1 large clove garlic

¼ cup (2 fl oz/60 ml) buttermilk

1½ cups (12 oz/375 g) plain whole yogurt

2 Tbsp fresh lemon juice

Salt and freshly ground pepper

FOR THE DILLED SHRIMP

¼ lb (125 g) bay shrimp, coarsely chopped

1 Tbsp chopped dill

Salt and freshly ground pepper

A very refreshing and visually enticing soup, this is perfect for a luncheon or summertime buffet. The dilled shrimp topping gives it substance.

Put the cucumbers, green onions, and garlic into a food processor and pulse to finely chop. Add the buttermilk, yogurt, and lemon juice, and purée. Season with salt and pepper. Transfer to a covered container and refrigerate for 1 hour.

To make the dilled shrimp, put the shrimp and the dill in a small bowl and stir to combine. Season with salt and pepper.

Serve the soup, topped with the dilled shrimp.

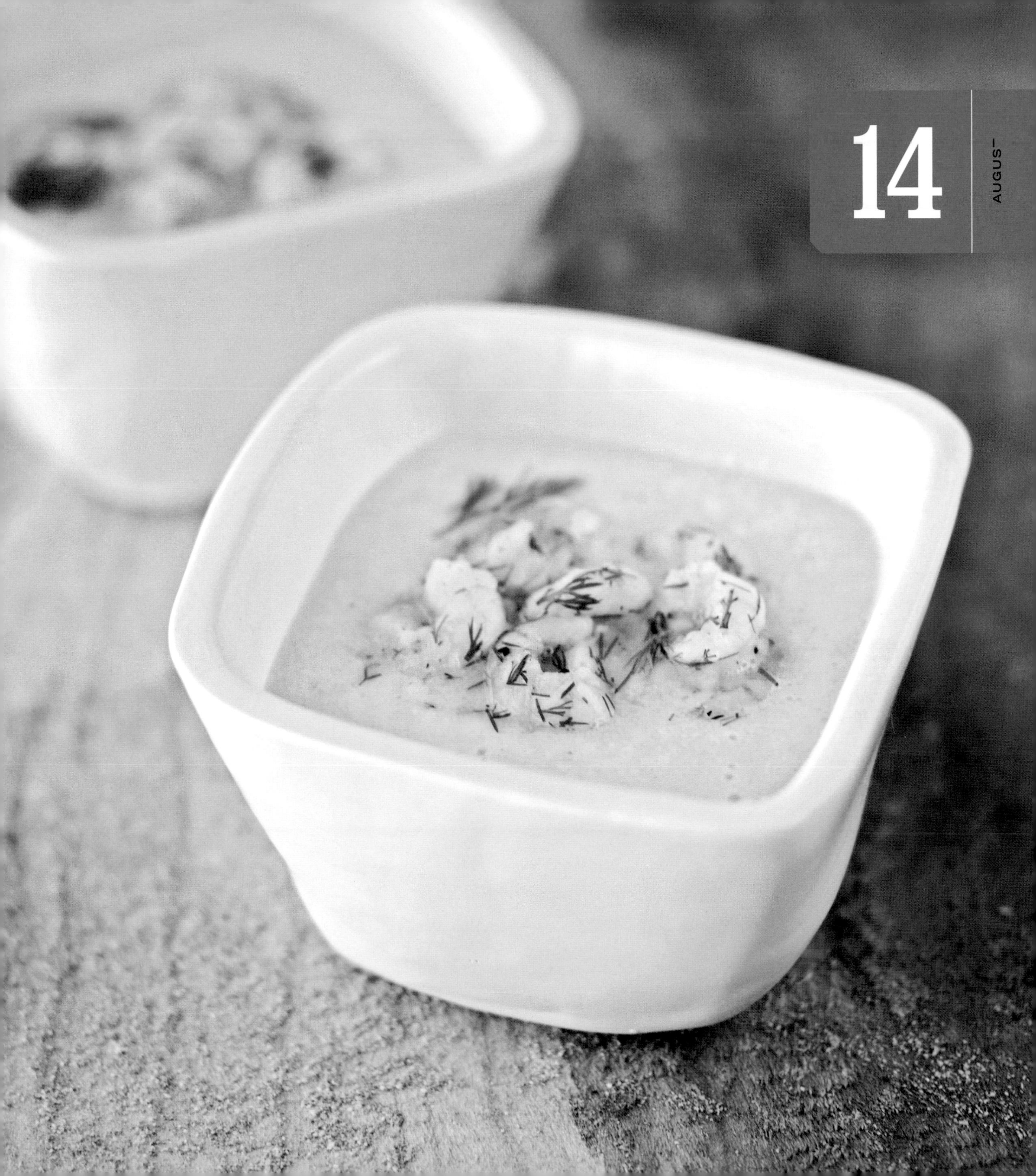
14
AUGUS

15

This soup can also be served smooth: after cooking the vegetables, purée them in batches in a blender. The charred eggplant turns silky and almost creamy, and the pleasant smoky flavor pervades the soup.

CHARRED EGGPLANT SOUP WITH CUMIN & GREEK YOGURT

serves 6–8

1 Tbsp olive oil, plus more for brushing

2 large eggplants (about 2½ lb/1.25 kg total), peeled and cut crosswise into slices 1 inch (2.5 cm) thick

3 ripe tomatoes (about 1¼ lb/625 g total), cored, halved, and seeded

3 carrots, peeled and finely chopped

5 shallots, finely chopped

3 cloves garlic, minced

¾ tsp minced thyme

¼ tsp ground cumin

1 cup (8 fl oz/250 ml) dry white wine

5 cups (40 fl oz/1.25 l) chicken or vegetable broth

Salt and freshly ground pepper

½ cup (4 oz/125 g) Greek-style plain yogurt (optional)

Prepare a charcoal or gas grill for direct-heat cooking over medium-high heat. Brush the grate with oil. Brush the eggplant slices and tomato halves with oil and arrange on the grill directly over the heat. Cook, turning as needed, until softened and nicely grill-marked, about 8 minutes for the tomatoes and 10 minutes for the eggplant. Transfer to a cutting board. When cool enough to handle, peel and discard the skins from the tomatoes. Coarsely chop the eggplant slices.

In a large, heavy pot, warm the 1 Tbsp oil over medium-high heat. Add the carrots and sauté until just beginning to soften, about 4 minutes. Add the shallots, garlic, thyme, and cumin and cook, stirring occasionally, until fragrant, about 2 minutes. Add the tomatoes, chopped eggplant, wine, and broth and bring to a boil. Reduce the heat to low, cover partially, and simmer for 20 minutes to blend the flavors. Season with 1½ tsp salt and pepper to taste. Serve, garnished with a dollop of yogurt, if using.

16

This is a soup inspired by the classic side dish of creamed corn. Serve with warm focaccia and a mixed green salad with mandarin oranges and sliced ripe avocado—and a grilled steak, of course.

CREAMY CORN SOUP WITH BACON & SAGE

serves 6

5 slices thick-cut bacon

2 Tbsp unsalted butter

1 Tbsp olive oil

2 leeks, white and pale green parts, chopped

5 sage leaves, chopped

4 cups (32 fl oz/1 l) chicken broth

6 cups (2¼ lb/1 kg) fresh corn kernels (from about 12 ears) or 6 cups frozen

2 Tbsp heavy cream

Salt and freshly ground pepper

In a large, heavy pot, cook the bacon over medium heat, turning once, until crispy, about 8 minutes. Transfer the bacon to paper towels to drain. When it is cool enough to handle, crumble into bite-sized pieces. Set aside.

In the same pot, melt the butter with the oil over medium heat. Add the leeks and sauté until soft, about 4 minutes. Add the sage and cook, stirring to combine, for 1 minute. Add the broth and bring to a boil over medium-high heat. Add the corn and cook for 5 minutes. Remove from the heat and let cool slightly.

Purée half of the soup in a blender. Return to the pot, stir in the cream, and warm through over medium-low heat. Season with salt and pepper and serve, topped with the crumbled bacon.

17

AVOCADO SOUP WITH LIME JUICE & RUM

serves 4–6

2 ripe avocados

4 cups (32 fl oz/1 l) very cold chicken broth

1½ cups (12 fl oz/360 ml) very cold heavy cream

¼ cup (2 fl oz/60 ml) white rum

1 tsp curry powder

Salt

¼ cup (2 fl oz/60 ml) fresh lime juice, plus more to taste

This soup, inspired by the tropics, must be served right away or the avocado will begin to brown. Serve in clear shot glasses garnished with lime slices as a starter for a brunch or an alfresco cocktail party.

Peel and pit the avocados and chop coarsely. Transfer to a blender along with the chicken broth, cream, rum, curry powder, 1 tsp salt, and the ¼ cup (2 fl oz/60 ml) lime juice. Blend until smooth.

Taste and add more lime juice and salt as needed until the soup is bright-tasting. Serve right away in chilled bowls or glasses.

18

SNAP PEA & SUCCOTASH SOUP WITH PARSLEY-MINT PISTOU

serves 4–6

¼ cup (2 fl oz/60 ml) olive oil

1 yellow onion, chopped

4 cloves garlic, minced

6 cups (48 fl oz/1.5 l) chicken broth

1 lb (500 g) lima beans in the pod, shelled (about 2 cups)

3 cups (18 oz/560 g) corn kernels (from about 6 ears), or 3 cups frozen

6 oz (185 g) sugar snap peas, trimmed and halved on the diagonal

Salt and freshly ground pepper

FOR THE PISTOU

1 cup (1 oz/30 g) flat-leaf parsley

½ cup (½ oz/15 g) mint leaves

2 small cloves garlic

2 green onions, white and tender green parts, chopped

¼ cup (2 oz/60 ml) olive oil

2 Tbsp fresh lemon juice

Pistou is a sauce from Provence classically made with garlic, basil, and olive oil. Here, parsley and mint stand in for the basil, adding a delicious flavor and vibrant color to the soup.

In a large, heavy pot, warm the oil over medium-high heat. Add the onion and garlic and sauté until translucent, about 5 minutes. Add the broth and bring to a boil. Add the lima beans and cook until tender, 12–15 minutes. Add the corn and cook for 3 minutes. Add the sugar snap peas and continue to cook for 3 minutes. Season with salt and pepper.

To make the pistou, put the parsley, mint, garlic, and green onion into a food processor and pulse until finely chopped. Add the oil, lemon juice, ¼ tsp salt, and ⅛ tsp pepper and pulse to combine.

Serve the soup, topped with a dollop of pistou.

19

ICED MELON SOUP WITH CHAMPAGNE & GINGER

serves 4–6

5 cups (30 oz/940 g) coarsely chopped cantaloupe or honeydew melon

1 Tbsp peeled and grated fresh ginger

1 Tbsp fresh lemon juice

3 cups (24 fl oz/750 ml) dry Champagne or sparkling wine, well chilled

1–2 Tbsp confectioners' sugar

Mint sprigs for garnish

A touch of sparkle and spice makes this an elegant start to a summer supper. Use the sweetest and juiciest cantaloupe or honeydew melon you can find, and garnish with sliced strawberries or whole raspberries, if you like.

Purée the melon and ginger in a blender, food processor, or food mill. If you use a processor or blender, force the purée through a strainer set inside a bowl, pressing hard on the solids with a wooden spoon. Stir in the lemon juice. Cover tightly and refrigerate until well chilled, at least 2 hours or up to overnight.

Stir in the Champagne. Stir in just enough of the sugar to bring out the melon flavor without making the soup overly sweet. Serve, garnished with the mint sprigs.

20

SPICY POBLANO SOUP WITH TORTILLA STRIPS

serves 4–6

2 Tbsp unsalted butter

1 small white onion, chopped

4 poblano chiles (about ¾ lb/375 g), roasted (left), peeled, seeded, and chopped

2 green bell peppers, roasted (left), peeled, seeded, and chopped

1 small russet potato, peeled and diced

1½ tsp ground cumin

¾ tsp ground coriander

3 cups (24 fl oz/750 ml) chicken broth

⅓ cup (3 fl oz/80 ml) heavy cream

Salt

FOR THE TORTILLA STRIPS

Canola oil for frying

2 corn tortillas, halved and then cut into ¼-inch (6-mm) strips

¼ cup (2 oz/60 g) sour cream

To roast chiles or bell peppers, preheat the broiler. Cut the chile or pepper in half lengthwise and remove the stem and seeds. Place cut side down on a baking sheet and broil 5 inches (13 cm) from the heat source until the skin blackens and blisters, about 6 minutes. Remove from the broiler, cover loosely with foil, and let steam and cool for 10 minutes. Peel away the skins.

In a large, heavy pot, melt the butter over medium-high heat. Add the onion and sauté until soft, about 5 minutes. Add the poblanos, bell peppers, potato, cumin, coriander, and broth and bring to a boil. Reduce the heat to low and simmer until the potatoes are very tender, about 25 minutes. Remove from the heat and let cool slightly.

Working in batches, purée the soup in a blender. Return to the pot, add the cream, and bring just to a boil. Turn off the heat and season to taste with salt.

To make the tortilla strips, pour ¼ inch (6 mm) of oil into a small frying pan and place over high heat. When the oil is very hot (a tortilla strip dropped into it should sizzle immediately), fry the tortilla strips in batches until they are browned, about 2 minutes per side. Transfer to paper towels to drain and season with salt while they are still hot.

Serve, topped with a dollop of sour cream and several fried tortilla strips.

21

To make rouille, in a blender, combine 2 seeded dried chiles, 4 cloves garlic, 1 Tbsp dried bread crumbs, 2 large egg yolks, and ½ teaspoon sea salt and process until a paste forms. With the motor running, drizzle in ½ cup (4 fl oz/125 ml) extra-virgin olive oil in a slow, steady stream, processing until the mixture is creamy and smooth. Store in the refrigerator in an airtight container for up to 1 week. Makes ¾ cup (6 fl oz/180 ml).

BOUILLABAISSE
serves 6–8

¼ cup (2 fl oz/60 ml) olive oil

1 yellow onion, chopped

2 leeks, white parts only, coarsely chopped

1 orange zest strip

2 tomatoes, peeled (page 172) and coarsely chopped

1 fennel stalk, about 6 inches (15 cm) long, thinly sliced

2 cloves garlic, crushed

2 thyme sprigs

1 bay leaf

Salt and freshly ground pepper

2 cups (16 fl oz/500 ml) dry white wine

5 boiling potatoes (about 1½ lb/750 g), peeled and cut into slices ½ inch (12 mm) thick

¼ tsp saffron threads

2 lb (1 kg) firm-fleshed fish steaks or fillets, cut into 1½-inch (4-cm) chunks

2 lb (1 kg) tender-fleshed whole fish, cleaned, cut into 1½-inch (4-cm) chunks

1 lb (500 g) mussels, scrubbed and debearded

Boiling water as needed

¾ cup (6 fl oz/180 ml) Rouille (left)

8 slices country-style bread, toasted and rubbed with 1 clove garlic

1 Tbsp minced flat-leaf parsley

In a large, heavy pot, warm the oil over medium-high heat. Add the onion and leeks and sauté until translucent, 2–3 minutes. Stir in the orange zest, tomatoes, fennel, garlic, thyme, and bay leaf. Season with ½ tsp salt and ½ tsp pepper. Add the wine, the potatoes, and 1 cup (8 fl oz/250 ml) water and bring to a boil. Reduce the heat to low, cover, and simmer until the potatoes are nearly tender, about 25 minutes.

Raise the heat to medium-high and bring the soup to a rolling boil. Stir in the saffron. Place the firm-fleshed fish on top of the soup, add just enough boiling water as needed to cover, and boil until the fish is just half-cooked, about 7 minutes. Add the tender-fleshed fish, the mussels, discarding any that do not close to the touch, and just enough boiling water as needed to cover. Boil just until the tender-fleshed fish separates easily with a fork and the mussels open, 3–4 minutes. Discard any unopened mussels. »→

Stir 2–3 Tbsp of the broth into the rouille. Place a slice of toasted bread in the bottom of each bowl. Top with the fish, mussels, and potatoes. Ladle the broth over the top and sprinkle with the parsley. Serve, passing the remaining rouille at the table.

22

This colorful soup makes use of the best that summer has to offer. The tomato broth is partially puréed to add satisfying thickness to the soup.

TOMATO, ZUCCHINI & FRESH CORN SOUP
serves 4–6

2 zucchini, trimmed, halved, and sliced

3 Tbsp olive oil

Salt and freshly ground pepper

1 yellow onion, chopped

5 cloves garlic, minced

4 plum tomatoes, chopped

4 cups (32 fl oz/1 l) vegetable or chicken broth

1 cup (6 oz/180 g) corn kernels (from about 2 ears)

⅓ cup (½ oz/15 g) chopped basil

Preheat the oven to 400°F (200°C). Toss the zucchini with 1 Tbsp of the oil and season with salt and pepper. Spread on a baking sheet and roast for 20 minutes. Set aside.

In a large, heavy pot, warm the remaining 2 Tbsp oil over medium-high heat. Add the onion and garlic and sauté until soft, about 5 minutes. Add the tomatoes, stir to combine, and cook for 3 minutes. Add the broth and bring to a boil. Reduce the heat to low and simmer for 20 minutes. Remove from the heat and let cool slightly.

Purée half of the soup in a blender. Return to the pot and season with salt and pepper. Return the soup to a boil, add the corn, and cook for 5 minutes. Add the zucchini and stir in the basil. Serve.

AUGUST

23

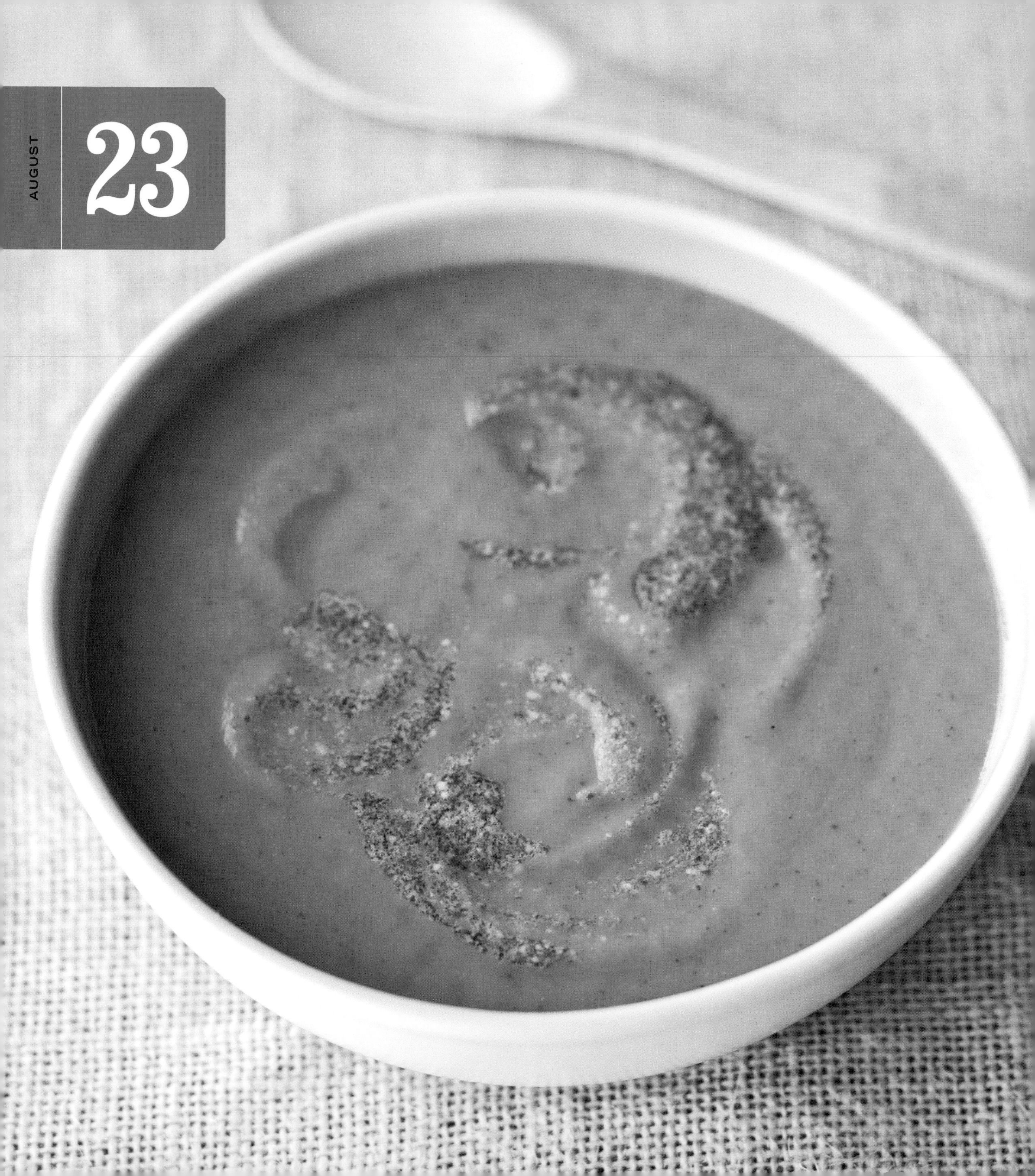

23

To make the sun-dried tomato pesto, in a food processor, mince 1 clove garlic. Coarsely chop and add ½ cup (2½ oz/ 75 g) drained oil-packed sun-dried tomatoes, 2 Tbsp olive oil, 2 Tbsp finely chopped basil, and 2 Tbsp pine nuts. Season with salt and pepper. Process to form a thick paste, adding more oil if needed.

ROASTED SUMMER VEGETABLE SOUP WITH PESTO

serves 4–6

2 leeks, white and pale green parts, finely chopped

4 carrots, peeled and cut into 2-inch (5-cm) pieces

2 zucchini, cut into 2-inch (5-cm) pieces

2 Asian eggplants, cut into 2-inch (5-cm) pieces

2 large tomatoes, quartered

2 potatoes (about 10 oz/315 g), peeled and cut into 2-inch (5-cm) pieces

4½ cups (36 fl oz/1.1 l) chicken broth, or more as needed

2 Tbsp olive oil

Salt and freshly ground pepper

2 Tbsp finely chopped basil

2 Tbsp fresh lemon juice

Basil Pesto (page 118) or Sun-Dried Tomato Pesto (left) for serving

Preheat the oven to 425°F (220°C). In a large, heavy roasting pan, combine the leeks, carrots, zucchini, eggplants, tomatoes, and potatoes. Add ½ cup (4 fl oz/125 ml) of the broth and the oil, season with salt and pepper, and mix until the vegetables are well coated. Roast, turning once, until the vegetables are softened, about 40 minutes. Remove from the oven and let cool slightly.

Working in batches, purée the vegetables with ½ cup (4 fl oz/125 ml) of the broth. Transfer to a large saucepan and stir in the remaining 3½ cups (28 fl oz/875 ml) broth, the basil, and the lemon juice. If needed, add more broth for the desired consistency. Cook over low heat for 3 minutes to blend the flavors. Season with salt and pepper.

Serve, garnished with the pesto.

24

Cinnamon and fresh ginger are unexpected spices to enhance the flavors of ripe summer berries. Serve with a scoop of vanilla ice cream for a gorgeous and unique summertime dessert. You can easily make this using frozen fruit in the winter.

SPICED BERRY SOUP

serves 4

1½ lb (750 g) strawberries, hulled and halved

1 lb (500 g) raspberries

¾ cup (6 fl oz/180 ml) cranberry juice cocktail

1 cinnamon stick

1½ tsp peeled and grated fresh ginger

⅓ cup (3 oz/90 g) sugar

In a large saucepan, combine the strawberries, raspberries, cranberry juice cocktail, cinnamon stick, ginger, and sugar over medium-low heat. Cook, stirring often, for 7 minutes. Remove from the heat, remove and discard the cinnamon stick, and let cool slightly.

Working in batches, purée the soup in a blender. Transfer to a covered container and refrigerate until thoroughly chilled, at least 3 hours. Serve.

25

MUSSELS IN SAFFRON BROTH

serves 4

1 tsp saffron threads

½ cup (4 fl oz/125 ml) dry white wine

2 Tbsp unsalted butter

2 Tbsp olive oil

1 small yellow onion, chopped

3 cloves garlic, sliced

1 cup (8 fl oz/250 ml) chicken broth

Salt and freshly ground pepper

2 lb (1 kg) mussels, scrubbed and debearded

2 Tbsp chopped flat-leaf parsley

Serving mussels family style makes such a beautiful presentation and is fun for all at the table. Serve this with plenty of bread, because you will be fighting over the last drop of this flavorful broth.

Using your fingers, gently crush the saffron into a small bowl and add the white wine. Set aside.

In a large, heavy pot, melt the butter with the oil over medium-high heat. Add the onion and garlic and sauté until soft, about 5 minutes. Add the saffron mixture and cook for 2 minutes. Add the broth and bring to a boil. Season with salt and pepper. Add the mussels, discarding any that do not close to the touch. Cover tightly and cook until the mussels open, 8–10 minutes.

Transfer the mussels and broth to a large bowl, discarding any unopened mussels. Sprinkle with the parsley and serve family style.

26

ROASTED TOMATO SOUP WITH CITRUS CRÈME FRAÎCHE

serves 4–6

4 lb (2 kg) plum tomatoes, halved lengthwise and seeded

5 Tbsp (3 fl oz/80 ml) olive oil

Salt and freshly ground pepper

1 yellow onion, chopped

3 cloves garlic, minced

2 cups (16 fl oz/500 ml) chicken broth

FOR THE CITRUS CRÈME FRAÎCHE

¼ cup (2 oz/60 g) crème fraîche or sour cream, at room temperature

Grated zest and juice of 1 lemon

It's not hard to make your own crème fraîche. Take 1 cup (8 fl oz/250 ml) cream, heat to lukewarm, add 1 Tbsp buttermilk, and let sit at room temperature for 12–48 hours to thicken and become tangy. Once you like the flavor and texture, refrigerate it.

Preheat the oven to 450°F (230°C). Arrange the tomatoes on a baking sheet. Drizzle with 3 Tbsp of the oil and season with salt and pepper. Toss gently and spread out in a single layer. Roast until the tomatoes are caramelized and very soft, about 25 minutes.

In a large, heavy pot, warm the remaining 2 Tbsp oil over medium-high heat. Add the onion and garlic and sauté until very soft, about 5 minutes. Stir in the tomatoes and sauté for 3–4 minutes. Add the broth, bring to a boil, reduce the heat to low, and simmer, uncovered, for 15 minutes to blend the flavors. Remove from the heat and let cool slightly.

Working in batches, purée the soup in a blender. Return to the pot and season with salt and pepper.

To make the citrus crème fraîche, in a bowl, combine the crème fraîche, the lemon zest, and 1 Tbsp of lemon juice. Using a whisk, blend well. Season with additional lemon juice and with salt and pepper.

Serve the soup, topped with a dollop of the citrus crème fraîche.

27

MISO SOUP WITH TOFU & LONG BEANS

serves 2

3 oz (90 g) firm tofu

Salt

¼ lb (125 g) Chinese long beans or green beans, cut into 1-inch (2.5-cm) pieces

1 piece kombu, about 3 inches (7.5 cm)

½ cup (½ oz/15 g) bonito flakes

2 Tbsp white miso paste

1 green onion, white and tender green parts, thinly sliced

In addition to being delicious, miso soup is said to enhance digestion and immunity. This is a very clean and light soup. If you can't find Chinese long beans, use Blue Lake or haricots verts. Serve with cold sesame noodles.

Drain the tofu and slice in half crosswise. Place both pieces of tofu on a plate and top with a second plate. Weigh down the top plate with a can. Let stand for 20 minutes to drain the tofu. Pour off any released water from the plate and cut the tofu into tiny cubes. Set aside.

Bring a small saucepan of water to a boil and add 1 Tbsp salt. Add the long beans and cook until crisp-tender, about 3 minutes. Drain the beans and set aside.

Put 3 cups (24 fl oz/750 ml) cold water and the kombu in a saucepan over medium heat. Bring to a boil and then remove and discard the kombu. Turn off the heat, add the bonito flakes, stir gently once, and let sit for 5 minutes. Strain the soup through a fine-mesh sieve and return the broth to the saucepan.

Put the miso paste in a small bowl and add ¼ cup (2 fl oz/60 ml) of the warm broth. Stir until the mixture is very smooth. Add the miso mixture to the saucepan and warm gently, taking care not to let the soup come to a boil. Add the tofu, long beans, and green onion and warm for just a few minutes. Serve.

28

ANGEL HAIR IN CHICKEN BROTH WITH TOMATOES & BASIL

serves 4

2 Tbsp olive oil

½ small yellow onion, thinly sliced

3 cloves garlic, minced

5 cups (40 fl oz/1.25 l) chicken broth

½ lb (250 g) angel hair pasta, broken into 2-inch (5-cm) pieces

4 plum tomatoes, chopped

⅓ cup (⅓ oz/10 g) chopped basil

Salt and freshly ground pepper

Grated Parmesan cheese for serving

A modern version of the classic chicken noodle soup, this summertime recipe is a great way to use leftover grilled chicken and the half-full box of angel hair pasta that's hanging around in your pantry waiting to be cooked.

In a large, heavy pot, warm the oil over medium heat. Add the onion and garlic and sauté until translucent, about 5 minutes. Add the broth and bring to a boil. Add the pasta, return to a boil, and cook, stirring once or twice, for 4 minutes. Add the tomatoes and cook 3 minutes. Turn off the heat, stir in the basil, and season with salt and pepper. Serve, topped with a generous amount of Parmesan.

29

LENTIL SOUP WITH SORREL

serves 4–6

2 Tbsp olive oil

1 yellow onion, chopped

3 cloves garlic, minced

Salt and freshly ground pepper

1 cup (7 oz/220 g) lentils

5 cups (40 fl oz/1.25 l) vegetable broth

⅓ cup (¾ oz/20 g) chopped sorrel

Grated zest and juice of 1 lemon

Sorrel is an herb that looks and acts a lot like spinach. As sorrel ages it becomes more acidic, so choose younger, smaller leaves for their subtle flavor. As this soup cools it will thicken, so you may need to add more broth when you reheat it. Substitute baby spinach if desired.

In a large, heavy pot, warm the oil over medium-high heat. Add the onion, garlic, 1 tsp salt, and ¼ tsp pepper and sauté until the onion is translucent, about 5 minutes. Add the lentils and broth and bring to a boil. Reduce the heat to low, partially cover, and simmer until the lentils are tender, about 40 minutes. Let cool slightly.

Working in batches, purée the soup in a blender. Return to the pot and stir in the sorrel and lemon zest and juice. Season with salt and pepper and serve.

30

ROMANO BEAN, ZUCCHINI & PARMESAN SOUP

serves 4–6

Romano beans, also known as Italian string beans, can be substituted with any snap pea. Use good-quality Parmesan and don't grate the cheese until just before you are ready to serve it for best flavor.

2 Tbsp olive oil

1 small yellow onion, finely chopped

2 cloves garlic, minced

3 small zucchini, trimmed, halved lengthwise, and cut into ½-inch (12-mm) slices

Salt and freshly ground pepper

4 cups (32 fl oz/1 l) chicken broth

½ lb (250 g) romano beans, ends trimmed and beans halved

1 can (14½ oz/15 oz) diced tomatoes

Grated Parmesan cheese for serving

In a large, heavy pot, warm the oil over medium heat. Add the onion and garlic and sauté until translucent, about 5 minutes. Add the zucchini, season with salt and pepper, and cook, stirring to combine, for 2 minutes. Add the broth and cook until the zucchini is tender, 6–8 minutes. Add the romano beans and tomatoes with their juices and cook for 5 minutes. Season with salt and pepper and serve, topped with Parmesan.

31

PORK PHO

serves 2

Pho is comfort food, Southeast Asian style. The light-bodied broth and zesty flavors satisfy without weighing you down. To slice the pork paper-thin, chill it in the freezer for half an hour.

3 oz (90 g) rice noodles

1 star anise

1 Tbsp coriander seeds

1 cinnamon stick

2 whole cloves

4 cups (32 fl oz/1 l) chicken broth

2-inch (5-cm) piece fresh ginger, peeled and minced

1 Tbsp Asian fish sauce

1 tsp sugar

¼ lb (125 g) pork tenderloin, cut into paper-thin slices

½ lime, cut into 4 wedges

2 Tbsp cilantro leaves

¼ red onion, thinly sliced

1 small red chile, seeded and thinly sliced

Hot sauce, such as Sriracha

In a bowl, combine the noodles with hot water to cover and let soak for 10 minutes. Drain and set aside.

In a small frying pan, combine the star anise, coriander seeds, cinnamon, and cloves. Toast the spices over medium heat, stirring frequently, until fragrant, 2–3 minutes.

In a large saucepan, combine the broth, ginger, fish sauce, sugar, and toasted spices. Bring to a boil over medium-high heat. Reduce the heat to low and simmer for 30 minutes. Strain the soup through a fine-mesh strainer and return to the pan. Return to a boil, add the noodles, and cook for 5 minutes.

Using tongs, remove the noodles from the soup and put in bowls. Top with half of the pork. Ladle the hot soup directly over the pork, adding enough to cover the noodles and cook the meat. Serve, passing the lime wedges, cilantro, red onion, chile, and hot sauce at the table.

1
**TUSCAN FARRO SOUP WITH
WHITE BEANS, TOMATOES & BASIL**
page 202

2
**POBLANO CHILE SOUP
WITH CORN & MUSHROOMS**
page 202

3
**TOMATO-BREAD SOUP
WITH BASIL OIL**
page 204

4
**GARLIC-SAGE SOUP WITH
POACHED EGGS & CROUTONS**
page 204

8
**CREAM OF FENNEL-LEEK PURÉE
WITH TOASTED ALMONDS**
page 207

9
LOBSTER & SWEET CORN CHOWDER
page 208

10
VEGETABLE-BARLEY SOUP
page 208

11
SPICY SEAFOOD & SAUSAGE GUMBO
page 209

15
MUSHROOM SOUP WITH CHICKEN
page 213

16
**PASTINA & KALE SOUP
WITH ANDOUILLE**
page 213

17
**SPICY BROCCOLINI &
CRANBERRY BEAN SOUP**
page 214

18
MINESTRONE WITH PESTO
page 214

22
**SCALLOPS & PANCETTA
IN SAFFRON BROTH**
page 216

23
**CHORIZO & CHICKEN STEW
WITH AVOCADO CREMA**
page 219

24
**SHIITAKE DUMPLINGS
IN KAFFIR LIME BROTH**
page 219

25
EGGPLANT & TOFU CURRY SOUP
page 220

29
**ROASTED PARSNIP & APPLE PURÉE
WITH GRUYÈRE TOASTS**
page 222

30
ITALIAN BEEF STEW
page 222

5
SPICY MEATBALL SOUP
page 205

6
ROASTED BUTTERNUT SQUASH SOUP
page 205

7
RIBOLLITA
page 207

12
LAMB & LENTIL SOUP WITH CILANTRO & PARSLEY
page 209

13
TURKEY & WHITE BEAN CHILI
page 210

14
GREEN CHILE STEW
page 210

19
CHICKEN & FARFALLE VEGETABLE SOUP
page 215

20
LEEK & POTATO SOUP WITH FRIED PROSCIUTTO
page 215

21
SWEET POTATO–CHIPOTLE SOUP
page 216

26
ROASTED PUMPKIN SOUP WITH CHINESE FIVE SPICE
page 220

27
BOURRIDE
page 221

28
ROASTED RED PEPPER & TOMATO SOUP
page 221

The glorious days of Indian summer are a boon to home cooks, offering late-harvest tomatoes, bell peppers, and eggplant as well as first-of-the season fall produce. Later in the month, draw on sweet potatoes, orange-fleshed squash, and other root vegetables for easy, nutritious, back-to-school soups. Cured meats and fresh sausages add satisfying bulk to stews and chilis as nights grow cooler.

september

1

TUSCAN FARRO SOUP WITH WHITE BEANS, TOMATOES & BASIL

serves 6

This wonderfully textured soup marries a handful of classic Tuscan flavors. The beans and farro make it hearty enough for a meal. Serve with an Italian red wine such as Chianti or Sangiovese.

½ cup (3 oz/90 g) farro

Salt and freshly ground pepper

3 Tbsp olive oil

1 large yellow onion, chopped

3 cloves garlic, minced

4 cups (32 fl oz/1 l) chicken broth

1 can (15 oz/470 g) cannellini or other white beans, drained

1 can (14½ oz/455 g) diced tomatoes

2 cups packed (2½ oz/75 g) baby spinach

½ cup (¾ oz/20 g) chopped basil

In a small saucepan, bring 1½ cups (12 fl oz/ 375 ml) water to a boil. Add the farro and a pinch of salt, reduce the heat to low, and cook, partially covered, until all the water is absorbed, 20–25 minutes.

In a large, heavy pot, warm the oil over medium-high heat. Add the onion and garlic and sauté until translucent, about 5 minutes. Add the broth and bring to a boil. Reduce the heat to low and add the beans, tomatoes with their juices, and farro. Bring to a simmer and cook, uncovered, for 10 minutes to blend the flavors. Add the spinach and basil and stir just until the spinach is wilted. Season with salt and pepper and serve.

2

POBLANO CHILE SOUP WITH CORN & MUSHROOMS

serves 6

Indian summer's chiles and the last corn of the season combine with fall's first mushrooms in this flavorful Latin-style soup. Crema is a thick, slightly sour cream sold in Mexican markets.

1 Tbsp canola oil

1 white onion, coarsely chopped

2 cloves garlic

2 cups (12 oz/375 g) fresh or frozen corn kernels

3 poblano chiles, roasted (page 191), peeled, seeded, and coarsely chopped

4 cups (32 fl oz/1 l) chicken broth

½ tsp dried oregano

2 Tbsp unsalted butter

½ lb (250 g) chanterelle, cremini, or other flavorful mushrooms, sliced

Salt and freshly ground pepper

½ cup (4 fl oz/125 ml) crema or sour cream, thinned with milk

3 oz (90 g) Muenster cheese or farmer's cheese, cut into ¼-inch (6-mm) cubes, at room temperature

In a large, heavy pot, warm the oil over medium-low heat. Add the onion and garlic and sauté until translucent, about 5 minutes. Raise the heat to medium and add half of the corn, half of the chiles, and 1 cup (8 fl oz/ 250 ml) of the broth. Bring to a simmer, stir in the oregano, and cook, uncovered, until the corn is tender, 10–15 minutes. Remove from the heat and let cool slightly.

Working in batches, purée the soup in a blender with ½ cup (4 fl oz/125 ml) of the remaining broth. Pass through a medium-mesh sieve back into the pot. Add the remaining 2½ cups (20 fl oz/625 ml) broth and bring to a simmer over medium-low heat.

Meanwhile, melt the butter in a frying pan over medium heat. Add the remaining chiles, the remaining corn, and the mushrooms and stir well. Season with salt and pepper and sauté until the mushrooms release their liquid and the liquid evaporates, about 8 minutes.

Add the mushroom mixture and the crema to the soup, stir well, cover, and simmer for 10 minutes to blend the flavors. Season with salt and pepper. Serve, garnished with the cheese.

3

SEPTEMBER

TOMATO-BREAD SOUP WITH BASIL OIL

serves 4–6

Called pappa al pomodoro in Italian, this soup combines a handful of favorite Italian ingredients: ripe tomatoes, bread (usually day old), olive oil, and basil. This version has cosmopolitan flair, with croutons, crisp-fried basil leaves, and a drizzling of basil oil as garnishes.

FOR THE BASIL OIL

1 cup (1 oz/30 g) packed basil leaves

¾ cup (6 fl oz/180 ml) extra-virgin olive oil

1 loaf country-style bread, crusts removed, cut into 1½-inch (4-cm) cubes

Salt and freshly ground pepper

6 Tbsp (3 fl oz/90 ml) extra-virgin olive oil, plus more for drizzling

3 celery ribs, minced

3 white onions, minced

2 carrots, peeled and minced

2 cloves garlic, minced

2 Tbsp tomato paste

2 lb (1 kg) plum tomatoes, peeled (page 172), seeded, and coarsely chopped

1 tsp sugar

To make the basil oil, bring a small saucepan of water to a boil. Have ready a bowl of ice water. Set aside 8 to 12 of the basil leaves. Blanch the remaining leaves in the boiling water for about 10 seconds. Drain, then plunge into the ice water. Drain again, and squeeze the leaves to remove as much water as possible. Transfer to a blender, add the oil, and pulse until the mixture is a uniform deep green. Strain the basil oil through a fine-mesh sieve lined with cheesecloth.

Preheat the oven to 350°F (180°C). Arrange the bread cubes in a single layer on a baking sheet, season with salt and pepper, and drizzle with olive oil. Bake until lightly toasted, about 10 minutes.

Meanwhile, in a large, heavy pot, warm 4 Tbsp (2 fl oz/60 ml) of the olive oil over medium heat. Add the celery, onions, carrots, and garlic and sauté until the vegetables are softened but not browned, about 10 minutes. Stir in the tomato paste and cook for 5 minutes. Add the tomatoes and sugar and season with salt and pepper. Simmer, stirring occasionally, until the tomatoes are softened, about 10 minutes.

Add the toasted bread cubes and 6 cups (48 fl oz/1.5 l) water to the pot. Stir to combine with the vegetables, bring to a ⟩⟩→

simmer over medium-high heat, and cook, uncovered and stirring often, until the bread has softened, about 15 minutes. Whisk the soup vigorously to break up the bread cubes. Keep warm.

In a small frying pan, warm the remaining 2 Tbsp olive oil over medium heat. Add the reserved basil leaves and fry, turning once, until crisp and slightly translucent, 30 seconds. Transfer to paper towels to drain and cool.

Serve the soup, garnished with the fried basil and drizzled with basil oil.

4

SEPTEMBER

GARLIC-SAGE SOUP WITH POACHED EGGS & CROUTONS

serves 6

20 cloves garlic, coarsely chopped

10 sage leaves

Salt and freshly ground pepper

6 eggs

Croutons (left)

2 Tbsp chopped flat-leaf parsley

6 Tbsp (3 fl oz/90 ml) extra-virgin olive oil

To make the croutons, remove the crusts from 4–6 slices of coarse country bread and cut the slices into cubes. Warm ⅓ cup (3 fl oz/80 ml) extra-virgin olive oil in a frying pan over medium-high heat. Add the bread cubes to the pan and fry, stirring often, until golden brown on all sides, 5–7 minutes. Transfer to paper towels to drain.

In a large, heavy pot, combine 8 cups (64 fl oz/2 l) water, the garlic, and the sage. Bring to a boil over high heat and boil until the garlic is soft, about 15 minutes. Remove from the heat. Using a slotted spoon, scoop out the sage and garlic. Discard the sage and mash the garlic with a fork. Return the garlic to the pot and season with salt and pepper.

Return the soup to a boil, then reduce the heat so that it gently simmers. Break each egg into a small bowl and slip into the simmering liquid. Cook until the whites are opaque but the yolks are still soft, about 2 minutes.

Using a slotted spoon, quickly and carefully lift the eggs from the soup and place in the bowls. Ladle some of the soup into each bowl, garnish with the croutons, and sprinkle with parsley. Drizzle with the oil and serve.

5

SPICY MEATBALL SOUP

serves 6

4 large russet potatoes (about 2 lb/1 kg)

1 lb (500 g) ground lean pork

1 white onion, one half minced, one half coarsely chopped

½ tsp dried oregano

Salt and freshly ground pepper

2 eggs, lightly beaten

1 lb (500 g) ripe tomatoes, chopped, or 1 can (14½ oz/455 g) diced tomatoes, drained

4 cups (32 fl oz/1 l) chicken broth

2 Tbsp canola oil

1 Tbsp all-purpose flour

1 jalapeño chile, partially slit open

1 flat-leaf parsley sprig, chopped

¼ cup (¼ oz/7 g) cilantro leaves for garnish

For this simple and filling Spanish-style soup, meatballs are enriched with grated potato and simmered in a base of tomato and parsley, then spiked with chile for a nice little kick.

Peel the potatoes and shred on the medium holes of a box grater-shredder. Wrap in a kitchen towel and squeeze out the excess liquid. In a bowl, combine the shredded potatoes, pork, minced onion, and oregano. Add 1 tsp salt and 1 tsp pepper, and toss to mix. Add the eggs and mix again. With your hands, roll the mixture into 1-inch (2.5-cm) balls.

In a blender, process the tomatoes and chopped onion until smooth, adding a little of the broth, if needed, to facilitate blending.

In a large, heavy pot, warm the oil over medium heat. Working in batches, gently add the meatballs and fry until lightly brown on all sides, about 10 minutes per batch. Using a slotted spoon, transfer the meatballs to a plate.

Return the pot to medium heat, sprinkle the flour into the hot oil in the pot, and cook, stirring, for about 4 minutes. Slowly pour in the tomato mixture, then add the chile and parsley. Cook, stirring occasionally, until the mixture thickens and darkens in color, about 3 minutes. Add the remaining broth and the meatballs and let the soup simmer, uncovered, for 10–15 minutes. Discard the chile. Season with salt and pepper and serve, garnished with the cilantro.

6

ROASTED BUTTERNUT SQUASH SOUP

serves 4–6

2½ lb (1.25 kg) butternut squash, halved

2 tsp olive oil

3 Tbsp unsalted butter

1 small yellow onion, chopped

1 Granny Smith apple, peeled, cored, and chopped

2 cloves garlic, chopped

2 cups (16 fl oz/500 ml) chicken broth, plus more as needed

Salt and ground white pepper

¼ tsp ground coriander

⅛ tsp grated nutmeg

Sour cream for garnish

Ground cinnamon for garnish

Roasting the squash gives this fall soup a smoky and sweet flavor, while the apple adds a hit of tartness. For a New England touch, serve with slices of sharp Vermont Cheddar for pressing to the bottom of the bowl—you'll get scrapings of savory melted cheese with every bite.

Preheat the oven to 400°F (200°C). Rub the cut sides of the squash with the oil. Place, cut side down, in the pan and roast until a knife easily pierces the skin, 45–50 minutes. Let cool, scoop out and discard the seeds, and scoop out the pulp.

In a large, heavy pot, melt the butter over medium heat. Add the onion and apple and sauté until softened, 10–12 minutes. Add the garlic and sauté for 1 minute. Add the broth, the squash pulp, 1 tsp salt, and ¼ tsp pepper. Bring to a boil, reduce the heat to low, cover, and simmer until slightly thickened, about 10 minutes. Let cool slightly.

Working in batches, purée the soup in a blender. Return to the pot, and stir in the coriander and nutmeg. Thin the soup to the desired consistency with additional broth and warm over low heat. Serve, garnished with the sour cream and a sprinkle of cinnamon.

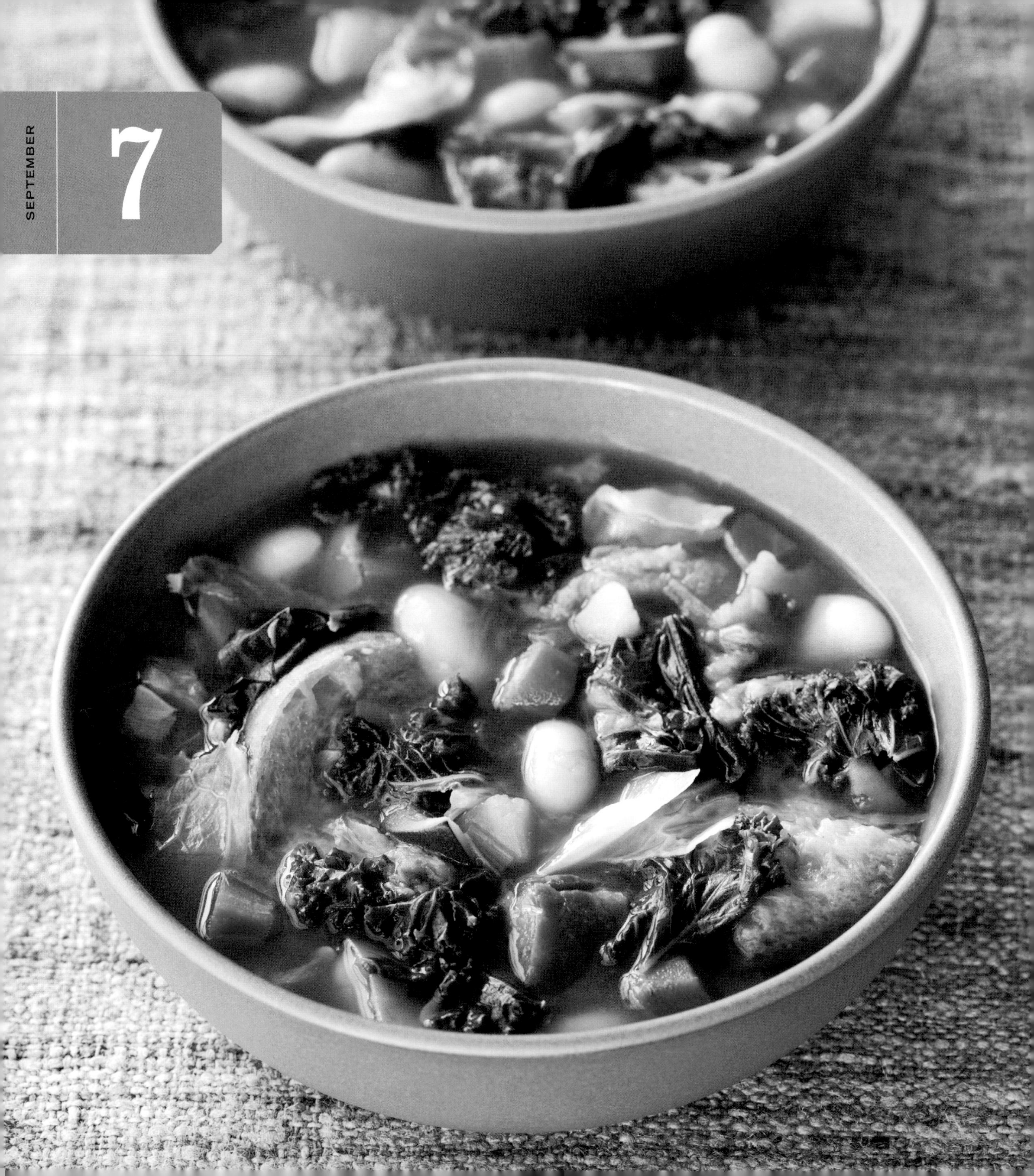

7

RIBOLLITA

serves 6–8

½ cup (4 fl oz/125 ml) extra-virgin olive oil, plus more for seasoning

2 carrots, peeled and coarsely chopped

2 celery stalks, chopped

2 yellow onions, coarsely chopped

2 potatoes, peeled and cut into chunks

2 zucchini, coarsely chopped

1 cup (6 oz/185 g) canned diced tomatoes

1 bunch Tuscan kale (lacinato kale), tough center stalks removed, leaves cut into thick strips

½ head savoy cabbage, coarsely chopped

1 bunch spinach, stemmed and coarsely chopped

1½ cans (21 oz/655 g) cannellini or other white beans, drained

Leaves from 3 thyme sprigs

Salt and freshly ground pepper

5 slices day-old country-style bread, toasted

This dish begins as a typical Tuscan vegetable soup, which you can eat as such on the first day. It becomes ribollita on the second day, when, as its name implies, it is reboiled with toasted bread added to thicken the soup. Because it's denser than most soups, some even serve it with a fork.

In a large, heavy pot over medium heat, warm the ½ cup oil. Add the carrots, celery, onions, potatoes, and zucchini and sauté until the vegetables are softened, 10–15 minutes. Stir in the tomatoes with their juices and 4 cups (32 fl oz/1 l) water, then add the kale, cabbage, and spinach. Raise the heat to high, bring to a simmer, reduce the heat to low, and let cook until the greens are tender, about 45 minutes.

Stir in the beans and cook over medium heat for 10 minutes. Add the thyme leaves and season with salt and pepper. Remove from the heat and let cool, then cover and refrigerate overnight.

The following day, preheat the oven to 350°F (180°C). Line a 2-qt (2-l) baking dish with the toasted bread slices and ladle the soup over the top. Bake, stirring occasionally with a wooden spoon so that the bread slices break apart and blend with the soup, 20–25 minutes. Continue baking without stirring until a lightly browned crust forms on top of the soup, 5–10 minutes longer.

Season generously with oil and freshly ground pepper and serve.

8

CREAM OF FENNEL-LEEK PURÉE WITH TOASTED ALMONDS

serves 4–6

2 fennel bulbs

2 Tbsp unsalted butter

2 leeks, white and pale green parts, chopped

¼ cup (2 fl oz/60 ml) dry white wine

2 cups (16 fl oz/500 ml) vegetable broth

½ cup (4 fl oz/125 ml) heavy cream

Salt and ground white pepper

¼ cup (1 oz/30 g) sliced almonds, toasted (left)

To toast the nuts, in a small frying pan, warm 1 Tbsp olive oil over medium heat. Add the almonds and cook, stirring constantly, until golden brown, about 3 minutes.

Remove the stalks and fronds from the fennel bulbs. Reserve a few fronds for garnish. Chop the fennel bulbs.

In a large, heavy pot, melt the butter over medium-high heat. Add the fennel and leeks and sauté until softened, about 10 minutes. Add the wine and cook for 5 minutes. Add the broth and bring to a boil. Reduce the heat to low and simmer, uncovered, until the vegetables are tender and the broth is flavorful, about 20 minutes. Let cool slightly.

Working in batches, purée the soup in a blender. Return to the pot and stir in the cream. Bring the soup to a gentle boil, remove from the heat, and season with salt and pepper.

Serve, topped with the almonds and garnished with fennel fronds.

9

Old-fashioned corn chowder reaches new heights when chunks of rosy lobster meat are added just before serving. For briny-sweet lobster, tender summer corn, buttery potatoes, and silky heavy cream, there's no better match than a crumbling of salty bacon. Ideal for a late-summer supper, serve this with a mixed green salad and warmed bread.

LOBSTER & SWEET CORN CHOWDER

serves 6–8

3 cooked lobsters (about 1½ lb/750 g each)

4 yellow onions

4 ears sweet corn, husked

1 cup (8 fl oz/250 ml) dry white wine

1 can (14½ oz/455 g) diced tomatoes

4 sprigs flat-leaf parsley, plus 4 Tbsp chopped

6 sprigs thyme

2 bay leaves

Salt and freshly ground pepper

6 slices bacon, cut crosswise into thin strips

2 Tbsp unsalted butter

1 tsp sweet paprika

5 Yukon gold potatoes (2½ lb/1.25 kg), peeled and cut into ¾-inch (2-cm) chunks

1½ cups (12 fl oz/375 ml) heavy cream

Remove the meat from the lobsters, cut into small pieces, and refrigerate. Put the shells in a large, heavy pot. Add 7 cups (56 fl oz/ 1.75 l) water and bring to a boil over high heat. Thinly slice 2 of the onions and add to the pot. Cut the kernels from the corn cobs. Add the cobs to the pot along with the wine, the tomatoes with their juices, the parsley sprigs, 4 of the thyme sprigs, the bay leaves, and ½ tsp salt. Reduce the heat to medium and simmer for 1½ hours, skimming off foam on the surface. Strain the lobster broth through a fine-mesh sieve into a large heatproof bowl. Discard the solids.

Finely chop the remaining 2 onions. In a large saucepan, sauté the bacon over medium heat until crisp, about 8 minutes. Transfer to paper towels to drain. Pour off all but 2 Tbsp fat from the pan and return to medium heat. Add the butter and chopped onions and sauté until softened, about 5 minutes. Add the paprika and cook until fragrant, about 1 minute. Add the potatoes, the remaining 2 thyme sprigs, and 6 cups (48 fl oz/1.5 l) of the lobster broth. Raise the heat to high and bring to a boil. Cover and cook until the potatoes just begin to soften, about 8 minutes. Using a wooden spoon, mash a few potato chunks against the side of the pan and stir into the liquid. Cook until ⟫⟫

the potatoes are tender, about 5 minutes. Reduce the heat to low and add the lobster meat, corn kernels, bacon, and cream. Add 2 tsp salt and season with pepper. Cook until the corn is tender and the lobster meat is warmed through, 6–8 minutes. Stir in the chopped parsley and serve.

10

Pearl barley is a barley from which the hard outer hull and germ have been removed, leaving small, cream-colored balls that look like the gems for which they are named. In this recipe, the tiny grains are used to thicken the soup, resulting in a pleasantly chewy texture.

VEGETABLE-BARLEY SOUP

serves 6

2½ qt (2.5 l) chicken or vegetable broth

½ cup (4 oz/125 g) pearl barley

2 carrots, peeled and diced

2 parsnips, peeled and diced

2 boiling potatoes, unpeeled and diced

1 rutabaga, peeled and diced

1 cup (2 oz/60 g) broccoli florets

1 tsp chopped thyme

1 tsp chopped oregano

1 Tbsp chopped flat-leaf parsley

In a large soup pot, bring the broth to a boil over high heat. Add the barley, reduce the heat to medium-low, cover, and simmer until almost tender, 15–20 minutes.

Raise the heat to medium-high and bring to a vigorous simmer. Add the carrots, parsnips, potatoes, rutabaga, broccoli, thyme, and oregano. Simmer, uncovered, until all the vegetables are tender, about 15 minutes.

Serve, garnished with the parsley.

11

SPICY SEAFOOD & SAUSAGE GUMBO

serves 6

8 Tbsp (4 fl oz/125 ml) canola oil

½ lb (250 g) okra, trimmed and cut into ½-inch (12-mm) slices

6 Tbsp (2 oz/60 g) all-purpose flour

1 large yellow onion, chopped

1 green bell pepper, chopped

1 red bell pepper, chopped

3 cloves garlic, minced

1 can (14½ oz/455 g) diced tomatoes

5 cups (40 fl oz/1.25 l) fish broth or bottled clam juice

2 bay leaves

2½ Tbsp Creole seasoning blend

Salt and freshly ground pepper

½ lb (250 g) andouille sausage, cut into 1-inch (2.5-cm) pieces

1 lb (500 g) large shrimp, shelled and deveined

1 cup (6 oz/185 g) fresh lump crabmeat, picked over for shell fragments

1 tsp filé powder

2 Tbsp finely chopped flat-leaf parsley

A nutty, slowly cooked brown roux adds a distinctive flavor to this stew, which boasts chunks of sweet shrimp, meaty poached chicken, and spicy andouille sausage in a complex, but not-too-thick broth.

In a large, heavy pot, warm 2 Tbsp of the oil over medium heat. Add the okra and sauté, stirring occasionally, until softened and browned, 15 minutes. Transfer to a bowl.

In the same pot, warm the remaining 6 Tbsp oil over medium heat for 2 minutes. Whisk in the flour until incorporated. Cook, stirring constantly, until dark brown, about 4 minutes. Add the onion, bell peppers, and garlic and sauté until softened, 8–10 minutes. Add the okra, tomatoes with their juices, broth, bay leaves, and Creole seasoning. Season with salt and pepper. Bring to a boil over medium-high heat, then reduce the heat to medium-low and simmer for 30 minutes to blend the flavors.

Stir in the sausage, shrimp, and crabmeat and cook until the sausage is heated through and the shrimp are pink, about 3 minutes. Sprinkle in the filé powder and stir for 30 seconds. Remove from the heat and discard the bay leaves. Serve, garnished with the parsley.

12

LAMB & LENTIL SOUP WITH CILANTRO & PARSLEY

serves 8

½ cup (3½ oz/105 g) dried small fava beans, picked over and rinsed

2 Tbsp olive oil

1 yellow onion, chopped

1 lb (500 g) boneless lamb shoulder, trimmed of fat and cut into ½-inch (12-mm) pieces

1 tsp ground ginger

½ tsp ground cinnamon

½ tsp ground turmeric

⅛ tsp caraway seeds, crushed

1 can (14½ oz/455 g) diced tomatoes

1 cup (7 oz/220 g) small green-brown lentils

8 saffron threads, steeped in 2 Tbsp warm water

½ cup (3½ oz/105 g) orzo or other small pasta

¼ cup (⅓ oz/10 g) chopped cilantro

¼ cup (⅓ oz/10 g) chopped flat-leaf parsley

Salt and freshly ground pepper

1 large lemon, cut into 8 wedges

To break the fast at day's end during Ramadan, Moroccans serve this sustaining soup, called harira. It is often made with chickpeas, but this version uses an earthy mix of dried fava beans and lentils. Choose small green-brown lentils, such as those grown in Umbria.

Put the dried beans in a bowl with cold water to cover and soak for at least 4 hours or up to overnight. Drain.

In a large, heavy pot, warm the oil over medium-high heat. Add the onion and lamb and sauté until the onions are soft and the meat is browned on all sides, 6–8 minutes. Add the ginger, cinnamon, turmeric, and caraway and cook, stirring, until the spices are fragrant, about 1 minute. Add the favas and 8 cups (64 fl oz/2 l) water and bring to a boil over high heat. Reduce the heat to medium-low, cover, and simmer until the beans are tender, about 1 hour. Add the tomatoes with their juices, lentils, and saffron with its steeping liquid. Cover and cook until the lentils are tender, about 1 hour, adding more water if needed.

About 10 minutes before serving, bring a large pot of salted water to a boil and cook the pasta until al dente, about 5 minutes, or according to package directions. Drain and add to the soup. Stir in the herbs and cook for 5 minutes to blend the flavors. Season with salt and pepper and serve, accompanied with the lemon wedges.

13

This is a basic, delicious, and reliable chili recipe. It easily feeds a large crowd, and it freezes beautifully. Serve right from the stove top and let guests create their own versions by garnishing with cheese, sour cream, cubed avocado, diced red onion, and cilantro leaves as desired.

TURKEY & WHITE BEAN CHILI
serves 6

2 Tbsp olive oil

1 yellow onion, chopped

2 cloves garlic, minced

1 red bell pepper, seeded and chopped

1 lb (500 g) ground turkey

1 Tbsp ground cumin

1 tsp pure ancho chile powder

1 tsp chili powder, plus more as needed

1 can (28 oz/875 g) diced tomatoes

1 can (15 oz/470 g) white beans, drained

2 Tbsp chopped cilantro

Grated Cheddar cheese for garnish

Minced red onion for garnish

In a large, heavy pot, warm the oil over medium-high heat. Add the onion, garlic, and bell pepper and sauté until soft, about 7 minutes. Add the ground turkey and cook, breaking up the meat, until browned, about 8 minutes. Stir in the cumin, ancho chile powder, and chili powder and cook for 2 minutes. Add the tomatoes with their juices and use the back of a wooden spoon to break them up in the pan. Add the beans, stir to combine, and bring to a boil. Reduce the heat to low and simmer, uncovered, stirring occasionally, until the flavors come together and the soup has thickened slightly, about 45 minutes.

Stir in the cilantro and season with salt and pepper. Serve, garnished with the cheese and red onion.

14

Commonly called simply chile verde, or "green chile," this easy-to-make, delicious dish is one of New Mexico's most popular traditional stews. Regional markets sell the state's green chiles both fresh and frozen. If you cannot find them, substitute Anaheims or poblanos.

GREEN CHILE STEW
serves 6

3 Tbsp toasted peanut oil or canola oil

2 lb (1 kg) boneless pork shoulder, trimmed and cut into ¾-inch (2-cm) cubes

1 white onion, chopped

2 cloves garlic, minced

½ lb (250 g) white or brown mushrooms, quartered

¾ lb (375 g) small yellow-fleshed potatoes, quartered lengthwise

1½ tsp coriander seeds, toasted and ground

1 tsp dried oregano

2 bay leaves

6 cups (48 fl oz/1.5 l) chicken broth

Salt

12–16 New Mexico green chiles (about 2 lb/1 kg), roasted (page 191), peeled, seeded, and chopped

6 Tbsp (3 oz/90 g) sour cream

Cilantro leaves for garnish

In a large, heavy pot, warm the oil over high heat. Working in batches, add the pork and brown well on all sides, 6–8 minutes per batch. Transfer to a plate.

Add the onion to the oil remaining in the pot and sauté over medium-high heat until lightly golden, about 4 minutes. Add the garlic and sauté for 1 minute. Add the mushrooms and sauté until the edges are browned, 3–4 minutes. Add the potatoes, coriander, oregano, and bay leaves and return the meat to the pot. Stir well, pour in the broth, and add 1 tsp salt. Bring to a boil, reduce the heat to medium, and simmer, uncovered, until the meat is just tender, about 30 minutes.

Add the chiles and simmer, uncovered, until the meat is very tender, about 20 minutes. Stir in another 1 tsp salt, then taste and adjust with more salt if necessary. Serve, garnished with the sour cream and cilantro.

SEPTEMBER

16

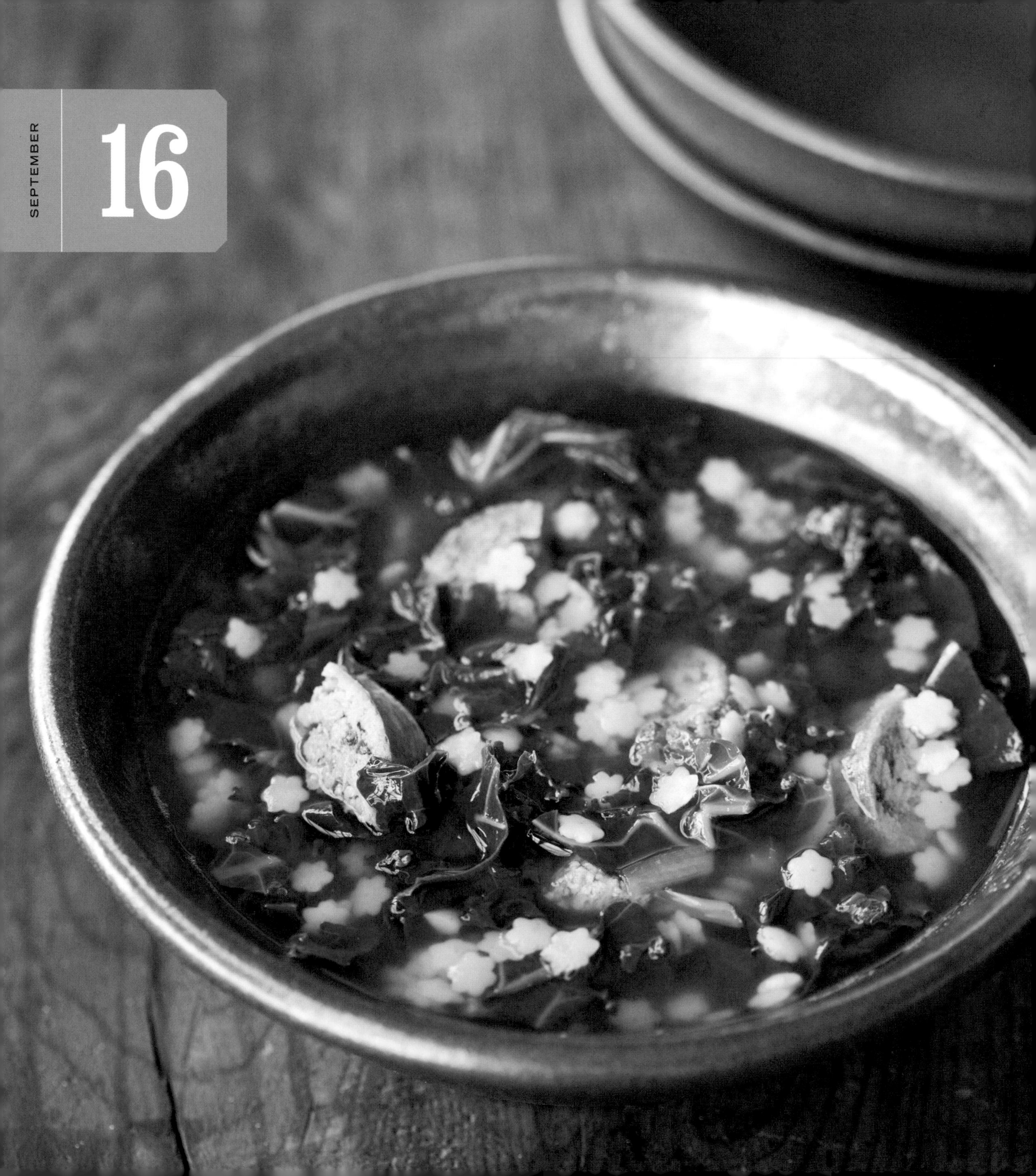

15

MUSHROOM SOUP
WITH CHICKEN

serves 4

1 oz (30 g) dried mushrooms, such as porcini

4 cups (32 fl oz/1 l) chicken broth

4 Tbsp (2 oz/60 g) unsalted butter

1 yellow onion, finely chopped

¾ lb (375 g) fresh cremini mushrooms, thinly sliced

¼ cup (1½ oz/45 g) all-purpose flour

Salt and ground white pepper

2 tsp soy sauce

1 lb (500 g) skinless, boneless chicken breast halves, cut crosswise against the grain into thin slices

1 cup (8 fl oz/250 ml) half-and-half

¼ cup (2 fl oz/60 ml) tawny port

Finely chopped flat-leaf parsley for garnish

Fresh mushrooms contain a lot of moisture, which is why it's important to sauté them well. Browning releases their liquid and softens their texture, and ensures that they won't dilute the soup when they are added to the pot.

In a saucepan, combine the dried mushrooms and broth. Cover, bring to a boil over medium-high heat, and cook for 5 minutes. Remove from the heat.

In a large, heavy pot, melt the butter over medium heat. Add the onion and sauté until softened, about 5 minutes. Add the cremini and sauté until softened, about 3 minutes. Sprinkle with the flour, season with salt and pepper, and cook, stirring, until the flour is incorporated and the mushrooms are coated, about 1 minute. Drain the soaked mushrooms through a coffee filter, reserving the liquid. Add the soaking liquid, drained mushrooms, and soy sauce to the pot and simmer, partially covered, until the mushrooms are tender and the flavors are blended, about 15 minutes. Remove from the heat and let cool slightly.

Working in batches, purée the soup, making sure to leave some texture. Return to the pot, add the chicken, and simmer over medium heat until opaque, 2–4 minutes. Add the half-and-half and port and simmer for about 1 minute to blend the flavors.

Serve, garnished with the parsley.

16

PASTINA & KALE SOUP
WITH ANDOUILLE

serves 4

1 cup (7 oz/200 g) small soup pasta, such as stelline, orzo, or dittalini

3 links andouille sausage (10 oz/315 g)

1 Tbsp olive oil

1 yellow onion, chopped

2 cloves garlic, minced

1 bunch kale, ribs removed, leaves chopped

4 cups (32 fl oz/1 l) chicken broth

1 Tbsp tomato paste

Salt and freshly ground pepper

Grated Parmesan cheese

This soup is flavor-packed, thanks to the spicy andouille, and nutrition-rich, thanks to the kale. Serve with bruschetta rubbed with garlic and topped with chopped ripe tomatoes and chopped fresh basil.

Bring a pot of salted water to a boil over high heat. Add the pasta and cook until al dente, according to package directions. Drain and set aside.

In a large, heavy pot, cook the sausage over medium heat until no longer pink in the center, about 15 minutes. Remove from the pot and cut into slices ¼ inch (6 mm) thick.

Add the oil to the pot and warm over medium-high heat. Add the onion and garlic and sauté until translucent, about 5 minutes. Add the kale, stir to coat, and sauté for 3–4 minutes. Add the broth and bring to a boil. Reduce the heat to low. Add the pasta, sausage, and tomato paste and stir well to combine. Simmer, stirring often, for 5 minutes. Season with salt and pepper and serve, topped with the Parmesan.

17

SPICY BROCCOLINI & CRANBERRY BEAN SOUP

serves 4–6

Fresh cranberry beans are beautiful in their red-and-white-striped shells, but if you can't find them, it's fine to use frozen or canned. Serve this brothy soup with a savory focaccia.

2 Tbsp olive oil

1 small yellow onion, finely diced

2 cloves garlic, minced

⅛ tsp red pepper flakes

Salt and freshly ground pepper

5 cups (40 fl oz/1.25 l) vegetable broth

1 lb (500 g) cranberry beans in pod, shelled

1 bunch broccolini, tough ends discarded, cut into ½-inch (12-mm) pieces

In a large, heavy pot, warm the oil over medium-high heat. Add the onion and garlic and sauté until translucent, about 5 minutes. Add the pepper flakes, ½ tsp salt, and ¼ tsp pepper and cook for 1 minute. Add the broth and bring to a boil. Add the beans and cook until they are tender, 15–20 minutes. Add the broccolini and cook for 5 minutes. Season to taste with salt and pepper and serve.

18

MINESTRONE WITH PESTO

serves 6

The best versions of this soup are made with fresh seasonal vegetables. Don't hesitate to use cabbage, green beans, eggplant, cauliflower, peas, zucchini, leeks, or whatever else looks good at the market or that you might have on hand. Simmering the rind from a wedge of Parmesan in the soup imparts a rich, deep flavor.

1 oz (30 g) dried porcini mushrooms

¼ cup (2 fl oz/60 ml) olive oil

1 yellow onion, chopped

2 carrots, peeled and chopped

1 celery rib, chopped

1 bunch Swiss chard, ribs removed, leaves chopped

3 Yukon gold or other boiling potatoes, peeled and chopped

1½ cups (8 oz/250 g) peeled, seeded, and diced butternut squash

4 tomatoes, peeled (page 172), seeded, and chopped, or 2 cups (12 oz/375 g) canned diced plum tomatoes with juices

2 lb (1 kg) cranberry beans in the pod, shelled, or 2 cups (8 oz/250 g) fresh shelled beans

1 piece Parmesan cheese rind

Salt and freshly ground pepper

1 cup (3½ oz/105 g) macaroni, tubetti, or other small soup pasta

¼ cup (2 fl oz/60 ml) Basil Pesto (page 118), or purchased pesto

Grated Parmesan cheese for serving

In a bowl, combine the mushrooms with 2 cups (16 fl oz/500 ml) hot water and soak for 30 minutes. Drain well, reserving the liquid. Strain the liquid through a coffee filter. Rinse the mushrooms well under cold running water. Drain well and chop.

In a large, heavy pot, warm the oil over medium heat. Add the onion, carrots, and celery and sauté until tender and golden, 10–15 minutes. Stir in the mushrooms, chard, potatoes, squash, tomatoes, beans, and cheese rind. Add the mushroom liquid and enough water to cover the vegetables by ½ inch (12 mm), bring to a simmer, and reduce the heat to low. Season with salt and pepper and cook uncovered, stirring occasionally, until the vegetables are soft, about 1½ hours, adding water as needed if the soup becomes too thick.

Add the pasta and cook, stirring frequently, until al dente, about 15 minutes or according to package directions. Remove the cheese rind from the pot and discard. Serve, topped with the pesto and passing the Parmesan at the table.

19

As the weather starts to cool, it's time for a back-to-school classic: chicken noodle soup. This one's full of healthy veggies and tender bowtie pasta. Simmering the stock requires little effort on busy weeknights, and leftovers are a cinch to pour into insulated containers for work or school the next day.

CHICKEN & FARFALLE VEGETABLE SOUP

serves 6

1 small chicken (3 lb/1.5 kg), quartered and skinned

1 large yellow onion, coarsely chopped

1 carrot, peeled and coarsely chopped

6 flat-leaf parsley sprigs, plus ¼ cup (⅓ oz/10 g) finely chopped parsley

1 tsp finely chopped thyme

2 bay leaves

3 celery ribs with leaves, cut into ½-inch (12-mm) pieces

½ small head savoy cabbage (6 oz/185 g), cored and coarsely chopped

½ lb (250 g) green beans, trimmed and cut into 1-inch (2.5-cm) pieces

2 cups (7 oz/210 g) farfalle pasta

1 Tbsp fresh lemon juice

Salt and freshly ground pepper

¾ cup (3 oz/90 g) grated Parmesan cheese

In a large, heavy pot, combine the chicken, onion, carrot, parsley sprigs, thyme, and bay leaves. Pour in 2½ qt (2.5 l) water and bring to a boil over high heat. Reduce the heat to medium-low and simmer, covered, until the chicken falls from the bone, about 1 hour.

Transfer the chicken to a plate. Strain the broth through a fine-mesh sieve and return to the pot. Discard the solids in the sieve. Once the chicken is cool enough to handle, remove the meat from the bones and discard the bones. Tear the meat into 1-inch (2.5-cm) pieces.

Add the celery, cabbage, green beans, and farfalle to the pot and simmer, covered, until the farfalle is al dente, 10–12 minutes or according to package directions. Add the chicken pieces, chopped parsley, and lemon juice. Season with salt and pepper. Cook, stirring occasionally, until the chicken is warmed through.

Serve, topped with the Parmesan.

20

Since they grow in sandy soil and grit becomes trapped within their layers, leeks always need a careful rinse. After slicing them lengthwise, hold them under cold running water and separate the layers with your fingers to clean them thoroughly.

LEEK & POTATO SOUP WITH FRIED PROSCIUTTO

serves 6–8

8 leeks (about 4 lb/2 kg), white and pale green parts

¼ cup olive oil

6 slices prosciutto (about 3 oz/90 g), cut into ribbons

Salt and freshly ground pepper

1½ tsp minced thyme

2 Tbsp all-purpose flour

8 cups (64 fl oz/2 l) chicken broth

5 Yukon gold potatoes (about 2½ lb/1.25 kg), peeled and cut into 1-inch (2.5-cm) chunks

2 small bay leaves

¼ cup (⅓ oz/10 g) chopped chives

Cut the leeks in half lengthwise and then cut each half crosswise into pieces ½ inch (12 mm) thick. In a large, heavy pot, warm the oil over medium heat. Add the prosciutto and sauté until crisp, about 6 minutes. Transfer to paper towels to drain.

Add the leeks and ½ tsp salt to the pot and stir to coat. Reduce the heat to medium-low, cover, and cook, stirring occasionally, until the leeks begin to soften, about 10 minutes. Add the thyme and flour and cook, stirring constantly, until the flour is incorporated.

Raise the heat to medium-high and, stirring constantly, slowly add the broth. Add the potatoes and bay leaves, season with pepper, cover, and bring to a boil. Reduce the heat to medium-low and simmer until the potatoes just start to become tender, about 6 minutes. Remove from the heat and let stand, covered, until the potatoes are tender all the way through, about 15 minutes. Discard the bay leaves and return the soup to a simmer. If desired, use the back of a large spoon to mash some of the potatoes against the side of the pot and stir them into the soup to thicken it.

Serve, garnished with the fried prosciutto and the chives.

21

SWEET POTATO–
CHIPOTLE SOUP

serves 4–6

2 Tbsp unsalted butter

1 small white onion, chopped

2 cloves garlic, minced

1 chipotle chile in adobo sauce, minced

2 sweet potatoes (1½ lb/750 g),
peeled and diced

4½ cups (36 fl oz/1.1 l) chicken broth

Salt and freshly ground pepper

1 Tbsp chopped chives

This soup has a mild chipotle flavor but you can adjust it to suit your desired level of heat by adding more. The soup can be made ahead, as it freezes beautifully. Serve with a red cabbage and apple slaw.

In a large, heavy pot, melt the butter over medium-high heat. Add the onion and garlic and sauté until translucent, about 5 minutes. Add the chipotle and potatoes and cook, stirring often, for 5 minutes. Add the broth and bring to a boil. Reduce the heat to low and simmer, uncovered, until the potatoes are very tender, 30–35 minutes. Remove from the heat and let cool slightly.

Working in batches, purée the soup in a blender. Return to the pot and season with salt and pepper. Serve, garnished with the chives.

22

SCALLOPS & PANCETTA
IN SAFFRON BROTH

serves 4

Large pinch of saffron threads

½ cup (4 fl oz/125 ml) dry white wine

3 oz (90 g) sliced pancetta, diced

2 Tbsp unsalted butter

2 shallots, finely chopped

½ cup (4 fl oz/125 ml) dry sherry

3 cups (24 fl oz/750 ml) chicken broth

Salt and freshly ground black pepper

12 large sea scallops (about 1¼ lb/625 total),
tough muscles removed

2 Tbsp olive oil

1 Tbsp chopped chervil or parsley

For this soup, you can substitute bay scallops, which are smaller, but cut the searing time in half. Shrimp or calamari are also good options. For a creamy version, stir in ½ cup (4 fl oz/ 125 ml) heavy cream after reducing the heat to low and before seasoning with salt and pepper.

Using your fingers, gently crush the saffron into a small bowl and add the white wine. Set aside.

In a large, heavy pot, cook the pancetta over medium-high heat, stirring often, until golden, about 4 minutes. Transfer to paper towels to drain. Set aside.

Add the butter and shallots to the pot and sauté until soft, about 5 minutes. Add the sherry and cook until the liquid evaporates, about 4 minutes. Add the saffron-wine mixture and cook until the liquid is reduced by half. Add the broth and bring to a boil. Reduce the heat to low and season with salt and pepper.

Warm a frying pan over high heat. Toss the scallops with the oil and season with salt and pepper. When the frying pan is very hot, add the scallops and sear on one side until lightly browned, 2–3 minutes. Flip the scallops and cook until lightly browned on the other side, 1–2 minutes.

Ladle the broth into shallow bowls. Place 3 scallops in each bowl, sprinkle with the reserved pancetta and chervil, and serve.

23

CHORIZO & CHICKEN STEW WITH AVOCADO CREMA

serves 4–6

1 skinless, boneless chicken breast half

½ lb (250 g) Mexican chorizo, cut into slices ½ inch (12 mm) thick

2 Tbsp olive oil

1 yellow onion, chopped

2 cloves garlic, minced

1 red bell pepper, seeded and chopped

4 cups (32 fl oz/1 l) chicken broth

1 Tbsp minced thyme

Salt and freshly ground pepper

FOR THE AVOCADO CREMA

1 avocado, pitted and peeled

¼ cup (2 oz/60 g) sour cream

1 Tbsp fresh lime juice

For the avocado crema, lime juice and sour cream are added to mashed avocados for a smooth, tangy version of guacamole. It melts into this soup, adding a creamy element and also helping to tame the spiciness of the chorizo.

In a small saucepan, combine the chicken breast with cold water to cover by 1 inch (2.5 cm) and bring to a boil over high heat. Reduce the heat to low and simmer until the chicken is cooked through, 15–18 minutes, skimming off any foam on the surface. Remove the chicken from the pan. When it is cool enough to handle, shred the meat.

Warm a large, heavy pot over medium-high heat. Add the chorizo and cook, stirring often, until browned on both sides, about 8 minutes. Transfer to a bowl. Add the oil and warm over medium-high heat. Add the onion and garlic and sauté until translucent, about 5 minutes. Add the bell pepper, stir to coat, and cook for 3 minutes. Add the shredded chicken, chorizo, broth, and thyme and simmer, uncovered, for about 15 minutes to blend the flavors. Season with salt and pepper.

To make the avocado crema, put the avocado in a small bowl and mash with a fork until creamy and smooth. Add the sour cream, the lime juice, and 2 large pinches of salt and stir to combine.

Serve the soup, accompanied with the avocado crema.

24

SHIITAKE DUMPLINGS IN KAFFIR LIME BROTH

serves 4

4 cups (32 fl oz/1 l) chicken broth

1 tsp peeled and minced fresh ginger

1 green onion, white and tender green parts, thinly sliced

5 kaffir lime leaves, torn in half

2 Tbsp soy sauce

2–3 drops Asian sesame oil

FOR THE SHIITAKE DUMPLINGS

2 oz (60 g) dried shiitake mushrooms

½ tsp peeled and minced fresh ginger

½ tsp soy sauce

¼ tsp dark Asian sesame oil

1 Tbsp minced green onion, white and light green parts, plus sliced dark green tops

Freshly ground pepper

24 wonton wrappers

Kaffir lime leaves are a popular ingredient in Southeast Asian cooking. They are highly aromatic and can be found in well-stocked grocery stores near other fresh herbs. If you can't find them you can substitute lime zest and a touch of fresh lime juice.

In a large saucepan, combine the broth, ginger, sliced green onion, kaffir lime leaves, and soy sauce and bring to a boil over medium-high heat. Reduce the heat to low and simmer for 10 minutes. Remove from the heat, add the drops of sesame oil to taste, cover, and let steep for 10 minutes. Strain the broth and return to the saucepan.

To make the dumplings, in a small bowl, combine the mushrooms with very hot water to cover. Soak for at least 30 minutes. Drain and finely chop. In a bowl, stir together the soaked mushrooms, ginger, soy sauce, ¼ tsp sesame oil, and minced green onion. Season with a pinch of pepper. Place 1 tsp of the mushroom mixture in the middle of each wonton wrapper. Using your fingers, apply a small amount of water on all sides of the wrapper. Fold the wrapper diagonally, forcing out any air bubbles as you press to seal. Take the 2 points on the longest side of the triangle and fold so that the tips meet. Apply a small amount of water on the tips and press firmly to stick together.

Return the broth to a gentle simmer. Add the dumplings and cook until tender, about 3 minutes. Using a slotted spoon and ladle, transfer the dumplings and broth to bowls. Serve, garnished with the green onion tops.

25

EGGPLANT & TOFU CURRY SOUP

serves 4

1 lb (500 g) extra-firm tofu

3 Tbsp unsalted butter

1 small yellow onion, sliced

1 lemongrass stalk, center white part only, smashed and thinly sliced

3 baby eggplants, cubed

1 red bell pepper, seeded and cut into thin strips

2 cans (15 oz/470 g each) light coconut milk

1–2 Tbsp Thai red curry paste

1 Tbsp Asian fish sauce

2 kaffir lime leaves, torn into pieces

½ cup (4 fl oz/125 ml) vegetable broth

2 Tbsp chopped cilantro

This is a flavorful curry soup that you can vary with many substitutions. In the winter, swap cubed sweet potato for the eggplant for a colorful and satisfying cold-weather curry. You can use any color of Thai curry paste (red, yellow, or green) that you have on hand.

Cut the tofu block in half crosswise. Place the tofu on a plate and top with a second plate. Weigh down the top plate with a can. Let stand for 20 minutes to press the water from the tofu. Pour off any water from the plate and cut the tofu into cubes.

In a large, heavy pot, melt the butter over medium heat. Add the onion and sauté until it begins to soften, about 4 minutes. Add the lemongrass, eggplant, and bell pepper and cook, stirring constantly, until the eggplant softens, 5–7 minutes. Transfer to a bowl.

Add the coconut milk, curry paste, fish sauce, kaffir lime leaves, and broth to the pot and cook until the liquid begins to thicken, about 5 minutes. Add the eggplant mixture and cook for 10 minutes. Add the tofu and cook, stirring well, for 3 minutes. Remove from the heat, stir in the cilantro, and serve.

26

ROASTED PUMPKIN SOUP WITH CHINESE FIVE SPICE

serves 4–6

1 small Sugar Pie pumpkin (about 3 lb/1.5 kg total weight), peeled, seeded, and diced

3 Tbsp olive oil

Salt and freshly ground pepper

2 Tbsp unsalted butter

1 small yellow onion, chopped

2 cloves garlic, minced

½ tsp Chinese five-spice powder

4½ cups (36 fl oz/1.1 l) vegetable broth

There is nothing more seasonally satisfying than pumpkin in the fall. You can also swap in butternut squash or sweet potatoes for this soup. Serve with a Waldorf salad of walnuts, raisins, and chopped apples.

Preheat the oven to 400°F (200°C). Line a baking sheet with parchment paper. In a bowl, toss the pumpkin with the oil and season with salt and pepper. Arrange in a single layer on the prepared pan and roast until tender, about 25 minutes.

In a large, heavy pot, melt the butter over medium-high heat. Add the onion and garlic and sauté until translucent, about 5 minutes. Add the five-spice powder, stir to combine, and cook for 1 minute. Add the pumpkin and broth and bring to a boil. Reduce the heat and simmer for about 15 minutes to blend the flavors. Remove from the heat and let cool slightly.

Working in batches, purée the soup in a blender. Return to the pot, season with salt and pepper, and serve.

27

BOURRIDE

serves 6

1½ lb (750 g) heads, tails, backbones, and other trimmings from nonoily fish

2 carrots, peeled and quartered

1 yellow onion, quartered

1 fennel bulb, stalks and fronds removed, quartered and cored

3 cloves garlic

1 celery rib, quartered

4 flat-leaf parsley sprigs

3 thyme sprigs

1 bay leaf

2-inch (5-cm) piece dried orange peel

Salt

2 cups (16 fl oz/500 ml) dry white wine

2 lb (1 kg) monkfish or other firm white-fleshed fish fillets, cut into 1-inch (2.5-cm) cubes

6 slices day-old country-style bread, each about 1 inch (2.5 cm) thick

1 cup (3 fl oz/250 ml) Aioli (left), or purchased aioli

6 egg yolks

Chopped flat-leaf parsley for garnish (optional)

To make aioli, in a blender, combine 8 cloves garlic, 1 tsp coarse sea salt, and 6 large egg yolks and process until a paste forms. With the motor running, add 2 cups (16 fl oz/ 500 ml) extra-virgin olive oil in a slow, steady stream. Process until the mixture is thick and creamy. Store in an airtight container in the refrigerator for up to 5 days. Makes about 2 cups (16 fl oz/500 ml).

In a large, heavy pot, combine the fish bones and trimmings, carrots, onion, fennel, garlic, celery, parsley, thyme, bay leaf, and orange peel. Add 1 tsp salt and 8 cups (64 fl oz/2 l) water. Bring to a boil over medium-high heat, regularly skimming off any scum and froth on the surface. Reduce the heat to low and simmer for 15 minutes. Add the wine, raise the heat to high, and bring to a boil. Reduce the heat to low and simmer for 15 minutes. Using a slotted spoon, remove and discard the solids. Line a colander with several layers of cheesecloth and strain the broth into a large saucepan. You should have about 6 cups (48 fl oz/1.5 l).

Place the pan over medium heat and bring the broth to a simmer. Add the monkfish and cook just until opaque throughout, about 5 minutes. Using the slotted spoon, transfer to a platter and loosely cover with foil to keep warm.

Place a bread slice in the bottom of each bowl. Ladle just enough broth into each bowl for the bread to absorb. ⟶

In a large bowl, whisk together half of the aioli and the egg yolks until well blended. Whisk in the remaining broth, adding it in a slow, steady stream. Pour into a clean saucepan and place over very low heat. Cook, stirring gently and being very careful not to let the mixture boil, until thickened to the consistency of light cream, 6–7 minutes.

Divide the fish among the bowls, ladle the creamy broth over the top, and garnish with the chopped parsley, if using. Serve, passing the remaining aioli at the table.

28

ROASTED RED PEPPER & TOMATO SOUP

serves 4–6

1 Tbsp unsalted butter

1 Tbsp olive oil

½ yellow onion, chopped

2 cloves garlic, minced

2 red peppers, roasted (page 191), peeled, seeded, and chopped

1 can (28 oz/875 g) diced tomatoes

2 Tbsp heavy cream

Salt and freshly ground pepper

How can you resist serving this classic soup with an old fashioned grilled cheese sandwich? Use smoked Cheddar on a sliced baguette to make several mini sandwiches. To save time, use store-bought roasted peppers.

In a large, heavy pot, melt the butter with the oil over medium-high heat. Add the onion and garlic and cook until translucent, about 5 minutes. Add the peppers, stir to coat, and cook for 3 minutes. Add the tomatoes with their juices, bring to a boil, reduce the heat to low, and simmer, uncovered, for 20 minutes to blend the flavors. Remove from the heat and let cool slightly.

Working in batches, purée the soup in a blender. Return to the pot, stir in the cream, and bring the soup just to a boil. Remove from the heat, season with salt and pepper, and serve.

29

Parsnips and apples are a great flavor pairing: the apples brighten the earthiness of the parsnips. Don't skip the melted Gruyère toasts in this recipe, as dipping them into the soup is a delicious experience.

ROASTED PARSNIP & APPLE PURÉE WITH GRUYÈRE TOASTS

serves 4–6

6 parsnips, peeled and chopped (about 4 cups)

1 Tbsp olive oil

Salt and freshly ground pepper

3 Tbsp unsalted butter

1 small yellow onion, chopped

¼ tsp grated nutmeg

2 Granny Smith apples, peeled, cored, and chopped, plus apple slices for garnish

6 cups (48 fl oz/1.5 l) chicken broth

Salt and ground white pepper

FOR THE GRUYÈRE TOASTS

4 oz (125 g) Gruyère cheese, shredded

1 loaf crusty bread, cut into slices ¼ inch (6 mm) thick

Preheat the oven to 400°F (200°C). Line a baking sheet with parchment paper. In a bowl, toss the parsnips with the oil and season with salt and pepper. Arrange in a single layer on the prepared pan and roast until beginning to caramelize, 25 minutes.

In a large, heavy pot, melt the butter over medium-high heat. Add the onion and sauté until translucent, about 5 minutes. Add the nutmeg and cook for 1 minute. Add the apples, stir to coat, and cook until they begin to soften, about 5 minutes. Add the broth and parsnips and bring to a boil. Reduce the heat to low and simmer, uncovered, until the parsnips are tender, about 20 minutes. Remove from the heat and let cool slightly.

Working in batches, purée the soup in a blender. Return to the pot and season with salt and pepper.

To make the Gruyère toasts, preheat the broiler to high. Put 2 Tbsp of the grated cheese on each bread slice. Arrange the slices on the baking sheet and broil until the cheese begins to melt, 2–3 minutes.

Serve the soup, garnished with apple slices. Place 1 or 2 Gruyère toasts on the side of each bowl.

30

Long cooking at a low temperature makes chuck steak wonderfully tender. Look for Italian (Romano) beans at farmers' markets, but if they evade you, regular green beans can easily substitute; just reduce the cooking time to about 15 minutes.

ITALIAN BEEF STEW

serves 4

3 Tbsp olive oil

1 beef chuck steak (about 2 lb/1 kg), trimmed

2 Tbsp red wine vinegar

2 large sweet onions, halved lengthwise, then cut crosswise into slices ½ inch (12 mm) thick

2 red bell peppers, seeded and cut into ½-inch (12-mm) strips

2 green bell peppers, seeded and cut into ½-inch (12-mm) strips

2 cups (16 fl oz/500 ml) beef broth

½ lb (250 g) Romano beans, cut into 2-inch (5-cm) pieces

½ lb (250 g) cremini mushrooms, thinly sliced

Salt and freshly ground pepper

In a large, heavy pot, warm 1 Tbsp of the oil over medium-high heat. Add the steak and cook, turning once, until richly browned on both sides, 4–6 minutes. Transfer to a plate. Add the vinegar and bring to a simmer. Stir to scrape up any browned bits on the bottom of the pot. Pour the liquid over the steak.

In the same pot, warm the remaining 2 Tbsp oil over medium-high heat. Add the onions and bell peppers and sauté until well browned, about 10 minutes. Add 2–3 Tbsp water if necessary to keep the vegetables from sticking. Slowly stir in the broth, scraping up any browned bits on the bottom of the pot. Return the meat to the pot and bring to a simmer. Reduce the heat to medium-low, cover, and simmer gently until the meat is very tender, about 2½ hours.

Add the beans and mushrooms, cover, and simmer until just tender, 20–30 minutes. Transfer the meat to a cutting board and cut it into bite-sized pieces. Return the meat to the pot, raise the heat to medium, and simmer until heated through, 2–3 minutes. Season with salt and pepper and serve.

1
CARROT-GINGER SOUP
page 226

2
CHEDDAR & HARD CIDER SOUP
WITH FRIED SHALLOTS
page 226

3
CURRIED LEEK & APPLE SOUP
page 228

4
CHICKEN CHOWDER
page 228

8
ROASTED CAULIFLOWER
& PARMESAN SOUP
page 231

9
ACORN SQUASH SOUP WITH
TOASTED WALNUT BUTTER
page 232

10
LEEK & SWISS CHARD SOUP
page 232

11
ROASTED VEGETABLE STEW
WITH COUSCOUS
page 233

15
SWEET POTATO–CORN CHOWDER
WITH AVOCADO
page 237

16
PUMPKIN-GINGER SOUP
page 237

17
WHITE BEAN, BROCCOLINI
& BRATWURST SOUP
page 238

18
ROASTED GARLIC & SHALLOT VELOUTÉ
WITH CRISPY PANCETTA
page 238

22
SQUASH SOUP WITH
SAGE BROWN BUTTER
page 240

23
CORN SOUP WITH
CHANTERELLES & THYME
page 243

24
CREAM OF PARSNIP SOUP
page 243

25
CREAMY BLACK BEAN PURÉE
WITH CHEESE STRAWS
page 244

29
ARTICHOKE & TOASTED BREAD
SOUP WITH SAGE
page 245

30
PEANUT-GINGER
SWEET POTATO SOUP
page 246

31
WILD RICE & RED CHARD
SOUP WITH ANDOUILLE
page 246

5

**BUTTERNUT SQUASH SOUP
WITH PEARS & ROSEMARY**
page 229

6

TURNIP, APPLE & POTATO SOUP
page 229

7

**SAFFRON FREGOLA
WITH SEAFOOD**
page 231

12

**CAULIFLOWER SOUP WITH
CHEDDAR & BLUE CHEESE**
page 233

13

CURRIED YELLOW LENTIL SOUP
page 234

14

**BEEF STEW WITH
TURNIPS & GREENS**
page 234

19

CREAM OF SPINACH SOUP
page 239

20

**VEGETABLES IN
COCONUT-LIME BROTH**
page 239

21

**INDIAN-SPICED
CHICKPEA STEW**
page 240

26

**PORK & ROASTED
TOMATILLO STEW**
page 244

27

MISO SOUP
page 245

28

CARROT & ASIAN PEAR PURÉE
page 245

Hearty roots and winter squashes bring warm colors to the autumn kitchen. The seasonal vegetables, from carrots and parsnips to butternut squashes and pumpkins, are ideal for turning into sweet and smooth purées seasoned with spicy ginger and earthy curry. Fall ales and ciders are also wonderful additions to the soup pot, subtly accenting meats or complementing sharp cheeses.

october

1

CARROT-GINGER SOUP

serves 4

2 Tbsp unsalted butter

1 large sweet onion such as Vidalia or Walla Walla, finely chopped

2 cloves garlic, minced

1 lb (500 g) carrots, cut into slices ¼ inch (6 mm) thick

Salt and freshly ground pepper

6 cups (1.5 l) chicken broth

1½ tsp peeled and grated fresh ginger

½ tsp freshly grated orange zest

Minced chives for garnish

Fresh carrots are puréed with sweet onions, garlic, and chicken broth for this bright orange soup, made even more vibrant-tasting with the addition of orange zest. Ginger adds a bit of spice to the finished soup, which has a pleasing spoon-coating consistency.

In a large, heavy pot, warm the butter over medium-low heat. When the butter has melted and the foam begins to subside, add the onion and sauté until it softens and is just translucent, 12–10 minutes. Add the garlic and sauté until fragrant, about 30 seconds. Add the carrots and salt to taste and stir to coat the carrots well with the butter.

Add 2 cups (16 fl oz/500 ml) of the broth, increase the heat to high, and bring to a boil. Reduce the heat to a simmer, cover, and cook until the carrots are tender when pierced with the tip of a knife, about 20 minutes. Uncover, remove from the heat, and let cool slightly.

Working in batches, purée the soup in a blender. Return to the pot and warm over medium-low heat, gradually whisking in the remaining 4 cups broth. Stir in the ginger and orange zest. Reheat gently, stirring occasionally, until the soup is hot, about 10 minutes. Season with salt and pepper and serve, garnished with the chives.

2

CHEDDAR & HARD CIDER SOUP WITH FRIED SHALLOTS

serves 6–8

4 Tbsp (2 oz/60 g) unsalted butter

2 yellow onions, chopped

1 celery rib, chopped

1 Yukon gold potato, peeled and chopped

2 cloves garlic, minced

2 Tbsp all-purpose flour

2½ cups (20 fl oz/625 ml) chicken broth

2½ cups (20 fl oz/625 ml) hard apple cider

1 cup (8 fl oz/250 ml) half-and-half

2 bay leaves

2 thyme sprigs

2 Tbsp applejack or Calvados brandy

¾ lb (375 g) English Cheddar cheese, shredded

Salt and freshly ground pepper

Fried Shallots (page 28)

Apples and Cheddar, a classic tart and sharp pairing—does it get any better? In fact it can, when thinly slivered shallot rings take a dive into hot oil for a crispy, crunchy, oniony topping. Serve a crisp, lightly dressed salad on the side, and ready yourself for the compliments from your dinner companions.

In a large, heavy pot, melt 3 Tbsp of the butter over medium-high heat. Add the onions, celery, potato, and garlic and stir. Reduce the heat to low, cover, and cook, stirring occasionally, until the vegetables are softened, about 12 minutes. Sprinkle the flour over the vegetables and cook, stirring constantly, until the flour is incorporated. While stirring constantly, gradually add the broth, cider, and half-and-half. Raise the heat to medium-high, add the bay leaves and thyme sprigs, and bring to a boil. Reduce the heat to low and simmer to blend the flavors, about 10 minutes.

Remove the bay leaves and thyme sprigs from the soup and discard. Remove the soup from the heat and let cool slightly.

Working in batches, purée the soup in a blender. Pour into a clean pot. Stir in the applejack. Off the heat, while whisking constantly, gradually add the cheese one handful at a time. Continue whisking until all the cheese is melted. Place over medium-low heat, stir in 1 tsp salt and pepper to taste, and cook gently, stirring often, until heated through, about 10 minutes.

Taste and adjust the seasoning. Serve, garnished with the fried shallots.

2 OCTOBER

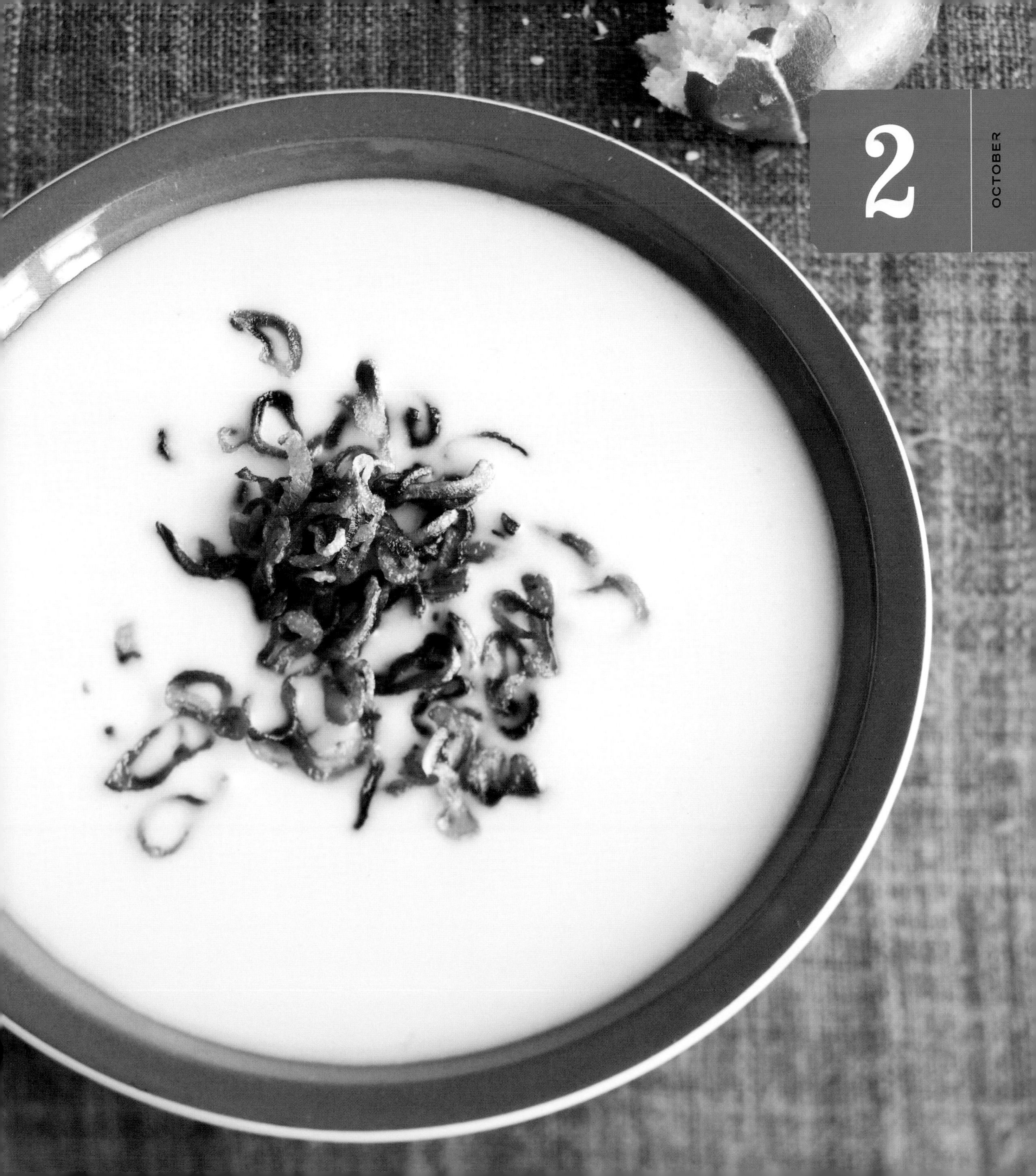

3

*This fragrant,
savory soup makes
excellent cool-
weather fare and is
the perfect start to
any holiday meal.
It is also just as tasty
when served chilled.
Reserve 4–6 thin
slices of the tender
green portion
of the leeks for
garnish, if desired.*

CURRIED LEEK & APPLE SOUP

serves 6

1 Tbsp unsalted butter

3 large crisp apples, such as Golden
Delicious, pippin, or Granny Smith, peeled,
cored, and cut into ½-inch (12-mm) dice

2 celery ribs, thinly sliced

2 tsp Madras curry powder

4 large leeks, white part and 2 inches
(5 cm) of the green, halved lengthwise
and sliced crosswise

4 cups (32 fl oz/1 l) vegetable broth

1 small russet potato, peeled and
cut into ½-inch (12-mm) dice

½ cup (4 fl oz/125 ml) milk

Salt and freshly ground pepper

In a large, heavy pot, melt the butter over
medium-low heat. Add the apples, celery,
curry powder, and leeks and stir well. Cook,
stirring occasionally, until the leeks soften,
about 5 minutes. Cover the pan and cook for
5 minutes, stirring once. Add the broth and
potato and bring to a boil over medium-high
heat. Reduce the heat to low, cover, and
simmer until the apples and potato are
tender when pierced with the tip of a knife,
about 20 minutes. Remove from the heat
and let cool slightly.

Working in batches, purée the soup in a
blender or food processor until smooth.
Return to the pot and stir in the milk.
Season with salt and pepper. Rewarm
over low heat without letting it come
to a boil. Serve.

4

*Tender hunks of
chicken replace the
typical fish, but
waxy potatoes and a
hit of bacon keep this
chowder true to its
roots. To save time,
buy a roast chicken
at your local deli to
make this chowder.*

CHICKEN CHOWDER

serves 4–6

3 slices thick-cut bacon

2 Tbsp unsalted butter

2 yellow onions, diced

2 celery ribs, diced

2 carrots, peeled and diced

3 cloves garlic, minced

3 cups (24 fl oz/750 ml) chicken broth

1¼ lb (625 g) Yukon gold potatoes,
peeled and diced

¼ tsp hot sauce, such as Tabasco

Salt and freshly ground pepper

4 cups (24 oz/750 g) cooked chicken,
cut into 1-inch (2.5-cm) pieces

In a large, heavy pot, cook the bacon over
medium heat, turning once, until browned,
5–7 minutes. Transfer to paper towels to
drain. Let cool, then crumble into pieces.

Add the butter to the bacon fat in the pan and
set over medium heat. Add the onions, celery,
carrots, and garlic. Sauté until the vegetables
are tender, about 12 minutes. Add the broth,
raise the heat to high, and bring to a boil.
Add the potatoes, hot sauce, 1 tsp salt, and
⅛ tsp pepper. Reduce the heat to medium-
low, cover, and simmer until the potatoes
are tender, 10–12 minutes. Add the chicken
and cook until heated through. Season with
salt and pepper and serve, sprinkled with
the crumbled bacon.

5

Piney, floral, and just a bit peppery, fresh rosemary is a flavorful herbal counterpoint to all the elements of this soup—not just the sweet pears, but also the lush, velvety butternut squash, and sweet onions that are puréed to a silky finish.

BUTTERNUT SQUASH SOUP WITH PEARS & ROSEMARY

serves 6–8

2 Tbsp unsalted butter

1 Tbsp canola oil

1 yellow onion, finely chopped

1 butternut squash (about 3 lb/1.5 kg), peeled, seeded, and cut into slices ¼ inch (6 mm) thick

6 cups (48 fl oz/1.5 l) chicken or vegetable broth

1 rosemary sprig, plus 1 tsp minced leaves

4 tsp firmly packed light brown sugar

3 large ripe but firm Anjou or Bartlett pears, peeled, cored, and cut into slices ¼ inch (6 mm) thick

½ cup (4 fl oz/125 ml) half-and-half

Salt and freshly ground pepper

In a large, heavy pot, melt 1 Tbsp of the butter with the oil over medium heat. Add the onion and sauté until softened and beginning to brown, about 7 minutes. Add the squash slices, broth, and rosemary sprig. Raise the heat to high and bring to a boil, then reduce the heat to medium-low, cover partially, and simmer until the squash is tender, about 20 minutes.

Meanwhile, preheat the oven to 500°F (260°C). In a small saucepan, melt the remaining 1 Tbsp butter. In a bowl, stir together the melted butter and 2 tsp of the brown sugar. Add the pear slices, reserving some for serving, and toss to coat. Spread in a single layer on a rimmed baking sheet and roast until the bottoms begin to brown, about 8 minutes. Turn, sprinkle with the minced rosemary, and continue roasting until tender and brown, about 7 minutes. Transfer to a plate and let cool.

Remove and discard the rosemary sprig from the pot. Remove from the heat and let cool slightly. Working in batches, purée the squash mixture in a blender. Pour the purée into a clean pot. Add the remaining 2 tsp brown sugar, the half-and-half, 2½ tsp salt, and pepper to taste and stir to combine. Place over medium-low heat and cook gently until heated through, about 10 minutes.

Serve, garnished with the pear slices.

6

Turnips can be a hard sell to non-vegetable-lovers, but whirled with apples and potatoes, their bold flavor is sweetened and mellowed. The important thing to remember is that the smaller and younger the turnip, the more mild and tender it is.

TURNIP, APPLE & POTATO SOUP

serves 4

2 Tbsp unsalted butter

1 small yellow onion, finely diced

1 tsp chopped thyme

1 bay leaf

Salt and ground white pepper

1 lb (500 g) turnips, peeled and cut into ½-inch (12-mm) chunks

2 tart apples, such as Braeburn, Granny Smith, Jonagold, or pippin, peeled, cored, and quartered

½ lb (250 g) Yukon gold potatoes, peeled and quartered

2 Tbsp crème fraîche or sour cream

2 Tbsp chopped flat-leaf parsley

In a large, heavy pot, melt the butter over medium-low heat. Add the onion, thyme, bay leaf, and a pinch of salt and sauté until the onion is tender, 10–12 minutes. Add the turnips, apples, potatoes, a pinch of salt, and 1 cup (8 fl oz/250 ml) water. Cover and simmer until the vegetables and apples are tender, 10–15 minutes. Add another 4 cups (32 fl oz/1 l) water, raise the heat to high, and bring to a boil. Reduce the heat to low and simmer, uncovered, for 20 minutes. Remove from the heat, remove the bay leaf, and let cool slightly.

Working in batches, purée the soup in a blender. Return to the pot and reheat. Thin the soup with water, if necessary, and season with salt and pepper. Serve, garnished with the crème fraîche and parsley.

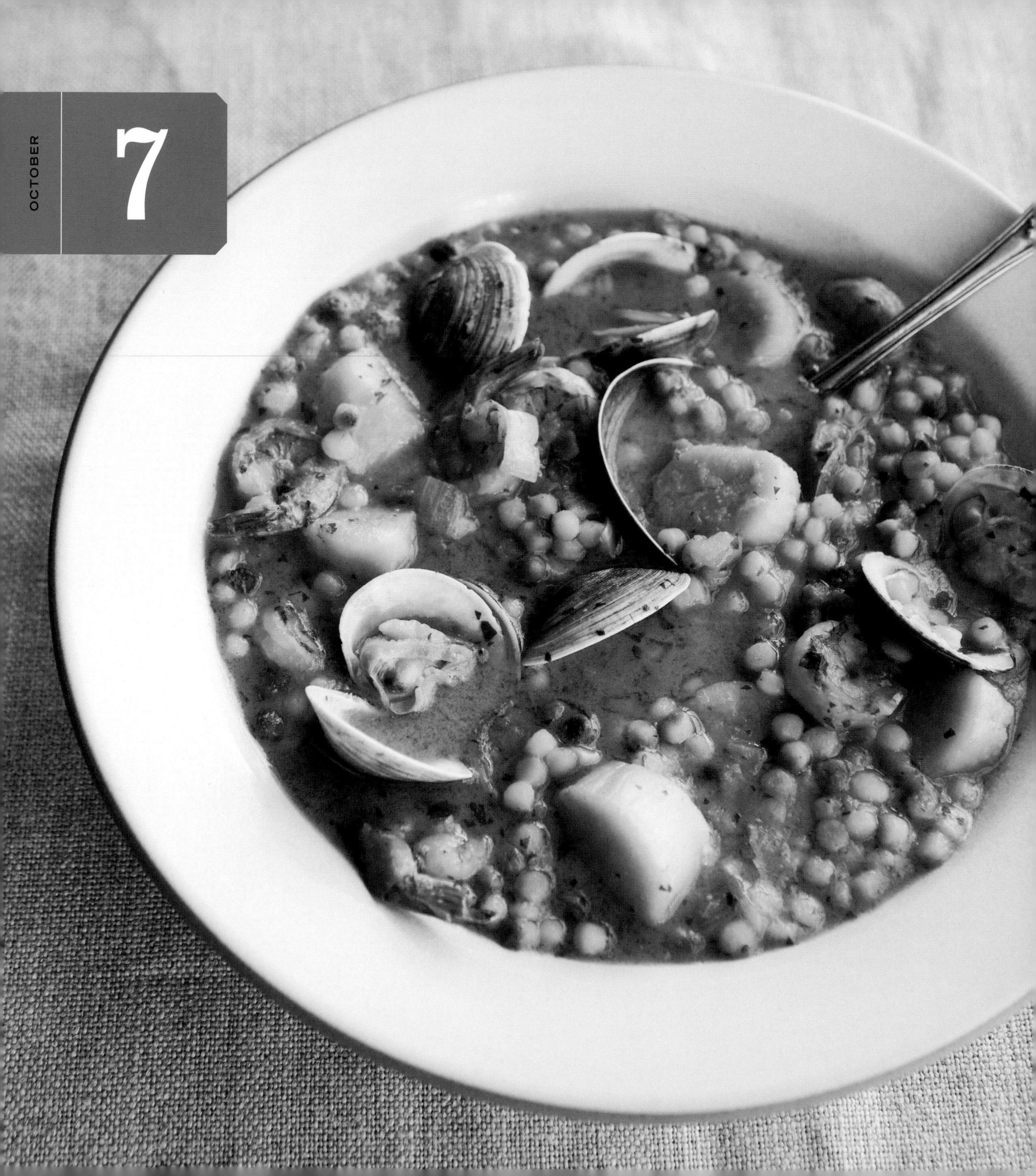

7

SAFFRON FREGOLA WITH SEAFOOD

serves 4

A bit of culinary exotica, fregola is a type of pasta from the Italian island of Sardinia. The more common Israeli couscous may be substituted. Serve this hearty stew with a refreshing butter lettuce and pear salad and plenty of crusty bread for dipping.

1 tsp saffron threads

¼ cup (2 fl oz/60 ml) dry white wine

2 Tbsp olive oil

½ lb (250 g) medium shrimp, shelled and deveined

½ lb (250 g) medium scallops, tough muscles removed

1 small yellow onion, chopped

2 cloves garlic, minced

2 cups (16 fl oz/500 ml) chicken broth

1 cup (6 oz/185 g) fregola (Sardinian couscous) or Israeli couscous

Salt and freshly ground pepper

½ lb (250 g) clams, scrubbed

2 Tbsp minced flat-leaf parsley

Crush the saffron in a bowl and add the white wine. Set aside.

In a large, heavy pot, warm 1 Tbsp of the oil over high heat. When the pan is very hot, add the shrimp and sear for 1 minute on each side (do not cook all the way through). Transfer to a bowl. Add the scallops and sear for 1 minute on each side, also without cooking all the way through. Transfer to the bowl with the shrimp.

Add the remaining 1 Tbsp oil, onion, and garlic to the same pot and sauté until soft, about 5 minutes. Add the saffron mixture and cook for 2 minutes. Add the broth and bring to a boil. Add the fregola, stir to combine, and reduce the heat to medium-low. Cook for 12 minutes. Season with salt and pepper.

Add the clams, discarding any that do not close to the touch. Cover the saucepan tightly and steam for 3 minutes. Remove the lid and quickly add the shrimp and scallops. Tightly cover the saucepan again and continue to cook just until the clams open and the shrimp and scallops are cooked through, about 3 minutes. Discard any unopened clams. Serve, sprinkled with the parsley.

8

ROASTED CAULIFLOWER & PARMESAN SOUP

serves 4–6

This soup might be your answer to getting more vegetables on the family table. Roasted cauliflower turns sweet, and Parmesan adds a salty-nutty complement. Use a good-quality Parmesan and serve with garlic bread and a green salad.

1 head cauliflower (about 2 lb/1 kg), stemmed and cut into florets

2 Tbsp olive oil

Salt and freshly ground pepper

2 Tbsp unsalted butter

1 yellow onion, chopped

3 cloves garlic, minced

3 cups (24 fl oz/750 ml) chicken broth, plus more as needed

½ cup (2 oz/60 g) grated Parmesan cheese

Preheat the oven to 400°F (200°C) and line a baking sheet with parchment paper. Toss the cauliflower with the oil and season with salt and pepper. Spread on the prepared baking sheet and roast in the oven until very tender, 30–35 minutes.

In a large, heavy pot, warm the butter over medium-high heat. Add the onion and garlic and sauté until translucent, about 5 minutes. Add the cauliflower and broth and bring to a boil. Reduce the heat to low and simmer for 15 minutes to blend the flavors. Remove from the heat and let cool slightly.

Working in batches, purée the soup in a blender or food processor. Return to the pot over low heat. If needed, add more broth, ¼ cup (2 fl oz/60 ml) at a time, until you achieve the desired consistency. Add the Parmesan and stir until melted. Season to taste with salt and pepper and serve.

9

*Autumn brings
the alluring sight
of market stands
featuring baskets
piled high with
winter squashes.
In this recipe,
butternut, Hubbard,
turban, or buttercup
squash can be
substituted for the
acorn squash, as can
pumpkin. A pretty
round of compound
butter melts over
the top of the soup,
spreading rich
walnut flavor.*

ACORN SQUASH SOUP WITH TOASTED WALNUT BUTTER

serves 6

4 acorn squashes, about 1 lb (500 g) each

1 Tbsp unsalted butter, at room temperature

2 slices bacon, finely chopped

1 large yellow onion, chopped

6 cups (48 fl oz/1.5 l) chicken broth

FOR THE TOASTED WALNUT BUTTER

¼ cup (1 oz/30 g) walnut halves

2 tsp walnut oil

Large pinch of sugar

Salt and freshly ground pepper

2 Tbsp unsalted butter, at room temperature

¼ cup (2 fl oz/60 ml) heavy cream

Large pinch of grated nutmeg

¼ cup (2 fl oz/60 ml) fresh orange juice

Preheat the oven to 375°F (190°C). Lightly oil a baking sheet.

Cut each squash in half through the stem end and place, cut sides down, on the prepared baking sheet. Bake until easily pierced with a knife, about 45 minutes. Remove from the oven and set aside until cool enough to handle, then scoop out the seeds and discard. Spoon the flesh into a bowl and set aside. Leave the oven set at 375°F (190°C).

In a large, heavy pot, melt the butter over medium heat. Add the bacon and onion and sauté until the onion is soft, about 10 minutes. Raise the heat to high, add the squash and broth, and bring to a gentle boil. Reduce the heat to medium and simmer, uncovered, until the squash is very soft, about 30 minutes.

Meanwhile, make the walnut butter. In a small bowl, toss together the walnuts, walnut oil, sugar, and salt and pepper to taste and spread out on a baking sheet. Toast until golden, 5–7 minutes. Remove from the oven, let cool, and chop finely. In a small bowl, using a fork, mash together the walnuts and butter. Season with salt and pepper. Spoon out the butter onto a piece of plastic wrap and, using the plastic wrap, shape into a log about 1 inch (2.5 cm) in diameter. Wrap and refrigerate until serving. »→

Remove the soup from the heat and let cool slightly. Working in batches, purée in a blender until smooth. Return to a clean saucepan over medium-low heat. Add the cream, nutmeg, orange juice, and salt and pepper to taste. Serve warm, garnished with slices of the walnut butter.

10

*Soup making does
not have to be
complicated, as
this recipe proves.
With just a few
ingredients—
including oniony
leeks, bittersweet
chard, and creamy
risotto rice—and
not much effort,
you can have a
flavorful, satisfying
dish in no time.*

LEEK & SWISS CHARD SOUP

serves 4

2 Tbsp unsalted butter

1 Tbsp olive oil

2 small leeks, white part and 2 inches (5 cm) of the green, cut into slices ½ inch (12 mm) thick

½ lb (250 g) Swiss chard, ribs removed, leaves cut into 1-inch (2.5-cm) pieces

6 cups (48 fl oz/1.5 l) chicken broth

½ cup (3½ oz/105 g) medium-grain rice such as Arborio

Salt and freshly ground pepper

¼ cup (1 oz/30 g) grated Parmesan cheese

In a large, heavy pot, melt the butter with the oil over low heat. Add the leeks and cook, stirring occasionally, until tender and golden, about 10 minutes. Add the chard and broth, raise the heat to medium, and bring to a simmer. Cook, stirring occasionally, until the chard wilts, about 10 minutes.

Add the rice and salt and pepper to taste. Cover and cook over low heat until the rice is tender, about 20 minutes. Stir in the Parmesan. Season with salt and pepper and serve.

11

ROASTED VEGETABLE STEW WITH COUSCOUS

serves 6

This is a vegetarian feast to tempt carnivores, with hearty roasted veggies and chickpeas simmered into a stew thick enough to serve over a bed of couscous. Purplish-black Kalamata olives impart full, briny flavor and a meaty texture.

8 carrots, peeled

1 eggplant, peeled

4 yellow crookneck squash

2 leeks, white and pale green parts, finely chopped

½ lb (250 g) small brussels sprouts, halved

3 Tbsp olive oil

4 cups (32 fl oz/1 l) chicken or vegetable broth

1 tsp finely chopped thyme leaves

Salt and freshly ground pepper

6 cloves garlic, minced

1 tomato, peeled (page 172) and diced

1 can (15 oz/470 g) chickpeas, drained

1 cup (5 oz/155 g) Kalamata olives, pitted and chopped

6 Tbsp finely chopped mixed herbs such as flat-leaf parsley, chives, and basil

¼ cup (1 oz/30 g) grated Parmesan cheese

1¼ cups (10 oz/315g) cooked couscous

Preheat the oven to 400°F (200°C).

Cut the carrots, eggplant, and squash into 1½-inch (4-cm) chunks. In a large roasting pan, combine with the leeks and brussels sprouts. Pour in the oil and 1 cup (8 oz/250 ml) of the broth. Add the thyme and salt and pepper to taste and mix to coat the vegetables evenly.

Roast, stirring occasionally, for 30 minutes. Add another 1 cup broth, the garlic, and tomato to the pan and continue roasting, stirring every 15 minutes, until the vegetables are very tender, about 30 minutes.

Add the remaining 2 cups (16 fl oz/500 ml) broth, the chickpeas, olives, and herbs to the pan and stir to combine. Taste and adjust the seasoning, and return to the oven for 5 minutes.

Spoon the vegetables into a large serving bowl and garnish with the Parmesan. Spoon the couscous into bowls, ladle the stew on top, and serve.

12

CAULIFLOWER SOUP WITH CHEDDAR & BLUE CHEESE

serves 4–6

Cauliflower has a mild flavor that marries nicely with cheese. Sharp Cheddar is stirred directly into this vegetable purée, and a few crumbles of potent blue cheese on top make the perfect cheese-lover's garnish.

2 Tbsp olive oil

1 yellow onion, sliced

3 cloves garlic, minced

½ tsp caraway seeds

2 lb (1 kg) cauliflower, stemmed and cut into florets

4 cups (32 fl oz/1 l) vegetable broth

1 cup (4 oz/125 g) shredded sharp Cheddar cheese

Salt and ground white pepper

¼ cup (1 oz/30 g) crumbled blue cheese

1 Tbsp finely chopped flat-leaf parsley

In a large, heavy pot, warm the oil over medium-high heat. Add the onion and sauté until softened, about 5 minutes. Add the garlic and caraway seeds and sauté for 1 minute.

Add the cauliflower and broth and bring to a simmer. Reduce the heat to medium and cook until the cauliflower is softened, 20–25 minutes. Remove from the heat and let cool slightly.

Working in batches, purée the soup in a blender or food processor until smooth. Return to the pot. Whisk in the Cheddar until completely incorporated. Season with salt and pepper.

Return the soup to medium heat and cook until heated through, about 2 minutes. Serve, sprinkled with the blue cheese and parsley.

13

*Serve this satisfying
Indian soup with
warmed naan or
other flatbread,
brushed with garlic
butter, if you're
feeling decadent.
For a smoother soup,
purée the lentil base
before adding the
onion mixture.*

CURRIED YELLOW LENTIL SOUP

serves 4

1 cup (7 oz/220 g) dried yellow lentils, picked
over and rinsed

½ tsp ground turmeric

1 tsp plus 2 Tbsp ghee or canola oil

1 tsp black mustard seeds

2 dried red chiles, chopped

1 yellow onion, sliced

2 cloves garlic, minced

2 tsp minced ginger

20 fresh or dried curry leaves

1 tsp garam masala

2 small tomatoes, quartered lengthwise

Salt

In a large, heavy pot, combine the lentils,
2 cups (16 fl oz/500 ml) water, the turmeric,
and the 1 tsp ghee over high heat. Bring to a
boil, stirring occasionally. Reduce the heat to
medium, cover, and simmer until the lentils
are tender, about 30 minutes.

In a frying pan, warm the remaining 2 Tbsp
ghee over medium-high heat. When hot,
add the mustard seeds and fry until they
turn gray and pop, about 2 minutes. Add the
chiles, onion, garlic, ginger, and curry leaves
and sauté until the onion is golden, about
5 minutes. Stir in the garam masala and
tomatoes and cook for 1 minute.

Pour the onion mixture into the cooked
lentils, add ½ tsp salt, and simmer for
5 minutes to blend the flavors. Serve.

14

*Turnips have a
delicately sweet
flavor when
young, but as they
mature they lose
their sweetness
and become
woody—so buy
them at their peak,
between October
and February.
The greens, which
are edible, should
be bright green
and garden fresh.
If unavailable,
substitute Swiss
chard, dandelion
greens, beet
greens, or kale.*

BEEF STEW WITH TURNIPS & GREENS

serves 6

¼ cup (2 fl oz/60 ml) olive oil

2 yellow onions, finely chopped

2 oz (60 g) bacon or pancetta, finely diced

3 lb (1.5 kg) chuck roast or sirloin tip,
cut into 1–1½-inch (2.5–4-cm) cubes

¼ cup (1½ oz/45 g) all-purpose flour

4 cloves garlic, minced

6 flat-leaf parsley stems, 2 thyme sprigs,
and 2 bay leaves tied together to make a
bouquet garni

1½ cups (12 fl oz/375 ml) dry red wine

3 cups (24 fl oz/750 ml) beef broth

1 Tbsp tomato paste

1 bunch turnips with greens, turnips cut into
½-inch (12-mm) chunks and leaves stemmed
and cut crosswise into strips

Salt and freshly ground pepper

In a large, heavy pot, warm the oil over
medium heat. Add the onions and bacon
and sauté until the onions are soft, about
10 minutes. Transfer to a plate.

Working in batches, add the beef to the
pot in a single layer and cook, turning
occasionally, until golden brown on all sides,
7–10 minutes. Transfer to a bowl. Return all
the meat to the pot, sprinkle with the flour,
and cook, stirring, until the meat is evenly
coated, about 1 minute. Return the onions
and bacon to the pot and add the garlic.
Add the bouquet garni to the pot.

Raise the heat to high, pour in the wine,
and bring to a boil, stirring to scrape up
any browned bits on the bottom of the pot.
Reduce the heat to medium and simmer,
stirring occasionally, until the liquid is
reduced by one-fourth, 3–5 minutes. Stir
in the broth and tomato paste. Bring
to a boil over high heat, reduce the heat to
low, cover, and simmer until the meat is
tender, 1½–2 hours.

Remove the bouquet garni and discard.
Add the turnips, cover, and cook until
tender, about 15 minutes. Add the turnip
greens, cover, and cook until wilted,
about 2 minutes. Season with salt and
pepper and serve.

OCTOBER

15

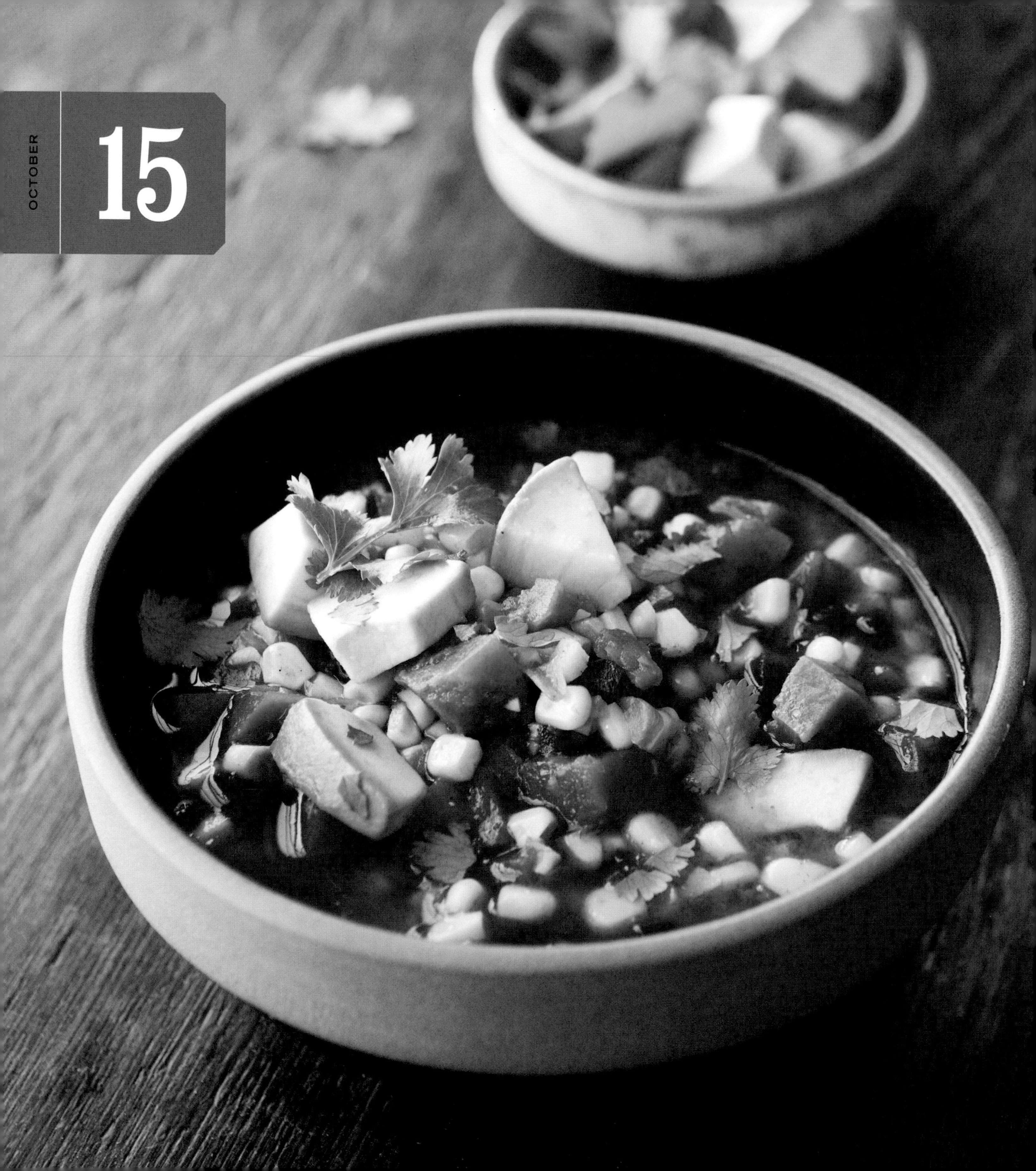

15

SWEET POTATO–CORN CHOWDER WITH AVOCADO

serves 6

2 Tbsp olive oil

1 small white onion, finely diced

2 cloves garlic, minced

2 tsp ground cumin

½ tsp ground coriander

Salt and freshly ground pepper

2 sweet potatoes (about 1½ lb/750 g total), peeled and diced

3 cups (24 fl oz/750 ml) vegetable or chicken broth

1 red bell pepper, seeded and finely diced

8 ears fresh corn, husks and silk removed and kernels cut from cobs, or 3½ cups (1 lb/500 g) thawed frozen corn kernels

2 Tbsp minced cilantro

1 ripe avocado, pitted, peeled, and diced

½ cup (4 oz/125 g) sour cream (optional)

Southwestern ingredients mingle in this surprisingly light chowder. It gets its creamy consistency not from dairy but by puréeing half of the soup. Serve with fresh tortilla chips and salsa.

In a large, heavy pot, warm the oil over medium-high heat. Add the onion and garlic and sauté until translucent, about 5 minutes. Add the cumin, coriander, and salt and pepper to taste and cook for 1 minute. Add the sweet potatoes, stir to coat, and cook for 3 minutes.

Add the broth, bring to a boil, and reduce the heat to low. Simmer until the sweet potatoes are tender, about 20 minutes. Add the red pepper and corn and cook until the vegetables are tender, 10 minutes. Remove from the heat and let cool slightly.

Purée half of the soup in a blender. Return to the pot. Stir in the cilantro and season with salt and pepper. Serve, garnished with the avocado and the sour cream, if desired.

16

PUMPKIN-GINGER SOUP

serves 6–8

2 lb (1 kg) Cheese or Sugar Pie pumpkin or winter squash such as butternut, Hubbard, or calabaza

6-inch (15-cm) piece peeled fresh ginger

2 Tbsp unsalted butter

1 yellow onion, chopped

1 carrot, peeled and chopped

1 celery rib, chopped

2 cloves garlic, minced

4 cups (32 fl oz/1 l) chicken broth, plus more as needed

Salt and freshly ground pepper

Heavy cream for garnish

Pumpkins for cooking differ from the jack-o'-lanterns that may be grinning crookedly on your porch this time of year. Look for Sugar Pie or Cheese varieties, which have dense, flavorful flesh.

Seed and peel the pumpkin, then cut the flesh into 2-inch (5-cm) chunks. Set aside.

Shred the ginger using the largest holes of a box grater. You should have about ¼ cup (1½ oz/45 g). Set aside.

In a large, heavy pot, melt the butter over medium heat. Add the onion, carrot, celery, and garlic and sauté until the vegetables soften, about 5 minutes.

Add the pumpkin and broth and bring to a boil over high heat. Reduce the heat to medium-low, cover partially, and simmer until the pumpkin is tender, about 25 minutes. Remove from the heat and let cool slightly.

Working in batches, purée the soup in a blender. Return to the pot and season with salt and pepper. Rewarm gently over medium-low heat. Serve, drizzled with cream.

17

WHITE BEAN, BROCCOLINI & BRATWURST SOUP

serves 4–6

3 Tbsp olive oil

¾ lb (375 g) bratwurst, cut into ¼-inch (6-mm) slices

1 yellow onion, chopped

4 cloves garlic, minced

1 can (14½ oz/455 g) diced tomatoes

4 cups (32 fl oz/1 l) chicken broth

1 bunch broccolini, cut into 1-inch (2.5-cm) pieces

1 can (14½ oz/455 g) white beans, drained

Salt and freshly ground pepper

This soup is very hearty and is great served with cold beer. You can substitute any type of sausage. Serve with Irish soda bread and a pot of butter.

In a large, heavy pot, warm 1 Tbsp of the oil over medium heat. Add the bratwurst and cook, stirring often, until browned on all sides, 7–8 minutes. Transfer to a bowl and set aside.

Add the remaining 2 Tbsp oil to the pot along with the onion and garlic. Sauté until very soft, about 5 minutes. Add the tomatoes with their juices and broth and bring to a boil. Add the broccolini and cook until tender, about 3 minutes. Reduce the heat to low, add the white beans and bratwurst, and simmer for 2 minutes to blend the flavors. Season with salt and pepper and serve.

18

ROASTED GARLIC & SHALLOT VELOUTÉ WITH CRISPY PANCETTA

serves 2

2 heads garlic

10 shallots

2 tsp olive oil

4 thyme sprigs, plus ¼ tsp minced leaves

2 oz (60 g) thinly sliced pancetta

2 Tbsp unsalted butter

1¼ cups (10 fl oz/310 ml) chicken broth

2 Tbsp heavy cream

Salt and freshly ground pepper

The French call it velouté when broth and cream are combined to make a "velvety" soup or sauce. This recipe yields only 2 cups (8 fl oz/250 ml), but a little goes a long way—it's a very rich soup meant to be served as a small first course. The recipe can be doubled easily.

Preheat the oven to 400°F (200°C). Cut off the tops of the garlic heads and the shallots to expose the bulbs. On a sheet of foil, place 1 head of garlic and half of the shallots, sprinkle with 1 tsp of the oil, and place 2 sprigs of thyme on top. Loosely close the foil. Repeat with a second piece of foil and the remaining garlic, shallots, oil, and thyme sprigs. Roast in the oven until very tender, about 1 hour and 10 minutes. When cool enough to handle, squeeze all the pulp from the skins of the garlic and shallots into a bowl.

In a saucepan, cook the pancetta over medium-high heat until crispy. Transfer to paper towels to drain. When cool enough to handle, crumble the pancetta. Add the butter to the saucepan and when melted, add the roasted garlic and shallots and the minced thyme and cook until translucent, about 6 minutes. Add the broth and bring to a boil. Stir in the cream and return to a boil. Reduce the heat to a simmer and cook for 5 minutes. Remove from the heat and let cool slightly.

Working in batches, purée the soup in a blender. Return to the pot and warm through over medium-low heat. Season with salt and pepper and serve, garnished with the crumbled pancetta.

19

In France, a pinch of freshly grated nutmeg accents many a béchamel sauce, used in gratins and all things creamy. Here, it is the secret ingredient lacing a simple spinach soup, creating a perfect foil for the dark greens.

CREAM OF SPINACH SOUP
serves 4

3 lb (1.5 kg) spinach, tough stems removed

2 cups (16 fl oz/500 ml) milk, plus more as needed

2 cups (16 fl oz/500 ml) chicken or vegetable broth

3 Tbsp unsalted butter

3 Tbsp all-purpose flour

Salt and freshly ground pepper

½ tsp grated nutmeg

½ cup (4 fl oz/125 ml) heavy cream

Put the spinach, with the rinsing water still clinging to the leaves, in a saucepan over medium heat, cover, and cook until wilted and tender, about 3 minutes. Drain the spinach and squeeze to extract as much water as possible. Using a food processor, process until finely chopped. Set aside.

Pour the 2 cups (16 fl oz/500 ml) milk and the broth into separate small saucepans and place over low heat. Heat both just until small bubbles form around the edge of the pan, then remove from the heat.

In a large, heavy pot, melt the butter over medium-low heat. When the foam begins to subside, add the flour and stir until smooth, about 2 minutes. Gradually add the hot milk while whisking gently. Cook, stirring often, until the mixture bubbles vigorously and has thickened, about 3 minutes. Gradually add the hot broth, whisking, and bring to a low boil. Cook until pale beige and opaque, about 3 minutes. Let cool slightly.

Add the spinach purée to the milk-broth mixture and stir until blended. Add 1 tsp salt, ⅛ tsp pepper, and the nutmeg. Reduce the heat to a bare simmer, cover, and cook for 10 minutes, stirring occasionally. Remove from the heat and let cool slightly.

Working in batches, purée the soup in the food processor. Return to the pot and stir in the cream. Reheat gently over low heat. If the soup seems too thick, thin it with milk, adding ¼ cup (2 fl oz/60 ml) at a time. Season with salt and pepper and serve.

20

This aromatic and creamy broth makes a great base for almost any combination of vegetables. You could also add thinly sliced poached chicken, prawns, or scallops.

VEGETABLES IN COCONUT-LIME BROTH
serves 4

1 Tbsp canola oil

1 shallot, minced

2 cloves garlic, minced

1-inch (2.5-cm) piece fresh ginger, peeled and minced

2 cans (14 oz/440 g each) coconut milk

4 cups (32 fl oz/1 l) vegetable broth

½ lb (250 g) small Yukon gold potatoes, quartered

3 oz (90 g) green beans, trimmed and halved on the diagonal

1 small red bell pepper, seeded and thinly sliced

Juice of 2 limes

Salt

In a large, heavy pot, warm the oil over medium-high heat. Add the shallot, garlic, and ginger and sauté until translucent, 2–3 minutes. Add the coconut milk and broth and bring to a boil. Add the potatoes and cook until tender, about 10 minutes. Add the green beans, red pepper, and lime juice and simmer for 4 minutes. Season to taste with salt and serve.

21

INDIAN-SPICED CHICKPEA STEW

serves 6

¾ cup (5 oz/155 g) dried chickpeas, picked over and rinsed

5 cups (40 fl oz/1.25 l) vegetable broth

1 lb (500 g) russet potatoes, peeled and diced

1 lb (500 g) tomatoes, peeled (page 172) and chopped

2 tsp garam masala

½ tsp ground ginger

½ tsp ground turmeric

Salt and freshly ground pepper

3 Tbsp chopped cilantro

Well seasoned but not too spicy, this cold-weather chickpea stew is an excellent source of protein. To save time, substitute 1 can (15 oz/470 g) chickpeas, drained and well rinsed, for the dried ones, decreasing the stock to 3 cups (24 fl oz/750 ml).

Put the chickpeas in a bowl with cold water to cover and soak for 3 hours. Drain.

In a large, heavy pot, bring the broth to a boil over high heat. Add the chickpeas, reduce the heat to medium, and simmer, uncovered, until almost tender, about 1½ hours. Add the potatoes, tomatoes, garam masala, ginger, and turmeric and continue to cook until the chickpeas and potatoes are tender, about 30 minutes. Remove from the heat and let cool slightly.

Purée half of the broth and vegetables in a blender or food processor. Return to the pot and season with salt and pepper. Reheat to serving temperature. Serve, garnished with the cilantro.

22

SQUASH SOUP WITH SAGE BROWN BUTTER

serves 4–6

1 butternut squash (2 lb/1 kg), peeled and diced

3 Tbsp olive oil

Salt and freshly ground pepper

2 Tbsp unsalted butter

1 yellow onion, chopped

2 cloves garlic, minced

4 cups (32 fl oz/1 l) vegetable broth

FOR THE SAGE BROWN BUTTER

¼ cup (2 oz/60 g) unsalted butter

6 sage leaves

Heavy cream for garnish (optional)

Butternut squash is the quintessential fall vegetable. Roasting the squash brings out its naturally nutty taste. When serving, drizzle the brown butter over the top of the soup, but do not stir, for an elegant presentation. Add a swirl of cream, if you like, along with the sage leaves.

Preheat the oven to 400°F (200°C) and line a baking sheet with parchment paper. Toss the squash with the oil and season with salt and pepper. Place on the prepared baking sheet and roast until tender, about 25 minutes.

In a large, heavy pot, melt the butter over medium-high heat. Add the onion and garlic and sauté until translucent, about 5 minutes. Add the roasted squash and broth and bring to a boil. Reduce the heat to low and simmer for 20 minutes to blend the flavors. Remove from the heat and let cool slightly.

Working in batches, purée the soup in a blender. Return to the pot and season with salt and pepper.

To make the sage brown butter, melt the butter in a small frying pan over low heat. Add the sage leaves and cook until the butter begins to brown and the sage is very aromatic, 3–4 minutes.

Serve the soup, drizzled with the brown butter, 1–2 sage leaves, and a swirl of cream, if desired.

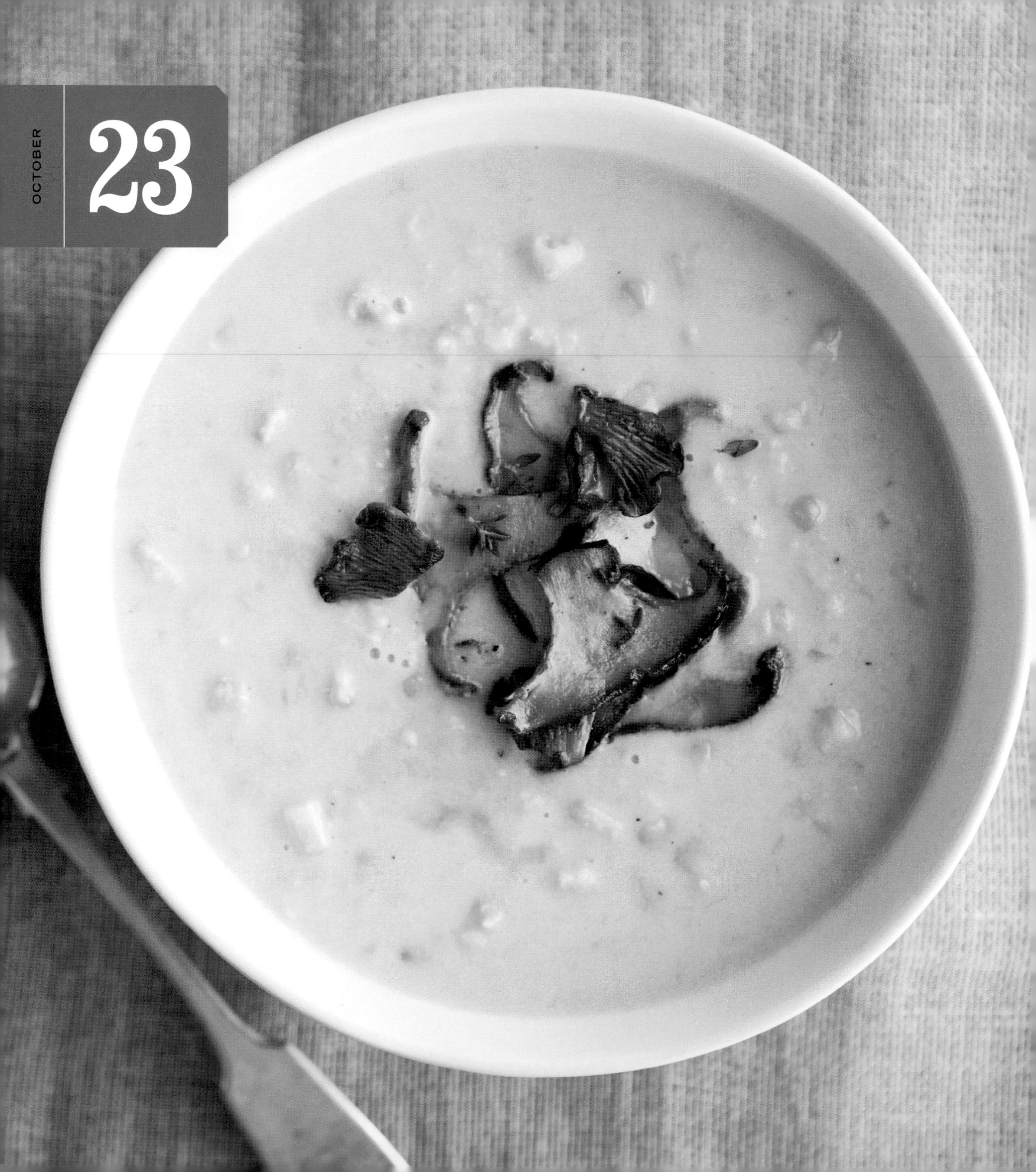

23

Slice the mushrooms crosswise to retain their shape. Chanterelles are beautiful, and you want diners to be able to see that you are serving a really special mushroom. Serve with warm croissants.

CORN SOUP WITH CHANTERELLES & THYME

serves 4

3 Tbsp unsalted butter

2 Tbsp olive oil

2 shallots, minced

4 cloves garlic, minced

4 cups (32 fl oz/1 l) chicken broth

2 packages (1 lb/500 g each) frozen corn kernels

¼ cup (2 fl oz/60 ml) heavy cream

Salt and freshly ground pepper

2 oz (60 g) chanterelle mushrooms, thinly sliced

½ tsp minced thyme leaves

In a large, heavy pot, warm 2 Tbsp of the butter and the oil over medium-high heat. Add the shallots and garlic and sauté until soft, about 3 minutes. Add the broth and bring to a boil. Add the corn and cook for 5 minutes. Remove from the heat and let cool slightly.

Purée half of the soup in a blender. Return to the pot and stir in the cream. Season with salt and pepper.

In a small frying pan, melt the remaining 1 Tbsp butter over medium-high heat. Add the mushrooms and thyme and sauté, stirring often, until the mushrooms release their liquid and caramelize slightly, about 4 minutes. Serve the soup, garnished with the chanterelles.

24

Cinnamon and nutmeg add an intriguing dimension to this soup, but parsnips are so sweet and flavorful that they could pull it off all on their own. For a fresh garnish, top with chopped parsley. This soup freezes well.

CREAM OF PARSNIP SOUP

serves 4–6

2 Tbsp unsalted butter

1 Tbsp olive oil

1 small yellow onion, chopped

2 celery ribs, chopped

2 cloves garlic, minced

½ tsp grated nutmeg

Pinch of ground cinnamon

6 parsnips (about 2½ lb/1.25 kg total), peeled and diced

6 cups (48 fl oz/1.5 l) chicken broth

½ cup (4 fl oz/125 ml) heavy cream

Salt and ground white pepper

In a large, heavy pot, melt the butter with the oil over medium-high heat. Add the onion, celery, and garlic and sauté until the vegetables are very soft, about 7 minutes. Add the nutmeg and cinnamon, stir to combine, and cook for 1 minute. Add the parsnips and the broth and bring to a boil. Reduce the heat to low and simmer until the parsnips are very soft, 45–55 minutes. Remove from the heat and let cool slightly.

Working in batches, purée the soup in a blender. Return to the pot, stir in the cream, and bring to a boil. Turn off the heat. Season to taste with salt and pepper and serve.

25

CREAMY BLACK BEAN PURÉE WITH CHEESE STRAWS

serves 4–6

*For a creative
appetizer at a
cocktail party, serve
this as "soup sips."
Put the soup into
clear shot glasses
and balance a cheese
straw across the
top rim of each
glass. Encourage
guests to dip their
straws and then
sip their soup.*

FOR THE CHEESE STRAWS

1 sheet puff pastry, thawed

½ cup (2 oz/60 g) finely shredded
Cheddar cheese

2 Tbsp olive oil

1 yellow onion, chopped

3 cloves garlic, minced

1 small jalapeño chile, seeded and minced

1½ tsp ground cumin

4 cans (15 oz/470 g each) black beans, drained

2¾ cups (22 fl oz/680 ml) chicken broth

Salt and freshly ground pepper

¼ cup (2 oz/60 g) sour cream

To make the cheese straws, preheat the
oven to 400°F (200°C) and line a baking sheet
with parchment paper. Roll out the puff
pastry to ⅛ inch (3 mm) thick on a floured
surface. Cut the pastry into 9 squares, each
about 3½ by 3½ inches (9 by 9 cm). Cut each
square in half diagonally to make 18 triangles.
Starting with the longest side, tightly roll up
each triangle and place, seam side down, on
the prepared baking sheet. Brush each roll
with water and sprinkle with cheese, gently
pressing with your fingers to help the cheese
stick to the pastry. Bake until the straws turn
golden brown, 18–20 minutes.

Meanwhile, in a large, heavy pot, warm
the oil over medium-high heat. Add the
onion and garlic and sauté until soft, about
5 minutes. Add the jalapeño and cumin
and cook, stirring often, for 2 minutes.
Add the black beans and broth and bring
to a boil. Reduce the heat to low and simmer
for 15 minutes. Remove from the heat and
let cool slightly.

Working in batches, purée the soup in a
blender or food processor. Return to the pot
and warm through over medium-low heat.
Season to taste with salt and pepper and
serve, topping each with a dollop of sour
cream. Serve with cheese straws on the side
for dipping. Pass the extra straws at the table.

26

PORK & ROASTED TOMATILLO STEW

serves 4–6

*This is one of those
stews that tastes
even better the
second day, when
all the flavors have
had time to come
together, so feel free
to make this one
ahead. Serve with
warm corn bread
and a green salad.*

1 lb (500 g) tomatillos, husked,
rinsed, and quartered

1 lb (500 g) plum tomatoes, quartered

4 Tbsp (2 fl oz/60 ml) olive oil

Salt and freshly ground pepper

1½ lb (750 g) pork loin, cut into ½-inch
(12-mm) cubes

1 white onion, chopped

3 cloves garlic, minced

2 cups (16 fl oz/500 ml) chicken broth

1 can (15 oz/470 g) white beans, drained

½ cup (4 oz/125 g) sour cream

Hot sauce for serving

Preheat the oven to 425°F (220°C). Put the
tomatillos and tomatoes on a baking sheet,
toss with 2 Tbsp of the oil, and season
with salt and pepper. Roast for 25 minutes,
stirring once. Set aside and lower the oven
temperature to 350°F (180°C).

Season the pork with salt and pepper. In a
large, heavy, ovenproof pot, warm 1 Tbsp of
the oil over medium-high heat. In 2 batches,
cook the pork until it is browned on all sides,
about 5 minutes per batch. Transfer the pork
to a bowl and set aside.

Add the remaining 1 Tbsp oil, the onion,
and the garlic to the pot and sauté until the
onion is translucent, about 5 minutes. Add
the pork, tomatillos, tomatoes, broth, and
beans and stir to combine. Cover, transfer
the pot to the oven, and cook for 1½ hours.

Season with salt and pepper and serve,
topped with a dollop of sour cream.
Pass hot sauce at the table.

27

This delicate soup is seasoned primarily with kombu or wakame (dried seaweed) and miso (fermented soybean paste), two Asian staples now commonly stocked by many grocers. Light and flavorful, this soup comes together very easily.

MISO SOUP

serves 4–6

3 oz (90 g) wakame

¾ tsp granulated dashi mixed with 6 cups (48 fl oz/1.5 l) hot water

6 Tbsp white miso paste

1 tsp rice vinegar

2 oz (60 g) soft tofu, cut into small cubes

3 green onions, white and tender green parts, thinly sliced on the diagonal

Soak the wakame in hot water to cover until soft, about 10 minutes. Drain and cut into thin strips.

In a large, heavy pot, bring the dashi mixture to a bare simmer over low heat. Whisk in the miso and vinegar and simmer for 5 minutes to blend the flavors. Stir in the wakame, tofu cubes, and green onions and serve.

28

Garam masala is a classic blend of Indian spices that adds beautiful depth to this sweet purée. Sautéing the spice mixture before adding the liquid toasts the spices, further enhancing their flavors.

CARROT & ASIAN PEAR PURÉE

serves 4–6

2 Tbsp olive oil

1 small yellow onion, chopped

2 cloves garlic, minced

2 tsp garam masala

8 carrots, peeled and chopped

2 ripe Asian pears, peeled, cored, and chopped

4 cups (32 fl oz/1 l) vegetable broth

Salt and ground white pepper

In a saucepan, warm the oil over medium-high heat. Add the onion and garlic and sauté until translucent, about 5 minutes. Add the garam masala, stir to combine, and cook for 1 minute. Add the carrots and pears, stir, and cook until the carrots begin to soften, 5–7 minutes. Add the broth and bring to a boil. Reduce the heat to low and simmer until the carrots are very tender, about 30 minutes. Remove from the heat and let cool slightly.

Working in batches, purée the soup in a blender. Return to the saucepan and heat through over medium-low heat. Season to taste with salt and pepper and serve.

29

A great way to use up leftover baguette, this is a very different take on classic tomato and bread soup. Because this soup, featuring earthy artichokes, is so hearty, serve it with a simple green salad topped with fresh figs and a balsamic vinaigrette.

ARTICHOKE & TOASTED BREAD SOUP WITH SAGE

serves 4

1 small loaf day-old Italian peasant bread, cut into ½-inch (12-mm) cubes (about 2 cups/2 oz/60 g)

3 Tbsp olive oil

Salt and freshly ground pepper

1 Tbsp unsalted butter

1 leek, white and pale green parts, chopped

2 cloves garlic, minced

7 sage leaves, chopped

2 cups (16 fl oz/500 ml) chicken broth

12 oz (375 g) frozen artichoke hearts

Preheat the oven to 350°F (180°C). Spread the bread cubes on a baking sheet, toss with 2 Tbsp of the oil, and season with salt and pepper. Bake until golden brown and toasted, about 10 minutes. Set aside.

In a large, heavy pot, melt the butter with the remaining 1 Tbsp oil and the butter over medium-high heat. Add the leek and garlic and sauté for 4 minutes. Add the sage and continue to sauté for 1 minute. Add the broth and 2 cups (16 fl oz/500 ml) water and bring to a boil. Add the artichoke hearts, reduce the heat to medium-low, and simmer until the artichokes are soft and heated through, about 10 minutes. Add the toasted bread, stir to combine, and cook for 5 minutes. Remove from the heat and let cool slightly.

Working in batches, purée the soup in a blender. Return to the pot and warm through over medium-low heat. Season with salt and pepper and serve.

30

PEANUT-GINGER SWEET POTATO SOUP

serves 4–6

2 Tbsp unsalted butter

1 small yellow onion, chopped

2 cloves garlic, minced

1 Tbsp peeled and minced fresh ginger

2 sweet potatoes (1½ lb/750 g total), peeled and diced

4½ cups (36 fl oz/1.1 l) vegetable broth

3 Tbsp creamy peanut butter

2 Tbsp minced cilantro

Salt and freshly ground pepper

Peanut butter ensures that this soup is a kid-pleaser. You can garnish with chopped peanuts for a little crunch. This would make a satisfying and nutritious dinner on Halloween night before you send the kids out for their sugar rush.

In a large, heavy pot, melt the butter over medium-high heat. Add the onion, garlic, and ginger and sauté until very soft, about 5 minutes. Add the sweet potatoes, stir to combine, and cook for 5 minutes. Add the broth and bring to a boil. Reduce the heat to low and simmer until the sweet potatoes are very tender, 30–35 minutes. Remove from the heat at let cool slightly.

Working in batches, purée the soup in a blender or food processor. Return to the pot over low heat, add the peanut butter, and stir until melted, about 4 minutes. Add the cilantro and season to taste with salt and pepper. Serve.

31

WILD RICE & RED CHARD SOUP WITH ANDOUILLE

serves 6

½ cup (3 oz/90 g) wild rice

2 cups (12 oz/375 g) cherry tomatoes

2 Tbsp olive oil

Salt and freshly ground pepper

4 links (12 oz/375 g) andouille sausage

1 yellow onion, finely diced

3 cloves garlic, minced

1 bunch red chard, tough stems removed, leaves and ribs chopped

6 cups (48 fl oz/1.5 l) chicken broth

A few rustic and wholesome ingredients come together in this soup to offer a satisfying and visually rich whole. Andouille sausages are spicy, so if you want to lower the heat you can substitute sweet Italian sausages.

Cook the wild rice according to package directions and set aside.

Preheat the oven to 500°F (260°C). In a bowl, toss the cherry tomatoes with 1 Tbsp of the oil and salt and pepper to taste. Spread out on a rimmed baking sheet and roast in the oven just until the tomatoes begin to split and caramelize, about 10 minutes. Set aside.

In a large, heavy pot, fry the sausages over medium-high heat until they are cooked through, about 15 minutes. Transfer to a cutting board and, when cool enough to handle, cut into ¼-inch (6-mm) slices. Set aside.

Add the remaining 1 Tbsp oil to the pot and warm over medium-high heat. Add the onion and garlic and sauté until soft, 5 minutes. Add the chard and cook, stirring often, for 4 minutes. Add the broth and bring to a boil, scraping up any browned bits on the bottom of the pot. Reduce the heat to low and let simmer. Add the rice, andouille, and tomatoes, stir to combine, and simmer for 5 minutes. Season with salt and pepper and serve.

1
SAVORY BARLEY SOUP WITH WILD MUSHROOMS & THYME
page 250

2
APPLE, LEEK & BUTTERNUT SQUASH SOUP
page 250

3
CELERY & RICE SOUP WITH PARSLEY
page 252

4
MUSHROOM, CARROT & LEEK SOUP WITH SHAVED PARMESAN
page 252

8
PUMPKIN-GRUYÈRE SOUP
page 255

9
CHICKEN-TOMATILLO SOUP WITH CHIPOTLE CHILES
page 256

10
POTATO-ROSEMARY SOUP
page 256

11
CURRIED CAULIFLOWER & CHICKEN STE
page 257

15
WHITE BEAN & HAM SOUP WITH CORN BREAD CROUTONS
page 261

16
PENNE & SQUASH SOUP WITH SAGE CROUTONS
page 261

17
KALE & SWEET POTATO SOUP WITH LAMB SAUSAGE
page 262

18
ORECCHIETTE, SAUSAGE & BROCCOLI IN BROTH
page 262

22
LEMONY RED LENTIL SOUP WITH FRIED SHALLOTS
page 264

23
PUMPKIN SOUP WITH SPICY PUMPKIN SEEDS
page 267

24
CREAM OF SUNCHOKE SOUP WITH PORCINI MUSHROOMS
page 267

25
TURKEY & JASMINE RICE SOUP WITH LEMONGRASS
page 268

29
SHRIMP BISQUE
page 270

30
TURKEY-NOODLE SOUP WITH SPINACH
page 270

5
PORK & POBLANO CHILI
page 253

6
**CHESTNUT—CELERY ROOT SOUP
WITH BACON & SAGE CROUTONS**
page 253

7
**CELERY ROOT PURÉE
WITH CARAMELIZED APPLES**
page 255

12
CHEDDAR CHEESE SOUP WITH ALE
page 257

13
**MUSTARD GREENS & WILD
RICE SOUP WITH GRUYÈRE**
page 258

14
RED CABBAGE & APPLE SOUP
page 258

19
GOULASH
page 263

20
TOMATO-FENNEL BROTH WITH CLAMS
page 263

21
TOMATO BISQUE
page 264

26
**GARLICKY GREENS, ROAST PORK
& WHITE BEAN SOUP**
page 268

27
**CARROT SOUP WITH
BACON & CHESTNUT CREAM**
page 269

28
**SPICED BROTH WITH ROASTED
ACORN SQUASH & KALE**
page 269

This month's bracing winds and touches of frost call for making hearty, long-simmered dishes. Slow-cooked stews of succulent beef or lamb are just the thing for cozy evenings at home, as is hearty vegetarian fare featuring toothsome grains, beans, and mushrooms. When the harvest wanes toward the end of the month, it's a good time to take advantage of leftover roasts to make easy rice and noodle soups.

november

1

SAVORY BARLEY SOUP WITH WILD MUSHROOMS & THYME

serves 4

½ oz (15 g) dried porcini mushrooms

½ cup (4 fl oz/125 ml) dry white wine

1 Tbsp olive oil

½ cup (2 oz/60 g) chopped shallots

2 cloves garlic, minced

8 oz (250 g) cremini mushrooms, chopped

1 tsp minced fresh thyme, or ½ tsp dried

Salt and freshly ground pepper

3 cups (24 fl oz/750 ml) chicken broth

¾ cup (6 oz/185 g) pearl barley

1 Tbsp tomato paste

2 tsp fresh lemon juice

Barley, an excellent source of minerals and fiber, deserves its renaissance in the modern kitchen. Thanks to a partial puréeing, this creamy soup supports meaty fall mushrooms. Add a Parmesan rind to the broth as it simmers for a boost in flavor.

Rinse the porcini well to remove any dirt or grit. In a small saucepan, bring the wine to a simmer. Remove from the heat and add the porcini. Let stand for 15 minutes, then drain the porcini over a bowl, reserving the liquid, and finely chop.

In a large, heavy pot over medium-high heat, warm the oil. Add the shallots and garlic. Sauté until the shallots are wilted, 3–5 minutes. Add the cremini, thyme, ¼ tsp salt, and ¼ tsp pepper. Cook until the cremini release their liquid and begin to brown, 4–5 minutes. Add the reserved mushroom soaking liquid and bring to a boil, scraping up any browned bits from the pan bottom.

Add the broth, barley, tomato paste, 3 cups (24 fl oz/750 ml) water, and the chopped porcini to the pot. Cover and simmer until the barley is tender to the bite, 45–50 minutes. Remove from the heat and let cool slightly.

Purée about 1 cup (8 fl oz/250 ml) of the soup in a blender. Return to the pot, heat until just hot, and stir in the lemon juice. Season with salt and pepper and serve.

2

APPLE, LEEK & BUTTERNUT SQUASH SOUP

serves 8

1 or 2 butternut squashes (about 4 lb/ 2 kg total), halved, seeded, peeled, and cut into chunks

1 lb (500 g) tart apples, peeled, cored, and quartered, plus 1 small tart apple, unpeeled, halved, cored, and thinly sliced

1 large leek, white and pale green parts, thickly sliced

4 large cloves garlic

2 Tbsp chopped sage, plus whole leaves for garnish (optional)

2 tsp ground cumin

Salt and freshly ground pepper

3 Tbsp olive oil

4 cups (32 fl oz/1 l) chicken broth

1 cup (8 fl oz/250 ml) hard cider or dry white wine

½ cup (4 oz/125 g) crème fraîche or sour cream

Apples, leeks, and cider create a complexity of flavor that makes this winter squash purée rich in character and in little need of embellishment. To save time, substitute 2½ lb (1.25 kg) butternut squash chunks from the produce section. Accompany with a warm baguette and bottle of dry French cider.

Preheat the oven to 425°F (220°C). Place the squash, quartered apples, leek, and garlic on a rimmed baking sheet. Sprinkle with 1 Tbsp of the chopped sage and 1 tsp of the cumin. Season with salt and pepper. Drizzle with the oil, stir to coat, and spread the apples and vegetables in a single layer.

Roast, stirring 2 or 3 times, until the squash is fork-tender and all the vegetables and apples are golden, 20–25 minutes. Remove from the oven.

Working in batches, process in a food processor until a coarse purée forms. With the motor running, pour in 1–1½ cups (8–12 fl oz/250–375 ml) of the broth and process until nearly smooth. Transfer the purée to a large, heavy pot over medium heat. Stir in the remaining broth, the cider, and the remaining 1 Tbsp chopped sage and 1 tsp cumin and bring just to a simmer, stirring often. Season with salt and pepper.

Ladle the soup into shallow bowls and top each serving with 1 Tbsp crème fraîche. Float a few apple slices in each bowl. Garnish with sage leaves, if using, and serve.

3

CELERY & RICE SOUP WITH PARSLEY

serves 6

Aromatic celery joins parsley and bay in this fragrant rice-based soup. Celery leaves don't deserve to be trimmed away and discarded, as they often are. Tender and herblike, the leaves are put to good use in this soup as a pretty garnish.

3 Tbsp unsalted butter

1 yellow onion, finely chopped

½ cup (3 oz/90 g) finely chopped celery

1 small bay leaf

Salt

6 cups (48 fl oz/1.5 l) chicken broth

⅓ cup (2½ oz/75 g) long-grain white rice

2 Tbsp finely chopped pale green celery leaves

2 Tbsp finely chopped flat-leaf parsley

¼ cup (2 fl oz/60 ml) extra-virgin olive oil

In a large, heavy pot, melt the butter over medium heat. Reduce the heat to medium-low and sauté the onion, celery, bay leaf, and a pinch of salt until the onion and celery are tender, about 15 minutes. Add the broth and bring to boil. Reduce the heat to low, add the rice, and simmer until the rice is tender, about 20 minutes. Season with salt.

In a bowl, stir together the celery leaves, parsley, and oil. Season with salt. Serve, garnished with the celery leaf mixture.

4

MUSHROOM, CARROT & LEEK SOUP WITH SHAVED PARMESAN

serves 4

This light, flavorful soup is a perfect first course. The broth combines rich chicken and beef broths for complexity, and carries a colorful array of finely cut vegetables, topped with a few thin shavings of Parmesan.

2 Tbsp unsalted butter

2 Tbsp canola oil

4 carrots, peeled and cut into strips 3 inches (7.5 cm) long by ¼ inch (6 mm) wide by ¼ inch (6 mm) thick

2 leeks, white part only, halved lengthwise and sliced crosswise ¼ inch (6 mm) thick

1 lb (500 g) shiitake mushrooms, stems discarded and caps cut into strips ¼ inch (6 mm) wide

¼ lb (125 g) white mushrooms, thinly sliced

3 cloves garlic, minced

3 cups (24 fl oz/750 ml) beef broth

3 cups (24 fl oz/750 ml) chicken broth

Salt and freshly ground pepper

Parmesan cheese shavings for garnish

In a large, heavy pot, melt the butter with the oil over medium-high heat. When hot, add the carrots and cook, stirring, until slightly softened, 2–3 minutes. Add the leeks and cook, stirring, until slightly softened, 3–4 minutes. Add the shiitake and white mushrooms and the garlic and cook, stirring, until the mushrooms are softened and beginning to wilt, about 5 minutes.

Add the beef and chicken broths, ½ tsp salt, and ¼ tsp pepper and simmer, uncovered, until all the vegetables are tender, about 15 minutes. Season with salt and pepper. Serve, garnished with the cheese shavings.

5

PORK & POBLANO CHILI

serves 6–8

4 Tbsp (2 fl oz/60 ml) olive oil

2 lb (1 kg) pork shoulder, cut into ½-inch (12-mm) cubes

Salt and freshly ground pepper

1 yellow onion, chopped

4 cloves garlic, minced

2 poblano chiles, seeded and diced

2 Tbsp ground cumin

2 tsp chili powder

1 can (28 oz/875 g) diced tomatoes

2 cups (16 fl oz/500 ml) chicken broth

¼ cup (⅓ oz/10 g) minced cilantro

Packed with flavor and heat, this chili will satisfy a crowd. Serve with traditional chili accompaniments and warm tortillas.

In a large, heavy pot, warm 2 Tbsp of the oil over medium-high heat. Season the pork with salt and pepper. In batches, cook the pork until it is browned on all sides, 6–8 minutes per batch. Transfer to a bowl and set aside.

Add the remaining 2 Tbsp oil, onion, garlic, and poblanos to the same pot and cook until the vegetables are soft, 5–7 minutes. Add the cumin and chili powder and cook for 1 minute. Add the tomatoes, broth, and pork and bring to a boil. Reduce the heat to low and simmer for 1 hour. Stir in the cilantro, season with salt and pepper, and serve.

6

CHESTNUT–CELERY ROOT SOUP WITH BACON & SAGE CROUTONS

serves 6–8

6 slices bacon

1 yellow onion, chopped

3 celery ribs, chopped

¼ tsp celery seed

6 cups (48 fl oz/1.5 l) chicken broth

1 celery root (about 1 lb/500 g), peeled and chopped

1 jar (15 oz/470 g) steamed peeled chestnuts, chopped

½ cup (4 fl oz/125 ml) half-and-half

Salt and freshly ground pepper

Sage Croutons (page 261)

Fresh sage just hints at bitterness, but asserts woodsy flavor. Here, with salty bacon, it accents the mellow sweetness of chestnuts and celery root. Try sage in other fall soups. Even a single leaf, browned in butter until fragrant and floated atop a serving, will add distinction.

In a large, heavy pot, cook the bacon over medium heat, turning once, until crisp, about 8 minutes. Transfer to paper towels to drain. Let cool, then crumble.

Pour off all but 2 Tbsp of the bacon fat from the pot and return to medium heat. Add the onion and celery and sauté until softened, about 7 minutes. Add the celery seed and cook, stirring often, until fragrant, about 1 minute. Add the broth, raise the heat to medium-high, and bring to a boil. Add the celery root and chestnuts and return to a boil, then reduce the heat to low, cover partially, and simmer until the celery root is tender when pierced with the tip of a knife, about 25 minutes. Remove from the heat and let cool slightly.

Working in batches, purée the soup in a blender. Transfer to a clean pot. Add the half-and-half, 1½ tsp salt, and pepper to taste and place over medium-low heat. Cook gently, stirring occasionally, until heated through, about 10 minutes. Season with salt and pepper. Serve, garnished with the bacon and croutons.

NOVEMBER

7

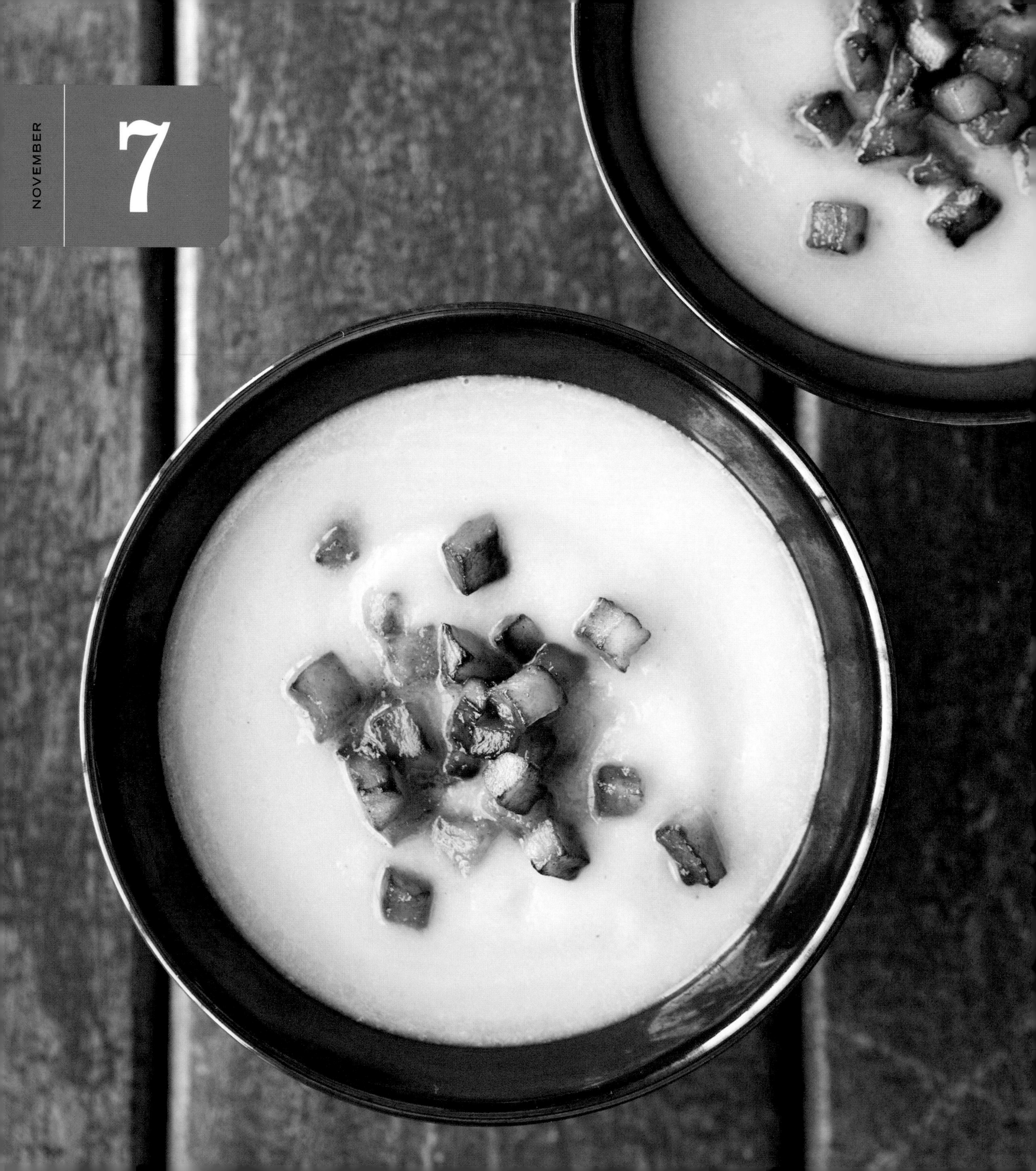

7

Celery root is just what it sounds like, the root of a variety of celery plant. It's sometimes labeled celeriac. Its subtle flavor stands out best in simple preparations like this one. This soup freezes well, without the caramelized apples.

CELERY ROOT PURÉE WITH CARAMELIZED APPLES

serves 4

2 Tbsp unsalted butter

1 leek, white and pale green parts, chopped

2 celery roots (2 lb/1 kg total), peeled and chopped

3½ cups (28 fl oz/875 ml) vegetable broth

FOR THE CARAMELIZED APPLES

1 Tbsp unsalted butter

1 small Granny Smith apple, peeled, cored, and cut into tiny cubes

¼ tsp dark brown sugar

2 Tbsp half-and-half

Salt and ground white pepper

In a large, heavy pot, warm the butter over medium-high heat. Add the leek and sauté until soft, about 4 minutes. Add the celery roots, stir to coat, and sauté for 2 minutes. Add the broth and bring to a boil. Reduce the heat to low and simmer until the celery root is very tender, 25–30 minutes. Remove from the heat and let cool slightly.

While the soup is cooling, make the caramelized apples. In a frying pan, melt the 1 Tbsp butter over medium-high heat until it foams. Add the apple and sauté for 4 minutes. Sprinkle with the brown sugar, stir to combine, and cook until the apples begin to caramelize, about 3 minutes. Remove from the heat and set aside.

Working in batches, purée the soup in a blender. Return to the pot over medium heat, add the half-and-half, and return just to a gentle boil. Turn off the heat and season with salt and pepper. Serve, garnished with the caramelized apples.

8

Gruyère, with its nutty and buttery flavor, is a good match for sweet pumpkin. Use the smallest holes on a box grater to grate the cheese to ensure easy and even melting in the soup.

PUMPKIN-GRUYÈRE SOUP

serves 4–6

2 Tbsp unsalted butter

1 shallot, minced

2 cloves garlic, minced

¼ lb (125 g) Gruyère cheese, finely grated

2 cans (15 oz/470 g each) pumpkin purée

Pinch of grated nutmeg

2 cups (16 fl oz/500 ml) chicken broth

2 Tbsp heavy cream

Salt and freshly ground pepper

In a large, heavy pot, melt the butter over medium-high heat. Add the shallot and garlic and cook until very soft, 3–4 minutes. Add half of the Gruyère and stir until the cheese begins to melt. Add the pumpkin, nutmeg, and broth, stir, and bring to a boil. Reduce the heat to low and simmer for 15 minutes. Stir in the cream. Season with salt and pepper, top with the remaining Gruyère, and serve.

9

NOVEMBER

A rich base for the broth provides depth of flavor in this soup: chipotle chiles add smokiness and heat, the adobo sauce lends a sweet-tartness, and tangy tomatillos balance with a bright, almost citrusy, flavor. The garnishes offer an inviting range of fresh colors and textures.

CHICKEN-TOMATILLO SOUP WITH CHIPOTLE CHILES

serves 6–8

8 cups (64 fl oz/2 l) chicken broth

1½ lb (750 g) skinless, boneless chicken breast halves

1 oregano sprig

10 cilantro sprigs

9 cloves garlic, crushed

1 lb (500 g) tomatillos, husked, rinsed, and chopped

1 white onion, chopped

2 large chipotle chiles in adobo, minced, plus 1 Tbsp adobo sauce

1½ Tbsp canola oil

Salt and freshly ground pepper

4 tsp fresh lime juice

1 ripe avocado

Tortilla Strips (page 191)

1½ cups (9 oz/280 g) cherry or grape tomatoes, quartered

½ lb (250 g) cotija or feta cheese, crumbled

In a large, heavy pot, combine the broth, chicken breasts, oregano and cilantro sprigs, and 3 of the garlic cloves and bring to a boil over medium-high heat. Reduce the heat to low, cover, and simmer until the chicken is opaque throughout, 15–20 minutes.

Transfer the chicken to a plate. Strain the broth through a fine-mesh sieve into a large heatproof bowl. Discard the solids in the sieve. Wipe out the pot and set aside. Once the chicken is cool enough to handle, shred the meat into bite-sized pieces and set aside.

In a food processor, combine the tomatillos, onion, chipotle chiles and adobo sauce, and the remaining 6 garlic cloves and process to a smooth purée. In the clean pot, heat the oil over high heat. Add the tomatillo mixture and fry, stirring occasionally, until the liquid evaporates, the color darkens, and the mixture is fragrant, about 15 minutes. ⤳

Add the broth and bring to a simmer. Cook, stirring occasionally, to blend the flavors, about 10 minutes. Add 1½ tsp salt, 3 tsp of the lime juice, the shredded chicken, and pepper to taste and simmer until the chicken is heated through, about 5 minutes.

Meanwhile, pit, peel, and dice the avocado and toss with the remaining 1 tsp lime juice.

Taste the soup and adjust the seasoning. Serve, garnished with the tortilla strips, avocado, tomatoes, and cheese.

10

NOVEMBER

Crushing the cooked potatoes instead of puréeing them gives this soup an interesting texture. There is no milk or cream here, but the soup is satisfying nonetheless. Fresh thyme can be substituted for the rosemary.

POTATO-ROSEMARY SOUP

serves 4–6

2 tsp olive oil

½ small shallot, minced

6 cups (48 fl oz/1.5 l) chicken broth

1 lb (500 g) Yukon gold or other all-purpose potatoes, peeled and cut into large pieces

1 tsp minced rosemary

1 bay leaf

Salt and freshly ground pepper

In a large, heavy pot, warm the oil over medium heat. Add the shallot and sauté until translucent, 1–2 minutes. Pour in the broth and bring to a boil. Add the potatoes, half of the rosemary, the bay leaf, and ¼ tsp pepper. Cover partially, reduce the heat to low, and simmer until the potatoes are tender when pierced with a fork, 15–20 minutes.

Remove the pot from the heat and discard the bay leaf. Using a fork or potato masher, crush the potatoes into small chunks. Season with salt and serve, garnished with the remaining rosemary.

11

Humble chicken thighs have their moments of glory, especially in stews and curries. Where their white-meat counterparts would overcook and tighten, thigh meat develops succulence with slow cooking, emerging spiced and flavorful.

CURRIED CAULIFLOWER & CHICKEN STEW

serves 4

1 small yellow onion, coarsely chopped

2 Tbsp peeled and chopped fresh ginger

3 cloves garlic, chopped

1 Tbsp curry powder

Salt

2 Tbsp corn or peanut oil

¾ lb (375 g) tomatoes, seeded and chopped

1 can (13½ fl oz/420 ml) coconut milk

1 lb (500 g) skinless, boneless chicken thighs, cut into large cubes

1 small head cauliflower, stemmed and cut into florets

¼ lb (125 g) green beans, trimmed and cut into 2-inch (5-cm) pieces

Steamed rice for serving

In a blender, combine 1 Tbsp water and the onion, ginger, and garlic and process until a paste forms. In a small bowl, stir together the curry powder and ½ tsp salt.

Heat a large frying pan over high heat until very hot and add the oil. Add the onion-garlic paste and sauté just until it begins to brown, about 5 minutes. Stir in the spice mixture and sauté until fragrant, about 10 seconds. Add the tomatoes and cook, stirring occasionally, until they begin to break down, about 5 minutes. Stir in the coconut milk and ½ cup (4 fl oz/125 ml) water, bring to a simmer, and stir in the chicken pieces. Cover, reduce the heat to low, and simmer until the stew thickens, about 20 minutes.

Uncover and stir in the cauliflower and green beans. Re-cover and continue to cook until the vegetables are tender, 15–20 minutes. Season to taste with salt. Serve the stew spooned over the rice.

12

This soup brings together a classic pub combination. Compared to American-style lagers, British ales have a heavier body and a more assertive taste. To match that flavor, the sharper the Cheddar, the better. Serve with beer bread or warm pretzels.

CHEDDAR CHEESE SOUP WITH ALE

serves 4–6

½ cup (4 oz/125 g) unsalted butter

1 leek, white and pale green parts, thinly sliced

1 carrot, peeled and cut into ½-inch (12-mm) dice

1 celery rib, cut into ½-inch (12-mm) dice

Salt and freshly ground black pepper

½ cup (2½ oz/75 g) all-purpose flour

½ tsp dry mustard

4 cups (32 oz/1 l) chicken broth

1 bottle (12 fl oz/375 ml) good-quality ale such as Bass or Newcastle

2 cups (8 oz/250 g) shredded sharp Cheddar cheese

¼ cup (1 oz/30 g) grated Parmesan cheese

Pinch of cayenne pepper

1 tsp Worcestershire sauce

In a large, heavy pot, melt the butter over medium heat. Add the leek, carrot, and celery and sauté until softened, about 10 minutes. Season with salt and pepper.

Stir in the flour and mustard until incorporated and cook for about 1 minute. Add the broth and ale and bring to a simmer over high heat. Reduce the heat to medium and cook, whisking to break up any lumps of flour, until the mixture is slightly thickened, about 5 minutes.

Add the cheeses and whisk constantly until completely melted, 3–5 minutes. Do not let the soup boil, or it may develop a stringy texture. Stir in the cayenne and Worcestershire sauce. Season with salt and pepper and serve.

13

MUSTARD GREENS & WILD RICE SOUP WITH GRUYÈRE
serves 4

1 cup (6 oz/185 g) wild rice

3 Tbsp unsalted butter

½ lb (250 g) white mushrooms, thinly sliced

Salt and freshly ground pepper

½ cup (4 fl oz/125 ml) dry sherry

1 Tbsp olive oil

1 yellow onion, chopped

5 cloves garlic, minced

5 cups (40 fl oz/1.25 l) chicken broth, plus more as needed

1 bunch mustard greens, coarsely chopped

¼ lb oz (125 g) Gruyère cheese, coarsely shredded

It takes only minutes to cook mustard greens, so be careful not to let the peppery leaves get soggy. Melted Gruyère on top brings the soup together. Serve with warm herbed popovers (simply add chopped fresh herbs such as chives or thyme to popover batter).

In a small saucepan, cook the wild rice according to package directions.

In a frying pan, melt 2 Tbsp of the butter over medium-high heat. Add the mushrooms and season with salt and pepper. Sauté until the mushrooms release their liquid and turn golden, about 5 minutes. Add the sherry and bring to a simmer, stirring to scrape up any browned bits on the pan bottom, and cook for 2 minutes. Remove from the heat and set aside.

In a large, heavy pot, melt the remaining 1 Tbsp butter with the oil over medium-high heat. Add the onion and garlic and sauté until translucent, about 5 minutes. Add the 5 cups broth (40 fl oz/1.25 l) and the mushrooms with all their juices, and bring to a boil. Reduce the heat to medium-low and simmer for 10 minutes. Add the wild rice and mustard greens and simmer, stirring occasionally, for 5 minutes. Season with salt and pepper and serve, topped with the shredded cheese.

14

RED CABBAGE & APPLE SOUP
serves 4

4 Golden Delicious apples, about 1 lb (500 g) total

2 Tbsp unsalted butter

1 yellow onion, minced

1 head red cabbage, about ¾ lb (375 g), cored and very thinly sliced

¼ cup (2 fl oz/60 ml) red wine vinegar

4½ cups (36 fl oz/1.1 l) beef broth

Salt and freshly ground pepper

2 tsp fresh lemon juice

⅓ cup (3 oz/80 g) sour cream (optional)

¼ cup (⅓ oz/10 g) chopped dill

This hearty and delicious soup gets an extra burst of flavor from the shredded apple added just before serving. Golden Delicious apples are sweet, but if you want a sharper-flavored, crisper variety, choose Granny Smith instead.

Leaving them unpeeled, cut 2 of the apples into quarters, core them, and then cut into 1-inch (2.5-cm) cubes. Set aside.

In a large, heavy pot, melt the butter over medium heat. When it is foaming, add the onion and sauté until translucent, 2–3 minutes. Add the apple cubes and sauté until softened slightly, 3–4 minutes. Add the cabbage and sauté, stirring often, until it glistens and the color has lightened, 5–6 minutes. Add the vinegar and bring to a simmer, stirring to scrape up any browned bits on the pan bottom. Add the broth, ½ tsp salt, and ½ tsp pepper and bring to a boil over medium-high heat. Reduce the heat to low, cover, and simmer until the cabbage and apples are tender, about 15 minutes.

While the soup is simmering, peel, halve, and core the remaining 2 apples, then shred them finely on a box grater. Place in a small bowl, add the lemon juice, and toss to coat. Set aside.

When the soup is ready, remove from the heat and stir in three-fourths of the shredded apples. Serve, topped with sour cream, if using, and sprinkled with the remaining shredded apples and the dill.

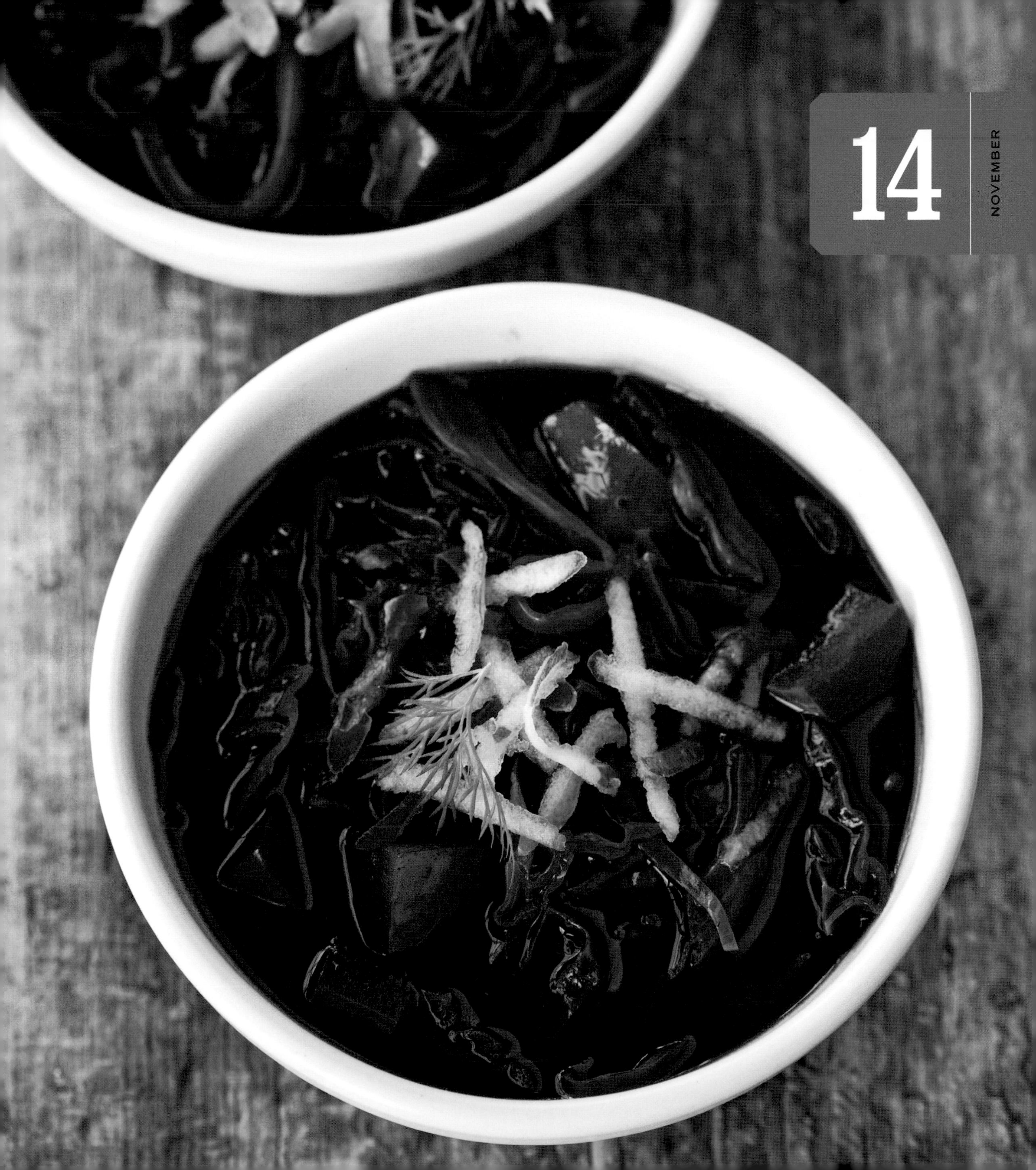

NOVEMBER 15

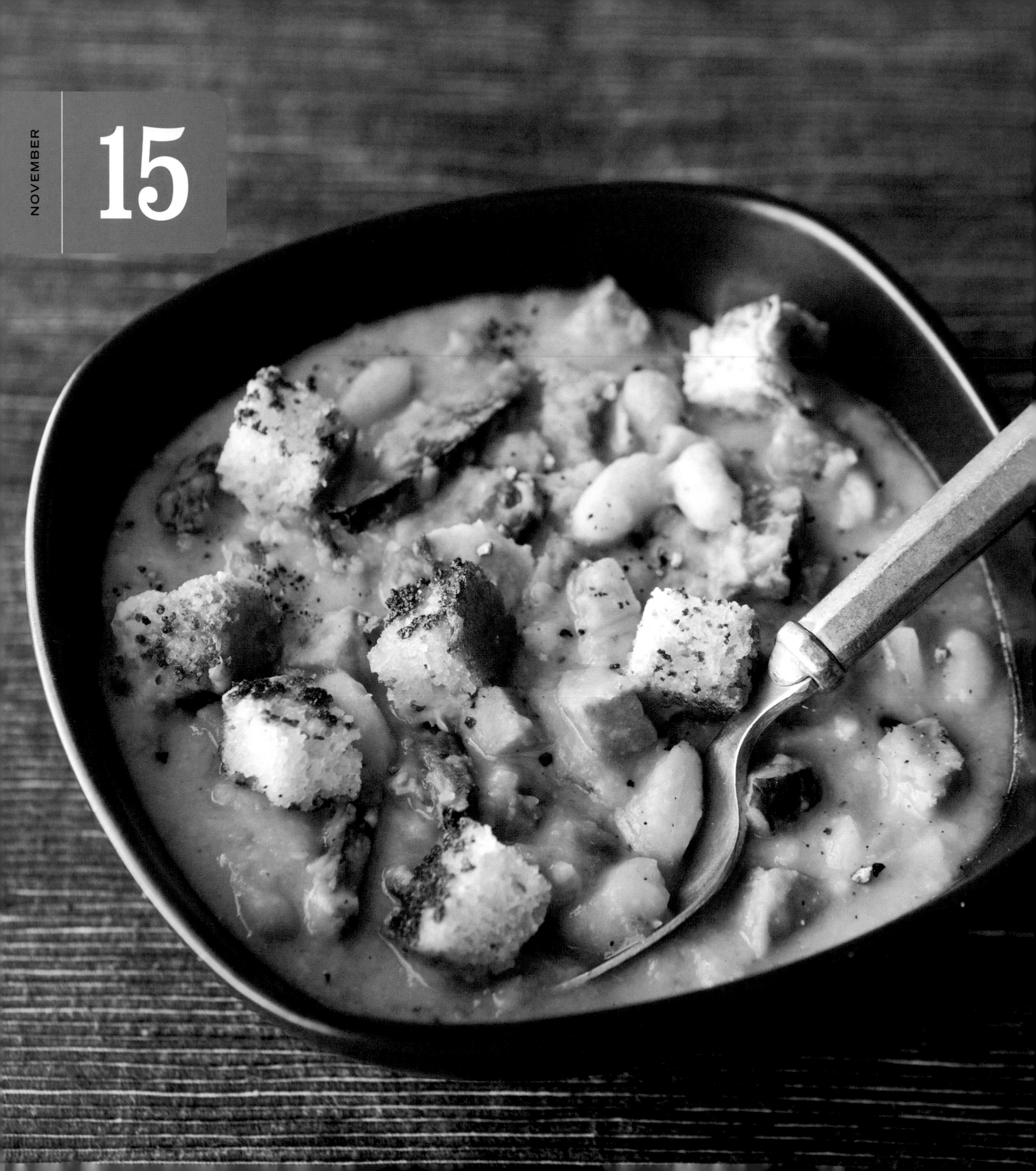

15

WHITE BEAN & HAM SOUP WITH CORN BREAD CROUTONS

serves 4–6

4 slices thick-cut bacon

½ lb (250 g) cooked ham steak, cubed

1 Tbsp olive oil

1 small yellow onion, diced

3 cloves garlic, minced

2 celery ribs, diced

2 cups (16 fl oz/500 ml) chicken broth

2 cans (15 oz/470 g each) white beans, drained

Salt and freshly ground pepper

FOR THE CORN BREAD CROUTONS

1 Tbsp unsalted butter

1 small loaf corn bread, cut into ½-inch (12-mm) cubes

To save time, purchase already-made corn bread. Make sure your pan is really hot when you add the corn bread cubes to ensure that they get a nice golden sear (but work fast so that the butter doesn't burn). Pass extra croutons at the table.

Set a large, heavy pot over medium-high heat. Add the bacon and cook until crispy, about 8 minutes. Transfer to paper towels to drain. Let cool, then crumble into bite-sized pieces. Set aside in a bowl. Add the ham to the pot and cook, stirring often, until browned, about 4 minutes. Add the ham to the bowl with the bacon.

Add the oil, onion, garlic, and celery to the pot and sauté until the vegetables are soft, about 5 minutes. Add the broth and beans and bring to a boil. Reduce the heat to low and simmer for 10 minutes. Remove from the heat and let cool slightly.

Purée half of the soup in a blender. Return to the pot along with the ham and bacon and stir to combine. Season with salt and pepper.

To make the corn bread croutons, in a frying pan, melt the butter over medium heat. Add the corn bread cubes and cook, turning once, until they are golden brown on both sides.

Serve, topped with the croutons.

16

PENNE & SQUASH SOUP WITH SAGE CROUTONS

serves 6

1 Tbsp plus 1 tsp olive oil

2 lb (1 kg) butternut squash, halved lengthwise and seeded

Salt and freshly ground pepper

6 oz (185 g) penne pasta

1 Tbsp unsalted butter

3 slices bacon, coarsely chopped

1 large yellow onion, coarsely chopped

6 cups (48 fl oz/1.5 l) chicken broth

Pinch of grated nutmeg

¾ cup (3 oz/90 g) coarsely shredded Gruyère cheese

18 flat-leaf parsley leaves

Sage Croutons (left)

To make the sage croutons, in a large bowl, toss together ½ lb (250 g) cubed crustless country-style bread, 2 Tbsp olive oil, and 1 Tbsp chopped sage. Season with salt and pepper. Bake in a preheated 350°F (190°C) oven for about 10 minutes, until crisp and golden.

Preheat the oven to 375°F (190°C). Coat a baking sheet with the 1 tsp olive oil. Place the squash on the baking sheet cut side down. Bake the squash until soft, about 1 hour. With a large spoon, scoop the squash pulp from the skin and discard the skin.

In a large pot, bring 4 qt (4 l) water to a boil over high heat. Add 2 tsp salt and the penne and cook until al dente, 10–12 minutes, or according to package directions. Drain the penne and toss it immediately with the 1 Tbsp oil.

In a large, heavy pot, melt the butter over medium heat. Add the bacon and onion and cook, uncovered, until the onion is soft, about 10 minutes. Add the squash and broth and simmer, uncovered, until the squash falls apart, about 30 minutes. Remove from the heat and let cool slightly.

Working in batches, purée the soup in a blender or food processor. Return to the pot. Add the penne, nutmeg, and salt and pepper to taste. Stir to mix well and serve, garnished with the Gruyère, parsley, and croutons.

17

KALE & SWEET POTATO SOUP WITH LAMB SAUSAGE

serves 6–8

3 sweet potatoes (about 2 lb/1 kg total), cut into 1½-inch (4-cm) chunks

2 Tbsp olive oil

Salt and freshly ground pepper

½ lb (250 g) lamb sausage, such as merguez

1 large yellow onion, finely chopped

4 cloves garlic, minced

2 tsp minced thyme

8 cups (64 fl oz/2 l) chicken broth

1 large red potato, peeled and cut into ¾-inch (2-cm) pieces

1 small bunch kale (about 1 lb/500 g), ribs removed, leaves cut crosswise into ¼-inch (6-mm) pieces

North African in origin, merguez is a lamb or beef sausage spiced with chiles or harissa. Starchy sweet potatoes and leafy kale make perfect foils for the spicy sausage.

Preheat the oven to 450°F (230°C). Line a rimmed baking sheet with foil. In a large bowl, toss together the sweet potatoes, 1½ Tbsp of the oil, and salt and pepper to taste. Spread in a single layer on the prepared baking sheet and roast until barely tender, about 20 minutes.

In a large, heavy pot, heat the remaining ½ Tbsp oil over medium heat. Add the sausage and cook, turning occasionally, until browned all over, about 8 minutes. Transfer to paper towels to drain. Add the onion to the pot and sauté until softened, about 5 minutes. Stir in the garlic and thyme and cook until fragrant, about 45 seconds. Add 3 cups (24 fl oz/750 ml) of the broth, raise the heat to high, and bring to a boil, using a wooden spoon to scrape up any browned bits from the bottom of the pot. Add the red potato, cover, and cook until tender, about 25 minutes. Meanwhile, cut the sausage into slices ½ inch (12 mm) thick.

Use a wooden spoon to mash the potatoes against the side of the pot, then stir them into the soup to thicken it. Add the sausage and remaining 5 cups (40 fl oz/1.25 l) broth and bring to a boil. Reduce the heat to low and simmer for 10 minutes to blend the flavors. Raise the heat to medium, add salt and pepper to taste, the roasted sweet potatoes, and the kale and cook, stirring often, until the kale is tender, about 8 minutes. Taste and adjust the seasoning and serve.

18

ORECCHIETTE, SAUSAGE & BROCCOLI IN BROTH

serves 6

8 cups (64 fl oz/2 l) chicken broth

½–1 tsp red pepper flakes

1 lb (500 g) spicy Italian sausage

1½ lb (750 g) broccoli, trimmed and cut into florets

Salt and freshly ground pepper

12 oz (375 g) orecchiette pasta

Serve this hearty pasta soup as a starter or main course, using orecchiette or other medium-sized pasta shapes. For a more authentic Italian touch, use broccoli rabe, a robust, pleasantly bitter cousin to broccoli.

In a large, heavy pot, bring the broth and red pepper flakes to a boil over medium heat. Reduce the heat to low and simmer for 20 minutes.

Using a fork, prick the skins of the sausages. In a frying pan, cook the sausages over medium heat until lightly browned on all sides and cooked through, 15–20 minutes. Transfer to paper towels to drain and cool. Cut the sausages into rounds and add to the broth. Add the broccoli and simmer until tender, about 15 minutes.

In a large pot, bring 5 quarts (5 l) water to a boil over high heat. Add 1 Tbsp salt and the orecchiette and cook until al dente, about 12 minutes, or according to package directions. Drain well.

Add the orecchiette to the broth and season to taste with salt and pepper. Stir to mix well and serve.

19

GOULASH

serves 4

3 Tbsp olive oil

4 leeks, white and light green parts only, finely chopped

2 tsp caraway seeds

1 red bell pepper, seeded and chopped

2 lb (1 kg) stewing beef, cut into 1-inch (2.5-cm) cubes

3 Tbsp sweet Hungarian paprika

3 cups (24 fl oz/750 ml) chicken, beef, or vegetable broth

1 can (14½ oz/455 g) diced tomatoes

3 cloves garlic, minced

1 Yukon gold potato, peeled and chopped

1 parsnip, peeled and chopped

2 carrots, peeled and chopped

Salt and freshly ground pepper

¼ cup (⅓ oz/10 g) finely chopped flat-leaf parsley

½ cup (4 oz/125 g) sour cream

The traditional beef stew of Hungary is defined by sweet Hungarian paprika. Unlike most paprikas, which add little but color, this dark red powder has a rich, aromatic flavor that captures the essence of the dried and milled peppers from which it is made.

In a large, heavy pot, warm the oil over medium-high heat. Add the leeks and caraway seeds and sauté until the leeks are softened, about 5 minutes. Add the bell pepper and sauté until softened, about 2 minutes.

Add the beef and paprika and sauté until the beef is evenly browned on all sides, 7–10 minutes.

Raise the heat to high, add the broth, and bring to a boil, stirring to scrape up any browned bits on the bottom of the pot. Reduce the heat to medium-low, cover partially, and simmer until the meat is fork-tender, 30–40 minutes.

Stir in the tomatoes and juice, garlic, potato, parsnip, carrots, and salt and pepper to taste. Cook, partially covered, until all the vegetables are tender, about 20 minutes. Stir in the parsley. Taste and adjust the seasoning. Serve, garnished with the sour cream.

20

TOMATO-FENNEL BROTH WITH CLAMS

serves 4

1 cup (6 oz/180 g) cherry tomatoes

2 Tbsp olive oil

Salt and freshly ground pepper

1 Tbsp unsalted butter

2 cloves garlic, sliced

2 small fennel bulbs, stalks and fronds removed, cored, and sliced

2 shallots, minced

½ cup (4 fl oz/125 ml) dry white wine

1 cup (8 fl oz/250 ml) chicken broth

2 lb (1 kg) clams, scrubbed

¼ cup (⅓ oz/10 g) chopped flat-leaf parsley

If you prefer a more pronounced licorice flavor, seek out anise bulbs for this soup. For a milder flavor, replace the fennel with 1 chopped yellow onion and 2 chopped celery ribs.

Preheat the oven to 500°F (260°C). Spread the cherry tomatoes on a baking sheet, toss with 1 Tbsp of the oil, and season with salt and pepper. Roast the tomatoes just until they soften and begin to split, about 7 minutes.

In a large, heavy pot, warm the butter and the remaining 1 Tbsp oil over medium-high heat. Add the garlic, fennel, and shallots and sauté until soft, about 5 minutes. Add the white wine and cook for 2 minutes. Add the broth and tomatoes and bring to a boil. Season with salt and pepper.

Add the clams to the pot, discarding any that do not close to the touch. Cover tightly and cook until the clams open, 8–10 minutes, discarding any unopened clams. Transfer the clams and broth to a serving bowl, sprinkle with the parsley, and serve family style.

21

A generous addition of cream turns this tomato bisque a warm, deep pink. With minimal hands-on cooking time, it makes a good weeknight supper. Serve with warmed crusty French or Italian bread.

TOMATO BISQUE
serves 4–6

2 Tbsp unsalted butter

⅓ cup (1½ oz/45 g) chopped shallots

2 cloves garlic, minced

2½ cups (20 fl oz/625 ml) vegetable broth

3 Tbsp long-grain white rice

Salt and ground white pepper

1 can (28 oz/875 g) crushed plum tomatoes

1 Tbsp torn basil leaves

1 cup (8 fl oz/250 ml) heavy cream

3 drops Tabasco sauce

Croutons for garnish

In a large saucepan, melt the butter over medium-low heat. Add the shallots and garlic and sauté until softened, about 3 minutes. Add the broth, rice, and ½ tsp salt and bring to a boil. Reduce the heat to low, cover, and cook until the rice is soft, 20–25 minutes.

Add the tomatoes and basil. Cover and simmer for 10 minutes. Remove from the heat and let cool slightly.

Purée in a blender until smooth, then push through a sieve with the back of a ladle and return to the saucepan over low heat. Whisk in the cream, ¼ tsp salt, ⅛ tsp pepper, and the Tabasco and reheat gently. Taste and adjust the seasoning and serve, garnished with the croutons.

22

An ancient preparation—this is the biblical "mess of pottage" for which Esau sold his birthright—red lentil soup remains common today in Egypt and Lebanon. Red lentils cook more quickly than other varieties, so are ideal for soups and puréeing.

LEMONY RED LENTIL SOUP WITH FRIED SHALLOTS
serves 4

2 Tbsp olive oil

1 yellow onion, chopped

1 tsp ground cumin

½ tsp ground coriander

Pinch of red pepper flakes

1 cup (7 oz/220 g) split red lentils, picked over and rinsed

1 carrot, peeled and finely chopped

1 tomato, peeled (page 172), seeded, and chopped

4 cups (32 fl oz/1 l) vegetable broth

Salt and freshly ground pepper

Juice of ½ lemon, plus 1 lemon cut into 4 wedges

Fried Shallots (page 28)

In a large, heavy pot, warm the oil over medium-high heat. Add the onion and sauté until soft, about 5 minutes. Add the cumin, coriander, and red pepper flakes and cook, stirring, until the spices are fragrant, about 30 seconds.

Add the lentils, carrot, tomato, and broth. Season with 1 tsp salt and a few grinds of pepper. Bring to a boil, reduce the heat to medium, cover, and simmer until the lentils fall apart and the carrots are soft, about 40 minutes. Remove from the heat and let cool slightly.

Working in batches, purée the soup in a blender. Return to the pot, add the lemon juice, and warm through over medium heat, stirring occasionally.

Serve, garnished with the fried shallots and accompanied with the lemon wedges.

23

The best part about this recipe is that it uses almost the entire pumpkin, and the seeds from the pumpkin are roasted to use for the garnish. Pack leftover toasted pumpkin seeds in your child's lunchbox for a fun treat.

PUMPKIN SOUP WITH SPICY PUMPKIN SEEDS

serves 6

1 small pumpkin (about 3 lb/1.5 kg), such as Sugar Pie, peeled, seeded, and chopped

2 Tbsp olive oil

Salt and freshly ground pepper

3 Tbsp unsalted butter

1 yellow onion, chopped

2 cloves garlic, minced

1 tsp ground cumin

½ tsp ground coriander

4 cups (32 fl oz/1 l) chicken broth

FOR THE SPICY PUMPKIN SEEDS

½ cup (2 oz/60 g) pumpkin seeds, cleaned

1 tsp canola oil

Salt

¼ tsp cayenne pepper

¼ tsp ground cumin

Pinch of ground cinnamon

Preheat the oven to 400°F (200°C) and line a baking sheet with parchment paper. Toss the pumpkin with the oil, season with salt and pepper, and spread on the prepared baking sheet. Roast the pumpkin until soft and caramelized, 30–35 minutes.

In a large, heavy pot, warm the butter over medium-high heat. Add the onion and garlic and sauté until translucent, about 5 minutes. Add the cumin and coriander and cook for 1 minute. Add the broth and pumpkin and bring to a boil. Reduce the heat to low and simmer for 25 minutes. Remove from the heat and let cool slightly.

Working in batches, purée the soup in a blender or food processor. Return to the pot and season with salt and pepper.

To make the spicy pumpkin seeds, lower the oven temperature to 350°F (180°C) and line a baking sheet with parchment paper. In a bowl, toss the seeds with the oil. In another bowl, combine 1 tsp salt, the cayenne, cumin, and cinnamon. Add the pumpkin seeds to the spice mixture and stir to coat. Spread the seeds in a single layer on the prepared baking sheet and bake, stirring once, until golden brown, 10–12 minutes. Serve the soup garnished with the pumpkin seeds.

24

Sunchokes are a very curious-looking vegetable that are usually available from the end of October through March. It takes some time to peel them, but they produce a very mellow and delicious flavor similar to that of artichokes.

CREAM OF SUNCHOKE SOUP WITH PORCINI MUSHROOMS

serves 4

4 Tbsp (2 oz/60 g) unsalted butter

2 Tbsp olive oil

2 leeks, white and pale green parts, chopped

2 lb (1 kg) sunchokes (Jerusalem artichokes), peeled and thinly sliced

3 cups (24 fl oz/750 ml) vegetable broth

2 Tbsp heavy cream

Salt and ground white pepper

2 oz (60 g) porcini mushrooms, thinly sliced

1 Tbsp finely chopped chives

In a large saucepan, melt 2 Tbsp of the butter with the oil over medium-high heat. Add the leeks and sauté until soft, about 4 minutes. Add the sunchokes and sauté for 4 minutes. Add the broth and bring to a boil. Reduce the heat to low and simmer for 25 minutes, until the sunchokes are very tender. Remove from the heat and let cool slightly.

Working in batches, purée the soup in a blender. Return to the saucepan and stir in the cream. Bring to a gentle boil. Turn off the heat and season with salt and pepper.

In a small frying pan, melt the remaining 2 Tbsp butter over medium-high heat. Add the porcini and season with salt and pepper. Sauté until soft and golden, about 4 minutes.

Serve, topped with the porcini and chives.

25

TURKEY & JASMINE RICE SOUP WITH LEMONGRASS

serves 6–8

Lemongrass is citrusy and lightly herbal in taste, with a crisp, refreshing aroma. The fragrant herb shines new light on a familiar turkey soup that also receives a flavor boost from ginger, garlic, hot chiles, and jasmine rice.

1-inch (2.5-cm) piece fresh ginger

3 serrano chiles

2 tsp canola oil

1 yellow onion, finely chopped

3 cloves garlic, minced

4 lemongrass stalks, center white part only, smashed and minced

3 carrots, peeled and thinly sliced

8 cups (64 fl oz/2 l) chicken or turkey broth

1 cup (8 fl oz/250 ml) dry white wine

¾ cup (5 oz/155 g) jasmine rice or other long-grain white rice

Leftover shredded cooked turkey meat

Salt and freshly ground pepper

Peel the ginger, cut it into 4 equal slices, and crush each piece with the flat side of a chef's knife. Seed and mince 2 of the serrano chiles; cut the remaining chile crosswise into very thin rings and set aside.

In a large, heavy pot, warm the oil over medium heat. Add the onion and sauté until softened, about 5 minutes. Stir in the garlic, minced chiles, and lemongrass and cook until fragrant, about 45 seconds. Raise the heat to high, add the ginger, carrots, broth, and wine and bring to a boil. Stir in the rice, turkey, 2 tsp salt, and pepper to taste, reduce the heat to low, and simmer until the rice is tender, about 15 minutes. Remove and discard the ginger pieces.

Season the soup with salt and pepper and serve, garnished with the reserved chile slices.

26

GARLICKY GREENS, ROAST PORK & WHITE BEAN SOUP

serves 4–6

The next time you roast a pork tenderloin for dinner, roast two and then you'll be halfway to this soup for another night. Serve with warmed crusty bread and a glass of Pinot Noir.

1 small pork tenderloin (about ¾ lb/375 g)

4 Tbsp (2 fl oz/60 ml) olive oil

7 cloves garlic, minced

Salt and freshly ground pepper

½ yellow onion, chopped

1 bunch kale, ribs removed, leaves chopped

3 cups (24 fl oz/750 ml) chicken broth

4 plum tomatoes, seeded and chopped

1 can (15 oz/470 g) cannellini or other white beans, drained

Preheat the oven to 400°F (200°C). Place the pork tenderloin on a baking sheet and drizzle with 2 Tbsp of the oil. Rub about 2 cloves worth of the minced garlic over the meat and season with salt and pepper. Roast in the oven until the pork is cooked through and a thermometer inserted into the thickest part registers 140°–150°F (60°–65°C), about 25 minutes. Transfer to a cutting board, let rest for at least 10 minutes, then cut into small cubes.

In a large, heavy pot, warm the remaining 2 Tbsp oil over medium-high heat. Add the remaining garlic and the onion and sauté until translucent, about 5 minutes. Add the kale and sauté for 4 minutes. Add the broth, tomatoes, beans, and pork and stir to combine. Simmer over low heat for 10 minutes to blend the flavors. Season with salt and pepper and serve.

27

For convenience, look for vacuum-packed steamed peeled chestnuts. The hard outer shells and bitter inner skins have already been peeled away, saving you from a labor of love. Avoid chestnuts packed in water in cans—they have poor texture and lack flavor.

CARROT SOUP WITH BACON & CHESTNUT CREAM

serves 8–10

4 slices bacon

¼ cup (2 oz/60 g) unsalted butter

1 yellow onion, chopped

1 leek, white and pale green parts, chopped

2 lb (1 kg) carrots, peeled and thinly sliced

1 russet potato, peeled and diced

6–8 cups (48–64 fl oz/1.5–2 l) chicken broth

FOR THE CHESTNUT CREAM

½ cup (2 oz/60 g) purchased steamed peeled chestnuts

¼ cup (2 fl oz/60 ml) chicken broth

⅓ cup (3 oz/90 g) crème fraîche or sour cream

Pinch of grated nutmeg

Salt and freshly ground pepper

2 Tbsp minced chives

In a large, heavy pot, fry the bacon over medium heat, turning once, until crisp, 6 minutes. Transfer to paper towels to drain. When cool, crumble the bacon and set aside.

Pour off the bacon fat from the pot, return the pan to medium heat, and add the butter. When the butter has melted, add the onion and leek and sauté until golden, about 10 minutes. Add the carrots, potato, and 6 cups (48 fl oz/1.5 l) of the broth and bring to a boil over high heat. Reduce the heat to low, cover partially, and simmer until all the vegetables are tender, about 45 minutes.

Meanwhile, make the chestnut cream. In a small saucepan, combine the chestnuts and broth over low heat. Bring to a simmer, cover, and cook until the chestnuts are tender, about 15 minutes. Remove from the heat and let cool slightly. Transfer to a blender, add the crème fraîche and nutmeg, and purée. Transfer to a small bowl and set aside.

Remove the vegetables from the heat and let cool slightly. Working in batches, purée in a blender. Return to the pot. If the soup is too thick, add broth as needed to thin to the desired consistency. Season with salt and pepper. Reheat the soup to serving temperature over low heat. Serve, topped with a swirl of the chestnut cream and the chives and bacon.

28

Lining a baking sheet with parchment paper will ensure that roasted vegetables keep their flavorful caramelized outer layer and that they don't end up stuck to the sheet. Plus, it makes cleanup a whole lot easier!

SPICED BROTH WITH ROASTED ACORN SQUASH & KALE

serves 4–6

1 acorn squash, peeled, seeded, and cubed

3 Tbsp olive oil

Salt and freshly ground pepper

¼ lb (125 g) thick-cut bacon, cut into ½-inch (12-mm) pieces

1 white onion, finely diced

2 cloves garlic, minced

1 tsp allspice

½ tsp grated nutmeg

¼ tsp ground cinnamon

1 bunch kale, ribs removed, and leaves cut crosswise into ½-inch (12-mm) strips

6 cups (48 fl oz/1.5 l) chicken broth

Preheat the oven to 400°F (200°C) and line a baking sheet with parchment paper. Toss the squash with 2 Tbsp of the oil, season with salt and pepper, and spread on the prepared baking sheet. Roast the squash until tender but not mushy, about 20 minutes.

In a large, heavy pot, cook the bacon over medium-high heat until crispy, about 10 minutes. Transfer the bacon to paper towels to drain. Add the remaining 1 Tbsp oil to the bacon fat in the pot. Add the onion, garlic, allspice, nutmeg, and cinnamon and cook, stirring frequently, until the onion is soft, 5–7 minutes. Add the kale and squash, stir to coat, and cook for 3 minutes. Add the broth, bring to a simmer, and cook for 10 minutes to blend the flavors. Stir in the bacon, season with salt and pepper, and serve.

29

Shells are the secret behind many a great seafood soup. For this bisque, you cook the shrimp, peel them, and then sauté the shells alone before returning them to the simmering stock. This concentrates the rich flavors.

SHRIMP BISQUE

serves 8

5 thyme sprigs

5 flat-leaf parsley sprigs

1 small yellow onion, quartered

1 small carrot, peeled and quartered

8 peppercorns

2 bay leaves

1½ lb (750 g) shrimp in the shell, preferably with the heads on

⅓ cup (3 fl oz/80 ml) olive oil

1 bottle (24 fl oz/750 ml) dry white wine

Salt and freshly ground pepper

4 cups (32 fl oz/1 l) heavy cream

In a large, heavy pot, combine 6 cups (48 fl oz/1.5 l) water, the thyme, parsley, onion, carrot, peppercorns, and bay leaves. Bring to a boil over medium-high heat. Add the shrimp and cook just until opaque, 1–2 minutes. Using a slotted spoon, transfer the shrimp to a colander and rinse under cold running water. Reduce the heat to low so the broth simmers.

Cover and refrigerate 8 shrimp in the shell. Peel the remaining shrimp, reserving the heads and shells. Chop the shrimp, cover, and refrigerate.

In a frying pan, warm the oil over medium-high heat. When hot, add the shrimp heads and shells and sauté until fragrant and beginning to brown, 5–8 minutes. Reduce the heat to medium and sauté for 15 minutes. Add the shells to the broth and cook until reduced to 2 cups (16 fl oz/500 ml), about 45 minutes. Using the slotted spoon, remove the herbs, vegetables, and shells and heads and discard. Add the wine, raise the heat to high, and bring to a boil. Reduce the heat to low and simmer, uncovered, until reduced to 3 cups (24 fl oz/750 ml), 30–40 minutes. Season with 1 tsp salt.

Add the cream, raise the heat to medium-high, and heat, stirring, until small bubbles form along the edge of the pan. Reduce the heat to medium and simmer, stirring frequently, until reduced to about 4 cups (32 fl oz/1 l) and the soup is thick and ⇢

creamy, about 20 minutes. Taste and adjust the seasoning with salt. Strain the soup through a fine-mesh sieve. Pour into a clean pot and heat over medium heat, stirring, until small bubbles form along the edge of the pan. Remove from the heat and cover.

To serve, divide the chopped shrimp among bowls. Ladle the soup on top, float a reserved unpeeled shrimp in the center of each bowl, sprinkle with pepper, and serve.

30

A noodle soup is the perfect way to finish off the last bits of meat from a turkey roast. If you just can't take one more day of the bird, stick this in your freezer and save it for another time.

TURKEY-NOODLE SOUP WITH SPINACH

serves 8–10

2 Tbsp olive oil

1 yellow onion, chopped

3 cloves garlic, minced

3 carrots, peeled and finely diced

4 celery ribs, finely diced

1½ Tbsp minced thyme

8 cups (64 fl oz/2 l) chicken broth

½ lb (250 g) wide egg noodles

2½ cups (15 oz/470 g) shredded cooked turkey meat

2 cups (2 oz/60 g) packed spinach leaves

Salt and freshly ground pepper

In a large, heavy pot, warm the oil over medium-high heat. Add the onion, garlic, carrots, celery, and thyme and sauté until the carrots begin to soften, about 8 minutes. Add the broth and bring to a boil. Add the egg noodles and cook until al dente, about 5 minutes. Add the turkey and spinach and stir to combine. Simmer the soup for 5 minutes to blend the flavors. Season to taste with salt and pepper and serve.

1
TOMATO SOUP WITH SMOKED PAPRIKA & BACON
page 274

2
CREAM OF ONION SOUP
page 274

3
SPLIT PEA SOUP
page 276

4
CHESTNUT SOUP
page 276

8
ROASTED SHALLOT & CRAB BISQUE
page 279

9
WEEKNIGHT HUNGARIAN BEEF STEW
page 280

10
TURKEY STEW WITH FIGS & MADEIRA
page 280

11
SWEET POTATO SOUP WITH CHEDDAR & CAVIAR CROUTONS
page 281

15
SHORT RIB STEW WITH PAPRIKA SOUR CREAM
page 285

16
RUTABAGA & CARROT SOUP
page 285

17
CLASSIC BEEF & RED WINE STEW
page 286

18
TURKEY MULLIGATAWNY
page 286

22
CRAB RANGOONS IN CHILE-LIME BROTH
page 288

23
BROCCOLI SOUP WITH PARMESAN-LEMON FRICO
page 291

24
ROOT VEGETABLE CHILI WITH ORANGE & CILANTRO
page 291

25
LOBSTER BISQUE
page 292

29
ESCAROLE & WHITE BEAN SOUP WITH ROSEMARY
page 293

30
RICE SOUP WITH PORK DUMPLINGS
page 294

31
CHILLED BEET & CUCUMBER SOUP
page 294

5
JERUSALEM ARTICHOKE SOUP WITH HAZELNUT-ORANGE BUTTER
page 277

6
POTATO–CELERY ROOT SOUP
page 277

7
ORZO, DELICATA SQUASH & CHICKEN SOUP WITH SAGE
page 279

12
ITALIAN-STYLE CLAM SOUP WITH PASTA
page 281

13
CHICKEN & HOMINY SOUP WITH ANCHO CHILES
page 282

14
OYSTER STEW WITH ROSEMARY
page 282

19
SHIITAKE BROTH WITH BUTTER-POACHED LOBSTER & CHIVES
page 287

20
NORTH AFRICAN CHICKPEA SOUP
page 287

21
WEDDING SOUP
page 288

26
LINGUIÇA & POTATO STEW WITH TWO PAPRIKAS
page 292

27
GINGER CHICKEN SOUP
page 293

28
CURRIED CREAM OF CELERY SOUP
page 293

With the winter holidays in full swing, soups become festive party fare that can often be made ahead. Luxurious ingredients such as oysters and lobster star in creamy, special-occasion bisques. Dress up bowls to suit the season with citrusy butters, fried herbs, or decadent caviar. Between parties, nourish and rebuild yourself with lean vegetable chilis, protein-packed chickpea stews, and clean-tasting broths.

december

1

TOMATO SOUP WITH SMOKED PAPRIKA & BACON

serves 4–6

4 slices thick-cut bacon

1 Tbsp unsalted butter

1 yellow onion, chopped

2 cloves garlic, minced

2 cans (28 oz/875 g each) crushed tomatoes

3 Tbsp heavy cream

1¼ tsp smoked paprika

Salt and freshly ground pepper

Classic tomato soup gets a punch with smoked paprika and crumbled bacon. Serve with savory panini, such as provolone and arugula or Cheddar and sage.

In a large, heavy saucepan, fry the bacon over medium heat, turning once, until crispy, 8–10 minutes. Transfer to paper towels. Let cool, then crumble.

Add the butter to the pan and melt over medium heat. Add the onion and garlic and sauté until very soft, about 5 minutes. Add the tomatoes and bring to a boil. Reduce the heat to low and simmer for 20 minutes. Remove from the heat and let cool slightly.

Working in batches, purée the soup in a blender. Return to the saucepan and add the cream, paprika, and ½ tsp salt. Return just to a boil, turn off the heat, taste, and adjust the seasoning.

Serve, topped with the crumbled bacon and a generous grinding of pepper.

2

CREAM OF ONION SOUP

serves 4

5 Tbsp (2½ oz/75 g) unsalted butter

1½ lb (750 g) sweet onions, such as Vidalia or Walla Walla, thinly sliced

2 cups (16 fl oz/500 ml) milk, plus more if needed

2 cups (16 fl oz/500 ml) chicken or vegetable broth

3 Tbsp all-purpose flour

Salt and freshly ground pepper

½ cup (4 fl oz/125 ml) heavy cream

½ cup (4 fl oz/125 ml) dry sherry

Onions, the aromatic base of so many silky cream soups, are allowed to shine on their own in this preparation. Favorite varieties such as Walla Walla, Maui, or Vidalia (named after the places they are grown) deliver a natural sweetness. This soup complements a savory roast.

In a large frying pan, melt 2 Tbsp of the butter over medium heat. Add the onions, reduce the heat to low, cover, and sauté until softened, about 5 minutes. Uncover and continue sautéing until golden, 10–12 minutes. Let cool slightly, then finely chop the onions in a food processor.

Pour the 2 cups (16 fl oz/500 ml) milk and the broth into separate small saucepans and place over low heat. Heat both just until small bubbles form around the edge of the pan, then remove from the heat.

In a large, heavy pot, melt the remaining 3 Tbsp butter over medium-low heat. When the foam begins to subside, sprinkle in the flour and whisk until smooth, about 2 minutes. Gradually add the hot milk while whisking and cook, stirring often, until the mixture bubbles vigorously and has thickened, about 3 minutes. Gradually add the hot broth, whisking, and bring to a low boil. Cook until pale beige and opaque, about 3 minutes. Let cool slightly.

Add the chopped onions to the pot and season with salt and pepper. Reduce the heat to a bare simmer, cover, and cook for 10 minutes, stirring occasionally. Remove from the heat and let cool slightly.

Working in batches, purée the soup in a blender or food processor. Return to the pot and stir in the cream. Place over low heat and reheat gently, stirring constantly. If the soup seems too thick, thin it with a little milk to the desired consistency. Taste and adjust the seasoning. Stir in the sherry, heat through, and serve.

3

SPLIT PEA SOUP

serves 4

1 Tbsp olive oil

1 yellow onion, finely diced

1 celery rib, thinly sliced

2 small carrots, peeled and thinly sliced

1 cup (7 oz/220 g) dried green or yellow split peas, picked over and rinsed

4 cups (32 fl oz/1 l) chicken or vegetable broth

6 slices bacon

2 Tbsp finely chopped flat-leaf parsley

½ tsp finely chopped marjoram

½ tsp finely chopped thyme

Salt and freshly ground pepper

You can substitute the fresh marjoram and thyme with dried in this recipe; just use half as much. Always use fresh parsley in recipes; it is easy to find and tastes infinitely better than dried parsley.

In a large, heavy pot, warm the oil over medium heat. Add the onion and sauté until softened, 3–5 minutes. Add the celery and carrots and sauté just until slightly softened, 3 minutes.

Add the split peas, broth, 2 slices of the bacon, parsley, marjoram, and thyme. Reduce the heat to medium-low and bring to a simmer. Cover partially and cook until the peas are tender, 50–60 minutes. Remove from the heat, discard the bacon, and let cool slightly.

Meanwhile, in a frying pan, fry the remaining 4 slices bacon over medium heat, turning once, until crisp, 8–10 minutes. Transfer to paper towels to drain. Let cool, then crumble.

Coarsely purée 2 cups (16 fl oz/500 ml) of the soup in a food processor and return to the pot. Season with salt and pepper to taste, return the soup to medium heat, and simmer for 5 minutes. Taste and adjust the seasoning.

Serve, garnished with the crumbled bacon.

4

CHESTNUT SOUP

serves 4–6

3 Tbsp unsalted butter

1 yellow onion, diced

1 celery rib, diced

3½ cups (28 fl oz/875 ml) chicken broth

2 cups (16 oz/500 g) purchased steamed peeled chestnuts

Salt and freshly ground pepper

1 cup (8 fl oz/250 ml) half-and-half

2 Tbsp brandy

Fried Shallots (page 28)

When making this soup, look for vacuum-packed steamed peeled chestnuts, which will save you the trouble of peeling. Choose a food processor in this instance, rather than a blender, as it will most smoothly purée the nuts.

In a large saucepan, melt the butter over medium heat. Add the onion and celery and sauté until softened, about 10 minutes. Add the broth, chestnuts, ½ tsp salt, and ¼ tsp pepper. Bring to a boil, reduce the heat to low, cover, and simmer until the chestnuts break up easily when pressed against the side of the pan, about 30 minutes.

Working in batches, purée the soup in a food processor. Pour through a medium-mesh sieve, pushing on the solids with the back of a spoon to extract as much liquid as possible. Discard the solids.

Return the soup to the saucepan and stir in the half-and-half and brandy. Simmer until heated through. Taste and adjust the seasoning and serve, garnished with the fried shallots.

5

JERUSALEM ARTICHOKE SOUP WITH HAZELNUT-ORANGE BUTTER

serves 6

To make the hazelnut-orange butter, finely chop ¼ cup (1¼ oz/37 g) toasted and skinned hazelnuts. Mix with 2 Tbsp softened butter and 1 tsp orange zest and season to taste with salt and pepper. Roll into 6 teaspoon-sized balls and refrigerate until ready to serve.

3 Tbsp unsalted butter

3 celery ribs with leaves, diced

3 large yellow onions, diced

2½ tsp ground coriander

3 lb (1.5 kg) Jerusalem artichokes, unpeeled, cut into 1-inch (2.5-cm) pieces

2 large strips orange zest

9 cups (2¼ qt/2.25 l) chicken broth

3 Tbsp fresh orange juice

Salt and freshly ground pepper

Hazelnut-Orange Butter (left)

In a large, heavy pot, melt the butter over medium heat. Add the celery and onions and sauté until the vegetables are soft, about 10 minutes. Add the coriander and sauté for about 1 minute. Add the Jerusalem artichokes, orange zest, and broth and bring to a boil over high heat. Reduce the heat to medium-low and simmer, uncovered, until the Jerusalem artichokes are soft, about 30 minutes.

Remove the Jerusalem artichokes from the broth and let cool slightly. Remove the orange zest and discard. Working in batches, purée the soup in a blender. Strain the purée through a fine-mesh sieve into a clean saucepan. Add the orange juice and mix well. Season with salt and pepper.

Reheat the soup to serving temperature over medium heat. Serve, placing a piece of the flavored butter in the center of each helping.

6

POTATO–CELERY ROOT SOUP

serves 4–6

Nutty celery root enlivens familiar potatoes for this comforting and satisfying cold-weather soup. Because celery root quickly turns brown after cutting, immerse it in water mixed with lemon juice to keep the purée a lovely ivory color.

1½ lb (750 g) celery root

Juice of ½ lemon

3 Tbsp unsalted butter

6 cups (18 oz/560 g) thinly sliced leeks, white and pale green parts

1 large yellow onion, sliced

4 cups (32 fl oz/1 l) chicken broth, plus more as needed

Salt

1 lb (500 g) russet potatoes, peeled and diced

1 tsp dried tarragon

Chopped chives for garnish

Trim and peel the celery root and cut into ¼-inch (6-mm) cubes. Put the cubes into a bowl filled with water and the lemon juice.

In a large, heavy pot, melt the butter over medium-low heat. Add the leeks and onion and sauté until tender, about 15 minutes. Drain the celery root. Add the celery root, broth, and 1 tsp salt to the pot and bring to a boil. Reduce the heat to low, cover, and simmer for 10 minutes. Add the potatoes, cover, and simmer until the potatoes and celery root are tender, about 15 minutes. Remove from the heat and let cool slightly.

Purée 3 cups (24 fl oz/750 ml) of the soup in a blender. Return to the pot and add the tarragon. Reheat gently, then adjust the consistency with up to 1 cup (8 fl oz/250 ml) more broth. Taste and adjust the seasoning. Serve, garnished with the chives.

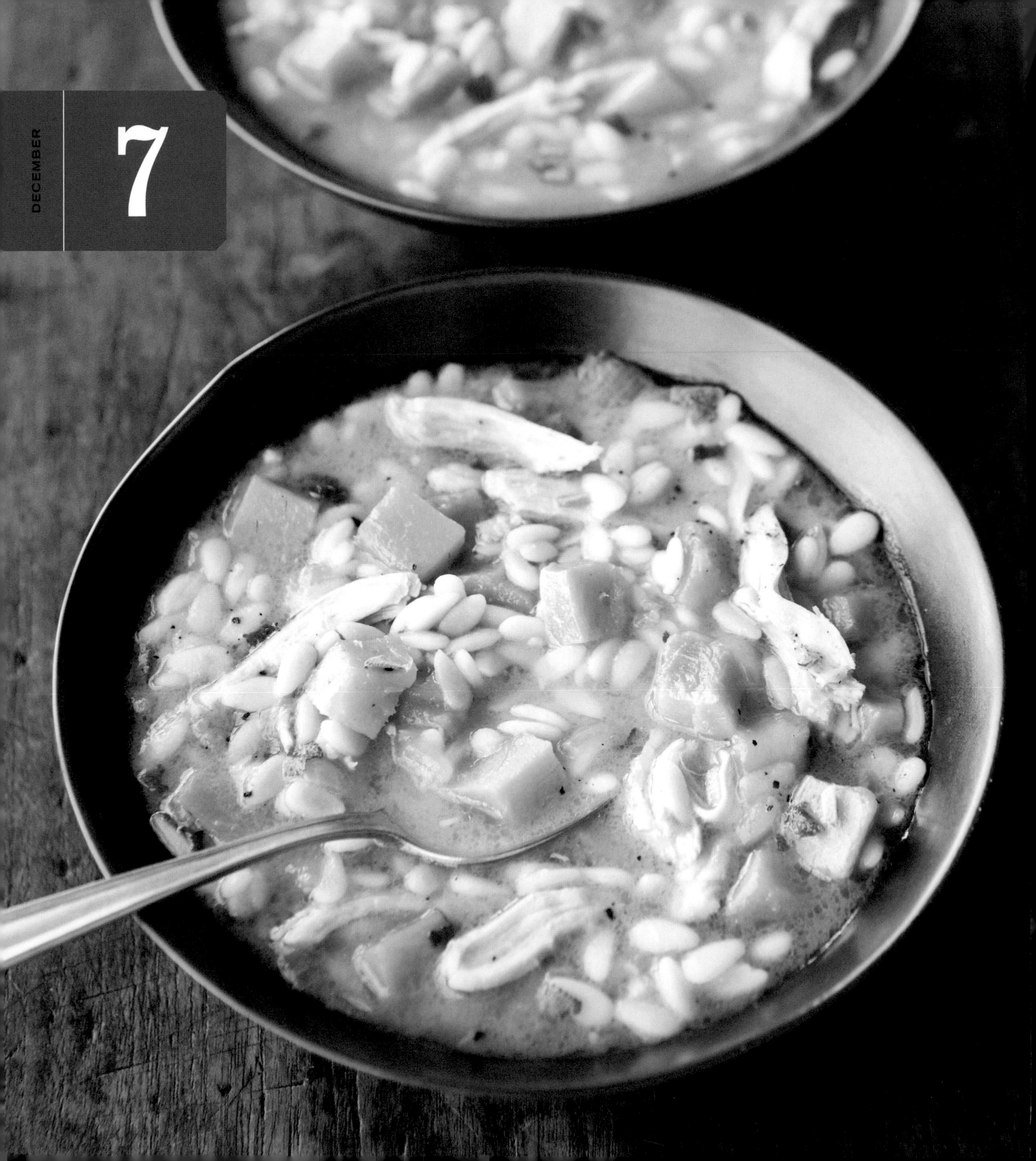

7

You can save time making this colorful and plentiful soup by using leftover rotisserie or roasted chicken. You can also substitute a different type of squash, or sweet potatoes. Make it meatless by omitting the chicken, substituting vegetable broth, and serving with shaved Parmesan.

ORZO, DELICATA SQUASH & CHICKEN SOUP WITH SAGE

serves 4–6

4 delicata squash (2¾ lb/4 kg total), peeled, seeded, and cubed

3 Tbsp olive oil

Salt and freshly ground pepper

2 small skinless, boneless chicken breast halves (about ¾ lb/375 g total)

1 cup (7 oz/220 g) orzo

3 Tbsp unsalted butter

1 small yellow onion, chopped

3 cloves garlic, minced

5 sage leaves, torn into pieces

4 cups (32 fl oz/1 l) chicken broth

Preheat the oven to 400°F (200°C) and line a baking sheet with parchment paper. Toss the squash with 2 Tbsp of the oil, season with salt and pepper, and spread on the prepared baking sheet. Place the chicken on another baking sheet, brush with the remaining 1 Tbsp oil, and season with salt and pepper. Place the squash on the top rack in the oven and the chicken on the lower rack. Roast until the chicken is cooked through and a thermometer inserted into the thickest part reaches 160°F (71°C), about 20 minutes. Remove the chicken from the oven and continue to roast the squash until it is tender and caramelized, about 10 minutes longer. When the chicken is cool enough to handle, shred it into bite-sized pieces.

Put 6 cups (48 fl oz/1.5 l) water in a saucepan over medium-high heat and bring to a boil. Add ½ tsp salt and the orzo and cook for 7 minutes. Drain the pasta and set aside.

In a large, heavy pot over medium-high heat, melt the butter. Add the onion, garlic, and sage and sauté until soft, about 5 minutes. Add the broth and bring to a boil. Add the orzo, shredded chicken, and squash and reduce the heat to low. Simmer for 15 minutes, then season to taste with salt and pepper and serve.

8

Mild-flavored shallots, sweetened with roasting, and shredded king crab meat star in this special seafood bisque worth adding to your holiday repertoire. Dry sherry, the iconic wine of Spain, provides an elegant underpinning for the briny-sweet flavors.

ROASTED SHALLOT & CRAB BISQUE

serves 6–8

1 lb (500 g) shallots, peeled

2 Tbsp olive oil

¾ cup (4 oz/125 g) canned diced tomatoes

Pinch of cayenne pepper

⅓ cup (2½ oz/75 g) white rice

4 cups (32 fl oz/1 l) crab, shellfish, or fish broth

½ cup (4 fl oz/125 ml) dry white wine

Shredded crabmeat from 1 lb (500 g) cooked king crab legs

⅓ cup (3 fl oz/80 ml) dry sherry

1 cup (8 fl oz/250 ml) half-and-half

1 Tbsp fresh lemon juice

Salt and ground white pepper

¼ cup (½ oz/15 g) minced chives

Preheat the oven to 400°F (200°C). In a bowl, toss the shallots with 1 Tbsp of the oil. Spread in a single layer on a rimmed baking sheet and roast in the oven for 20 minutes. Stir the shallots and continue roasting until browned and tender, about 20 minutes more.

In a large saucepan, warm the remaining 1 Tbsp oil over medium heat. Add two-thirds of the roasted shallots, the tomatoes with their juices, cayenne, and rice and stir to mix well. Add the crab broth and wine, raise the heat to high, and bring to a boil. Reduce the heat to low, cover, and simmer until the rice is completely tender, about 30 minutes. Remove from the heat and let cool slightly. Meanwhile, finely chop the remaining roasted shallots and set aside.

Working in batches, purée the soup in a blender. Pour into a clean pot. Add the chopped roasted shallots, crabmeat, sherry, half-and-half, lemon juice, 2¼ tsp salt, and pepper to taste. Place over medium-low heat and cook gently, stirring occasionally, until heated through, about 10 minutes. Taste and adjust the seasoning and serve, garnished with the chives.

9

WEEKNIGHT HUNGARIAN BEEF STEW

serves 4–6

2 Tbsp olive oil

2 lb (1 kg) boneless beef chuck, trimmed and cut into 1½-inch (4-cm) pieces

2 large yellow onions, chopped

Salt and freshly ground pepper

3 large cloves garlic, minced

1½ Tbsp sweet smoked paprika

2 Tbsp tomato paste

4 cups (32 fl oz/1 l) beef broth

1 lb (500 g) boiling potatoes, quartered

1 red bell pepper, seeded and cut into ½-inch (12-mm) strips

2 carrots, peeled and cut into 1-inch (2.5-cm) chunks

Hungary's iconic paprika dish gets a weeknight remix, proof that stew can be a hassle-free dinner option. A mere twenty minutes of active work plus some simmering time, and you have a tempting, saucy beef preparation to dish up for family or friends. Buttered egg noodles are a must.

In a large, heavy pot, warm the oil over high heat. Add the beef and onions, season with salt and pepper, and cook, stirring frequently, until the beef is browned and the onions begin to caramelize, about 10 minutes. Stir in the garlic, paprika, and tomato paste. Add the broth, bring to a boil, reduce the heat to low, cover, and braise until the meat is nearly fork-tender, about 1 hour.

Add the potatoes, bell pepper, and carrots and continue to braise, covered, until the vegetables are tender, 25–30 minutes. Taste and adjust the seasoning. Serve.

10

TURKEY STEW WITH FIGS & MADEIRA

serves 8

2 Tbsp canola oil

1 whole bone-in turkey breast, 3½–4 lb (1.5–2 kg)

¼ cup (2 oz/60 g) unsalted butter

2 large yellow onions, cut in half lengthwise and then crosswise into slices ½ inch (12 mm) thick

4 large carrots, peeled and cut into slices ½ inch (12 mm) thick

1 sweet potato, peeled and cut into ½-inch (12-mm) dice

1½ cups (8 oz/250 g) dried Calimyrna figs, stemmed and cut in half

3 cups (24 fl oz/750 ml) chicken broth

1 cup (8 fl oz/250 ml) Madeira wine

Salt and freshly ground pepper

A boned, rolled turkey breast used in place of the bone-in breast simplifies the preparation. Serve with a soft bread, like challah, and a baby spinach salad dressed with mustard vinaigrette.

In a large, heavy pot, warm the oil over medium-high heat. Add the turkey breast and brown on both sides, turning once, about 8 minutes.

Turn the turkey breastbone up and add the butter. When the butter melts, add the onions, carrots, sweet potato, and figs, stir to coat evenly with the butter, and cook until the vegetables begin to soften, about 8 minutes. Add the chicken broth and Madeira and bring to a simmer. Reduce the heat to medium-low, cover, and simmer gently for 2 hours.

Turn the turkey breast over, remove the bones, and continue to simmer gently, uncovered, until the turkey is tender and cooked through and the vegetables are soft, about 30 minutes.

Transfer the turkey breast to a cutting board and cut it across the grain into slices ½ inch (12 mm) thick. Cut the slices into bite-sized pieces, return to the pot, and stir to mix in with the vegetables. Heat to serving temperature, season with salt and pepper, and serve.

11

This silky sweet potato purée boasts unusual flavors and a striking presentation when topped with slices of baguette and bubbling oven-browned cheese. A final dollop of inky black caviar elevates it to the realm of swanky starters, fit for a special occasion.

SWEET POTATO SOUP WITH CHEDDAR & CAVIAR CROUTONS

serves 8

8 baguette slices, ¼ inch (6 mm) thick

2 Tbsp olive oil

2 large sweet potatoes
(1½–2 lb/750 g–1 kg total)

4 cups (32 fl oz/1 l) chicken broth,
plus 2–4 cups (16 –32 fl oz/250 ml–1 l)
more as needed

Salt and ground white pepper

¼ lb (125 g) white Cheddar cheese, shredded

2 oz (60 g) black caviar

Preheat the oven to 350°F (180°C).

Arrange the baguette slices in a single layer on a baking sheet and brush with 1½ Tbsp of the oil. Toast in the oven until lightly golden, about 15 minutes. Turn and toast until lightly golden on the second side, about 8 minutes. Set aside.

Rub the sweet potatoes with the remaining ½ Tbsp olive oil and place on a baking sheet. Bake until the skin is wrinkled and the flesh is easily pierced with a fork, 1–1½ hours. Remove from the oven. When the potatoes are cool enough to handle, cut in half lengthwise and scoop the flesh into a large, heavy pot. Add 4 cups of the broth and whisk until smooth, adding more broth as needed to achieve a creamy but soupy consistency. Place over medium-high heat and bring to just below a boil, stirring often. Add ½ tsp pepper and salt to taste. Reduce the heat to low and simmer while you finish making the croutons.

Preheat the broiler. Sprinkle the toasted baguette slices with the cheese and arrange on a baking sheet. Broil just until the cheese melts, about 3 minutes.

To serve, ladle the soup into bowls. Spoon a dollop of caviar on top of each crouton and float a crouton in each bowl of soup.

12

A light seafood supper can be a welcome break from richer holiday fare at this time of year. Serve with slices of toasted bread rubbed with cut garlic cloves and spread with aioli.

ITALIAN-STYLE CLAM SOUP WITH PASTA

serves 6

Salt and freshly ground black pepper

¼ lb (125 g) small pasta shells

1 Tbsp extra-virgin olive oil

3 cups (24 fl oz/750 ml) fish broth

1 cup (8 fl oz/250 ml) dry white wine

2 cups (12 oz/375 g) canned diced tomatoes

4 cloves garlic, minced

6 flat-leaf parsley sprigs, tied together, plus
3 Tbsp finely chopped flat-leaf parsley

½ tsp chopped thyme

2 bay leaves

Cayenne pepper

4 lb (2 kg) clams, scrubbed

In a large pot, bring 3 quarts (3 l) water to a boil over high heat. Add 2 tsp salt and the pasta and cook until al dente, 12–15 minutes or according to package directions. Drain the pasta and toss it immediately with the olive oil. Set aside.

In a large pot, combine the broth, wine, 2 cups (16 fl oz/500 ml) water, the tomatoes with their juices, garlic, parsley sprigs, thyme, bay leaves, and cayenne to taste and bring to a boil over high heat. Reduce the heat to medium-low and simmer, covered, for 15 minutes. Remove and discard the parsley and bay leaves.

Add the clams to the pot, discarding any that do not close to the touch, and simmer, covered, shaking the pot occasionally, until the clams open, 3–5 minutes. Using a slotted spoon, remove the clams, discarding any unopened ones, and let them cool slightly. Remove the clams from the shells and discard the shells.

Return the clams to the pot. Add the pasta and chopped parsley and season with salt and pepper. Simmer until the pasta is heated through, about 1 minute, and serve.

13

*Ancho chiles have
very little heat, but
they are rich with
flavor—raisin,
leather, tobacco,
and even cocoa
characterize their
amazing complexity.
Anchos give this
hearty posole-
inspired soup
lusciousness and
depth. Mild-tasting
hominy balances the
robust flavors, and
cilantro and lime
are sprightly
finishing touches.*

CHICKEN & HOMINY SOUP WITH ANCHO CHILES

serves 6–8

4 large ancho chiles, stemmed and seeded, flesh torn into pieces

1⅔ cups (13 fl oz/395 ml) boiling water

3 lb (1.5 kg) bone-in, skin-on chicken thighs

Salt and freshly ground pepper

2 tsp canola oil, or as needed

2 yellow onions, finely chopped

4 cloves garlic, minced

1 Tbsp ground cumin

1 Tbsp minced oregano

6 cups (48 fl oz/1.5 l) chicken broth

1 can (14½ oz/455 g) diced tomatoes

2 cans (29 oz/910 g each) hominy, drained

¼ cup (¼ oz/7 g) cilantro leaves

1 lime, cut into wedges

In a heatproof bowl, soak the chiles in the boiling water until softened, about 25 minutes. Transfer the chiles and their soaking liquid to a blender and purée. Strain though a fine-mesh sieve, pressing on the solids to extract as much liquid as possible. Discard the solids. Set the purée aside.

Season the chicken generously with salt and pepper. In a large, heavy pot, warm the oil over medium-high heat. In batches, place the chicken, skin side down, in the pot and cook until golden brown, about 5 minutes. Turn and cook until golden brown on the second side, about 5 minutes. Transfer to a large plate. Repeat to brown the remaining chicken, adding more oil to the pot if needed. When the chicken is cool enough to handle, remove the skin.

Pour off all but 1 Tbsp of fat from the pot and place over medium heat. Add about three-fourths of the chopped onions and sauté until softened, about 5 minutes. Stir in the garlic, cumin, and oregano and cook until fragrant, about 1 minute. Raise the heat to high, add the broth, bring to a simmer, and stir to scrape up any browned bits on the bottom of the pot. Add the chicken and any accumulated juices, the tomatoes with ⟫

their juices, and 1½ tsp salt and bring to a boil. Reduce the heat to low, cover partially, and simmer until the chicken is tender, about 40 minutes.

Transfer the chicken to a bowl. When cool enough to handle, shred the meat and discard the bones. Stir the shredded chicken, hominy, and chile purée into the pot. Simmer for about 15 minutes to blend the flavors. Season with salt and pepper, then stir in the cilantro. Serve, garnished with the remaining chopped onion and lime wedges.

14

*A traditional holiday
food, oysters are at
their best during
the winter months
in most climates.
If you live in an area
where oysters are
plentiful, you can
shuck your own or
buy freshy shucked;
you will need about
36 oysters in the
shell. If not, or if
you are short on
time, use those sold
in glass jars at fish
and butcher shops.*

OYSTER STEW WITH ROSEMARY

serves 8–10

1 Tbsp unsalted butter

1 Tbsp canola oil

1 small yellow onion, finely chopped

2 celery ribs, finely chopped

¼ cup (2 fl oz/60 ml) dry white wine or vermouth

6 cups (48 fl oz/1.5 l) chicken broth

Salt and ground white pepper

1 cup (8 fl oz/250 ml) half-and-half or cream

3 pints (3 lb/1.5 kg) shucked oysters with their liquor

1 Tbsp minced rosemary, plus more for garnish

In a large, heavy pot, melt the butter with the oil over medium heat. Add the onion and celery and sauté until the onion is translucent, about 3 minutes. Add the wine and cook, stirring occasionally, for 3–4 minutes. Add the broth and season with salt and pepper to taste. Reduce the heat to low, cover, and simmer for 5 minutes.

Stir the half-and-half into the broth mixture and simmer, uncovered, for 5 minutes. Add the oysters and their liquor and simmer, uncovered, until the oysters have plumped up and their edges are curled, about 3 minutes. Stir in the 1 Tbsp rosemary. Season with salt and pepper and serve, garnished with the remaining rosemary.

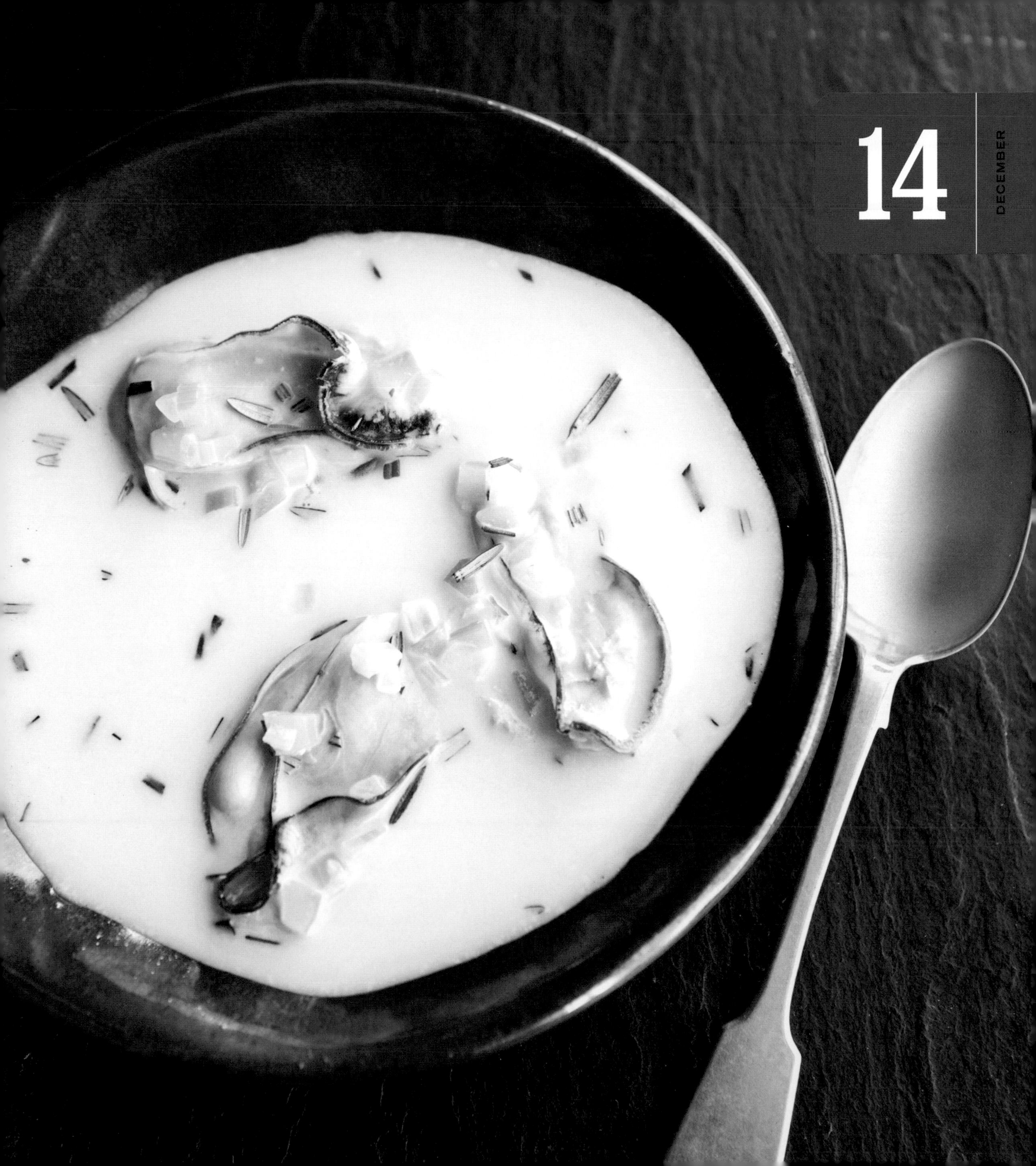

14 DECEMBER

DECEMBER

15

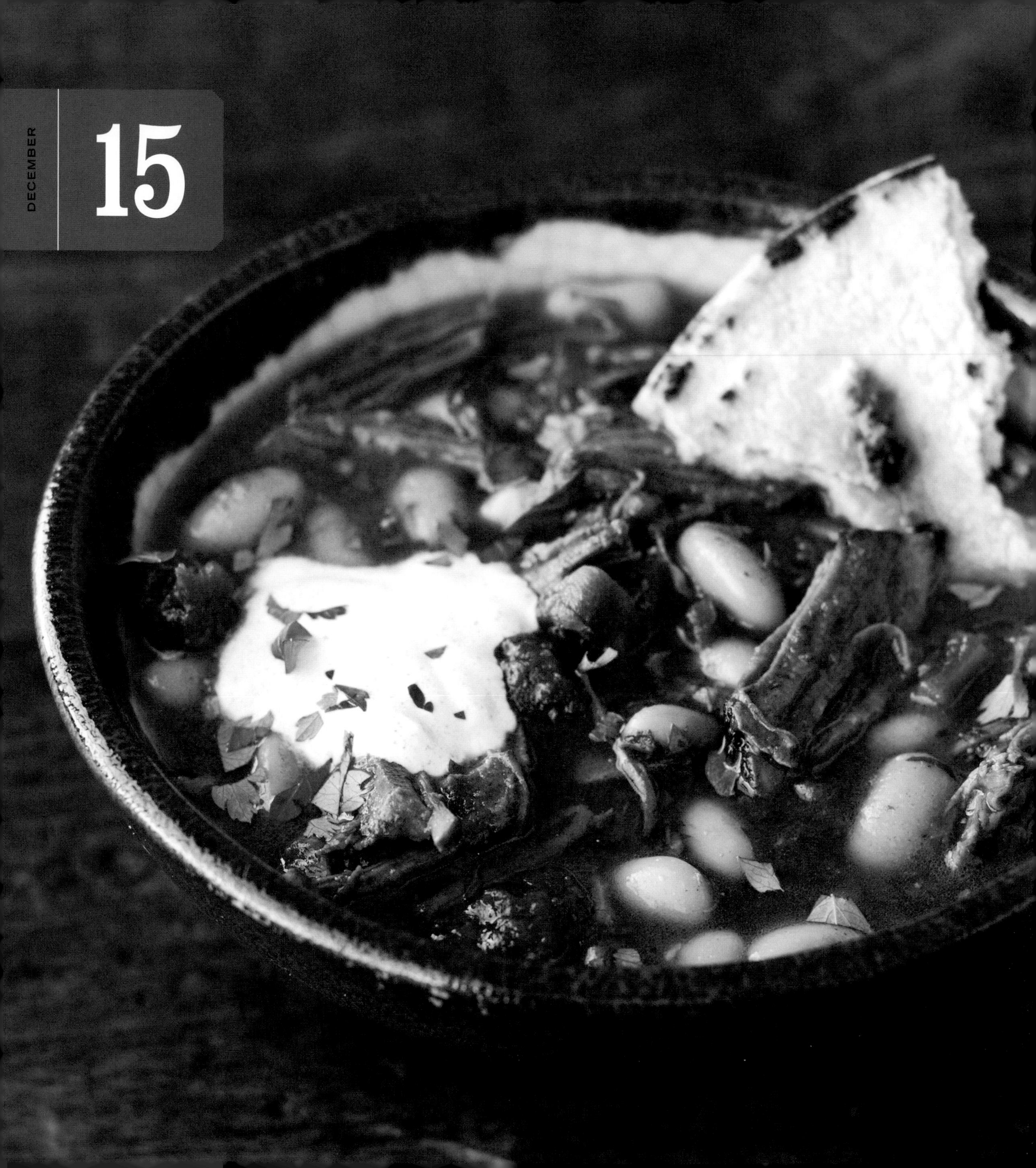

15

Short ribs braise slowly in the oven and come out caramelized and tender. This savory stew uses the shredded meat and the braising liquid. This is a great way to use leftover short rib meat (and if you don't have any leftover braising liquid, you can use beef broth).

SHORT RIB STEW WITH PAPRIKA SOUR CREAM
serves 4

3 lb (1.5 kg) short ribs, halved

Salt and freshly ground pepper

2 Tbsp olive oil

1 yellow onion, chopped

6 cloves garlic, minced

2 celery ribs, chopped

1 carrot, peeled and chopped

3 cups (24 fl oz/750 ml) dry red wine

2 bay leaves

4½ cups (36 fl oz/1.1 l) beef broth

1 can (15 oz/470 g) cannellini or other white beans, drained

1 can (14½ oz/455 g) diced tomatoes

¼ cup (⅓ oz/10 g) chopped flat-leaf parsley

FOR THE PAPRIKA SOUR CREAM

⅔ cup (5½ oz/170 g) sour cream

1 tsp fresh lemon juice

½ tsp smoked paprika

Salt

Season the short ribs with salt and pepper and refrigerate for at least 6 hours. Remove from the refrigerator, bring to room temperature, and season again with salt and pepper.

Preheat the oven to 350°F (180°C). In a large sauté pan, warm the oil over high heat until very hot. Sear the short ribs until they are browned on all sides, 6–8 minutes, then transfer to a large, heavy ovenproof pot.

Reduce the heat under the sauté pan to medium, add the onion, garlic, celery, and carrot, and sauté for 5 minutes. Add the wine and bay leaves, raise the heat to high, and boil until the liquid has been reduced by half, 10–12 minutes. Add the broth and bring to a boil. Pour the contents of the sauté pan into the pot. Cover tightly, transfer to the oven, and cook for 2½ hours.

Remove the short ribs from the pot and, when they are cool enough to handle, remove the meat from the bones and shred into bite-sized pieces. Strain the braising liquid and reserve 1¼ cups (10 fl oz/310 ml); discard the vegetables left in the strainer. ⟫

Put the shredded meat and the reserved braising liquid back into the pot and set over medium heat. Stir in the beans and the tomatoes with their juices and bring to a boil over medium-high heat. Stir in the parsley and season with salt and pepper.

To make the paprika sour cream, in a bowl, stir together the sour cream, lemon juice, paprika, and ¼ tsp salt. Serve the stew, topped with a generous dollop of the paprika sour cream.

16

Rutabagas, also known as Swedes or yellow turnips, are often ignored because people just don't know what to do with them. They are sweet and very flavorful when roasted. Paired with carrots and allspice, they simmer into a delicious soup.

RUTABAGA & CARROT SOUP
serves 4–6

2 rutabagas (21 oz/655 g total), peeled and chopped

4 carrots, peeled and chopped

1 Tbsp olive oil

Salt and freshly ground pepper

2 Tbsp unsalted butter

1 yellow onion, chopped

2 cloves garlic, minced

½ tsp allspice

5 cups (40 fl oz/1.25 l) vegetable broth, plus more as needed

Preheat the oven to 400°F (200°C) and line a baking sheet with parchment paper. Toss the rutabagas and carrots with the oil and season with salt and pepper. Spread the vegetables on the prepared baking sheet and roast in the oven until tender, 20–25 minutes.

In a large, heavy pot, melt the butter over medium-high heat. Add the onion and garlic and sauté until the onion is translucent, about 5 minutes. Add the allspice, stir, and cook for 2 minutes. Add the broth and bring to a boil. Add the roasted rutabagas and carrots, reduce the heat to low, and simmer for 15 minutes. Remove from the heat and let cool slightly.

Working in batches, purée the soup in a blender. Return to the pot, add more broth if needed to achieve the desired consistency, season to taste with salt, and serve.

17

CLASSIC BEEF & RED WINE STEW

serves 6

This recipe is quintessential French bistro fare. The term "daube" typically refers to a rich, savory stew of beef in red wine. Accompany the stew with celery root purée or coarse country bread and a salad, with a platter of cheeses to follow.

3 lb (1.5 kg) boneless beef chuck, trimmed and cut into 2-inch (5-cm) pieces

3 Tbsp brandy

2 whole cloves

2 yellow onions, coarsely chopped

½ carrot, peeled and sliced

1 celery rib, sliced

8 cloves garlic, coarsely chopped

1 bay leaf

4–5 sage leaves, coarsely chopped

2 Tbsp chopped flat-leaf parsley

1–2 tsp thyme leaves

Salt and freshly ground pepper

2 large strips orange zest

1 bottle (750 ml) dry red wine

2 Tbsp (1 oz/30 g) dried porcini mushrooms

3 slices (2½ oz/75 g) pancetta or salt pork, diced

4 cups (32 fl oz/1 l) beef broth

3 Tbsp tomato juice

In a large nonaluminum bowl, combine the beef, brandy, cloves, onions, carrot, celery, garlic, bay leaf, sage, parsley, thyme, ¼ tsp ground pepper, the orange zest, wine, and dried porcini. Cover and refrigerate overnight or for up to 2 days.

Bring the beef and vegetables to room temperature. Using a slotted spoon, transfer them to a platter and pat the meat dry with paper towels. Reserve the remaining marinade.

Preheat the oven to 325°F (165°C). In a large, heavy ovenproof pot, fry the pancetta over medium heat until it renders its fat, 3–5 minutes. Using a slotted spoon, transfer to paper towels to drain, reserving the fat in the pot. Working in batches, add the meat and vegetables and brown them on all sides, seasoning with salt and pepper as they brown, about 7 minutes for each batch. Transfer to a platter. Add the marinade to the pot, raise the heat to high, and bring to a boil. Reduce the heat to medium and simmer, skimming off any foam on the surface, ⟫→

until the liquid is reduced by one-third, about 8 minutes. Add the broth and simmer until reduced by one-third, about 8 minutes.

Reduce the heat to low and return the meat, vegetables, and bacon to the pot. Cover and cook in the oven until the meat is tender, 2½–3 hours.

Using a slotted spoon, transfer the meat and vegetables to a plate. Spoon off any fat from the cooking liquid. Set the pot over high heat and cook, stirring, until the liquid is reduced by about half and is richly flavored, about 10 minutes. Return the meat and vegetables to the pot and stir in the tomato juice. Season with salt and pepper and serve.

18

TURKEY MULLIGATAWNY

serves 4

Leftover turkey can be put to good use in this Anglo-Indian soup. Curry powder is responsible for the vibrant yellow color. Lentils may replace the rice, but will require longer simmering.

3 Tbsp unsalted butter

½ boneless, skinless turkey breast (about 1½ lb/750 g), cubed

1 yellow onion, finely chopped

3 celery ribs, finely chopped

2 carrots, peeled and finely chopped

1 clove garlic, minced

1 Tbsp Madras curry powder

4 cups (32 fl oz/1 l) chicken broth

½ cup (3½ oz/105 g) long-grain white rice

1 cup (8 oz/250 g) plain yogurt

Salt and freshly ground pepper

In a large, heavy pot, melt the butter over medium heat. Add the turkey and sauté until lightly browned, about 7 minutes. Transfer to a plate. Add the onion, celery, carrots, and garlic to the pot and sauté until the onion is translucent, about 5 minutes. Stir in the curry powder and cook, stirring, for 2 minutes to blend the flavors.

Add the broth and turkey to the vegetables and bring to a simmer over high heat. Reduce the heat to medium, add the rice, and cook, uncovered, until the rice is tender and the turkey is cooked through, 15–20 minutes. Stir in the yogurt and simmer for 10 minutes to blend the flavors. Season with salt and pepper and serve.

19

This is a very relaxed recipe when it comes to the ingredient list. It is absolutely fine to use frozen and thawed lobster tails. Be sure to keep the meat in the shells during poaching. This will ensure that they keep their shape, making for a better presentation when you slice them.

SHIITAKE BROTH WITH BUTTER-POACHED LOBSTER & CHIVES

serves 6

1 oz (30 g) dried shiitake mushrooms

2 Tbsp olive oil

1 small yellow onion, chopped

2 cloves garlic, minced

½ lb (250 g) fresh white mushrooms, diced

¼ cup (2 fl oz/60 ml) dry white wine

¼ cup (2 fl oz/60 ml) soy sauce

2 thyme sprigs

1 cup (8 oz/250 g) unsalted butter

2 lobster tails, in their shells

1 Tbsp chopped chives

Put the shiitakes in a small bowl, cover with very hot water, and soak for at least 30 minutes. Drain, reserving the soaking liquid. Remove the stems from the mushrooms and thinly slice. Strain the soaking liquid through a coffee filter and reserve ¾ cup (6 fl oz/180 ml).

In a large, heavy pot, warm the oil over medium-high heat. Add the onion, garlic, and white mushrooms and sauté for 5 minutes. Add the wine, soy sauce, thyme, the reserved mushroom soaking liquid, and 2 cups (16 fl oz/500 ml) water and bring to a boil. Reduce the heat to low and simmer for 1 hour. Strain the liquid, discarding the solids, and return the broth to the saucepan. Add the sliced shiitakes and keep warm over low heat.

To poach the lobster, in a very small saucepan, melt the butter slowly over medium-low heat, skimming off any foam that rises to the top. Add the lobster tails and poach, turning the tails once and frequently spooning the butter over the exposed parts, until they are cooked all the way through, 5–7 minutes. Transfer the lobster tails to a cutting board, remove the meat from the shells, and cut into ½-inch (12-mm) slices.

To serve, ladle the broth and mushrooms into shallow bowls. Place the lobster slices in the center of each bowl, garnish with the chives, and serve.

20

This easy stew comes together with a few fresh veggies, convenient canned chickpeas, and seasonings that are probably already lurking in your spice cabinet. The result is a wholesome vegetarian meal, a nice change of pace from what can otherwise be an overly indulgent time of year.

NORTH AFRICAN CHICKPEA SOUP

serves 4

2 Tbsp olive oil, plus more for drizzling

1 carrot, peeled and finely chopped

¼ yellow onion, finely chopped

1 tomato, finely chopped

1 small red bell pepper, seeded and finely chopped

Salt and freshly ground black pepper

½ tsp ground cumin

¼ tsp ground turmeric

½ tsp cayenne pepper

2 cans (14½ oz/455 g each) chickpeas, drained

2 small zucchini, trimmed and chopped

5 cups (40 fl oz/1.25 l) chicken broth

In a large, heavy pot, warm the 2 Tbsp oil over medium heat. Add the carrot and onion and sauté until slightly softened, about 3 minutes. Add the tomato, bell pepper, 1 tsp salt, cumin, turmeric, and cayenne. Sauté until fragrant, about 1 minute.

Add the chickpeas, zucchini, and broth. Raise the heat to medium-high and bring to a boil. Reduce the heat to medium-low and simmer, uncovered, until the zucchini is tender and the flavors are blended, about 15 minutes. Season to taste with salt and black pepper and serve, drizzled with oil.

21

*Good enough
to serve at any
celebratory meal,
this Italian soup
traditionally
included different
cuts of pork and
a large variety
of vegetables,
which were slowly
simmered together
until the ingredients
were pronounced
"married." Here
is an updated and
streamlined version.*

WEDDING SOUP

serves 6

3 qt (3 l) chicken broth

1 lb (500 g) dinosaur kale, escarole,
or other sturdy greens, stems and ribs
removed, leaves cut into bite-sized pieces

3 large carrots, peeled and chopped

1 celery rib, chopped

FOR THE MEATBALLS

1 lb (500 g) ground pork

2 eggs, lightly beaten

½ cup (2½ oz/75 g) minced yellow onion

½ cup (2 oz/60 g) fine dried bread crumbs

½ cup (2 oz/60 g) grated
pecorino romano cheese

Salt and freshly ground pepper

3 Tbsp olive oil

Grated pecorino romano for garnish

In a large, heavy pot, bring the broth to a
boil over high heat. Add the kale, carrots,
and celery, reduce the heat to low, and
simmer until the vegetables are tender,
about 30 minutes.

Meanwhile, to make the meatballs, combine
the pork, eggs, onion, bread crumbs, pecorino,
1 tsp salt, and several grindings of pepper in
a large bowl and mix well. For each meatball,
scoop up 1 teaspoon of the pork mixture,
form into a meatball, and place on a plate.

In a large frying pan, warm the oil over
medium-high heat. In batches, gently
add the meatballs and brown on all sides,
about 5 minutes per batch. Using a slotted
spoon, carefully add them to the soup
and simmer gently over low heat until
the meatballs are cooked through, about
10 minutes. Season with salt and pepper
and serve, garnished with pecorino.

22

*Rangoons are
usually deep-fried
Asian dumplings.
These are not fried
but simmered in
broth and served
as a soup. This
soup is best eaten
right away, as the
rangoons tend to fall
apart when reheated.
Be careful not to
overspice your broth;
you can always add
more chile and let it
simmer longer.*

CRAB RANGOONS IN CHILE-LIME BROTH

serves 4–6

2 cups (16 fl oz/500 ml) vegetable broth

1 Tbsp soy sauce

4 kaffir lime leaves, torn

½ tsp seeded and chopped red chile

FOR THE CRAB RANGOONS

¼ lb (125 g) fresh lump crabmeat,
picked over for shell fragments

2 Tbsp cream cheese, at room temperature

1 tsp canola oil

1 tsp chopped chives, plus 1 Tbsp
finely chopped chives

Salt and freshly ground pepper

24 wonton wrappers

Combine the broth, 2 cups (16 fl oz/500 ml)
water, the soy sauce, lime leaves, and
chopped chile in a large, heavy pot and put
over medium-high heat. Bring to a boil,
then reduce the heat to low and simmer for
5 minutes. Strain the broth, discard the solids,
and return the broth to the pot. Set aside off
the heat or keep warm over low heat.

To prepare the crab rangoons, in a small bowl,
combine the crabmeat, cream cheese, oil, 1 tsp
chives, ½ tsp salt, and ¼ tsp pepper. Place
1 tsp of the crab mixture in the middle of a
wonton wrapper. Using your fingers, apply
a small amount of water on all edges of the
wrapper. Fold the wrapper diagonally, forcing
out any air bubbles as you press to seal. Take
the 2 points on the longest side of the triangle
and fold so that the tips meet. Apply a small
amount of water on one of the tips and press
firmly to stick together. Repeat to use the
remaining wrappers and filling.

Return the broth to a boil, reduce to a simmer,
and carefully add the crab rangoons. Cook
for 3 minutes to warm through, then serve,
garnished with the finely chopped chives.

DECEMBER

23

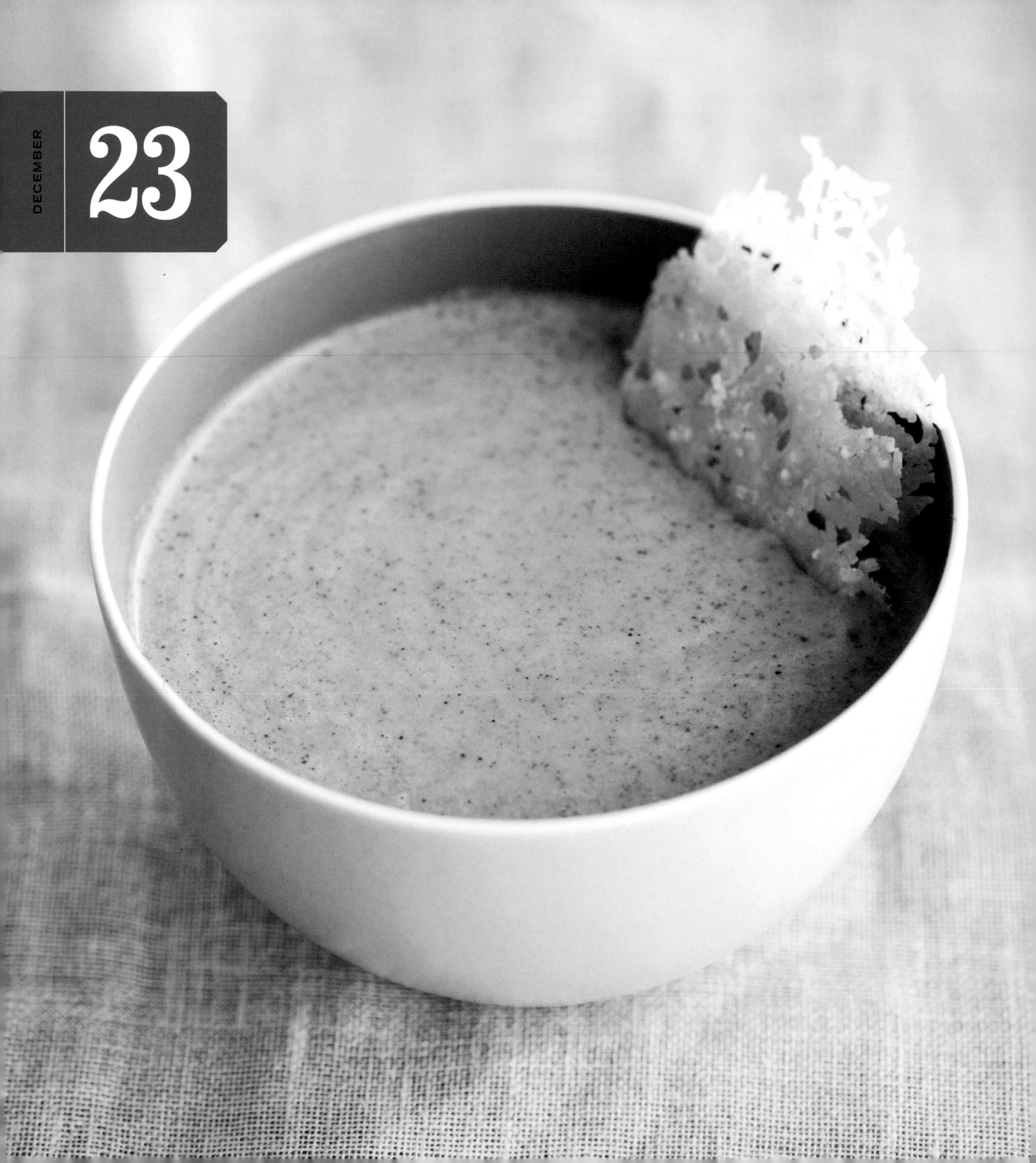

23

This recipe uses all of the broccoli: the florets (where most of the nutrition is) and the stems (filled with fiber). Make extra frico and store in an airtight container for up to 5 days. The frico makes a delicious appetizer on its own.

BROCCOLI SOUP WITH PARMESAN-LEMON FRICO

serves 4–6

2 Tbsp olive oil

1 small yellow onion, chopped

3 cloves garlic, minced

1 large bunch broccoli, cut into small florets, stems peeled and coarsely chopped

3 cups (24 fl oz/750 ml) chicken broth

½ cup (4 fl oz/125 ml) heavy cream

Salt and freshly ground pepper

FOR THE PARMESAN-LEMON FRICO

½ cup (2 oz/60 g) grated Parmesan cheese

2 tsp grated lemon zest

In a large, heavy pot, warm the oil over medium-high heat. Add the onion and garlic and sauté until very soft, about 5 minutes. Add the broccoli, stir, and cook for about 2 minutes. Add 2 cups (16 fl oz/500 ml) of the broth, cover, and cook for 6 minutes. Remove from the heat and let cool slightly.

Working in batches, purée the soup in a blender or food processor with the remaining 1 cup (8 fl oz/250 ml) broth. Return to the pot and stir in the cream. Return the soup to a gentle boil and cook for 2 minutes. Season with salt and pepper. Keep warm over low heat.

To make the Parmesan-lemon frico, preheat the oven to 400°F (200°C) and line a baking sheet with parchment paper. In a small bowl, stir together the Parmesan and lemon zest. Transfer a heaping teaspoonful of the cheese mixture onto the prepared baking sheet and use your fingers to flatten the mound. Repeat with the remaining cheese mixture, placing the mounds 1 inch (2.5 cm) apart. Bake the frico until golden brown, 3–5 minutes. Let cool on the baking sheet, then carefully lift using a spatula.

Ladle the soup into bowls, top each with 2 frico, and serve.

24

This is a fantastic version of the often ho-hum vegetarian chili. Orange zest adds a clean citrus zing. Serve with cheesy quesadillas and a green salad.

ROOT VEGETABLE CHILI WITH ORANGE & CILANTRO

serves 4

2 Tbsp olive oil

1 yellow onion, chopped

2 cloves garlic, minced

2 tsp ground cumin

1 tsp ground coriander

1 tsp chili powder

1 sweet potato (¾ lb/375 g), peeled and diced

2 parsnips (½ lb/250 g total), peeled and diced

1½ cups (12 fl oz/375 ml) vegetable broth

1 can (14½ oz/455 g) diced tomatoes

1 can (15 oz/470 g) pinto beans, drained

2 Tbsp fresh orange juice

½ tsp smoked paprika

2 Tbsp chopped cilantro

Salt and freshly ground pepper

In a large, heavy pot, warm the oil over medium-high heat. Add the onion and garlic and sauté until the onion is translucent, about 5 minutes. Add the cumin, coriander, and chili powder, stir, and cook for 2 minutes. Add the sweet potato and parsnips, stir, and cook for 4 minutes. Add the broth and bring to a boil. Reduce the heat to low and cook until the vegetables are soft, about 15 minutes. Add the tomatoes with their juices and pinto beans and continue to cook, stirring occasionally, for 10 minutes.

Stir in the orange juice and paprika. Turn off the heat, stir in the cilantro, season with salt and pepper, and serve.

25

The intense flavor of this rich soup derives from a combination of shellfish and beef broths. Indulge in good lobster meat, and you won't need many other ingredients to let it shine. This is a luxurious treat for the season.

LOBSTER BISQUE

serves 4–6

2 Tbsp unsalted butter

¼ cup (1 oz/30 g) chopped shallots

½ cup (4 fl oz/125 ml) dry white wine

2 cups (16 fl oz/500 ml) shellfish broth

1 cup (8 fl oz/250 ml) beef broth

3 Tbsp long-grain white rice

1 Tbsp tomato paste

¾ lb (375 g) cooked lobster meat, picked over for shell fragments

1 cup (8 fl oz/250 ml) heavy cream

Salt

⅛ tsp cayenne pepper

In a large saucepan, melt the butter over medium-low heat. Add the shallots and sauté until softened, about 5 minutes. Raise the heat to medium, stir in the wine, and bring to a boil. Add the shellfish and beef broths, rice, and tomato paste and return to a boil. Reduce the heat to low, cover, and simmer until the rice is soft, 20–25 minutes. Add ½ lb (250 g) of the lobster meat to the saucepan, remove from the heat, and let cool slightly.

Working in batches, purée the soup in a blender. Return to the saucepan. Stir in the cream, ½ tsp salt, and the cayenne pepper and rewarm gently over medium-low heat. Serve, garnished with the reserved lobster meat.

26

Linguiça is a spicy Portuguese sausage, which brings heat to this stew. Garnish with sour cream and serve with a cold lager.

LINGUIÇA & POTATO STEW WITH TWO PAPRIKAS

serves 4–6

½ lb (250 g) linguiça, cut into ¼-inch (6-mm) slices

2 Tbsp olive oil

1½ yellow onions, chopped

3 cloves garlic, minced

1 yellow bell pepper, seeded and diced

2 tsp smoked paprika

1 tsp sweet paprika

1 russet potato, peeled and diced

3 cups (24 fl oz/750 ml) chicken broth

1½ Tbsp tomato paste

1 Tbsp heavy cream

2 Tbsp chopped flat-leaf parsley

Salt

Warm a large, heavy pot over medium-high heat. Add the linguiça and brown on both sides, 5–7 minutes. Transfer to a bowl.

Warm the oil in the pot over medium-high heat. Add the onion, garlic, and bell pepper and sauté until the vegetables are softened, about 5 minutes. Add the smoked and sweet paprikas and cook for 1 minute. Add the potato, stir, and cook for 2 minutes. Add the broth and tomato paste and bring to a boil. Reduce the heat to low, add the linguiça, and simmer for about 30 minutes to blend the flavors. Stir in the cream and parsley, season with salt, and serve.

27

The addition of snow peas, sesame oil, soy sauce, and ginger gives traditional chicken soup an Asian spin. With fresh veggies and precooked chicken, the recipe becomes dead simple—just add everything to the pot.

GINGER CHICKEN SOUP

serves 4–6

2 qt (2 l) chicken broth

2 cups (6 oz/185 g) thinly sliced cremini or stemmed shiitake mushrooms

½ cup (2½ oz/75 g) chopped snow peas

1 Tbsp peeled and minced fresh ginger

4 green onions, white and tender green parts, thinly sliced on the diagonal

2 Tbsp soy sauce

Salt and freshly ground pepper

1½ cups (9 oz/280 g) shredded cooked chicken

1 tsp Asian sesame oil

Pour the broth into a large, heavy pot and bring to a boil. Add the mushrooms, snow peas, ginger, green onions, soy sauce, 1 tsp salt, and the shredded chicken. Reduce the heat to low and simmer until heated through, about 5 minutes. Stir in the sesame oil and ⅛ tsp pepper. Taste and adjust the seasoning. Serve.

28

When sautéed with butter and other aromatics, celery's slightly tangy flavor is accentuated. For an even more pronounced flavor, swap in celery root for the celery and increase the amount of broth to achieve the desired consistency.

CURRIED CREAM OF CELERY SOUP

serves 4–6

2 Tbsp unsalted butter

1 yellow onion, chopped

1½ lb (750 g) celery, coarsely chopped

1 Tbsp curry powder

3 cups (24 fl oz/750 ml) vegetable broth

¼ cup (2 fl oz/60 ml) heavy cream

Salt and freshly ground pepper

In a large, heavy pot, melt the butter over medium-high heat. Add the onion and celery and sauté until the celery is very soft, about 10 minutes. Add the curry powder, stir, and cook for 1 minute. Add the broth and bring to a boil. Reduce the heat to low and simmer for 30 minutes. Remove from the heat and let cool slightly.

Working in batches, purée the soup in a blender. Return to the pot, stir in the cream, and bring just to a boil. Turn off the heat, season with salt and pepper, and serve.

29

Escarole is a type of endive, and it needs only to be wilted in this dish, where it adds a beautiful green color and a bit of texture. Use your best-quality olive oil to finish the soup.

ESCAROLE & WHITE BEAN SOUP WITH ROSEMARY

serves 8–10

2¼ cups (1 lb/500 g) dried white beans, picked over and rinsed

2 Tbsp extra-virgin olive oil, plus more for drizzling

2 yellow onions, chopped

3 cloves garlic, minced

4 cups (32 fl oz/1 l) chicken broth, plus more as needed

2 rosemary sprigs

½ head escarole, cut into 1-inch (2.5-cm) ribbons

Salt and freshly ground pepper

Place the dried beans in a bowl with cold water to cover and soak overnight. Drain.

In a large, heavy pot, warm the 2 Tbsp oil over medium-high heat. Add the onions and garlic and cook until translucent, 8–10 minutes. Add the white beans, the 4 cups broth, and the rosemary and bring to a boil. Reduce the heat to low, cover tightly, and simmer, adding more broth as needed to keep the beans covered, until the beans are very tender, 50–60 minutes. Remove from the heat, remove and discard the rosemary sprigs, and let cool slightly.

Purée half of the soup in a blender, return to the pot, and set over medium-low heat. Stir in the escarole until it is wilted. Add more broth if needed to achieve the desired consistency and season well with salt and pepper. Serve, drizzled with oil.

30

RICE SOUP WITH PORK DUMPLINGS

serves 6

6 cups (48 fl oz/1.5 l) chicken broth

1 Tbsp preserved radish or turnip, or tamarind paste (optional)

2 Tbsp Asian fish sauce, or to taste

Ground white pepper

¼ lb (125 g) ground pork shoulder

1½ cups (7½ oz/235 g) cooked long-grain white rice, preferably jasmine

3 Tbsp coarsely chopped cilantro

3 Tbsp chopped green onion, white and pale green parts

¼ cup (2 fl oz/60 ml) garlic oil

In many parts of the world, soup is a breakfast food, and such is the case for Thailand's traditional "khao tom moo," a rice soup inflected with tiny pork balls and garlic oil. It makes a wonderful, satisfying lunch or supper, too.

In a large saucepan, combine the broth, preserved radish, if using, fish sauce, and ⅛ tsp pepper. Bring to a boil over high heat, then reduce to medium heat. Adjust the heat to maintain a gentle simmer.

To make each dumpling, use your fingers to break off about 1 tsp of the pork and roll it into a tiny ball. Drop the balls, a few at a time, into the simmering broth and cook for 1 minute. Add the rice and simmer until the rice is soft and the soup is slightly thickened, about 5 minutes.

Serve, garnished with the cilantro, green onion, and garlic oil.

31

CHILLED BEET & CUCUMBER SOUP

serves 8

2 lb (1 kg) beets (about 8 beets), trimmed

1 yellow onion, quartered

8 cups (64 fl oz/2 l) chicken broth

1 Tbsp sugar

2 English cucumbers, peeled, seeded, and cut into thin strips, plus thinly sliced cucumber rounds for serving

2 Tbsp fresh lemon juice

2 Tbsp rice wine vinegar

Salt and freshly ground pepper

¼ cup (⅓ oz/10 g) finely chopped dill

1 cup (8 oz/250 g) nonfat plain yogurt or lowfat sour cream (optional)

Eastern Europe has given rise to many versions of the peasant soup of beets known as borscht, commonly served with dark rye bread. This vegetarian version makes a cool, festive, and bright soup to cleanse the palate and ring in the new year. For a party, garnish with tangy yogurt, a few feathers of dill, and a dollop of caviar.

In a large, heavy pot, combine the beets, onion, broth, 1 cup (8 fl oz/250 ml) water, and the sugar over medium-high heat. Cover and bring to a boil. Reduce the heat to low and simmer, covered, until the beets are tender, 45–60 minutes.

Using a slotted spoon, transfer the beets to a colander. Reserve the cooking liquid. Peel the beets under cold running water. Cut 3 of the beets in half. Cut the remaining beets into strips 1 inch (2.5 cm) long and ¼ inch (6 mm) wide. Cover and refrigerate the beet strips.

Strain the cooking liquid through a fine-mesh sieve into a large bowl. Remove and discard the onion. Purée the 6 beet halves and 1 cup (8 fl oz/250 ml) of the strained liquid in a food processor and add the purée to the remaining strained liquid in the bowl. Cover and refrigerate until well chilled, at least 4 hours or overnight.

Add the beet strips, cucumber strips, lemon juice, vinegar, ½ tsp salt, ¼ tsp pepper, and half of the dill to the chilled beet mixture. Stir to mix well.

Serve, garnished with the yogurt, if using, the cucumber slices, and the remaining dill.

SOUPS BY INGREDIENT

A

Almonds
Carrot & Coconut Purée with Curried Almonds, 96
Chicken Stew with Olives & Almonds, 40
Cold Almond Soup with Grapes, 133

Apples
Apple, Leek & Butternut Squash Soup, 250
Curried Leek & Apple Soup, 228
Red Cabbage & Apple Soup, 258
Roasted Parsnip & Apple Purée
with Gruyère Toasts, 222
Turnip, Apple & Potato Soup, 229

Artichokes
Artichoke, Spring Pea & Mint Soup, 75
Artichoke & Quinoa Soup with Green Garlic, 90
Artichoke Soup with Camembert Crostini, 118
Artichoke Soup with Morel Butter, 60
Artichoke & Toasted Bread Soup with Sage, 245

Asparagus
Asparagus-Chervil Purée
with Lemon Mascarpone, 88
Asparagus Soup with Poached
Eggs & Crispy Prosciutto, 93
Crab & Asparagus Egg Flower Soup, 123
Cream of Asparagus Soup, 58
Leek & Asparagus Vichyssoise, 113
Lemony Asparagus & Rice Soup with Parmesan, 65
Simple Asparagus Soup, 125

Avocados
Avocado Soup with Lime Juice & Rum, 190
Avocado Soup with Shrimp & Salsa, 150
Cold Zucchini & Avocado Soup, 120
Crab & Avocado Soup, 173

B

Barley
Barley-Leek Soup with Mini Chicken Meatballs, 21
Cranberry Bean & Barley Soup, 27
Roasted Root Vegetable & Barley Stew, 37
Savory Barley Soup with Wild
Mushrooms & Thyme, 250
Vegetable Barley Soup, 208

Beans. See also Black beans; Chickpeas; White beans
Bean & Elbow Pasta Soup with Basil Pesto, 118
Cranberry Bean & Barley Soup, 27
Cranberry Bean & Pappardelle Soup, 63
Egg-Lemon Soup with Fava Beans
& Fried Garlic Chips, 124
Fava Bean & Farfalle Soup, 95
Fava Bean Soup, 89
Fresh Green Bean Soup, 184
Lima Bean, Pea & Zucchini Purée with Pesto, 135
Minestrone with Pesto, 214
Miso Soup with Tofu & Long Beans, 197
Pinto Bean Soup with Toasted Jalapeños, 159

Provençal Minestrone, 150
Ramen Noodles with Edamame & Mushrooms, 148
Red Bean & Andouille Soup, 112
Romano Bean, Zucchini & Parmesan Soup, 198
Root Vegetable Chili with Orange & Cilantro, 291
Silken Lima Bean Soup with Ham Croûtes, 160
Snap Pea & Succotash Soup
with Parsley-Mint Pistou, 190
Spicy Broccolini & Cranberry Bean Soup, 214
Stone Soup, 46
Three-Bean Soup with Linguiça, 76
Vegetarian Chili, 13

Beef. See also Veal
Baby Bok Choy & Beef Noodle Soup, 66
Balsamic Beef Stew, 94
Beef Borscht, 16
Beef & Mushroom Soup with Farro, 69
Beef Pho, 47
Beef Stew with Orange Zest & Red Wine, 52
Beef Stew with Turnips & Greens, 234
Chili con Carne, 34
Classic Beef & Red Wine Stew, 286
Five-Spice Beef Stew, 12
Gingery Beef Broth with Soba Noodles
& Bok Choy, 22
Goulash, 263
Italian Beef Stew, 222
Short Rib Stew with Paprika Sour Cream, 285
Steak & Potato Soup with Fried Shallots, 28
Weeknight Hungarian Beef Stew, 280

Beets
Beef Borscht, 16
Chilled Beet & Cucumber Soup, 294
Golden Beet Soup with Dilled Goat Cheese, 130
Roasted Beet Purée with Feta, 142

Black beans
Black Bean Chili, 100
Black Bean Soup with Meyer Lemon
Crème Fraîche, 51
Creamy Black Bean Purée with
Cheese Straws, 244
Cuban Black Bean Soup, 148

Black-eyed peas
Black-Eyed Pea Soup with Herbs & Garlic, 46
Black-Eyed Pea Stew, 77

Bread
Artichoke & Toasted Bread Soup with Sage, 245
Summer Panzanella Soup with Tiny Pasta, 171
Tomato-Bread Soup with Basil Oil, 204

Broccoli
Broccoli & Cheddar Soup, 23
Broccoli-Leek Soup, 61
Broccoli Soup with Parmesan-Lemon Frico, 291
Cream of Broccoli Soup, 96

Broccolini
Orecchiette, Sausage & Broccolini in Broth, 262
Spicy Broccolini & Cranberry Bean Soup, 214
White Bean, Broccolini & Bratwurst Soup, 238

C

Cabbage & bok choy
Baby Bok Choy & Beef Noodle Soup, 66
Kielbasa & Sauerkraut Soup, 102
Napa Cabbage Soup with Pork & Bean Sprouts, 71
Red Cabbage & Apple Soup, 258
Savoy Cabbage, Fontina & Rye Bread Soup, 22

Carrots
Carrot & Asian Pear Purée, 245
Carrot & Coconut Purée with Curried Almonds, 96
Carrot-Ginger Soup, 226
Carrot Soup with Bacon & Chestnut Cream, 269
Chilled Carrot Soup with
Ginger & Orange Zest, 106
Curried Carrot Purée, 117
Kumquat-Carrot Purée with
Toasted Fennel Seeds, 24
Mushroom, Carrot & Leek Soup
with Shaved Parmesan, 252
Rutabaga & Carrot Soup, 285

Cauliflower
Cauliflower & Roasted Garlic Purée, 12
Cauliflower Soup with
Cheddar & Blue Cheese, 233
Cauliflower Soup with Chervil, 63
Creamy Cauliflower Soup
with Crispy Prosciutto, 45
Curried Cauliflower & Chicken Stew, 257
Roasted Cauliflower & Parmesan Soup, 231

Celery
Celery, Leek & Oyster Bisque, 45
Celery & Rice Soup with Parsley, 252
Curried Cream of Celery Soup, 293

Celery root
Celery Root Purée with Caramelized Apples, 255
Chestnut-Celery Root Soup
with Bacon & Sage Croutons, 253
Potato-Celery Root Soup, 277

Chard
Fennel Broth with Chard & Chorizo, 77
Leek & Swiss Chard Soup, 232
Wild Rice & Red Chard Soup with Andouille, 246
Winter Greens & Shiitake Soup
with Poached Eggs, 34

Cheese
Broccoli & Cheddar Soup, 23
Cauliflower Soup with
Cheddar & Blue Cheese, 233
Cheddar Cheese Soup with Ale, 257
Cheddar & Hard Cider Soup
with Fried Shallots, 226

Cheese & Arugula Ravioli Soup, 144

Parmesan Broth with Lemon,
Chicken & Spinach, 66

Parmesan Straciatella with Kale, 48

Pumpkin-Gruyère Soup, 255

Cherries

Chilled Sour Cherry Soup with Tarragon, 120

Sour Cherry–Riesling Soup, 137

Chestnuts

Chestnut–Celery Root Soup
with Bacon & Sage Croutons, 253

Chestnut Soup, 276

Chicken

Barley-Leek Soup with Mini Chicken Meatballs, 21

Burmese Chicken Curry Soup, 167

Chicken Chili with Piquillo Peppers, 15

Chicken & Chipotle Soup with Avocado & Lime, 72

Chicken Chowder, 228

Chicken & Farfalle Vegetable Soup, 215

Chicken & Hominy Soup with Ancho Chiles, 282

Chicken-Lemongrass Soup, 99

Chicken Soup with Gnocchi, Basil & Parmesan, 171

Chicken Stew with Buttermilk-Chive Dumplings, 42

Chicken Stew with Olives & Almonds, 40

Chicken-Tomatillo Soup with Chipotle Chiles, 256

Chicken & Wild Rice Soup with Ginger, 70

Chorizo & Chicken Stew with Avocado Crema, 219

Classic Chicken Noodle Soup, 16

Curried Cauliflower & Chicken Stew, 257

Fideo & Chicken Soup with Queso Fresco, 183

Five-Spice Chicken Noodle Soup, 112

Ginger Chicken Soup, 293

Israeli Couscous Soup with Curry,
Chicken & Spinach, 119

Mexican Lime Soup with Chicken, 166

Mushroom Soup with Chicken, 213

Orzo, Delicata Squash
& Chicken Soup with Sage, 279

Parmesan Broth with Lemon,
Chicken & Spinach, 66

Poached Chicken Soup with Spinach, 180

Udon Noodle Soup with Chicken & Spinach, 88

Chickpeas

Chickpea, Porcini & Farro Soup, 39

Chickpea & Roasted Tomato Soup
with Fried Rosemary, 78

Curried Chickpea Stew, 142

Indian-Spiced Chickpea Stew, 240

Moroccan-Spiced Vegetarian Chili, 108

North African Chickpea Soup, 287

Roman Chickpea Soup, 138

Chile peppers

Chicken & Hominy Soup with Ancho Chiles, 282

Creamy Poblano Chile Soup, 143

Garlicky Pork & Chile Soup, 185

Green Chile Stew, 210

Poblano Chile Soup with Corn & Mushrooms, 202

Roasted Chile & Corn Soup with
Farmer's Cheese, 172

Spicy Poblano Soup with Tortilla Strips, 191

Clams

Cioppino, 18

Citrusy Seafood Soup, 23

Clams in Fennel Broth with Parsley Vinaigrette, 99

Italian-Style Clam Soup with Pasta, 281

Manhattan Clam Chowder, 95

Mediterranean Fish Stew, 156

New England Clam Chowder, 41

Saffron Fregola with Seafood, 231

Tomato-Fennel Broth with Clams, 263

Corn

Chilled Curried Corn Soup, 183

Chipotle Corn Purée with
Bay Shrimp & Avocado Salsa, 168

Corn Soup with Chanterelles & Thyme, 243

Corn & Zucchini Soup with Crumbled Bacon, 161

Creamy Corn Soup with Bacon & Sage, 189

Lobster & Sweet Corn Chowder, 208

Poblano Chile Soup with Corn & Mushrooms, 202

Roasted Chile & Corn Soup
with Farmer's Cheese, 172

Snap Pea & Succotash Soup
with Parsley-Mint Pistou, 190

Spicy Corn Soup, 156

Sweet Corn Chowder with Bacon, 130

Sweet Potato–Corn Chowder with Avocado, 237

Three-Potato Chowder with Corn,
Cilantro & Lime, 147

Tomato, Zucchini & Fresh Corn Soup, 192

Couscous

Israeli Couscous Soup with Curry,
Chicken & Spinach, 119

Saffron Fregola with Seafood, 231

Crabmeat

Cioppino, 18

Crab & Asparagus Egg Flower Soup, 123

Crab & Avocado Soup, 173

Crab Rangoons in Chile-Lime Broth, 288

Lump Crab in Tomato-Rosemary Broth, 135

Roasted Shallot & Crab Bisque, 279

Spicy Seafood & Sausage Gumbo, 209

Sun-Dried Tomato Soup with Crab, 42

Cucumbers

Chilled Beet & Cucumber Soup, 294

Chilled Cucumber-Buttermilk Soup
with Dilled Shrimp, 186

Chilled Cucumber-Yogurt Soup
with Lemon & Mint, 154

Cucumber-Dill Soup, 132

Cucumber & Green Grape Gazpacho, 160

Gazpacho, 159

D, E

Dashi with Scallops, Watercress & Soba Noodles, 87

Duck, Seared, & Beet Greens Soup, 40

Eggplant

Charred Eggplant Soup with
Cumin & Greek Yogurt, 189

Eggplant & Tofu Curry Soup, 220

Ratatouille Soup, 178

Roasted Eggplant Soup with Mint, 157

Roasted Summer Vegetable Soup with Pesto, 195

Eggs

Asparagus Soup with Poached Eggs
& Crispy Prosciutto, 93

Egg-Lemon Soup with Fava Beans
& Fried Garlic Chips, 124

Garlic-Sage Soup with Poached Eggs
& Croutons, 204

Parmesan Straciatella with Kale, 48

Spinach & Vermicelli Soup with Fried Egg, 126

Escarole

Escarole & White Bean Soup with Rosemary, 293

Ham, Bean & Escarole Soup, 54

F, G

Farro

Beef & Mushroom Soup with Farro, 69

Chickpea, Porcini & Farro Soup, 39

Tuscan Farro Soup with White Beans,
Tomatoes & Basil, 202

Fennel

Clams in Fennel Broth with Parsley Vinaigrette, 99

Cream of Fennel-Leek Purée
with Toasted Almonds, 207

Fennel Broth with Chard & Chorizo, 77

Fennel-Celery Bisque, 28

Fennel Vichyssoise, 124

Tomato-Fennel Broth with Clams, 263

Fish. See also Shellfish

Bouillabaisse, 192

Bourride, 221

Brazilian Fish Stew, 147

Citrusy Seafood Soup, 23

Five-Spice Broth with Salmon
& Onion Dumplings, 76

Mediterranean Fish Stew, 156

Miso with Black Cod & Green Onions, 162

Potato-Leek Purée with Smoked Salmon & Dill, 106

Smoked Trout Chowder, 30

Soba Noodles & Seared Salmon
in Ginger–Green Onion Broth, 138

Garlic

Garlic-Sage Soup with Poached Eggs
& Croutons, 204

Green Garlic and New Potato Soup, 58

Roasted Garlic & Shallot Velouté
with Crispy Pancetta, 238

Grapes
    Cold Almond Soup with Grapes, 133
    Cucumber & Green Grape Gazpacho, 160

H, J, K

Ham
    Creamy Mushroom Soup with Ham & Peas, 101
    Ham, Bean & Escarole Soup, 54
    White Bean & Ham Soup with
        Corn Bread Croutons, 261
    Yellow Split Pea Soup with Ham, 52
Jerusalem artichokes
    Cream of Sunchoke Soup with
        Porcini Mushrooms, 267
    Jerusalem Artichoke Soup with
        Hazelnut-Orange Butter, 277
Kale
    Garlicky Greens, Roast Pork
        & White Bean Soup, 268
    Kale & Sweet Potato Soup with Lamb Sausage, 262
    Kale & White Bean Soup, 17
    Parmesan Straciatella with Kale, 48
    Pastina & Kale Soup with Andouille, 213
    Sausage & Kale Soup, 53
    Spiced Broth with Roasted
        Acorn Squash & Kale, 269
    Wedding Soup, 288
Kumquat-Carrot Purée with Toasted Fennel Seeds, 24

L

Lamb
    Irish Lamb Stew, 70
    Kale & Sweet Potato Soup with Lamb Sausage, 262
    Lamb & Dried Apricot Stew, 82
    Lamb & Lentil Soup with Cilantro & Parsley, 209
    Moroccan Lamb Stew, 17
Lamb sausages
    Kale & Sweet Potato Soup with Lamb Sausage, 262
Leeks
    Broccoli-Leek Soup, 61
    Chilled Potato & Leek Soup, 78
    Curried Leek & Apple Soup, 228
    Leek & Asparagus Vichyssoise, 113
    Leek & Potato Soup with Blue Cheese, 29
    Leek & Potato Soup with Fried Prosciutto, 215
    Leek Soup with Pancetta & Bread Crumbs, 85
    Leek & Swiss Chard Soup, 232
Lemongrass
    Chicken-Lemongrass Soup, 99
    Lemongrass Soup with Shrimp & Chile, 41
Lentils
    Curried Yellow Lentil Soup, 234
    Green Lentil Soup, 113
    Lamb & Lentil Soup with Cilantro & Parsley, 209

Lemony Red Lentil Soup with Fried Shallots, 264
Lentil & Andouille Soup, 100
Lentil Soup with Pasta & Sage, 53
Lentil Soup with Sorrel, 197
Vegetable-Lentil Soup with Sherry, 30
Lobster
    Cioppino, 18
    Lobster Bisque, 292
    Lobster & Sweet Corn Chowder, 208
    Shiitake Broth with Butter-Poached
        Lobster & Chives, 287

M

Matzo Ball Soup, 87
Meat. See Beef; Lamb; Pork; Veal
Melon
    Cool Honeydew-Mint Soup, 143
    Iced Melon Soup with Champagne & Ginger, 191
    Melon & Prosciutto Soup with
        Mascarpone Cheese, 149
    Two Melon Soups, 168
    Watermelon Gazpacho with
        Goat Cheese Croûtes, 178
Miso paste
    Miso Soup, 245
    Miso Soup with Shrimp & Pea Shoots, 69
    Miso Soup with Tofu & Long Beans, 197
    Miso with Black Cod & Green Onions, 162
Mushrooms
    Beef & Mushroom Soup with Farro, 69
    Corn Soup with Chanterelles & Thyme, 243
    Cream of Sunchoke Soup with
        Porcini Mushrooms, 267
    Creamy Mushroom Soup with Ham & Peas, 101
    Mushroom, Carrot & Leek Soup with
        Shaved Parmesan, 252
    Mushroom & Madeira Soup with Brie Cheese, 108
    Mushroom-Quinoa Soup, 109
    Mushroom Soup with Chicken, 213
    Mushroom Soup with Thyme & Green Onions, 64
    Ramen Noodles with Edamame & Mushrooms, 148
    Savory Barley Soup with
        Wild Mushrooms & Thyme, 250
    Shiitake Broth with Butter-Poached
        Lobster & Chives, 287
    Shiitake Dumplings in Kaffir Lime Broth, 219
    Shrimp, Mushroom & Sorrel Soup, 60
    Three-Mushroom Purée with Sherry, 94
    Winter Greens & Shiitake Soup with
        Poached Eggs, 34
Mussels
    Bouillabaisse, 192
    Cioppino, 18
    Mediterranean Fish Stew, 156
    Mussel Chowder, 165

Mussels in Saffron Broth, 196
Mussels in Tomato & Cream Broth, 21
Seafood Stew with Saffron,
    Serrano Ham & Almonds, 48
Spicy Coconut Curry Seafood Soup, 114
Mustard Greens & Wild Rice Soup with Gruyère, 258

N, O, P

Nectarine, Roasted, Soup with Mint, 173
Noodles
    Baby Bok Choy & Beef Noodle Soup, 66
    Beef Pho, 47
    Burmese Chicken Curry Soup, 167
    Classic Chicken Noodle Soup, 16
    Dashi with Scallops, Watercress
        & Soba Noodles, 87
    Fideo & Chicken Soup with Queso Fresco, 183
    Five-Spice Chicken Noodle Soup, 112
    Gingery Beef Broth with Soba Noodles
        & Bok Choy, 22
    Noodle Soup with Lemongrass & Tofu, 173
    Pork Pho, 198
    Ramen Noodle Soup with Sugar Snap Peas, 114
    Ramen Noodles with Edamame & Mushrooms, 148
    Roast Pork & Udon Noodle Soup, 24
    Shrimp & Spinach Noodle Soup, 90
    Soba Noodle Soup, 157
    Soba Noodles & Seared Salmon
        in Ginger-Green Onion Broth, 138
    Spicy Coconut Broth with
        Udon Noodles & Shrimp, 137
    Turkey-Noodle Soup with Spinach, 270
    Udon Noodle Soup with Chicken & Spinach, 88
Onions
    Caramelized Onion Soup with
        Gorgonzola Croutons, 84
    Cream of Onion Soup, 274
    French Onion Soup, 11
    Sweet Onion Soup with Blue Cheese Toasts, 123
    Three-Onion Soup with
        Cambozola Grilled Cheese, 65
Oysters
    Celery, Leek & Oyster Bisque, 45
    Oyster Stew with Rosemary, 282
Parsnips
    Cream of Parsnip Soup, 243
    Roasted Parsnip & Apple Purée
        with Gruyère Toasts, 222
Pasta. See also Couscous; Noodles
    Angel Hair in Chicken Broth with
        Tomatoes & Basil, 197
    Bean & Elbow Pasta Soup with Basil Pesto, 118
    Cheese & Arugula Ravioli Soup, 144
    Chicken & Farfalle Vegetable Soup, 215
    Cranberry Bean & Pappardelle Soup, 63

Fava Bean & Farfalle Soup, 95
Italian-Style Clam Soup with Pasta, 281
Lentil Soup with Pasta & Sage, 53
Orecchiette, Sausage & Broccolini in Broth, 262
Orecchiette in Aromatic Broth, 36
Orzo, Delicata Squash &
    Chicken Soup with Sage, 279
Pasta & Bean Soup with Fontina, 37
Pasta in Broth with Chives, 71
Pastina & Kale Soup with Andouille, 213
Pea Shoot & Pasta Soup, 117
Penne & Squash Soup with Sage Croutons, 261
Roman Chickpea Soup, 138
Spinach & Vermicelli Soup with Fried Egg, 126
Summer Panzanella Soup with Tiny Pasta, 171
Tortellini & Escarole Soup, 27
Tortellini in Broth, 167
Vegetable Soup with Annellini, 136
Vegetable-Tortellini Soup, 101
Zucchini Soup with Pasta & Mint, 141
Peach & Riesling Soup, 185
Pears
    Butternut Squash Soup with Pears & Rosemary, 229
    Spanish-Style Pear, Pumpkin & Bean Soup, 36
Peas
    Artichoke, Spring Pea & Mint Soup, 75
    Creamy Pea Soup with Citrus Oil & Chives, 64
    Pea & Arborio Rice Purée, 77
    Pea & Mint Purée with Lemon, 111
    Pea Shoot & Pasta Soup, 117
    Ramen Noodle Soup with Sugar Snap Peas, 114
    Snap Pea & Succotash Soup with
        Parsley-Mint Pistou, 190
    Sweet Pea Dumplings in Gingery
        Green Onion Broth, 174
    Venetian Rice & Pea Soup, 84
Peppers. See also Chile peppers
    Acquacotta, 180
    Chilled Red Pepper & Fennel Soup
        with Indian Spices, 172
    Chilled Yellow Pepper Soup with Chives, 149
    Gazpacho, 159
    Roasted Red Pepper Purée with
        Spicy Corn Salsa, 141
    Roasted Red Pepper Soup with
        Goat Cheese & Harissa, 162
    Roasted Red Pepper & Tomato Soup, 221
    Smoky Red Pepper Soup, 181
    Yellow Gazpacho with Lemon-Basil Ricotta, 186
Pork. See also Ham; Pork sausages
    Garlicky Greens, Roast Pork
        & White Bean Soup, 268
    Garlicky Pork & Chile Soup, 185
    Green Chile Stew, 210
    Napa Cabbage Soup with Pork & Bean Sprouts, 71

Pork Pho, 198
Pork & Poblano Chili, 253
Pork & Roasted Tomatillo Stew, 244
Pork Stew with Prunes & Sweet Potatoes, 75
Posole, 13
Rice Soup with Pork Dumplings, 294
Roast Pork & Udon Noodle Soup, 24
Soba Noodle Soup, 157
Spicy Meatball Soup, 205
Wedding Soup, 288
Wonton Soup, 109
Pork sausages
    Chorizo & Chicken Stew with Avocado Crema, 219
    Fennel Broth with Chard & Chorizo, 77
    Kielbasa & Sauerkraut Soup, 102
    Lentil & Andouille Soup, 100
    Linguiça & Potato Stew with Two Paprikas, 292
    Orecchiette, Sausage & Broccolini in Broth, 262
    Pastina & Kale Soup with Andouille, 213
    Red Bean & Andouille Soup, 112
    Sausage & Kale Soup, 53
    Spicy Sausage & Broccoli Rabe Soup, 11
    Spicy Seafood & Sausage Gumbo, 209
    Three-Bean Soup with Linguiça, 76
    White Bean, Broccolini & Bratwurst Soup, 238
    Wild Rice & Red Chard Soup with Andouille, 246
Potatoes. See also Sweet potatoes
    Chilled Potato & Leek Soup, 78
    Green Garlic and New Potato Soup, 58
    Irish Lamb Stew, 70
    Leek & Potato Soup with Blue Cheese, 29
    Leek & Potato Soup with Fried Prosciutto, 215
    Potato-Celery Root Soup, 177
    Potato-Leek Purée with Smoked Salmon & Dill, 106
    Potato-Rosemary Soup, 256
    Steak & Potato Soup with Fried Shallots, 28
    Three-Potato Chowder with Corn,
        Cilantro & Lime, 147
Poultry. See Chicken; Duck; Turkey
Pumpkin
    Pumpkin-Ginger Soup, 237
    Pumpkin-Gruyère Soup, 255
    Pumpkin Soup with Spicy Pumpkin Seeds, 267
    Roasted Pumpkin Soup with
        Chinese Five Spice, 220
    Spanish-Style Pear, Pumpkin & Bean Soup, 36

Q, R, S

Quinoa
    Artichoke & Quinoa Soup with Green Garlic, 90
    Mushroom-Quinoa Soup, 109
    Quinoa in Lemon Broth with
        Greens & Parmesan, 136

Rice. See also Wild rice
    Avgolemono, 15
    Celery & Rice Soup with Parsley, 252
    Lemony Asparagus & Rice Soup with Parmesan, 65
    Pea & Arborio Rice Purée, 77
    Rice Soup with Pork Dumplings, 294
    Turkey & Jasmine Rice Soup with Lemongrass, 268
    Venetian Rice & Pea Soup, 84
Rutabaga & Carrot Soup, 285
Salmon
    Five-Spice Broth with Salmon
        & Onion Dumplings, 76
    Potato-Leek Purée with Smoked Salmon & Dill, 106
    Soba Noodles & Seared Salmon
        in Ginger-Green Onion Broth, 138
Sausages. See Lamb sausages; Pork sausages
Scallops
    Cioppino, 18
    Dashi with Scallops, Watercress
        & Soba Noodles, 87
    Saffron Fregola with Seafood, 231
    Scallops & Pancetta in Saffron Broth, 216
Shallots
    Roasted Garlic & Shallot Velouté
        with Crispy Pancetta, 238
    Roasted Shallot & Crab Bisque, 279
Shellfish. See also Clams; Crabmeat; Lobster;
    Mussels; Scallops; Shrimp
    Calamari Stew, 161
    Celery, Leek & Oyster Bisque, 45
    Oyster Stew with Rosemary, 282
    Spicy Coconut Curry Seafood Soup, 114
Shrimp
    Avocado Soup with Shrimp & Salsa, 150
    Cajun Shrimp Soup, 184
    Chilled Cucumber-Buttermilk Soup
        with Dilled Shrimp, 186
    Cioppino, 18
    Gingery Broth with Prawns & Green Onions, 126
    Lemongrass Soup with Shrimp & Chile, 41
    Mediterranean Fish Stew, 156
    Miso Soup with Shrimp & Pea Shoots, 69
    Saffron Fregola with Seafood, 231
    Seafood Stew with Saffron,
        Serrano Ham & Almonds, 48
    Shrimp, Mushroom & Sorrel Soup, 60
    Shrimp Bisque, 270
    Shrimp & Spinach Noodle Soup, 90
    Spicy Coconut Broth with
        Udon Noodles & Shrimp, 137
    Spicy Coconut Curry Seafood Soup, 114
    Spicy Seafood & Sausage Gumbo, 209
    Thai Hot & Sour Soup, 93
    Tomato Broth with Shrimp, Feta & Oregano, 54
    Tom Yum with Shrimp, 166

Sorrel Purée with Torn Croutons, 85

Spinach
    Cream of Spinach Soup, 239
    Creamy Spinach-Leek Soup, 125
    Parmesan Broth with Lemon,
        Chicken & Spinach, 66
    Poached Chicken Soup with Spinach, 180
    Spinach Soup with Sumac & Feta, 102
    Spinach & Vermicelli Soup with Fried Egg, 126
    Udon Noodle Soup with Chicken & Spinach, 88

Split peas
    Split Pea Soup, 276
    Yellow Split Pea Soup with Ham, 52

Squash. See also Pumpkin; Zucchini
    Acorn Squash Soup with
        Toasted Walnut Butter, 232
    Apple, Leek & Butternut Squash Soup, 250
    Butternut Squash Soup with Pears & Rosemary, 229
    Chilled Summer Squash Soup, 132
    Moroccan-Spiced Vegetarian Chili, 108
    Orzo, Delicata Squash
        & Chicken Soup with Sage, 279
    Penne & Squash Soup with Sage Croutons, 261
    Roasted Butternut Squash Soup, 205
    Spiced Broth with Roasted
        Acorn Squash & Kale, 269
    Squash Soup with Sage Brown Butter, 240
    Thai Squash & Coconut Milk Soup, 51

Squid
    Calamari Stew, 161
    Spicy Coconut Curry Seafood Soup, 114

Strawberries
    Spiced Berry Soup, 195
    Strawberry-Lemon Soup, 125
    Strawberry-Rhubarb Soup with Prosecco, 144

Sweet potatoes
    Kale & Sweet Potato Soup with Lamb Sausage, 262
    Peanut-Ginger Sweet Potato Soup, 246
    Pork Stew with Prunes & Sweet Potatoes, 75
    Steak & Potato Soup with Fried Shallots, 28
    Sweet Potato–Chipotle Soup, 216
    Sweet Potato–Corn Chowder with Avocado, 237
    Sweet Potato Soup with Cheddar
        & Caviar Croutons, 281
    Three-Potato Chowder with Corn,
        Cilantro & Lime, 147

T

Tofu
    Eggplant & Tofu Curry Soup, 220
    Miso Soup with Tofu & Long Beans, 197
    Noodle Soup with Lemongrass & Tofu, 173

Tomatillos
    Chicken-Tomatillo Soup with Chipotle Chiles, 256
    Pork & Roasted Tomatillo Stew, 244

Tomatoes
    Acquacotta, 180
    Angel Hair in Chicken Broth with
        Tomatoes & Basil, 197
    Chickpea & Roasted Tomato Soup
        with Fried Rosemary, 78
    Chunky Heirloom Tomato & Basil Soup, 165
    Cream of Tomato Soup, 18
    Gazpacho, 159
    Lump Crab in Tomato-Rosemary Broth, 135
    Mussels in Tomato & Cream Broth, 21
    Old-Fashioned Tomato & Rice Soup, 30
    Roasted Red Pepper & Tomato Soup, 221
    Roasted Tomato Soup with
        Citrus Crème Fraîche, 196
    Roasted Tomato Soup with
        Serrano Ham & Burrata, 133
    Summer Panzanella Soup with Tiny Pasta, 171
    Sun-Dried Tomato Soup with Crab, 42
    Tomato, Zucchini & Fresh Corn Soup, 192
    Tomato Bisque, 264
    Tomato-Bread Soup with Basil Oil, 204
    Tomato Broth with Shrimp, Feta & Oregano, 54
    Tomato-Fennel Broth with Clams, 263
    Tomato Soup with Smoked Paprika & Bacon, 274
    Tomato Soup with White Wine & Shallots, 181
    Yellow Gazpacho with Lemon-Basil Ricotta, 186

Trout, Smoked, Chowder, 30

Turkey
    Turkey & Jasmine Rice Soup with Lemongrass, 268
    Turkey Meatball Soup with Arugula, 111
    Turkey Mulligatawny, 286
    Turkey-Noodle Soup with Spinach, 270
    Turkey Soup with Chipotle & Lime, 29
    Turkey Stew with Figs & Madeira, 280
    Turkey & White Bean Chili, 210
    Vietnamese Turkey Meatballs in Broth
        with Red Onion & Herbs, 174

Turnips
    Beef Stew with Turnips & Greens, 234
    Turnip, Apple & Potato Soup, 229

V

Veal Stew with Tarragon, 89

Vegetables. See also specific vegetables
    Minestrone with Pesto, 214
    Provençal Minestrone, 150
    Ribollita, 207
    Roasted Root Vegetable & Barley Stew, 37
    Roasted Summer Vegetable Soup with Pesto, 195
    Roasted Vegetable Stew with Couscous, 233
    Root Vegetable Chili with Orange & Cilantro, 291
    Spring Vegetable Soup, 82
    Stone Soup, 46

Vegetable Barley Soup, 208
Vegetable-Lentil Soup with Sherry, 30
Vegetables in Coconut-Lime Broth, 239
Vegetable Soup with Annellini, 136
Vegetable-Tortellini Soup, 101

W

Watercress Soup, 119

White beans
    Bean & Elbow Pasta Soup with Basil Pesto, 118
    Chicken Chili with Piquillo Peppers, 15
    Escarole & White Bean Soup with Rosemary, 293
    Garlicky Greens, Roast Pork
        & White Bean Soup, 268
    Ham, Bean & Escarole Soup, 54
    Kale & White Bean Soup, 17
    Pasta & Bean Soup with Fontina, 37
    Ribollita, 207
    Turkey & White Bean Chili, 210
    Tuscan Farro Soup with White Beans,
        Tomatoes & Basil, 202
    White Bean, Broccolini & Bratwurst Soup, 238
    White Bean & Ham Soup with
        Corn Bread Croutons, 261

Wild rice
    Chicken & Wild Rice Soup with Ginger, 70
    Mustard Greens & Wild Rice Soup
        with Gruyère, 258
    Wild Rice & Red Chard Soup with Andouille, 246
    Wild Rice Soup with Bacon, 61

Wonton Soup, 109

Z

Zucchini
    Cold Zucchini & Avocado Soup, 120
    Corn & Zucchini Soup with Crumbled Bacon, 161
    Lima Bean, Pea & Zucchini Purée with Pesto, 135
    Romano Bean, Zucchini & Parmesan Soup, 198
    Simple Zucchini Soup, 154
    Tomato, Zucchini & Fresh Corn Soup, 192
    Zucchini Soup with Pasta & Mint, 141

SOUPS BY TYPE

ASIAN-STYLE SOUPS

Baby Bok Choy & Beef Noodle Soup, 66
Beef Pho, 47
Burmese Chicken Curry Soup, 167
Chicken-Lemongrass Soup, 99
Chicken & Wild Rice Soup with Ginger, 70
Crab & Asparagus Egg Flower Soup, 123
Crab Rangoons in Chile-Lime Broth, 288
Dashi with Scallops, Watercress & Soba Noodles, 87
Eggplant & Tofu Curry Soup, 220
Five-Spice Broth with Salmon & Onion Dumplings, 76
Five-Spice Chicken Noodle Soup, 112
Ginger Chicken Soup, 293
Gingery Beef Broth with
    Soba Noodles & Bok Choy, 22
Gingery Broth with Prawns & Green Onions, 126
Lemongrass Soup with Shrimp & Chile, 41
Miso Soup, 245
Miso Soup with Shrimp & Pea Shoots, 69
Miso with Black Cod & Green Onions, 162
Napa Cabbage Soup with Pork & Bean Sprouts, 71
Noodle Soup with Lemongrass & Tofu, 173
Poached Chicken Soup with Spinach, 180
Pork Pho, 198
Ramen Noodle Soup with Sugar Snap Peas, 114
Ramen Noodles with Edamame & Mushrooms, 148
Rice Soup with Pork Dumplings, 294
Roasted Pumpkin Soup with
    Chinese Five Spice, 220
Roast Pork & Udon Noodle Soup, 24
Shiitake Dumplings in Kaffir Lime Broth, 219
Shrimp & Spinach Noodle Soup, 90
Soba Noodle Soup, 157
Soba Noodles & Seared Salmon
    in Ginger–Green Onion Broth, 138
Spicy Coconut Broth with
    Udon Noodles & Shrimp, 137
Spicy Coconut Curry Seafood Soup, 114
Sweet Pea Dumplings in Gingery
    Green Onion Broth, 174
Thai Hot & Sour Soup, 93
Thai Squash & Coconut Milk Soup, 51
Tom Yum with Shrimp, 166
Udon Noodle Soup with Chicken & Spinach, 88
Vietnamese Turkey Meatballs in Broth
    with Red Onion & Herbs, 174
Wonton Soup, 109

CHILI

Black Bean Chili, 100
Chicken Chili with Piquillo Peppers, 15
Chili con Carne, 34
Moroccan-Spiced Vegetarian Chili, 108
Pork & Poblano Chili, 253

Root Vegetable Chili with Orange & Cilantro, 291
Turkey & White Bean Chili, 210
Vegetarian Chili, 13

CHILLED SOUPS

Avocado Soup with Lime Juice & Rum, 190
Avocado Soup with Shrimp & Salsa, 150
Chilled Beet & Cucumber Soup, 294
Chilled Carrot Soup with Ginger & Orange Zest, 106
Chilled Cucumber-Buttermilk Soup
    with Dilled Shrimp, 186
Chilled Cucumber-Yogurt Soup
    with Lemon & Mint, 154
Chilled Curried Corn Soup, 183
Chilled Potato & Leek Soup, 78
Chilled Red Pepper & Fennel Soup
    with Indian Spices, 172
Chilled Sour Cherry Soup with Tarragon, 120
Chilled Summer Squash Soup, 132
Chilled Yellow Pepper Soup with Chives, 149
Cold Almond Soup with Grapes, 133
Cold Zucchini & Avocado Soup, 120
Cool Honeydew-Mint Soup, 143
Crab & Avocado Soup, 173
Cucumber-Dill Soup, 132
Cucumber & Green Grape Gazpacho, 160
Curried Carrot Purée, 117
Fennel Vichyssoise, 124
Gazpacho, 159
Iced Melon Soup with Champagne & Ginger, 191
Leek & Asparagus Vichyssoise, 113
Melon & Prosciutto Soup with
    Mascarpone Cheese, 149
Peach & Riesling Soup, 185
Roasted Beet Purée with Feta, 142
Roasted Nectarine Soup with Mint, 173
Sour Cherry–Riesling Soup, 137
Spiced Berry Soup, 195
Strawberry-Lemon Soup, 125
Strawberry-Rhubarb Soup with Prosecco, 144
Two Melon Soups, 168
Watercress Soup, 119

CHOWDER

Chicken Chowder, 228
Lobster & Sweet Corn Chowder, 208
Manhattan Clam Chowder, 95
Mussel Chowder, 165
New England Clam Chowder, 41
Smoked Trout Chowder, 30
Sweet Corn Chowder with Bacon, 130
Sweet Potato–Corn Chowder with Avocado, 237
Three-Potato Chowder with Corn,
    Cilantro & Lime, 147

FRUIT SOUPS

Chilled Sour Cherry Soup with Tarragon, 120
Cold Almond Soup with Grapes, 133
Cool Honeydew-Mint Soup, 143
Cucumber & Green Grape Gazpacho, 160
Iced Melon Soup with Champagne & Ginger, 191
Melon & Prosciutto Soup with
    Mascarpone Cheese, 149
Peach & Riesling Soup, 185
Roasted Nectarine Soup with Mint, 173
Sour Cherry–Riesling Soup, 137
Spiced Berry Soup, 195
Strawberry-Lemon Soup, 125
Strawberry-Rhubarb Soup with Prosecco, 144
Two Melon Soups, 168

GRAIN-BASED SOUPS & STEWS

Artichoke & Quinoa Soup with Green Garlic, 90
Avgolemono, 15
Barley-Leek Soup with Mini Chicken Meatballs, 21
Beef & Mushroom Soup with Farro, 69
Celery & Rice Soup with Parsley, 252
Chicken & Wild Rice Soup with Ginger, 70
Chickpea, Porcini & Farro Soup, 39
Cranberry Bean & Barley Soup, 27
Lemony Asparagus & Rice Soup with Parmesan, 65
Mushroom Quinoa Soup, 109
Mustard Greens & Wild Rice Soup with Gruyère, 258
Old-Fashioned Tomato & Rice Soup, 30
Pea & Arborio Rice Purée, 77
Quinoa in Lemon Broth with Greens & Parmesan, 136
Rice Soup with Pork Dumplings, 294
Roasted Root Vegetable & Barley Stew, 37
Savory Barley Soup with
    Wild Mushrooms & Thyme, 250
Turkey & Jasmine Rice Soup with Lemongrass, 268
Tuscan Farro Soup with White Beans,
    Tomatoes & Basil, 202
Vegetable Barley Soup, 208
Venetian Rice & Pea Soup, 84
Wild Rice & Red Chard Soup with Andouille, 246
Wild Rice Soup with Bacon, 61

PASTA, COUSCOUS & NOODLES

Baby Bok Choy & Beef Noodle Soup, 66
Bean & Elbow Pasta Soup with Basil Pesto, 118
Beef Pho, 47
Burmese Chicken Curry Soup, 167
Cheese & Arugula Ravioli Soup, 144
Chicken & Farfalle Vegetable Soup, 215
Classic Chicken Noodle Soup, 16
Cranberry Bean & Pappardelle Soup, 63
Dashi with Scallops, Watercress & Soba Noodles, 87

Fava Bean & Farfalle Soup, 95
Fideo & Chicken Soup with Queso Fresco, 183
Five-Spice Chicken Noodle Soup, 112
Gingery Beef Broth with
    Soba Noodles & Bok Choy, 22
Israeli Couscous Soup with Curry,
    Chicken & Spinach, 119
Italian-Style Clam Soup with Pasta, 281
Lentil Soup with Pasta & Sage, 53
Moroccan Lamb Meatball & Couscous Soup, 72
Noodle Soup with Lemongrass & Tofu, 173
Orecchiette, Sausage & Broccolini in Broth, 262
Orecchiette in Aromatic Broth, 36
Orzo, Delicata Squash & Chicken Soup with Sage, 279
Pasta & Bean Soup with Fontina, 37
Pasta in Broth with Chives, 71
Pastina & Kale Soup with Andouille, 213
Pea Shoot & Pasta Soup, 117
Penne & Squash Soup with Sage Croutons, 261
Pork Pho, 198
Provençal Minestrone, 150
Ramen Noodle Soup with Sugar Snap Peas, 114
Ramen Noodles with Edamame & Mushrooms, 148
Roasted Vegetable Stew with Couscous, 233
Roast Pork & Udon Noodle Soup, 24
Roman Chickpea Soup, 138
Saffron Fregola with Seafood, 231
Shrimp & Spinach Noodle Soup, 90
Soba Noodle Soup, 157
Soba Noodles & Seared Salmon
    in Ginger–Green Onion Broth, 138
Spicy Coconut Broth with
    Udon Noodles & Shrimp, 137
Spinach & Vermicelli Soup with Fried Egg, 126
Summer Panzanella Soup with Tiny Pasta, 171
Tortellini & Escarole Soup, 27
Tortellini in Broth, 167
Turkey-Noodle Soup with Spinach, 270
Udon Noodle Soup with Chicken & Spinach, 88
Vegetable Soup with Annellini, 136
Vegetable-Tortellini Soup, 101
Zucchini Soup with Pasta & Mint, 141

PURÉED SOUPS

Acorn Squash Soup with Toasted Walnut Butter, 232
Apple, Leek & Butternut Squash Soup, 250
Artichoke Soup with Camembert Crostini, 118
Artichoke Soup with Morel Butter, 60
Artichoke & Toasted Bread Soup with Sage, 245
Asparagus-Chervil Purée with Lemon Mascarpone, 88
Asparagus Soup with Poached Eggs
    & Crispy Prosciutto, 93
Avocado Soup with Lime Juice & Rum, 190
Avocado Soup with Shrimp & Salsa, 150

Broccoli & Cheddar Soup, 23
Broccoli-Leek Soup, 61
Broccoli Soup with Parmesan-Lemon Frico, 291
Butternut Squash Soup with Pears & Rosemary, 229
Carrot & Asian Pear Purée, 245
Carrot & Coconut Purée with Curried Almonds, 96
Carrot-Ginger Soup, 226
Carrot Soup with Bacon & Chestnut Cream, 269
Cauliflower & Roasted Garlic Purée, 12
Cauliflower Soup with Cheddar & Blue Cheese, 233
Cauliflower Soup with Chervil, 63
Celery Root Purée with Caramelized Apples, 255
Cheddar & Hard Cider Soup with Fried Shallots, 226
Chestnut–Celery Root Soup with
    Bacon & Sage Croutons, 253
Chestnut Soup, 276
Chilled Carrot Soup with Ginger & Orange Zest, 106
Chilled Cucumber-Buttermilk Soup
    with Dilled Shrimp, 186
Chilled Cucumber-Yogurt Soup with
    Lemon & Mint, 154
Chilled Curried Corn Soup, 183
Chilled Red Pepper & Fennel Soup
    with Indian Spices, 172
Chilled Summer Squash Soup, 132
Chilled Yellow Pepper Soup with Chives, 149
Chipotle Corn Purée with
    Bay Shrimp & Avocado Salsa, 168
Cold Almond Soup with Grapes, 133
Cold Zucchini & Avocado Soup, 120
Cool Honeydew-Mint Soup, 143
Corn & Zucchini Soup with Crumbled Bacon, 161
Crab & Avocado Soup, 173
Cream of Asparagus Soup, 58
Cream of Broccoli Soup, 96
Cream of Fennel-Leek Purée with
    Toasted Almonds, 207
Cream of Onion Soup, 274
Cream of Parsnip Soup, 243
Cream of Spinach Soup, 239
Cream of Sunchoke Soup with
    Porcini Mushrooms, 267
Creamy Black Bean Purée with Cheese Straws, 244
Creamy Cauliflower Soup with Crispy Prosciutto, 45
Creamy Pea Soup with Citrus Oil & Chives, 64
Creamy Poblano Chile Soup, 143
Creamy Spinach-Leek Soup, 125
Cucumber-Dill Soup, 132
Cucumber & Green Grape Gazpacho, 160
Curried Carrot Purée, 117
Curried Cream of Celery Soup, 293
Curried Leek & Apple Soup, 228
Fava Bean Soup, 89
Fennel-Celery Bisque, 28
Fresh Green Bean Soup, 184

Golden Beet Soup with Dilled Goat Cheese, 130
Green Garlic and New Potato Soup, 58
Iced Melon Soup with Champagne & Ginger, 191
Jerusalem Artichoke Soup with
    Hazelnut-Orange Butter, 277
Kumquat-Carrot Purée with Toasted Fennel Seeds, 24
Leek & Asparagus Vichyssoise, 113
Leek & Potato Soup with Blue Cheese, 29
Leek Soup with Pancetta & Bread Crumbs, 85
Lemony Red Lentil Soup with Fried Shallots, 264
Lentil Soup with Sorrel, 197
Lima Bean, Pea & Zucchini Purée with Pesto, 135
Lobster Bisque, 292
Melon & Prosciutto Soup with Mascarpone Cheese, 149
Mushroom & Madeira Soup with Brie Cheese, 108
Pea & Arborio Rice Purée, 77
Peach & Riesling Soup, 185
Pea & Mint Purée with Lemon, 111
Peanut-Ginger Sweet Potato Soup, 246
Potato-Leek Purée with Smoked Salmon & Dill, 106
Pumpkin-Ginger Soup, 237
Pumpkin Soup with Spicy Pumpkin Seeds, 267
Ratatouille Soup, 178
Roasted Beet Purée with Feta, 142
Roasted Butternut Squash Soup, 205
Roasted Cauliflower & Parmesan Soup, 231
Roasted Chile & Corn Soup with Farmer's Cheese, 172
Roasted Eggplant Soup with Mint, 157
Roasted Garlic & Shallot Velouté
    with Crispy Pancetta, 238
Roasted Nectarine Soup with Mint, 173
Roasted Parsnip & Apple Purée
    with Gruyère Toasts, 222
Roasted Pumpkin Soup with Chinese Five Spice, 220
Roasted Red Pepper Purée with Spicy Corn Salsa, 141
Roasted Red Pepper Soup with
    Goat Cheese & Harissa, 162
Roasted Red Pepper & Tomato Soup, 221
Roasted Shallot & Crab Bisque, 279
Roasted Summer Vegetable Soup with Pesto, 195
Roasted Tomato Soup with Citrus Crème Fraîche, 196
Roasted Tomato Soup with Serrano Ham & Burrata, 133
Rutabaga & Carrot Soup, 285
Silken Lima Bean Soup with Ham Croûtes, 160
Simple Asparagus Soup, 125
Smoky Red Pepper Soup, 181
Sorrel Purée with Torn Croutons, 85
Sour Cherry–Riesling Soup, 137
Spiced Berry Soup, 195
Spicy Poblano Soup with Tortilla Strips, 191
Squash Soup with Sage Brown Butter, 240
Strawberry-Lemon Soup, 125
Strawberry-Rhubarb Soup with Prosecco, 144
Sun-Dried Tomato Soup with Crab, 42

Sweet Potato–Chipotle Soup, 216
Three-Mushroom Purée with Sherry, 94
Tomato Bisque, 264
Tomato Soup with Smoked Paprika & Bacon, 274
Tomato Soup with White Wine & Shallots, 181
Turnip, Apple & Potato Soup, 229
Two Melon Soups, 168
Watercress Soup, 119

STEWS

Balsamic Beef Stew, 94
Beef Stew with Orange Zest & Red Wine, 52
Beef Stew with Turnips & Greens, 234
Black-Eyed Pea Stew, 77
Bouillabaisse, 192
Brazilian Fish Stew, 147
Calamari Stew, 161
Chicken Stew with Buttermilk-Chive Dumplings, 42
Chicken Stew with Olives & Almonds, 40
Chorizo & Chicken Stew with Avocado Crema, 219
Cioppino, 18
Classic Beef & Red Wine Stew, 286
Curried Cauliflower & Chicken Stew, 257
Curried Chickpea Stew, 142
Five-Spice Beef Stew, 12
Goulash, 263
Green Chile Sterw, 210
Indian-Spiced Chickpea Stew, 240
Irish Lamb Stew, 70
Italian Beef Stew, 222
Lamb & Dried Apricot Stew, 82
Linguiça & Potato Stew with Two Paprikas, 292
Mediterranean Fish Stew, 156
Moroccan Lamb Stew, 17
Oyster Stew with Rosemary, 282
Pork & Roasted Tomatillo Stew, 244
Pork Stew with Prunes & Sweet Potatoes, 75
Roasted Root Vegetable & Barley Stew, 37
Roasted Vegetable Stew with Couscous, 233
Short Rib Stew with Paprika Sour Cream, 285
Spicy Seafood & Sausage Gumbo, 209
Turkey Stew with Figs & Madeira, 280
Veal Stew with Tarragon, 89
Weeknight Hungarian Beef Stew, 280

TOPPINGS & GARNISHES

Aioli, 220
Avocado Crema, 219
Basil Oil, 204
Basil Pesto, 118
Bay Shrimp & Avocado Salsa, 168
Blue Cheese Toasts, 123
Bruschetta, 135

Camembert Crostini, 118
Caramelized Apples, 255
Cheese Straws, 244
Chestnut Cream, 269
Citrus Crème Fraîche, 196
Citrus Oil, 64
Corn Bread Croutons, 261
Fried Garlic Chips, 124
Fried Rosemary, 78
Fried Shallots, 28
GarlicCroutons, 61
Goat Cheese Croûtes, 178
Gruyère Toasts, 222
Hazelnut-Orange Butter, 277
Lemon-Basil Ricotta, 186
Lemon Mascarpone, 88
Meyer-Lemon Crème Fraîche, 51
Paprika Sour Cream, 285
Parmesan-Lemon Frico, 291
Parsley-Mint Pistou, 190
Pistou, 150
Rouille, 192
Sage Brown Butter, 240
Sage Croutons, 261
Salsa, 150
Spicy Corn Salsa, 141
Spicy Pumpkin Seeds, 267
Sun-Dried Tomato Pesto, 195
Toasted Walnut Butter, 232
Tortilla Strips, 191

VEGETARIAN SOUPS & STEWS

Acquacotta, 180
Asparagus-Chervil Purée with Lemon Mascarpone, 88
Black Bean Chili, 100
Black Bean Soup with Meyer Lemon Crème Fraîche, 51
Butternut Squash Soup with Pears & Rosemary, 229
Carrot & Asian Pear Purée, 245
Cauliflower Soup with Chervil, 63
Celery Root Purée with Caramelized Apples, 255
Charred Eggplant Soup with
  Cumin & Greek Yogurt, 189
Chickpea, Porcini & Farro Soup, 39
Chilled Carrot Soup with Ginger & Orange Zest, 106
Chilled Sour Cherry Soup with Tarragon, 120
Cold Almond Soup with Grapes, 133
Cold Zucchini & Avocado Soup, 120
Cool Honeydew-Mint Soup, 143
Cream of Onion Soup, 274
Cream of Spinach Soup, 239
Cream of Sunchoke Soup with
  Porcini Mushrooms, 267
Cream of Tomato Soup, 18

Creamy Pea Soup with Citrus Oil & Chives, 64
Creamy Spinach-Leek Soup, 125
Cuban Black Bean Soup, 148
Cucumber-Dill Soup, 132
Cucumber & Green Grape Gazpacho, 160
Curried Chickpea Stew, 142
Curried Cream of Celery Soup, 293
Curried Leek & Apple Soup, 228
Curried Yellow Lentil Soup, 234
Eggplant & Tofu Curry Soup, 220
Fava Bean Soup, 89
Fennel Vichyssoise, 124
Fresh Green Bean Soup, 184
Garlic-Sage Soup with Poached Eggs & Croutons, 204
Indian-Spiced Chickpea Stew, 240
Lemony Red Lentil Soup with Fried Shallots, 264
Lentil Soup with Sorrel, 197
Minestrone with Pesto, 214
Miso Soup, 245
Moroccan-Spiced Vegetarian Chili, 108
Mushroom-Quinoa Soup, 109
Pea & Arborio Rice Purée, 77
Peach & Riesling Soup, 185
Peanut-Ginger Sweet Potato Soup, 246
Quinoa in Lemon Broth with Greens & Parmesan, 136
Ribollita, 207
Roasted Beet Purée with Feta, 142
Roasted Eggplant Soup with Mint, 157
Roasted Nectarine Soup with Mint, 173
Roasted Red Pepper & Tomato Soup, 221
Roasted Root Vegetable & Barley Stew, 37
Roasted Vegetable Stew with Couscous, 233
Root Vegetable Chili with Orange & Cilantro, 201
Rutabaga & Carrot Soup, 285
Sorrel Purée with Torn Croutons, 85
Sour Cherry–Riesling Soup, 137
Spiced Berry Soup, 195
Spicy Broccolini & Cranberry Bean Soup, 214
Squash Soup with Sage Brown Butter, 240
Strawberry-Rhubarb Soup with Prosecco, 144
Sweet Potato–Corn Chowder with Avocado, 237
Three-Mushroom Purée with Sherry, 94
Tomato Bisque, 264
Tomato-Bread Soup with Basil Oil, 204
Tomato Soup with White Wine & Shallots, 181
Turnip, Apple & Potato Soup, 229
Two Melon Soups, 168
Vegetable Barley Soup, 208
Vegetable-Lentil Soup with Sherry, 30
Vegetables in Coconut-Lime Broth, 239
Vegetarian Chili, 13
Watermelon Gazpacho with
  Goat Cheese Croûtes, 178

weldonowen

415 Jackson Street, Suite 200, San Francisco, CA 94111
www.weldonowen.com

SOUP OF THE DAY

Conceived and produced by Weldon Owen, Inc.
In collaboration with Williams-Sonoma, Inc.
3250 Van Ness Avenue, San Francisco, CA 94109

A WELDON OWEN PRODUCTION

Color separated in Hong Kong by Mission Productions
Printed and bound in China by Toppan-Leefung Printing Limited

First printed in 2011
20 19 18 17 16

Library of Congress Control Number: 2011925884

ISBN 13: 978-1-61628-167-0
ISBN 10: 1-61628-167-7

Weldon Owen is a division of
BONNIER

WILLIAMS-SONOMA, INC.

Founder and Vice-Chairman Chuck Williams

WELDON OWEN, INC.

CEO and President Terry Newell
VP, Sales and Marketing Amy Kaneko
Director of Finance Mark Perrigo

VP and Publisher Hannah Rahill
Associate Publisher Amy Marr
Editor Julia Humes
Assistant Editor Becky Duffett

Creative Director Emma Boys
Art Director Kara Church
Associate Art Director Diana Heom
Designer Anna Grace

Production Director Chris Hemesath
Production Manager Michelle Duggan
Color Manager Teri Bell

Photographer Erin Kunkel
Food Stylist Robyn Valarik
Prop Stylist Leigh Noe

ACKNOWLEDGMENTS

Weldon Owen wishes to thank the following people for their generous support in producing
this book: Donita Boles, David Bornfriend, Joe Budd, Sarah Putman Clegg, Judith Dunham,
David Evans, Alexa Hyman, Kim Laidlaw, Carolyn Miller, Julie Nelson, Jennifer Newens,
Elizabeth Parson, Hannah Rahill, Tracy White Taylor, Jason Wheeler, and Sharron Wood.